Captain Charles Fordyce,

14th Foot

by

Roy Randolph

January 2019

Copyright © 2019 Roy E. Randolph
All rights reserved

Contact information:
Roy Randolph
600 West Las Flores Avenue
Ridgecrest, California 93555

Cover design: Amy Ashworth
Front cover portrait by Amy Ashworth, © 2018 Roy E. Randolph. Pose taken by Captain Fordyce based on the portrait, "Lieutenant Colonel Stewart, 25th Regiment of Foot (later to become the King's Own Scottish Borderers)" at the King's Own Scottish Borderers Museum, The Barracks, Berwick upon Tweed, England. Used by permission.
Image of miniature frame on cover portrait from Wikimedia Commons. Public domain in the United States because it was published (or registered with the U.S. Copyright Office) before January 1, 1923.

Image of badge and motto for the cap worn by the grenadiers of the 14th Regiment of Foot on back cover based on a plaque in the Yorkshire Regimental Memorial, York Minster, York, England. © Chapter of York: Reproduced by kind permission.

Version: 201117

Library of Congress Control Number: 2018909926

ISBN: 978-0-692-17529-3

TABLE OF CONTENTS

Table of Contents iii
Foreword v
Acknowledgements and Credits ix
Introduction: A Circuitous Path 1
Chapter 1: Charles Fordyce's Family 15
Chapter 2: Deployed to Germany, Seven Years War
    Service, 1761 – 1763 26
Chapter 3: Deployed to Nova Scotia, 1766 - 1768 36
Chapter 4: Unrest in Boston, 1767 - 1768 48
Chapter 5: Deployed to Boston, 1768 – 1772 57
Chapter 6: Deployed to St. Vincent,
    the Carib War, 1772 -1773 77
Chapter 7: Deployed to St. Augustine, Florida, 1773 - 1775 90
Chapter 8: Lord Dunmore and the "Spirit of Faction" 107
Chapter 9: Deployed to Virginia, 1775 128
Chapter 10: The Battle of Great Bridge 149
Chapter 11: Tributes 170
Chapter 12: Significance of the Battle of Great Bridge 189
Epilogue 200
Appendix: Annotated List of Accounts of the
    Battle of Great Bridge 222
Notes 248
Select Bibliography 300
Index 310

Badge and motto worn on the caps of the grenadiers in the 14th Regiment of Foot. Image based on a plaque in the Yorkshire Regimental Memorial, York Minster, York, England. © Chapter of York: Reproduced by kind permission.

The 14th Regiment has been renamed and amalgamated with different regiments several times since the American Revolutionary War. In 1782 it was named the 14th (Bedfordshire) Regiment and later the 14th (Buckinghamshire) Regiment, the Prince of Wales's Own (West Yorkshire Regiment), the Prince of Wales's Own Regiment of Yorkshire and finally, in 2006, the Yorkshire Regiment, which is comprised of regiments formerly denominated the 14th/15th, 19th and 33rd/76th Foot.

The York Army Museum in York, England is home to an admirable and worthy collection of artifacts, paintings, histories and displays that feature and memorialize this over three-hundred-and fifty-year-old regiment. There is also a memorial enclave to the officers and men who died fighting in the regiment in the South Transept of York Minster in York. The image above is adapted from a photograph of a memorial plaque in the enclave. The white horse emblem and motto, *nec aspera terrent*, were worn on the bearskin caps of the grenadiers in the 14th Regiment. The Latin motto has various translations, including, "Let no difficulties deter" and "Afraid of no hardships." A motto Captain Fordyce and many of his grenadiers honored in the ultimate.

FOREWORD

My interest in Charles Fordyce stems from an interest in one of the lesser known battles of the American Revolutionary War, the Battle of Great Bridge, Virginia. I developed an interest in this battle when I was researching the military career of one of my ancestors, Thomas Hubbard, who *almost* fought in the battle and served several months in the theater of the Chesapeake Bay after the battle.

Even though the battle is not well known, it is considered by some students of the war as decisive, even pivotal—an assessment that lends an element of mystique to the event since such significance is inconsistent with the battle's relative obscurity. For me, the fact my ancestor almost fought at Great Bridge adds to the mystique and consequent appeal of the battle as a research topic.

Thomas Hubbard was in the 1st Virginia Regiment, sent from Williamsburg to reinforce Colonel William Woodford's 2nd Virginia Regiment—then on the way to Norfolk to dislodge the royally-appointed governor of Virginia, Lord Dunmore. Woodford had been blocked by a small but capable detachment of British troops at the village of Great Bridge, situated on the main road to Norfolk passing through marshlands south-west of the city.

Woodford and Dunmore's forces were at a standoff, cautiously eying each other from their camps on opposite sides of the Southern Branch of the Elizabeth River. Dunmore had intelligence of troops on the way to reinforce Colonel Woodford and although his intelligence was not always accurate, this time it was. Two regiments were on the way, the 1st Virginia from Williamsburg and the 2nd North Carolina Regiment from Salisbury.

Governor Dunmore would later explain his intelligence of Woodford's imminent reinforcement was one of the circumstances that prompted him to attack the entrenched troops of the

2nd Virginia Regiment on Saturday morning December 9, 1775. The reinforcements would arrive three days after the battle. Had they arrived earlier, it is likely the battle never would have occurred.

As I began to study the battle, I soon discovered my ancestor's close brush with fame—inasmuch as veterans of the battle are famous—and the amazing way a few hours can change the course of history, were only part of the mystique of this event. Considering the battle in the context of a multifaceted, intercontinental dispute, I was struck by the magnitude and number of uncertainties with which British and American war planners were struggling at the time.

Although New England had taken precedence as the primary theater in the looming war, I became convinced there had been a real possibility of Virginia and the South emerging as the theater where the definitive confrontations would occur in these early months of the conflict. I also became convinced one of the main reasons this did not happen was the British loss at Great Bridge.

At this point, I was convinced the Battle of Great Bridge was in fact an important if not decisive determinant in the way the Revolutionary War—and consequently Western civilization—unfolded. Having thus elevated the battle to such a level of significance, I naturally elevated the soldiers involved to the same level and I was impressed that neither the battle nor the participants, especially the British soldiers, have received the attention I concluded they merited.

One particular British soldier stood out, Captain Charles Fordyce. Fordyce led the British attack at the battle and was killed a few feet from the American entrenchments. He is named as the commander of the attacking force in the all the eyewitness and contemporary accounts of the battle and in the later histories that touch on the battle. In the shorter summaries of the battle, he is the only British soldier named. In Colonel Woodford's after-action reports, he is portrayed as a courageous, meritorious leader who deserved a better fate. In fact, Colonel Woodford buried Captain Fordyce with "full military honors." Both the American and

British participants in the battle described him as brave, gallant, courageous and resolute.

Other than these appellations—complementary as they are—accounts of the battle include little information from which a broader estimate of his character might be developed. Invariably, accounts of the Battle of Great Bridge list only Captain Fordyce's rank, his military unit, the 14th Regiment of Foot, his on-scene commander, Captain Samuel Leslie, and the fact he was the commander of the grenadier company in the regiment. But sparse as these details were, they were enough to locate vital records. His affiliation with the 14th Regiment proved to be the key to unlocking the mysteries of his career and family. This affiliation linked him to Scotland. The 14th Regiment originated in Scotland and linking Charles to Scotland resulted in the discovery of several documents relating to the Fordyce family, in particular, Charles' birth record. With that, I was able to develop a rudimentary genealogy.

Charles was from an aristocratic family and once I made connections to titled members of the family, this research in itself was quite fascinating. I address key relationships Charles had with influential military officers, politicians and courtiers in the book. But, glamorous as such relationships may be, they provide only one dimension of the man. I have tried to discover who Charles was in a broader context where family connections are important but where the importance of his experiences, his relationships with fellow officers, his opinions, his reactions and his interests are also addressed.

I believe Charles' story is remarkable and interesting—worth telling—because it brings an important epoch of history to life. But the main reason I commend Captain Fordyce as worthy of attention is because he seems to have been an honest, diligent, capable, respectful man who was true to himself, his country and in his case, to his king. I base this assessment on the entire body of research summarized in this text but especially on his performance at the Battle of Great Bridge.

Based on his military record, I believe he was the most experienced soldier on the field at Great Bridge. And based on first-hand accounts of both the American and British officers, the attack was not well conceived—through no fault of Charles'. It was the kind of attack a conceited officer would have abandoned as soon as the predicted and anticipated perils were realized. It was the kind of attack where too many elements of the operation failed from the outset. The kind of attack which could have been aborted and no aspersions regarding the courage and competence of the commander would have ever been made.

But Charles Fordyce, captain of the company of grenadiers in His Majesty's 14th Regiment of Foot, would let no difficulties deter. He chose to honor his commander-in-chief, a man of superior rank in the aristocracy but inferior in military experience and skill. At the risk of waxing sentimental, it can be said Captain Fordyce honored his King, his country and his regiment. He chose to obey his orders without reservation and without hesitation. He fought valiantly and in so doing, he—more than anyone else in this pivotal although historically neglected encounter—secured the otherwise minor Battle of Great Bridge a place on the list of major battles which not only deserve the name "turning point," but the more highly prized designation of "hard fought" as well. Based on the eyewitness accounts of the men and officers on both sides, a strong case can be made that the valor and spirit of Captain Fordyce triggered an extraordinary display of courage, honor, and respect throughout the ranks of the combatants at Great Bridge.

ACKNOWLEDGEMENTS AND CREDITS

ACKNOWLEDGEMENTS

Since most of my research has been performed "online" I am grateful for the many institutions that provide on-line catalogues, key-word search capabilities and digital images of their vast and wonderful archives. The following institutions have provided invaluable services, including direct access to digital records *via* the internet, quick-turnaround microfilm loans and traditional services at brick-and-mortar facilities. Without these services, this book could not have been written.

The National Archives of Great Britain at Kew, Richmond, Surrey, makes many of the colonial and military records of the Revolutionary War era available online. Through this institution, I was able to obtain excellent quality digital images of military muster rolls, letters of soldiers, wills, collections of correspondence related to specific deployments and the *Army Lists* and *Commission Books* for the 18th and 19th centuries. There is a modest fee for copies of some of these images, but the last two items mentioned—the *Army Lists* and *Commission Books*—are already on-line at the National Archives site and available at no charge.

The National Records of Scotland at the General Register House, 2 Princes Street, Edinburgh, is another vast archive which, at their "ScotlandsPeople" site, provides birth, deaths and marriage records from church registers beginning in 1553. This institution also contains collections of a wide range of rare records acquired as "gifts and deposits." These collections are searchable online. The original records in these collections are available for registered researchers at the General Register House in Edinburgh and the staff there are very helpful with the registration process and retrieval of records.

The Massachusetts Historical Society has a tremendous collection of records related to the Revolutionary War era including the

Annotated Newspapers of Harbottle Dorr, Jr. (internet access with no charge) and the "Frederick Lewis Gay transcripts, 1632-1786," which include the depositions British soldiers made in Boston as a consequence of altercations with the citizens of that city in the years leading up to the Revolutionary War.

The Héritage Project, Canadiana, at the Public Archives of Canada offers a wide range of records such as the "Haldimand Papers" (correspondence of General Frederick Haldimand) and "William Legge, 2nd Earl of Dartmouth fonds."

The Library of Congress has archives of every genre, including Revolutionary War era maps and illustrations, the *Journals of the Continental Congress*, a microfilmed collection of the "British Manuscripts Project" of 1941, which is available through interlibrary loans, the George Washington Papers, Thomas Jefferson Papers and similar collections for all the "founding fathers."

Founders Online at the US National Archives provides an archive of the correspondence of the key military and political figures involved in the American's fight for independence.

The Colonial Williamsburg Foundation provides a searchable archive and digital images of the various editions of the *Virginia Gazette* published in Williamsburg between 1736 and 1780.

The London Gazette from 1665 provides an "official" record of the promotions and assignments of military officers as well as announcements of Parliamentary proceedings and proclamations made by the king.

The Naval History and Heritage Command provides on-line access to the *Naval Documents of the American Revolution*.

Northern Illinois University provides a searchable version of one of the most widely cited references of Revolutionary War material, Peter Force's 1837 master work, *American Archives*.

The library of the University of Glasgow has an extensive collection of digital records and the staff there were very helpful in finding and providing copies of records.

The National Library of Scotland in Edinburgh has a wide variety of collections covering the 18th century, including the British Newspaper Archive. This resource is also available online for a modest fee.

Acknowledgements and Credits

Almost all of the maps presented in the book are from the Norman B. Leventhal Map & Education Center at the Boston Public Library. This Center is a vast repository of such maps and most are available as digital files at no charge.

The library of the Cerro Coso Community College in Ridgecrest California provided access to a number of databases such as the JSTOR (Journal Storage) database. This library was always helpful in acquiring resources through inter-library loans.

The Ridgecrest Branch of the Kern County Regional Library and the Family History Center of the Mormon Church in Ridgecrest provided film readers for reading records acquired in microfilm format.

The Huntington Library in San Marino California has extensive holdings of Revolutionary War era manuscripts and first editions of early histories and document collections such as Force's *American Archives* (1837) Fortescue's *Correspondence of King George III* (1928), Sibbald Scott's *The British Army: Its Origin, Progress, and Equipment* and Edward Curtis' *The Organization of the British Army in the American Revolution*—just to name a few.

In addition to these institutions, those of us doing research in the 21st century have access to the most extensive collection of books and periodicals in human history *via* collections digitized and promulgated by entities such as Google Books, Project Gutenberg and the Hathi Trust, with the support of numerous universities.

Two members of the School of History, Classics and Archaeology at the University of Edinburgh met with me on short notice to discuss graduate studies at the University. Professor Frank Cogliano provided information on the Masters in Research program and introduced me to Dr. David Kaufman, Program Director of the MSc in History (Online). Dr. Kaufman tutored me on searching the "gifts and deposits" holdings at the National Records of Scotland. With his direction and encouragement, I was able to find the letters of Thomas Fordyce (Charles' father) and acquire invaluable data on Charles' family.

In the course of my research, my wife and I visited the cemetery at Ayton Church to view the memorials to John Fordyce and his wife Katherine Maxwell, Captain Fordyce's brother and sister-in-law. These memorials were in the "Fordyce Aisle" –part of the original church Captain Fordyce may have attended but now a ruin, completely overgrown with ivy. The Session Clerk of the Ayton and District Churches, Mr. Bill Stewart, met us at the cemetery, directed us to the Fordyce Aisle and proceeded to cut away the ivy so we could enter the aisle and view the memorials. Without his help, I could not have found the memorials.

Early in my research, I was pleased to establish contact with Mr. Peter Williamson, a British soldier who served with the 14th Regiment during the Malayan Emergency in the 1950s. Mr. Williamson took the time to describe the extensive training he received in jungle warfare and recount some of his experiences in Malaysia, which helped me appreciate the difficulties Captain Fordyce would have encountered in St. Vincent in 1773. He also read the proof of the book and provided very encouraging feedback.

The cover of the book was designed by Amy Ashworth, a young woman talented as a librarian, designer, artist, student of 18th century literature, wife and mother of three. It was a pleasure to work with her on this project and witness her creativity and skill. Ms. Ashworth also did the cover portrait of Captain Fordyce. Since there are no known portraits of Captain Fordyce, this portrait is an interpretation. It is done in colored pencil in the style of an 18th century miniature. The pose taken by Captain Fordyce is based on the portrait, "Lieutenant Colonel Stewart, 25th Regiment of Foot (later to become the King's Own Scottish Borderers)" at the King's Own Scottish Borderers Museum, The Barracks, Berwick upon Tweed, England. The uniform is based on photographs of actual uniforms in the York Army Museum in York, England, sample portraits, cartoons of military uniforms and photographs of re-enactors from the non-profit organization, "His Majesty's 14th Regiment of Foot." I supplied all the information and images on the uniform and reviewed the final product, so if the portrait is inaccurate in that respect, the fault is mine.

Finally, I would like to thank two people who have taken time from their busy schedules and put aside their interests to review the book and provided encouragement of all kinds. My brother, Rex Randolph, read the book first and gave very sound advice on logic and the lack thereof as well as grammar and spelling. My wife, Lorraine, is an excellent critic, speller and grammarian. She is also an avid reader, although Revolutionary War history is not a genre of choice. She read the book and made astute corrections and recommendations. She also accompanied me on research jaunts, spending much more time in libraries, records offices, battlefields and cemeteries than she could have ever imagined growing up to the sounds of the Beach Boys in Orange County, California.

CREDITS

Figure 1. World map. Public Domain, https://commons.wikimedia.org/w/index.php?curid=1545382.

Figure 2. Samuel William Reynolds; after Sir Joshua Reynolds, Caleb Whitefoord, 1734 - 1810. Diplomat and wit, National Galleries of Scotland. Bequeathed by William Finlay Watson 1886. Used by permission.

Figure 3. Thomas Gainsborough, The Honourable Mrs Graham (1757 - 1792), National Galleries of Scotland. Bequest of Robert Graham of Redgorton 1859. Used by permission.

Figure 4. George Romney, Jane Maxwell, Duchess of Gordon, c 1749 - 1812. Wife of the 4th Duke of Gordon (With her son, George Duncan, 1770 - 1836. Marquess of Huntly, later 5th Duke of Gordon. General), National Galleries of Scotland. Purchased 1972 with help from the Pilgrim Trust. Used by permission.

Figure 5. Jefferys, Thomas, d. 1771, and Sayer, Robert, ? d 1725-1794. *A new map of Nova Scotia, and Cape Britain.* Map. 1768. Norman B. Leventhal Map & Education Center. https://collections.leventhalmap.org/search/commonwealth:cj82ks15w (January 05, 2019).

Figure 6. Revere, Paul, and Sewell, Alfred L. *A view of part of the town of Boston in New-England and Brittish [sic] ships of war landing their troops! 1768*. Map. 1870. Norman B. Leventhal Map & Education Center. https://collections.leventhalmap.org/search/commonwealth:4m90f850d (January 5, 2019).

Figure 7. Norman, John. *Plan of the town of Boston, with the attack on Bunkers-Hill, in the peninsula of Charlestown, the 17th of June, 1775*. Map. 1781. Norman B. Leventhal Map & Education Center. https://collections.leventhalmap.org/search/commonwealth:st74cw36c (January 5, 2019).

Figure 9. Page, Thomas Hyde, Sir, Montresor, John, and Faden, William. *Boston, its environs and harbour, with the rebel works raised against that town in 1775*. Map. 1777. Norman B. Leventhal Map & Education Center. https://collections.leventhalmap.org/search/commonwealth:wd376798v (January 5, 2019).

Figure 10. Jefferys, Thomas, d. 1771. *St. Vincent, from an actual survey made in the year 1773*. Map. 1775. Norman B. Leventhal Map & Education Center. https://collections.leventhalmap.org/search/commonwealth:6t053r22n (January 5, 2019).

Figure 11. Dunn, Samuel, d. 1794, Carver, Jonathan, and Robert Laurie and James Whittle. *A new map of the United States of North America with the British dominions on that continent &c*. Map. 1794. Norman B. Leventhal Map & Education Center. https://collections.leventhalmap.org/search/commonwealth:w9505s603 (January 5, 2019).

Figure 12. Sir Joshua Reynolds, John Murray, 4th Earl of Dunmore, National Galleries of Scotland. Purchased 1992 with contributions from the Art Fund and the National Heritage Memorial Fund. Used by permission.

Figure 14. Annotated drawing by the author based on *A view of the Great Bridge near Norfolk in Virginia where the action happened between a detachment of the 14th Regt: & a body of the rebels*. Original sketch attributed to Hastings, Francis Rawdon-Hastings, Marquess of, 1754-1826. William L. Clements Library Image Bank. Public domain: "Published anywhere before 1924 and public domain in the U.S."

INTRODUCTION: A CIRCUITOUS PATH

Charles Fordyce commanded the company of British soldiers that attacked the fortifications of Colonel William Woodford's 2nd Virginia Regiment at Great Bridge, Virginia, on December 9, 1775. Fordyce was a captain in the 14th Regiment of Foot, a British infantry regiment. He commanded the elite grenadier company in the regiment. He was Scottish by birth, 34 years old and an experienced combat veteran.

Captain Fordyce had taken a circuitous route of thousands of miles to get to Great Bridge that day, but one might argue it was not an arbitrary route. The trip connected "dots," which were the geographical locations where a British military unit was posted either in response to a crisis or in anticipation of a crisis requiring force of arms. The crises and anticipated crises were occurring as the result of the divergent interests of a government—the British Parliament—administering an expansive colonial empire, and the colonists in that empire, especially the Americans.

In the decades preceding the French and Indian War and during that war (1754-1763), the American colonists' interests in enlightenment philosophies—republicanism, egalitarianism, free trade, religious pluralism—were aroused. The arousal of these interests coincided with the colonists' rapidly growing appetites for just about every kind of resource, in particular, land, capital, infrastructure and favorable commercial arrangements. On the other hand, Great Britain, governor of the vast empire of which newly acquired North American territories were the centerpiece, was faced with the daunting prospect of paying the debt incurred during almost a decade of conflict on two continents—three including India. In addition, it was now Great Britain's responsibility to develop and fund the military and civil establishments necessary to secure, administer and develop the territories gained in the expensive wars.

So, at this crucial juncture, the priorities of Britain's governing oligarchy came to be at odds with those of the American colonists. The British government and the monarchy made paying for the war and securing the borders of their overgrown empire their highest priorities. The colonists were indifferent to Britain's war debts and they seemed to be satisfied their borders—the only borders they cared about—had been secured as a result of victory in the French and Indian War. Furthermore, they were convinced this outcome was due in large part to their own contributions of material and human resources.[1] They were also satisfied they could manage any additional security needs on an *ad hoc* basis. Certainly, they saw no need to pay British soldiers for protection. Free trade and land were their highest priorities, not debt relief and border security. Disagreements, confrontations and violence—crises—resulted when these priorities could not be reconciled.

༄

Charles' journey to Great Bridge took fourteen years—a relatively short time considering the number of dots to be connected and the complexity of the issues to be resolved at each dot. Inasmuch as Charles' journey does provide a set of geographical and chronological milestones of this extraordinary epoch—the epoch in which one of the world's great revolutions emerged—it is clear he had a "front row seat" on the making of modern history. A map of Charles' momentous journey is presented in Figure 1.

Charles joined the army in January 1761 and his journey to Great Bridge began a few months later when he was posted to Germany (Austria), fighting in the Seven Years War (French and Indian War in America). He was then a lieutenant in John Campbell's 88th or Highland Regiment. The Highland Regiments (Campbell's and Keith's) were part of an Anglo-Prussian alliance fighting a Franco-Austrian alliance. Charles' deployment to Germany is designated on the map of Figure 1 as the circled numeral "1" off the eastern coast of Scotland. Mainland Europe is not shown on the map but the fighting in which Charles was involved occurred in campaigns fought in the north-western region of modern Germany.

Introduction: A Circuitous Path

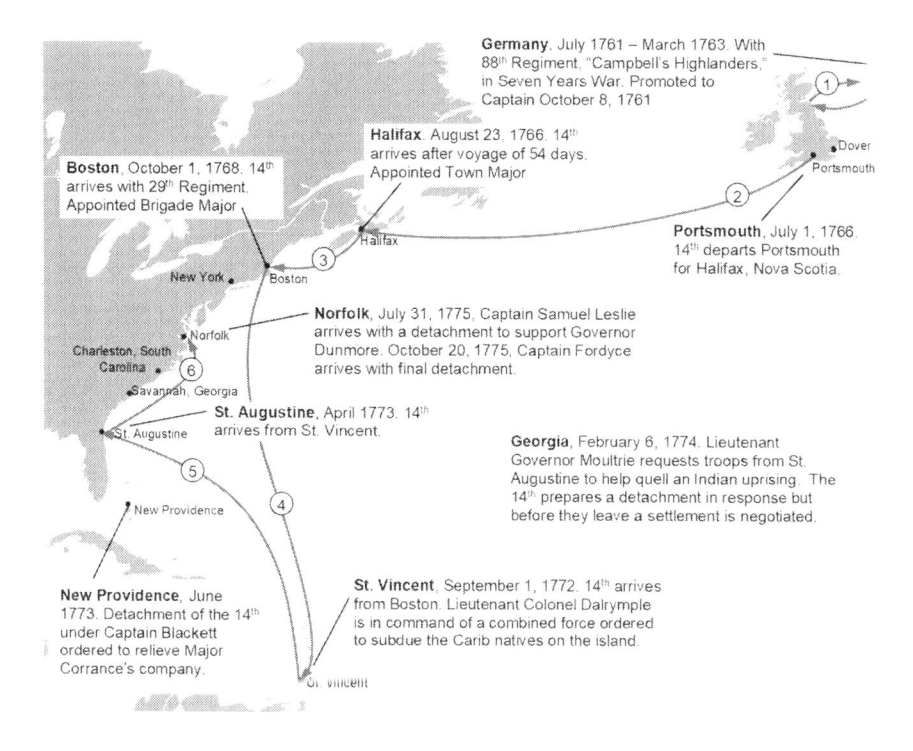

Germany, July 1761 – March 1763. With 88th Regiment, "Campbell's Highlanders," in Seven Years War. Promoted to Captain October 8, 1761

Halifax, August 23, 1766, 14th arrives after voyage of 54 days. Appointed Town Major

Boston, October 1, 1768. 14th arrives with 29th Regiment. Appointed Brigade Major

Portsmouth, July 1, 1766. 14th departs Portsmouth for Halifax, Nova Scotia.

Norfolk, July 31, 1775, Captain Samuel Leslie arrives with a detachment to support Governor Dunmore. October 20, 1775, Captain Fordyce arrives with final detachment.

St. Augustine, April 1773. 14th arrives from St. Vincent.

Georgia, February 6, 1774. Lieutenant Governor Moultrie requests troops from St. Augustine to help quell an Indian uprising. The 14th prepares a detachment in response but before they leave a settlement is negotiated.

New Providence, June 1773. Detachment of the 14th under Captain Blackett ordered to relieve Major Corrance's company.

St. Vincent, September 1, 1772. 14th arrives from Boston. Lieutenant Colonel Dalrymple is in command of a combined force ordered to subdue the Carib natives on the island.

Figure 1. Map of the Locations Where Charles Fordyce Served During His Military Career, 1761 – 1775.

For Britain and France, the war in Europe began with a proxy fight in North America. Neither country was satisfied with the balance of power in Europe following the War of the Austrian Succession (1740-1748) — the war fought to determine which dynasty should rule Austria. British historian George Louis Beer noted the treaty ending that war was "universally recognized" as "merely a truce" and that "combat would soon be resumed."[2]

The resumption of combat was particularly likely in the case of Britain and France since, in addition to the disputes over European borders, they had been engaged in an undeclared war over contested borders in North America for years. The disputes in Europe and North America were intertwined. Both Britain and

France could compensate for losses in one theater by gains in the other. They could also challenge their adversary in one theater by challenging them in the other.

By 1754, these disputes were at the forefront of British and French strategic maneuvering. The maneuvering involved innovative diplomacy but at the same time it seems both countries acceded to the proposition made famous by Carl von Clausewitz decades later that war is "the continuation of politics by different means."

To the extent war was wanted, the escalating belligerence displayed in frontier encounters between the rather unruly British and French proxies in America—traders, colonists, Indians and militias—made it likely hostilities sufficient to justify such a war would occur there before they would in Europe. Wanted or not, this proved to be the case. In 1754, skirmishing began along the Ohio River. Despite a flurry of diplomatic activity to forestall war in Europe, the proxy fighting in America, and alliances formed because of it, advanced British and French involvement in the larger fight over the European balance of power.

Although Charles was not in the army when the disputes over territorial boundaries in North America occurred (he was thirteen years old in 1754), the regiment in which he eventually would serve, the 14th Regiment of Foot, was directly involved in responding to those disputes. Inasmuch as this response led to the start of the French and Indian War in America and the congruent Seven Years War in Europe, the 14th Regiment played a tangential but dramatic role in the start of those wars.

Historians generally agree hostilities in the Seven Years War were precipitated by an obscure battle in America in 1754. Actual fighting may be traced to Lieutenant Governor Robert Dinwiddie of Virginia ordering twenty-one-year-old Major George Washington of the Virginia Militia to stop what he considered French encroachments into the Ohio territory on the frontier of Virginia.

Washington met with the French and Indians in the backcountry of Ohio and Pennsylvania in December of 1753 and attempted to negotiate a settlement. The negotiations were fruitless. Six months later—on May 28, 1754—in what appears to have been a preemptive strike to prevent a consolidation of French forces on the border, Washington attacked what he took to be a French reconnaissance party at Jumonville Glen—near Hopwood, Pennsylvania. In a short but deadly skirmish, Washington overpowered the French. In retaliation, Washington and his modest force were attacked at their outpost at Fort Necessity—near Farmington, Pennsylvania—a few weeks later. The preemptive attack at Jumonville Glen was touted as a victory for Washington, but he was obliged to surrender to the French after a determined defense at Fort Necessity.

Modest and remote as these engagements were, they were not inconsequential. Within a year, the King and Parliament formulated a more ambitious plan to curtail the alleged French invasions into British territory and, although still undeclared, the French and Indian War was underway. General Edward Braddock was selected to command the combined British and American force embodied to halt the French. At the time of his selection, Braddock was the colonel-commander of the 14th Regiment of Foot.

General Braddock sailed to Virginia in 1755 but the 14th Regiment was not part of the force he would command in North America. The 14th was in Gibraltar protecting that outpost from French and Spanish incursions. Two Irish regiments, the 44th and 48th Foot, comprised the brigade of regular troops employed in Braddock's campaign against the French and their Indian allies.[3]

The campaign was ill-fated. General Braddock and his staff showed a lack of appreciation for the logistics requirements associated with moving an army across a trackless mountain range as well as a lack of appreciation for the ferocity and skill of Native American warriors.[4] On July 9, 1755, in the first battle of the campaign, Braddock was severely wounded in a confused fight with the French and Indians. This was the Battle of the Monongahela or Braddock's Defeat, near present day Pittsburg, Pennsylvania. Four days later, on July 13, Braddock died of his wounds.

The operation was considered a debacle.[5] 19th-Century British historian Arthur Bradley noted some of the consequences of the battle in his history of the French and Indian War. These were far-reaching consequences. It is possible they affected the recruiting program the Governor of Virginia, Lord Dunmore, initiated twenty years later when he needed reinforcements to augment the detachment of the 14th Regiment sent to his aid in 1775. According to Mr. Bradley,

> The effect of this battle, which neither before nor since has had any exact parallel in British history, was prodigious. Shame and humiliation was felt in England, unbounded exultation in France, while the American colonists' faith in the invincibility of British soldiers was permanently shaken.[6]

There is also a fascinating coincidence that occurred in this campaign when General Braddock condescended to recruit experienced Indian fighters from the ranks of the American provincials. It seems one of the American officers with the experience Braddock needed was also desirous of a commission as a regular officer in Braddock's retinue. The American was George Washington, now Lieutenant Colonel in Virginia's provincial army.[7] Had Braddock offered Washington a commission as a regular officer, it is possible he would have joined Braddock's own 14th Regiment. Washington did serve as one of Braddock's *aides de camp*, and he was with Braddock at Monongahela the day he was shot. He tended to the dying general as the army retreated from the battle. When Braddock died the evening of July 13, Washington conducted his torchlight funeral service.[8]

One of the earliest assessments of Braddock's Defeat, probably made by an officer either present at the battle or nearby, offers a concise explanation of the significance of the battle in terms of Charles' deployment to fight the French in Germany six years later. He summarized, victory in this battle "would very probably have put an End to the Contest in America."[9] At this time, it is likely that putting an end to the contest in America would have postponed, if not precluded, the beginning of the contest in Europe and Charles' deployment there.

That said, Charles was in Germany with the 88th Regiment for almost two years and he was actively engaged. The battles in which he fought involved tens of thousands of troops and lasted days. The Scots Highlanders with whom he fought were credited with exemplary service. In 1763, at the war's end, he returned to Scotland with his regiment and was reassigned to the 14th Foot. Given the record of the Highlanders in the war and Charles' promotion to the rank of captain at just twenty years old, it is conceivable the young veteran was welcomed home as a hero.

The regiment was stationed in southern England between 1762 and 1766 but Charles was on leave in Scotland for part of this time. While there, he might have renewed his acquaintance with Lady Jane Maxwell—destined for fame as the Duchess of Gordon. His brother, John Fordyce, would marry Jane's sister, Katherine*, in 1767 and they were probably courting at this time.

༺ ༻

Britain and her allies were victorious in the Seven Years War—French and Indian War. But the enormous expense of the war, coupled with the enormous responsibility and cost of administering the vast territorial accessions victory bestowed, meant Parliament would end the policy Edmund Burke called "wise and salutary neglect"[10] for America. Under the auspices of mercantilism—the prevailing economic paradigm of rigid governmental control of trade balances—this meant taxes, regulation, monopolistic trade arrangements (protectionism), and strict enforcement of all these policies.

To develop and secure a favorable trade relationship with the Indian Nations in North America, now a much larger part of the empire and endowed with immeasurable natural wealth, the King issued the Proclamation of 1763, which set the boundary for westward expansion of the colonies. Two years later Parliament passed the Stamp Act to start raising revenue in the colonies to defray the costs of securing territorial borders. The Proclamation of 1763 was unpopular but difficult, if not impossible, to implement and enforce so it was ignored and evaded—behavior consistent with long-standing predilections of the colonists.[11]

The Stamp Act—a tax on paper and legal documents—was not ignored. It was vigorously and violently opposed by the colonists

---

* In some records, the spelling is Catherine. The spelling on her gravestone in the Ayton Parish Church cemetery, Ayton, Scotland, is Katherine. Visit by the author, April 25, 2018.

for at least three reasons. First, it was instigated by a legislative body, Parliament, in which the colonies were not represented. Second, the revenue raised was to be used to pay for British military forces deployed to America to secure borders the Americans insisted they could secure. Third, the Stamp Act was easy to implement and thus difficult to evade.

The vitriol and violence with which the act was met resulted in its repeal in 1766, a year after it was passed. But the acrimony engendered poisoned the relationship between Parliament and the colonies to the extent that raising revenue became a secondary goal of all future fiscal legislation. The assertion of Parliamentary authority came to be the primary goal. That goal was articulated unequivocally in an act passed with the repeal of the Stamp Act — the Declaratory Act. According to this legislation, the colonies were "subordinate unto, and dependent on, the imperial crown and Parliament of Great Britain," and the "King and Parliament of Great Britain had ... full power and authority to make laws and statutes of sufficient force to bind the colonies, and his Majesty's subjects in them, in all cases whatsoever."* This manifesto would underlie the deployments of the 14th Regiment for the next ten years, beginning with the deployment to Halifax, Nova Scotia in 1766. This deployment is labeled "2" in Figure 1.

༶

Charles arrived at Halifax with the 14th Regiment on August 23, 1766. The Stamp Act had been repealed by this time, so ostensibly this deployment was not in response to the furor over that legislation. It was a deployment made in compliance with a "plan of

---

* Not all the Lords acceded to the Declaratory Act, notable among the dissenters was jurist Charles Pratt, Lord Camden. In a speech during the debates on the bill, he denounced it as "absolutely illegal, contrary to the fundamental laws of nature, contrary to the laws of this [i.e., the English] constitution." *Parliamentary History of England*, Vol. 16, pp. 177, 178. Historian George Trevelyan believed the reason the arguments of men like Lord Camden were ineffectual was due to a firmly established system of "personal government" instituted and promoted by King George III. Trevelyan was convinced this policy caused the American Revolutionary War and kept it going. George Trevelyan, *The American Revolution*. Vol. 2, New York: Longmans, Green, and Co., 1917, p. 164 and Vol. 1, p. 218.

rotation" King George III instituted to relieve the troops on foreign deployments of the fatigue of years away from home and civilization.[12] But when the transports that brought the 14th to Nova Scotia returned to England they were empty.[13] This suggests there had been no rotation so, in this case, the troops in North America had been augmented. In any event, the 14th Regiment was now forward deployed on the North American Station to provide a means of more rapid reaction should follow-on acts of Parliament again elicit violence in the colonies.

Charles was named Town Major of Halifax a year after he arrived, an administrative posting and a position of responsibility on the regimental staff. Duty in Halifax was probably routine garrison duty with detachments sent out to nearby outposts from time-to-time to guard work parties and farmers from unlikely but conceivable Indian assaults or, in some cases, to help as laborers.

This calm would last two years for Charles and the men of the 14th Regiment, even though the Parliamentary acts that brought an end to the calm were enacted in June 1767, less than a year after the 14th arrived in Halifax. The acts in question—Revenue Acts—were sponsored by Charles Townshend and came to be known as the Townshend Acts. By these acts, import duties were levied on dozens of commodities, a Board of Customs Commissioners was established and the British Navy was coopted to maintain the various trade monopolies by curtailing smuggling.[14]

The colonists were disaffected by these new acts but they resorted to more civil means to express that disaffection than had been the case with the Stamp Act. Since the acts set duties on imports, the initial reaction in America was to cease importing and replace the imports with home-made goods. Citizens' groups established non-importation agreements and importers were exposed to the indignation and scorn of non-importers when their names were published in the local newspapers. However, in addition to this relatively temperate behavior, the Massachusetts' Assembly drafted a "Circular Letter" –distributed throughout the colonies—denouncing the Townshend Acts as unconstitutional and mobs threatened the Customs Commissioners by hanging their effigies in "Liberty Trees."

By June of 1768, Wills Hill, Lord Hillsborough, Secretary of State for the Colonies, had had enough of the intimidation, evasion and threats. He directed General Gage, commander of British forces in North America, to "order one regiment, or such force as you shall think necessary, to Boston, to be quartered in that town, and to give every legal assistance to the civil magistrate in the preservation of the public peace."[15] General Gage decided he needed two regiments for the job and ordered the 14th and 29th to Boston. So it was that Charles embarked on the third increment of his journey to the Battle of Great Bridge—the increment that took him to Boston in September 1768. This deployment is labeled "3" in Figure 1.

While in Halifax, Charles had heard and read of what might have been considered the seditious behavior of the American colonists. In Boston, he and the 14th Regiment would experience colonial outrage over taxation without representation first-hand. To their immediate discomfort, the regiment would learn of the bitter resentment a considerable number of Bostonians harbored over the quartering of British troops in their city. Boston was thus an active crisis point.

The soldiers were the representatives of what the more incensed colonists considered slave masters. As such, they were subjected to a steady stream of insults and abuses. Charles was appointed Brigade Major in Boston; a staff position similar to that of Town Major. Under the circumstances in Boston, his forbearance was put to numerous tests involving irate businessmen, insolent schoolboys, indignant magistrates, libelous newspaper reporters, exasperated soldiers and unscrupulous contractors.

On March 5, 1770, about eighteen months after the 14th and 29th Regiments entered Boston, the anger and resentment erupted in a melee between the soldiers and a club-wielding mob of citizens outraged at an alleged attack on a barber's apprentice. In the confrontation, soldiers in a detachment from the 29th Regiment fired on the mob and killed five civilians. This tragic episode—called the Boston Massacre by the Patriot faction—exposed the frightening level to which acrimony had risen in Boston. The shock of this violence forced immediate changes in the quartering of the British troops and provided some relief to the months of tension.[16] The soldiers were moved to Castle Island in Boston Harbor and a period of relative calm ensued. This lasted for the remainder of the time the 14th was in New England.

Charles was barracked on Castle Island with his regiment for the next two years. Then another instance of colonial disaffection raised fears of bloodshed. This time some 2,000 miles from Boston on the Island of St. Vincent. St. Vincent is part of an island chain in what was called the West Indies in 1772. France had ceded St. Vincent to Great Britain at the conclusion of the Seven Years War. The indigenous people on the Island, named Caribs by the French and British, were not inclined to be governed by either European power. The British were eager to open plantations on the island, which, in the colonial tradition, involved resettling the indigenous population, whether they agreed to such resettlement or not. The Caribs refused to move but unlike the situation in America, where the colonists outnumbered the natives, the natives outnumbered the colonists on St. Vincent. Under these conditions, the colonists on St. Vincent were only too happy to acknowledge their complete dependence on the mother country for protection. They appealed to the King and Parliament and in April 1772, Secretary Hillsborough initiated plans that resulted in the deployment of the 14th Regiment to St. Vincent to provide the requested protection.[17]

The deployment to St. Vincent, noted as "4" in Figure 1, may seem like an unnecessary detour on the way to Virginia, a detour that not only added time to an already lengthy overseas deployment but—because of the unhealthy tropical climate—greatly increased the risks of personnel losses due to disease. Of course, such losses would reduce the regiment's capability to respond to the "necessary" assignments associated with the increasing unrest in North America. (Just before the regiment left for St. Vincent, HMS *Gaspee* was burned by the Sons of Liberty off the coast of Rhode Island. This was the most provocative act of defiance in New England since the Stamp Act riots.)

Arguably, the mission to St. Vincent was a detour and the regiment was degraded significantly in terms of men fit for duty after the assignment. But since the colony of St. Vincent—including the natives—was to be just as subordinate and dependent as Massachusetts Bay, this deployment was no more or less a detour than any of the deployments the 14th Regiment was assigned.

That said, the costs of the Carib Campaign were indeed high. At its conclusion, Lieutenant Colonel Dalrymple—promoted to the local rank of Major General to lead the combined force on St. Vincent—reported 72 men had been killed, 110 died of disease and 428 were sick.[18] In the 14th Regiment, eleven men had been killed and twenty-six had died of disease. The losses meant it was a much-weakened regiment that sailed from St. Vincent to the garrison town of St. Augustine, Florida in 1773, and the losses would never be fully restored. For the remainder of their deployment in America, the 14th Regiment would be overextended both in terms of the duration of the deployment and their inventory of men and equipment.[19] Given this outcome, the deployment to St. Vincent did highlight the requirement for an extensive military capability inherent in a British colonial policy which mandated subordination, dependence and obedience were prerequisites to cooperation, development and commerce.

The campaign in St. Vincent was short. The 14th Regiment was there about nine months. They arrived in September of 1772 and within weeks of the signing of the treaty ending the conflict in February 1773, they set sail for St. Augustine. This deployment to Florida is labeled with the circled "5" in Figure 1.

Florida was not one of the thirteen original colonies. It was another prize of the Seven Years War, traded by Spain for Havana, Cuba, which had been captured by the British in 1763. As had been the case with the deployment to Halifax in 1766, the deployment to St. Augustine was nominally part of the rotation established by King George III. In this case, the 14th would be relieving the 29th Regiment, the same regiment they had joined in Halifax in 1766 and the same regiment that accompanied them to Boston in 1768. The 29th had been deployed to St. Augustine in 1771[20] and in 1773 they were finally on their way back to England.

Halifax had been, and remained, the staging area for British troops destined for service in Canada, New England and the Northern and Central colonies. Now St. Augustine came to be the staging area for troops destined for service in the Southern colonies—Georgia, South Carolina, North Carolina, Virginia and Maryland. As had been the case in Halifax, the troops in St. Augustine would perform routine garrison duty in a rather benign and even friendly environment. There would be one alarm of an Indian uprising in neighboring Georgia during their stay. It seems Captain Fordyce, in command of the garrison at the time, suspected the alarm was false, or at least overblown. He would negotiate with General Haldimand, acting Commander-in-Chief of the British forces during General Gage's furlough to England, and Governor James Wright of Georgia to delay deployment of regular troops. His delay tactic (never officially acknowledged as such) provided the contending parties the time they needed to resolve their differences without further violence. The 14th Regiment was never deployed to Georgia. With the exception of a detachment sent to New Providence in the Bahamas and a detachment that never left Boston, the regiment remained intact in St. Augustine for the two years they were deployed there.

Like they had in Halifax, Charles and the men of the 14th Regiment in St. Augustine would read of continued disaffection in the American colonies over the Townshend Acts. They would read of the way the Tea Act was characterized in Philadelphia as a "Precedent for every imposition the Parliament of Great Britain shall think proper to saddle us with."[21] They would read of the dumping of tea in Boston Harbor on December 16, 1773—an object lesson for Parliament known as the Boston Tea Party. They would read of the Boston Port Act—the closure of the Port of Boston as a result of the Tea Party. They would read of the first Continental Congress and the Articles of Association adopted by that body, which cited a "ruinous system of colony administration, adopted by the British ministry about the year 1763, evidently calculated for enslaving these colonies."[22] Finally they would read of General Gage's botched attempt to confiscate the arms in the magazine in Concord, Massachusetts on April 19, 1775 and of Governor Dunmore's attempt to do the same in Williamsburg a day later.

Within a few days of hearing of these latter incidents, Captain Fordyce and the men of the 14th would receive orders to deploy to

Virginia, the circled "6" in Figure 1. Here, command of the regiment would devolve to "his Excellency the Right Honorable John Earl of Dunmore, his Majesty's Lieutenant and Governor General of the said Colony and Dominion, and Vice Admiral of the same." Governor Dunmore intended to combine the regulars of the 14th Regiment with contingents of volunteers recruited among the Loyalists and freed slaves in Virginia to build a force of some one thousand men. With that force he would confront the Patriot forces that had driven him from the seat of government in Williamsburg after he seized the provincial gunpowder reserve.[23]

Captain Fordyce and his detachment of the 14th Regiment arrived in Norfolk, Virginia on October 20, 1775. Seven weeks later, on December 9, 1775, they would fight in the Battle of Great Bridge. For Charles, it was the final dot on the path of dots marking the locations of clashes over interests and priorities. Locations where impatient colonists, with aspirations for civil and religious liberties and commercial and territorial growth, challenged the authority of a detached king and his Parliament thought to be confounding those aspirations.

Invariably, the challenges had degenerated into military confrontations—the instigation of martial law—at a time when demands for British military forces were being made from every corner of the world. In one of the more obscure whims of history, a single British army regiment, the 14th Foot, was the regiment available when the king and Parliament made the decision to impose martial law at crisis points in North America and the West Indies during the eventful years between 1766 and 1775. As fate would have it, Charles Fordyce joined the 14th Regiment at this time of challenge and confrontation. So the account of his military career is the account of the sequence of confrontations that climaxed in the outbreak of war in America and, at that critical time, to the confrontation that fixed British intentions to make New England, Canada and the central colonies the seat of the war. That confrontation was the Battle of Great Bridge—Charles' final battle.

CHAPTER 1: CHARLES FORDYCE'S FAMILY

Charles Fordyce was born October 1, 1741 in Edinburgh, Scotland. He was baptized the day of his birth by his Uncle, the Rev. Mr. George Fordyce, Minister of the Gospel at Corstorphine,[1] a suburb of Edinburgh. Charles' father was Thomas Fordyce and his mother Elizabeth Whitefoord. Thomas Fordyce is called a "writer" in family histories and this refers to a "writer to the signet," or solicitor. He was also a businessman—a "factor" or agent in the York Buildings Company that administered the Port Seton glassworks. Thomas was the son of Alexander Fordyce, a minister of the Church of Scotland, and his wife, Anna Meldrum.

Charles' mother, Elizabeth Whitefoord, was the daughter of Sir Adam Whitefoord, 1st Baronet of Blairquhan, and Margaret Cathcart. Both the Whitefoords and Cathcarts were families of renown.[2] Margaret's brother, Charles, 8th Lord Cathcart, achieved the rank of major general in the army and served as a Scottish Peer in Parliament between 1732 and 1740. In 1727 he was appointed Groom of the Bedchamber to King George II. Lord Cathcart's son, the 9th Lord Cathcart (this would be Charles' first cousin once removed), was also a soldier. He was *aide de camp* to George II's son, the Duke of Cumberland. The 9th Lord achieved the rank of lieutenant general, was created a Knight of the Order of the Thistle and was wounded at the Battles of Fontenoy in 1745 and Culloden in 1746. Culloden was the battle that sealed the fate of the forces fighting to restore the British crown to the descendants of James VI of Scotland (James I of England and Ireland). These Scottish forces were called the Jacobites (Jacob is Latin for James). The British forces fighting for King George II won the battle. Lord Cathcart fought for the British at Culloden.

On the Whitefoord side, Elizabeth's oldest brother (Charles' uncle) was Lieutenant General Sir John Whitefoord, 2nd Baronet of

Blairquhan. Sir John's son (Charles' first cousin), the 3rd Baronet of Blairquhan—also named John—served as a major in the British Army but he is best known for his patronage of the poet Robert Burns.[3] This John Whitefoord was born in 1734. Robert Burns was born in 1759 so he would have been twenty-five years younger than Sir John and eighteen years younger than Charles. Given this age disparity, it is unlikely Charles ever met Burns, despite the patronage of his first cousin. Charles was with the 14th Regiment in America before Burns was in his teens, and this was before Burns and Sir John were acquainted.

Another of Elizabeth Whitefoord's brothers, Charles, was recognized for his role in negotiating the pardon of one of the Jacobite officers, Alexander Stewart, after the Battle of Culloden. The negotiations were carried on at the highest level of command in the British army, i.e., with the Duke of Cumberland. Colonel Whitefoord met with the Duke in person and appealed for Stewart's pardon. When that was refused, he requested Stewart's house, wife, children and property be exempt from the royal sanctions. That too was refused. At this point, according to Sir Walter Scott's account of the proceedings, Colonel Whitefoord laid his commission "… on the table before his Royal Highness with much emotion, and asked permission to retire from the service of a sovereign who did not know how to spare a vanquished enemy." This gesture disarmed the Duke—he was "struck, and even affected"—and Whitefoord's request was granted.[4]

Whitefoord's humanity and gallantry under circumstances of considerable risk qualify him as a man of courage and integrity. These family traits seem to have been inherited by Colonel Whitefoord's nephew, Charles Fordyce, because the record of his military career affirms he too was a humane and gallant man of integrity.

Colonel Whitefoord's son, Caleb Whitefoord (another of Charles Fordyce's first cousins), was appointed secretary of the commissioners sent to Paris after the Revolutionary War to conclude the peace with America. He was also well known as a writer and wit who was respected by contemporaries Samuel Johnson, Oliver Goldsmith, and Horace Walpole.[5] Caleb's circle of friends included the celebrated portrait painter, Sir Joshua Reynolds. A copy of an engraved portrait of Caleb is presented in Figure 2. Samuel William Reynolds did the engraving from a portrait by Joshua Reynolds. (Joshua Reynolds also painted portraits of Charles' and Caleb's cousin, the 9th Lord Cathcart and his wife, Jane Hamilton.)

Caleb was an intimate of Benjamin Franklin. He lived next door to Franklin on Craven Street when they both lived in London prior to the Revolutionary War. In fact, it seems it was this accidental but genuine friendship between Franklin and Whitefoord that led to his appointment to the Paris peace negotiations in 1782. He was acquainted with Franklin by 1762 and was linked with the literary luminaries Goldsmith and Johnson in the early 1770s. Franklin was in London between 1757 and 1762 then again between 1764 and 1775. Since Charles returned from Germany in 1763 and his regiment, the 14th Foot, was stationed in London in 1764, it is possible he spent some time with his cousin while there. If so, it is also possible he was introduced to his cousin's neighbor and friend, Benjamin Franklin.

Figure 2. Caleb Whitefoord, Charles' First Cousin. Whitefoord was a friend of Benjamin Franklin and secretary to the commission that concluded peace between Great Britain and the United States at Paris in 1782. Engraving by Samuel William Reynolds; after Sir Joshua Reynolds. National Galleries of Scotland. Used by permission.

Caleb was born in 1734 so he, like his cousin Sir John Whitefoord, was seven years older than cousin Charles Fordyce, but it seems Caleb and Charles knew each other and had some understanding of each other's status in their extended family. When Caleb's father died in 1753, he left him with an obligation to pay his cousin Charles a £100 legacy.[6] As a legacy, this seems rather modest, but it was half of the £200 necessary to purchase a commission as an ensign in the infantry in 1753,[7] so it may be Charles' uncle was already interested in supporting a military career for his then twelve-year-old nephew.

In addition to well-respected, high-ranking and influential military officers and diplomats, Charles' family was also affiliated with the highest ranking political figures of Scotland and England. He was related by blood or marriage to five of the sixteen Scottish Peers in the House of Lords. These were: Charles Cathcart, 9th Lord Cathcart, already noted as Charles' first cousin once removed, John Dalrymple, 5th Earl of Stair, Charles' second cousin once removed, John Campbell, 4th Earl of Loudoun, another second cousin once removed, John Murray, 4th Duke of Atholl, who was the husband of Charles' second cousin, Jane Cathcart and David Murray, 2nd Earl of Mansfield, who married Jane's sister Louisa Cathcart. This marriage took place on May 5, 1776—after Charles' death—so his connection to peer David Murray was posthumous. But even such a posthumous connection establishes Charles' proximity to the highest tier of the Scottish aristocracy, especially when combined with the other connections in place before his death.

One of these relations might have been the source of an interest in America years before Charles was posted there as a Captain in the 14th Regiment. In addition to his service as a Scottish Peer, John Campbell, the 4th Earl of Loudoun, served as the Commander-in-Chief of British forces in America and Governor of Virginia for a short time during the French and Indian War. He served less than two years in America between 1756 and 1758, during which time Charles would have been a teenager. Nevertheless, the fact his relative served in such an auspicious capacity could have piqued Charles' interest in Virginia and America during these formative years.

Charles' second cousins, Jane and Louisa Cathcart—just mentioned—along with their sister Mary, were celebrities in their own right as some of the most beautiful patricians of the day. Mary Cathcart, wife of Thomas Graham, 1st Baron Lynedoch, was particularly notable. Gainsborough's portrait of Mrs. Graham is one of the most popular works in the Scottish National Gallery and has been denominated by one critic as "the most charming

Gainsborough in the world."⁸ The portrait in question—presented here as Figure 3—was painted after Mary married in 1774, so it is unlikely Charles—in St. Augustine, Florida at the time—was aware of his second cousin's celebrity in terms of her beauty but in all likelihood he would have been aware of her advantageous marriage.

☙

Clearly, the connections to high-ranking military officers, paragons of the arts, powerful politicians and even royalty are solid in Charles' extended family. There is little evidence Charles exploited these connections but there is no reason to believe he did not enjoy them.

Despite Charles' close and actual encounters with the aristocrats and celebrities of his age—and there are more to be mentioned in this survey of his family and military service—his immediate family seems to have been one of modest but respectable means. According to one family historian, the Thomas Fordyce family lived in a "large dwelling house with garden in the 'Town' of Corstorphine" when Charles was born but moved from that location to Covenant Close on the Royal Mile in Edinburgh in 1742.⁹

Figure 3. Mary Cathcart, wife of Thomas Graham, 1ˢᵗ Baron Lynedoch. Portrait is considered "the most charming Gainsborough in the world." Mary was Charles' second cousin. Portrait by Thomas Gainsborough. National Galleries of Scotland. Used by permission.

Charles was the youngest of five children.[10] His oldest sibling, Adam, born June 15, 1732, was nine years his senior. The next in birth order was brother, George Thomas Fordyce, born Jun 25, 1734. A third brother, John Fordyce, was born May 3, 1736. Charles' only sister, Cathcart Fordyce, was born May 13, 1740.

That Charles was born in Edinburgh is established by his birth record, but it seems the family spent considerable time in Ayton, about 50 miles east and slightly south of Edinburgh, before and after Charles was born. In 1732, Charles' father, Thomas, received a Crown Charter for the "lands and the barony of Aytoun."[11] He wrote several letters to Mr. George Innes, Deputy Receiver General of the Land Tax and Cashier of the Royal Bank (Thomas' brother-in-law, Allan Whitefoord, was Receiver General) between 1738 and 1751 and all were sent from Ayton. In a letter from Ayton dated April 26, 1742, Mr. Fordyce tells Mr. Innes his son Charles—then seven months old—was teething and was also recovering from a rash. In the same letter, he mentioned how the entire family was benefiting from the change of air.[12]

In another letter from Ayton, written in 1746, when Charles was five years old, Thomas informs Mr. Innes he is concerned about the qualifications of a tutor he has hired for his sons (no mention is made of daughter Cathcart) which suggests he may have planned to educate the boys at home in Ayton. This possibility is reinforced by another statement in the same letter where Thomas concludes he may have to send his sons to Edinburgh if the tutor fails to qualify. Given that possibility, Mr. Fordyce asks Mr. Innes if he would inform him if he hears "of some good private teacher near Dickson's Close," noting that location "would be convenient for them."[13] Based on this inquiry, it is reasonable to conclude the family may have had a residence or access to lodgings in Edinburgh near Dickson's Close as well as Ayton.

༄

In Alexander Dingwall Fordyce's *Family Record of the Name of Dingwall Fordyce in Aberdeenshire*, Charles is listed as an "unconnected" Fordyce. That is, he is not listed in the summary of the Fordyce family of Ayton in which Charles' father, mother and brother, John Fordyce, are mentioned. In fact, in this *Family Record*, Charles is simply listed with the erroneous citation: "Charles Fordyce, Captain, 14th Regiment of Foot, died in St. Vincent's*, November, 1772, in a skirmish with the Caribs."[14] True, Charles was with the 14th Regiment in St. Vincent in 1772, and he was skirmishing with "Caribs," but he was not killed by the Caribs. The error in this citation no doubt stems from the erroneous report of Charles' death in numerous British newspapers and magazines covering the Carib War as it unfolded in 1772 and 1773.[15] All these reports are incorrect for the plain and simple reason Charles did not die in 1772 at St. Vincent. He died on December 9, 1775 in a battle with the 2nd Virginia Regiment at Great Bridge, Virginia.

Charles is absent from all the short histories of the Alexander and Thomas Fordyce families. But so are his brothers, Adam and George, and his sister, Cathcart. Despite this oversight, the birth records of the Edinburgh Parish make it clear all four of these individuals were the children of Thomas Fordyce and his wife, Elizabeth Whitefoord.[16]

Adam and George Fordyce may be absent from the family histories because they died young. This supposition is based on the fact their younger brother, John, succeeded his maternal uncle, Allan Whitefoord of Ballochmyle, as Receiver General of the Land Tax for Scotland in 1766. Although this does not seem to have been a hereditary office, it is likely the incumbent was influential in determining his successor and given the importance and potential of the office for both influence and wealth, the likely successor would be an elder son. Since the successor in question, John Fordyce, was not the eldest son—both Adam and George were older—it is natural to speculate Adam and George were dead, or they had already inherited appointments of greater worth than Receiver General of the Land Tax for Scotland. The supposition they inherited appointments of more worth than the Receiver General is difficult to support because, if they had achieved such influence, they would be recognized in the records for the given offices for their service. Since both Adam and George are not only

---

* Often St. Vincent was identified as St. Vincent's in 18th Century references.

absent from the family history but state history as well, it is reasonable to conclude they were dead in 1766 when their younger brother, John, succeeded their uncle as Receiver General of the Land Tax for Scotland.

That Charles was not considered a candidate in the succession is not surprising since he was the youngest of the four boys and since he was already a captain in His Majesty's 14th Regiment of Foot in 1766. In fact, it is likely Charles was in Halifax, Nova Scotia, when his brother was appointed Receiver General. Within two years, he would be in Boston. Within seven more years, he would be killed at the Battle of Great Bridge.

Several elements of Charles' family status and career conspired to relegate him to obscurity in the family lore. First, as just noted, he was the youngest child from a family of ministers, attorneys, businessmen and bankers—men named only on the margins of aristocratic circles. Second, he died rather young at 34 in what was still, in effect, a "police action." Third, although distinguished as having given his life for his country, some would argue his sacrifice was wasted in a high-risk, unnecessary gamble. Fourth, he was buried in an unmarked grave in a rural churchyard in an obscure village in America. These elements may provide a reasonable explanation for his absence from the Fordyce family lore, but—given what seems to have been a life rich in devotion, competence and courage—certainly not an acceptable one.

༄

Charles' well-known older brother, John, was, like Charles, born in Edinburgh. It seems he was somewhat of a prodigy—or at least shown the deference one might show a prodigy. In 1751, when he was 15 years old, his father arranged for him to attend a "fine academy" at "Heath near York." It is likely the academy in question was that run by Joseph Randall, and it was located at Heath near Wakefield in Yorkshire. The curriculum of the academy was quite broad, and included a course of study aimed at preparing young men for a career in the army.[17] In a letter requesting finances to support his son's education, Thomas Fordyce noted John would learn mathematics, geography, fortification, gunnery, drawing and French to "Qualify him for the army, which he intends to follow."[18]

There is no record of John ever serving in the army or attending the academy at Heath, but it is likely he received a good education, possibly through the offices of a private tutor at home either in Edinburgh or Ayton. It is also conceivable he attended the academy at Heath but took the course of study Randall offered to prepare young men for service in the "compting house" –today's business office. This possibility seems likely since John was appointed "merchant councillor [sic] and a director of the Royal Bank," in 1760, when he was 24 years old. When he succeeded his uncle, Allan Whitefoord, as Receiver General of the Land Tax in Scotland in 1766, he was 30 years old.[19]

John received considerable notoriety for his activities while Receiver General, but he would also be remembered for his connection to one of the most beautiful—and colorful—aristocrats of the 18th century, Jane Maxwell, Duchess of Gordon. John married Jane's older sister, Katherine, on January 28, 1767, just after taking over the position of Receiver General of the Land Tax. Later that year, on October 23, 1767, the newlyweds hosted the marriage of Jane to Alexander Gordon, 4th Duke of Gordon, at their home in Edinburgh.[20] A copy of George Romney's portrait of Jane with her son George Gordon, Marquis of Huntly, is presented in Figure 4.

It is possible John and Katherine met as children. As noted earlier, the Fordyces lived in Covenant Close on the High Street of the Royal Mile in Edinburgh. Based on the letter Thomas Fordyce wrote George Innes, wherein he mentions the convenience of finding a tutor for his sons near Dickson's Close—also on the High Street—it is possible the Fordyces had a residence nearer that location. The Maxwells also lived on the High Street at Hyndford's Close.

The Royal Mile is the street connecting Edinburgh Castle to Holyrood Palace. Hyndford's Close is about halfway between the castle and the palace and no more than two hundred yards from Covenant Close. Dickson's Close is about halfway between Hyndford's Close and Covenant Close. In an early 20th century gazetteer of Scotland, Hyndford's Close is listed at number 50 on the High

Street, Dickson's Close at number 118 and Covenant Close at number 162.[21] Given this proximity, the Fordyces and Maxwells were neighbors and it is reasonable to conclude the Fordyce boys would have known the Maxwell girls in their youth.

Charles left with his regiment for North America seven months before his brother married Katherine Maxwell and over a year before Katherine's sister married the Duke of Gordon. Under these circumstances, it is possible he never met the Maxwell sisters. On the other hand—as just noted—the Fordyces and Maxwells were neighbors, so Charles and Jane may have known each other for most of their lives. In any event, the protocols of etiquette would dictate their being introduced when Charles' brother John was courting Jane's sister Katherine, which was probably underway sometime after Charles returned from military service in Germany in 1763 and before his departure for North America in 1766. In fact, the record is clear that part of the time the 14th Regiment was stationed in Salisbury in southern England during 1765 and 1766, Charles was on leave in Scotland. He was there for over three months between November 1765 and March 1766.[22] He could have been introduced to the

Figure 4. Jane Maxwell, Duchess of Gordon, with her son George Gordon, Marquis of Huntly. Charles' brother, John Fordyce, married Jane's sister, Katherine Maxwell. Portrait by George Romney. National Galleries of Scotland. Used by permission.

Maxwell sisters at this time or, given the more likely possibility they were already well acquainted, this could have been an opportunity for Charles to bid his neighbors and future in-laws farewell before departing for North America.*

Since the Duchess of Gordon was John Fordyce's sister-in-law, it is reasonable to conclude he would have been a guest at the elegant soirees for which the Duchess was so well known. And these parties could have included the likes of Robert Burns and General Charles Cornwallis of Revolutionary War fame. Robert Burns memorialized the Duchess in one of his poems and he was a frequent guest of the Gordons. Cornwallis' oldest son, Lord Brome, married the Duchess of Gordon's fourth daughter, Louisa. It is possible Charles Fordyce was included in the rarified society surrounding the Duchess of Gordon, but if he were, he would have been on leave from the army since the 14th Regiment was so active in the Americas between 1766 and 1776. Even if he never met the Duchess, it is conceivable his social status and perhaps his career were influenced by his proximity to such celebrity, although in fairness to Charles, there is no record or hint of such influence.

---

* A very romantic and tragic love story persists involving Jane Maxwell, Duchess of Gordon, and an unknown British army officer. According to one of the earliest publications of the story, "As a girl she was strongly attached to a young officer, who reciprocated her passion. The soldier, however, was ordered abroad with his regiment." The tragedy involves a false report of the officer's death in America, an ensuing marriage to the Duke of Gordon, discovery of the false report and the heartbreak over the accidental but irretrievable denial of her only true love. This story has never been authenticated. That said, there are remarkable parallels between the life of the officer of the legend and that of Charles Fordyce. See, for example: "Death of the Duchess Gordon," "The Seaforth Papers: Letters from 1796 to 1843," *The North British Review*, Vol. 39, August – November 1863, Edinburg: Edmonston and Douglas, 1863, p. 344 and "A Chapter on Clerical Song-Writers in the North" James Anthony Froude, John Tulloch, editors, *Fraser's Magazine for Town and Country*, Vol. 76, July 1867, London: Longmans, Green and Company, 1867, p. 17.

CHAPTER 2: DEPLOYED TO GERMANY, SEVEN YEARS WAR SERVICE, 1761 – 1763

The first record of Charles' service in the army is the *Army Commission Book for 1761-1762*. In this document he is listed three times. First as "Charles Fordyce, Gent," a lieutenant in the Independent Company of Foot commanded by Captain Patrick Wilkie. According to the record, his commission was given at Saville House on January 8, 1761. Second, he is listed as "Charles Fordice, Gent, to be Lieutenant in Our 14th Regt of Foot commanded by Maj. Genl. Charles Jefferyes." This commission was given at St. James, August 24, 1761. Charles is listed a third time as "Fordyce, Esq. to be Captain of a Company (vice David Wedderburn Esq.) in our 88th Regiment of Foot or Highland Volunteers commanded by Lieutenant Colonel John Campbell." The date of this last commission is given as 8 October 1761.[1]

Charles is also included in another record of the officers of the British army known simply as the *Army List*. As with the *Commission Book*, there is some ambiguity in the first record of Charles' service in the *Army List*. This seems to stem from the fact two *Lists* were published for 1761. The first is distinguished as "Complete for 1761" and the second as "to November 1761." The "to November 1761" *List* seems to be the latest for that year. Charles is not included in the first *List* but he is included twice in the "to November 1761" *List*, first as a lieutenant in the 14th Regiment with a regimental date-of-rank of August 24, 1761 and an army date-of-rank of January 8, 1761.* In the same volume, his name appears a second time as "Capt Charles Fordyce" of the 88th Foot in the

---

* Two dates-of-rank were included in the *Army List*. The army date-of-rank was the date the officer entered the service. It did not change. The regimental date-of-rank was the date the officer joined the regiment or was promoted to the rank listed for the officer. This date changed with any promotion or reassignment.

Chapter 2: Deployed to Germany, Seven Years War Service, 1761 - 1763   27

"Additions since printing" section of the *List*. In the "Additions," his date-of-rank is October 8, 1761 and the citation includes the note: "*v*. Wedderburn (*pref*)."[2] This officer, David Wedderburn, is listed as a captain in the 88th Regiment in the first *List* for 1761.[3] Wedderburn was promoted to major of the 102nd Regiment on July 4, 1761.[4] The notation "*pref*" next to Charles' name in the November 1761 *Army List* is an abbreviation of "preferred" and it means he too had been promoted as opposed to purchasing the commission of the higher rank.

The date of the next year's *Army List* is designated as "for 1763" on the cover. Since none of the date entries in that *List* are beyond 1762, it is—in effect—the list for 1762, not 1763. Charles is included in this *List* as a captain in the 88th Regiment of Foot, Highland Volunteers, in Germany, with a date-of-rank in the regiment of October 8, 1761.[5] Another *List* was published for the year 1763 with the date designation of "to November 1763." In this *List*, Charles is identified as a captain in the 14th Regiment with a regimental date of rank of September 9, 1763 and an army date of rank of October 8, 1761.[6]

Born October 1, 1741, Charles would have been nineteen years old when commissioned a lieutenant in Patrick Wilkie's Independent Company on January 8, 1761, and a week over twenty years old when he received the commission of a captain on October 8 of that year. Normally, a young gentleman entered the army with the rank of ensign or second lieutenant. It was not unusual for this to occur when the candidate was no more than sixteen years old. Such a prescription begs the question, "Why did Charles enter the service as a nineteen-year-old lieutenant instead of a sixteen-year-old ensign?" There are three likely answers. First, even though there is no evidence to support it, he did receive some help from his influential relatives, second, he was commissioned an ensign or second lieutenant some time earlier and the record was lost or, third, there was an urgent need for officers and extraordinary enlistment incentives were offered. This latter answer is plausible and perhaps the best answer given the timing of Charles' service. That is, 1761 was a time of urgent need for both officers and men in the British army—a need resulting from the concentration of the French forces in Europe against Britain's ally, Prussia during the Seven Years War.

Given Charles joined the army on January 8, 1761—the date listed in the *Commission Book for 1761-1762*—his initial service occurred about a year after the formation of two "Highland Regiments" in Scotland in January 1760. These regiments were formed to support an alliance with Prussia negotiated in 1756. This Anglo-Prussian Alliance benefited the British in their war with France in that German armies threatened France in Europe enabling the British to bring more of their forces to bear on the French in North America.

The two regiments raised were the 87th and 88th, "Keith's and Campbell's Highlanders." Robert Murray-Keith commanded the 87th Regiment. He had been reassigned to this post from the 73rd Regiment of Foot where he held the rank of captain. John Campbell was reassigned to the 88th Regiment from the 78th Regiment of Foot where he was serving as a major under Lieutenant-Colonel, Commander Simon Fraser. King George II had established the 78th Regiment three years earlier in January 1757. It was also known as Fraser's Highlanders.[7]

It seems the 87th and 88th Regiments evolved from a smaller "Corps of Highlanders" King George II ordered Murray-Keith to form on August 25, 1759. By September 1759, 360 men of this newly organized corps were on their way to Shields on the northwest coast of England to embark for Germany. This modest contingent of Highlanders arrived in Greenstendorp, near Bremen before the end of October and they were reported to have "distinguished themselves greatly" in action at Eybach on January 7, 1760.[8]

Evidently Prince Ferdinand was impressed with the Highlanders and wanted more of them. Shortly after the action at Eybach, a correspondent to a party in London noted, "It is said Prince Ferdinand has wrote over, by all means to provide a large body of Highlanders, at the same time bestowing the highest encomiums on Major Keith's corps."[9]

A few days later another correspondent reported, "We are informed that Major Keith's Corps of Highlanders which is already augmented to 14 Companies, is to be further augmented, and divided into two Battalions of 1000 Men each, the one Battalion to be commanded by Major Keith, as Lieutenant Colonel Commandant, and the other by the above Colonel Campbell [i.e., Lieutenant Colonel John Campbell]."[10]

When the 87th and 88th Regiments were formed, Murray-Keith was promoted from captain to major. He would be promoted to lieutenant colonel on May 10, 1760. Campbell already ranked as a major when the 88th Regiment was formed, and he was promoted to lieutenant colonel on January 1, 1760.[11]

The 88th was called into action almost as soon as they joined Prince Ferdinand's army in Germany, fighting in battles at Warburg, July 31, 1760, Zurenberg, August 5, 1760 and Cloister Camp or Camphen in October 1760. Since Charles did not enter service until January of 1761, he would not have participated in these 1760-battles. It is likely he sailed for Germany in mid-April or early-May of 1761.[12]

Given Charles was "regimented" in the 88th by July 10, his first combat experience was likely the Battle of Fellinghausen (or Villinghausen) on July 15 and 16, 1761. This was one of the larger battles of the war, pitting 65,000 British, Hanoverians, Prussians, Brunswickers and Hessians against 92,000 French. After two days of fighting, the allied army was victorious and again, the Scots Highlanders were instrumental in the victory. In recognition of their accomplishments, none other than Prince Ferdinand himself noted "The soldier like perseverance of the Highland battalions, in resisting and repulsing the repeated attacks of the chosen troops of France, has deservedly gained them the highest honour." He took special note of the grenadiers adding, "The ardour and activity with which the grenadiers pushed and pursued the enemy, and the trophies they have taken, justly intitle them to the highest encomiums." He concluded, "… the intrepidity of the little band of Highlanders merits the greatest praise."[13]

Two skirmishes involving Highlanders were reported as occurring in the fall of 1761. The skirmishes were strikingly similar in that they both involved an outnumbered detachment of Highlanders obstinately defending their position until they were obliged to surrender. A British officer observed of one of the engagements, "On the 22ᵈ [of September], a body of 400 French attacked a party of 105 Highlanders that had been posted in Winter-Kasten, who, after a brave and obstinate defence, were obliged to surrender."[14] A report of this engagement was also published in the *Caledonian Mercury*, with the news "Lieutenant Campbell of the Highlanders was shot through the head"[15] with no mention of the particular Highland Regiment. The most likely regiment would be Charles Fordyce's own 88th since there was only one lieutenant Campbell in Keith's 87th Regiment at this time—Second Lieutenant Ronald Campbell—and there were six First Lieutenant Campbells in the 88th.[16]

Another such engagement at about the same time was reported in the *Oxford Journal*. The report referenced "Letters from the Allied Army" which "informed, that in the Beginning of this Month there happened a very sharp skirmish near Weissenstein, on the Frontiers of Hesse Cassel, between 70 Scotch Highlanders and some Hundreds of the French, in which the former had greatly the Advantage in the Beginning, and killed above a Hundred of the Enemy. But the French being reinforced with fresh Troops, and the Highlanders having exhausted all their Ammunition, after breaking their Firelocks in knocking them down, and pelting the Enemy with Stones, they were obliged to surrender Prisoners of War, but were exchanged for French Prisoners in a few Days after."[17] It is possible these two reports are addressing the same engagement. In any event, they record another display of Highland courage and determination, and since the engagement or engagements occurred well after Charles arrived in Germany, it is reasonable to conclude he was involved.

In early November 1761, Prince Ferdinand and his allied army engaged the French in another series of skirmishes near Embeck, Germany. In these skirmishes, the Marquis of Granby commanded the corps that included Campbell's and Keith's Highlanders. As had been the case in the previous engagements, the Highlanders distinguished themselves for their perseverance and determination. The corps endured extended periods under arms, long marches, inclement weather, and surprise attacks. Here

Chapter 2: Deployed to Germany, Seven Years War Service, 1761 - 1763 31

again, it is likely young Charles Fordyce was a part of this corps. He had been promoted to captain in the 88th Regiment on October 8, 1761. By the time of these November skirmishes, he could have been in command of one of the Highland companies in the regiment. According to an account of the action simply datelined "Hague, Nov, 17," with no other attribution, Lord Granby's force was attacked just as he was beginning to encamp at Foorwohle. His outposts were driven in, but according to the report, "his Lordship had the Satisfaction, in the Presence of Prince Ferdinand, to repulse the Enemy, and to pursue them quite back to the Huve [the French camp], with the greatest Spirit and Conduct." Granby was attacked again the next morning and "received the Enemy with the same Spirit as before, and repulsed them with a considerable Loss."[18]

That Lord Granby's force was able to fight with spirit and effect even when in the vulnerable disposition of making camp is testimony of a competent, alert, formidable fighting unit. In addition to these characteristics, it seems they were tough. In another account of the action near Embeck, a reporter for the *London Gazette* describes the privations the army endured noting the march to the encampment was at "Night, through a heavy Fall of Snow, and almost impassable Roads." The reporter concluded, "After the extraordinary Fatigue, which the Troops had under-gone, their very gallant Behaviour did them the highest Honour, and cannot be sufficiently commended."[19]

The next battle in which the Highlanders were involved was at Wilhelmsthal on June 24, 1762. 50,000 Allied troops surprised 70,000 French troops advancing on Sababurg and drove them back to Cassel. An artillery officer observed Lord Granby, at the head of the grenadiers and Highlanders, "attacked a Corps in a Wood under the Command of Gen. Stainville, and after a very heavy Fire for some Time, took four or five battalions Prisoners, mostly of the Grenadiers of France." This officer, like the reporters of the action at Embeck, was impressed with the spirit and skill of Granby's Corps. Of this engagement he summarized, "our Troops behaved with a Bravery not to be paralleled in History, especially our Grenadiers and Highlanders, who sent Prisoners (I dare say) more than their own Number out of the Wood."[20]

After the main battle at Wilhelmsthal, Lord Granby's Corps skirmished with the French near Homberg. In a report of one of the actions the Highlanders were described as pursuing and attacking the retreating enemy with "ardor and success."[21]

In all likelihood, the last battle in which Charles Fordyce was involved during his Seven Years War service was the Battle of Brucher Mühl (Brucher Mill) on September 21, 1762. This was part of the Combat of Amöneburg, which was the last campaign of the Seven Years War. Peace negotiations were already underway at the time of the battle and the Treaty of Paris, marking the official end of the war, would be finalized less than five months later on February 10, 1763. In fact, preliminary articles of peace would be signed on November 3, 1762.[22] Prince Ferdinand's representatives and those of the French Marshalls at Brucher Mühl would sign a convention there on November 15—two months after the battle—calling for a cessation of hostilities in response to the signing of the preliminary articles.[23]

The battle was fought over control of a bridge across the Ohme River at Brucher Mühl. The allied detachment guarding the bridge was small. 200 soldiers manned a redoubt on their side of the river, supported with artillery. The French posted artillery with which they could cannonade the redoubt on the high ground on their side of the river. The battle lasted fifteen hours and ended in a stalemate. One observer noted, "… from Break of Day till Dark Night, a most terrible Firing continued without Intermission. We maintained the Redoubt, and the Enemy the Mill. History, I believe, can scarce furnish an Instance of so obstinate a Dispute." Evidently this observer interviewed some of the participants in the battle to corroborate his conclusion since he also reported, "The oldest Soldiers say, they never saw so severe a Cannonade."[24]

Another observer noted the detachment at the redoubt had to be relieved every half hour. Of the relief effort he determined, "At first we supported the work with a whole battalion at a time;

afterwards with only 100 men; and towards evening with only 40 or 50; tho' our troops consisted but of 15 battalions, we made a shift to fight them all round before night, which perhaps is the most extraordinary thing that has happened this war."[25] This would have been a battle that tested the nerve and stamina of a young Captain Fordyce. Most of the troops in the relief battalions were from Lord Granby's Corps, so if all the relief battalions saw action, it is likely he led a company that spent half an hour at the redoubt.

Regardless of whether or not Charles participated in the most violent action in the battle, it would have been an engagement wherein the young officer learned valuable lessons regarding the effectiveness of a well-placed defensive position—especially a redoubt placed at a river crossing where it is difficult to bring to bear the mass of troops needed to breech it. In this engagement, the defense included artillery that effectively counterbalanced the artillery of the offense. This artillery was also critical to the effectiveness of the defense and it was probably apparent as the battle raged that without it, even the best-placed redoubt could not have withstood a concerted attack of French artillery and infantry.

Shortly after the Battle of Brucher Mühl and the signing of the preliminary articles of peace on November 3, 1762, reports of the impending dissolution of the Anglo-Prussian Alliance—at least in terms of allied military forces—were published in England. According to a report of November 18, "Express arrived from Prince Ferdinand and some Dispatchers from the Marquis of Granby; and we hear the Armies, will immediately separate, in consequence of the Preliminaries being signed, which seems to be very well relished by both Sides; for in Fact, there is nothing left for either of them to get but Wounds and Honour."[26]

Early in 1763 the English troops were marched to Williamstadt where they embarked transports for England. By March "the greatest part of the Highland Volunteers" had arrived at Yarmouth. Later that month, the *Derby Mercury* published a report of a battalion of Colonel Keith's Regiment and a battalion of Colonel Campbell's Regiment of Highlanders marching through Westminster for Highgate. Both Keith's and Campbell's Highland

Battalions were reported to be in Newcastle in April, "on their march to Scotland." Early in May reports were published of the marching of Campbell's Highlanders through Edinburgh to Stirling, where they were to be "broke," i.e., disbanded. According to reports published later in May, they were disbanded on May 9 in Linlithgow and Keith's Highlanders were disbanded in Perth on May 25, 1763.[27] After the 88th Regiment was disbanded, Charles would be reinstated in the 14th Regiment of Foot where he would remain for the rest of his military career.

The 14th was at Dover Castle when Charles was assigned to the 88th Regiment in 1761. In August 1761, while Charles was in Germany, a report was published in the *Newcastle Courant* that the 14th had been assigned to relieve the garrison at Gibraltar.[28] It is not clear the regiment provided this relief. A little over a year later, in November 1762, a report the 14th was still at Dover was published in the *Manchester Mercury*. Evidently the regiment was assigned to Sissinghurst in Kent at this time to guard French prisoners of war.[29] If any of the 14th did go to Gibraltar in 1761, it seems they had returned before Campbell's Highlanders were disbanded in May 1763 since they were reported to be in Exeter in February.[30] Charles could have rejoined the regiment there after the 88th was disbanded.

According to the February report, the 14th was undergoing a reduction by discharging "the old and disabled men." Such a reduction was, no doubt, prompted by the end of the Seven Years War—the same circumstance that would prompt the disbanding of Campbell's and Keith's Highlanders in May. The disbanding of regiments raised to fight the Seven Years War and reduction of regiments that were to remain in service resulted in considerable restructuring of the army in terms of manning. Sometime in 1763 Captain Herbert Whitfield left the 14th Regiment and on September 9, Charles took his place.[31] This marked the official recognition of Charles' return to the 14th.

Charles' service in the 88th Regiment of Highlanders had been intense. He was probably in Germany from July 1761 through February 1763—about twenty months. This service provided him

Chapter 2: Deployed to Germany, Seven Years War Service, 1761 - 1763 35

with a portfolio of experience few officers of his age and rank could match. During the Seven Years War, he fought in some of the largest battles of the 18th century. At the Battle of Villinghausen, he had been part of an allied force numbering 65,000 opposed by a French force of 92,000. A year later, at Wilhelmsthal, the allied force numbered 50,000 and the French 70,000. The concentration and duration of the cannonade at Brucher Mühl made it one of the most violent engagements of the war. Charles had proven himself as an officer and a soldier in his tour to Germany and it is likely he was considered a valuable asset in the down-sized army emerging from the war.

CHAPTER 3: DEPLOYED TO NOVA SCOTIA, 1766 - 1768

When twenty-seven-year-old King George III opened Parliament on December 17, 1765, he informed both Houses "matters of importance have occurred in some of my colonies in America, which will demand the most serious attention of parliament."[1] The matters of importance were matters related to the Americans' spirited rejection of the Stamp Act* for raising revenue to defray the expense of administering territories gained in the French and Indian War—Seven Years War. The King had approved the act on March 22, 1765 and it took effect on November 1.

By the time Parliament opened in December, the King would have known of the American reaction from contemporary newspaper accounts[2] and from official dispatches from his royal governors. In September, Cadwallader Colden, the Lieutenant Governor of New York, informed Secretary of State for the Colonies, Henry Seymour Conway,† "Soon after it was known Stamp Duties were by Act of Parliament to be paid in the Colonies, virulent papers were published in the Weekly Newspapers, fill'd with every falsehood that malice could invent to serve their purpose of exciting the People to disobedience of the Laws and to sedition. At first they only denied the authority of Parliament to lay internal Taxes in the Colonies, but at last they have denied the Legislative Authority of the Parliament in the Colonies."[3] Earlier that month, Lieutenant Governor Colden had written General Thomas Gage, Commander of British forces in North America, expressing his

---

* In effect, the Stamp Act was a sales tax on a particular product group, i.e., paper. The "stamp" in question was a watermark, stamp or imprint on the specific paper good that served as evidence the tax had been paid.
† Conway was Secretary of State for the Southern Department 12 July 1765 – 23 May 1766 and for the Northern Department 23 May 1766 – 20 January 1768.

opinion "The only method ... to prevent mischief is to have such a military Force present as may effectually discourage all opposition to the Laws." Prophetically, he went on to apprise the general of one of the precepts the British ministry never fully accounted for in developing their colonial policies and in planning and fighting the war in America, namely, "A Weak Force which the seditious can have any hopes of overcoming may be productive of great mischief."[4]

Philip York, the 2nd Earl of Hardwicke, noted in his response to the King's opening speech, "The state of affairs in America, which is the subject pointed out to us in the Speech, is indeed of the highest magnitude; if I had not heard that term so often misapplied, I should say the greatest in its extent and consequences, that ever came before parliament." And in their formal reply to the King, the members of the House of Lords agreed to "Proceed to the consideration of those weighty matters, with an attention equal to the importance of the subject, and with a resolution to do every thing which the exigency of the case may require." For some in the House of Lords, such exigencies included the use of military force. In a letter to his son after this short, pre-holiday session of Parliament ended, Lord Chesterfield noted, "The administration are for some indulgence and forbearance to those froward children of their mother country: the opposition are for taking vigorous, as they call them, but I call them violent measures; not less than *les dragonades*;* and to have the tax collected by the troops we have there."[5]

Some strategic thinkers in Britain had contemplated the utility of British troops "in guarding against Disobedience, or Defection amongst the Inhabitants of the Maritime Provinces," as early as 1762. At the time, it seems the disobedience or defection in question had to do with the provinces entertaining "some extraordinary

---

*French government policy instituted by Louis XIV in 1681 to intimidate Huguenot families into either leaving France or re-converting to Catholicism. This involved the billeting of ill-disciplined dragoons in Protestant households with implied permission to abuse the inhabitants and destroy or steal their possessions. Wikipedia.

opinions concerning their Relation to, & Dependance [sic] on their Mother-Country."[6] But this thinking had not been translated into strategic doctrine, so when the Stamp Act was passed the British military contingent in America had been reduced and what remained was still deployed against the Indian threat on the frontiers of the colonies.

The violence perpetrated in America in response to the Stamp Act was alarming and frightening. It was unprecedented and coupled with the unequivocal and universal rejection of the act of Parliament, the inhabitants of the Maritime Provinces certainly had demonstrated extraordinary opinions concerning their relation to, and dependence on their mother country. But despite these displays of rank insubordination, Parliament and the King recognized the limitations of their budget and inapt troop deployments.[7] They agreed to try and assuage the ire and delinquency of the outraged Americans by repealing the act on March 18, 1766.

However, there was a caveat to this conciliatory gesture. King George and some powerful members of Parliament were indignant at what they considered the disrespectful and barely sufferable display of American effrontery related to the Stamp Act. The King would later refer to its repeal as the "fatal compliance in 1766."[8] So at the same time the Stamp Act was repealed, Parliament passed the "Act for the Better Securing the Dependence of his Majesty's Dominions in America on the Crown of Great Britain"—better known as the Declaratory Act. In the preamble to the new act, Parliament inveighed, "the said colonies have been, are, and of right ought to be, subordinate unto, and dependent on, the imperial crown and Parliament of Great Britain; and that the King and Parliament of Great Britain had, hath, and of right ought to have, full power and authority to make laws and statutes of sufficient force to bind the colonies, and his Majesty's subjects in them, in all cases whatsoever."[9]

Indeed, this was a clear declaration of British authority—likely construed by the colonists as a severe rebuke of their alleged rebellious behavior. But, given what historian George Beer called the "anarchic conditions" prevailing at the time, it was simply a declaration.[10] The worth of the measure had to be questionable in light of the contempt the colonists had shown for British authority during the Stamp Act crisis. At the height of that crisis, the citizens of Elizabeth Town (now Elizabeth), New Jersey, erected a gallows in the village and published their vow "that the first person that either distributes or takes out Stamped Paper, shall be hung thereon without judge or jury."[11] Clearly the cooperative relationship between Mother Country and her American colonies had changed. Declarations would have to be enforced with means other than the nominal resources available to the British civil servants implementing regulations in formerly loyal and law-abiding communities. The default resource for such enforcement was the military.

The British had already taken steps to provide for the enforcement of their declaration and the tax bills that followed, although not as part of an integrated plan. The provisions were improvised and probably went unnoticed by both the British and the Americans at the time, but they were portentous.

To enforce their declarations, the British would need troops in place and ready to deploy rapidly. This meant redeploying troops already in America and upgrading the logistics infrastructure supporting the troops. On October 15, 1765, after news of the Stamp-Act riots in New England reached Britain, the Lords of the Admiralty were directed to "send immediate orders to Vice Admiral Alexander Colvill, Commander of H. M.'s naval forces on the North American station, to give such assistance to any of the Governors of the American colonies as may be called for, and particularly by transporting from Nova Scotia or other parts of that country any land forces which may be wanted for the suppression of tumults."[12] This was an impromptu reaction but it was prescient. Troops were redeployed, and a more capable infrastructure devised. Nova Scotia was to become the depot and staging area where many of the British troops employed in North America over the next fifteen years would make their first landfall.

Within weeks of the repeal of the Stamp Act, King George III ordered the 14th Regiment to North America. This deployment seems to have been part of the "plan of rotation" the King instituted some years earlier as "an encouragement to all corps to undertake any service they may be sent upon with spirit and alacrity"[13] and not a reaction to the Stamp Act or its repeal.

Regardless of why the 14th was ordered to North America at this time, their deployment was momentous. They would be in America for the next nine years.[14] During this time America and Great Britain would pontificate, maneuver and posture over the issues of authority and independence and finally come to blows. As the official embodiment of the King's authority during this time, the 14th Regiment would be one of the primary objects on which the ire of the King's "refractory" subjects would be visited.

༺

Charles rejoined the 14th Regiment after the 88th Regiment was disbanded in 1763—over two years before the momentous deployment to North America. In the November 1763 *Army List*, he is listed as a captain in the 14th with a date-of-rank of September 9, 1763. This date-of-rank put him last in rank of the six captains in the regiment despite his army date-of-rank* as a captain–recorded as October 8, 1761 in the same list. The other five captains were, in date-of-rank order, Jonathan Furlong, George James Bruere, Alexander Murray, William Blackett and Samuel Lindsey.

In the next *Army List*, that of March 1765, Charles is listed sixth out of seven captains, outranking Captain Edmund Mason. This year the field officers were Colonel Charles Jefferyes, Lieutenant Colonel William Napier and Major William Dalrymple. In the *Army List* of 1766—the year the regiment left for North America—Charles is fourth in rank of the seven Captains. At that time, the commander of the regiment was the Honorable William Keppel. William Dalrymple had been promoted to Lieutenant Colonel and Jonathan Furlong to major. Colonel Keppel did not accompany

---

* This army date-of-rank—October 8, 1761—is somewhat of a puzzle. It does coincide with Charles' replacing David Wedderburn as a captain in the 88th Regiment, but Charles was in the army prior to that. According to the *Army Commission Book*, he was commissioned a lieutenant in Patrick Wilkie's Independent Company nine months earlier, on January 8, 1761, and a lieutenant in the 14th Regiment on August 24, 1761. Nevertheless, Charles' dates-of-rank for the army and his captaincy as recorded in the *Army List* of November 1763 would not change during his career in the army.

the regiment to Halifax, so Lieutenant Colonel Dalrymple was the local commander.

Charles was a distant relation of Colonel Keppel through the marriage of one of his cousins, Mary Ann Cathcart. Charles and Lieutenant Colonel Dalrymple were also related. They were second cousins once removed. Dalrymple was the grandson of John Dalrymple, 1st Earl of Stair,[15] one of the key figures in the negotiations that led to the union of Scotland and England—the formation of Great Britain—in 1707.[16] This same Earl of Stair was Charles' Great-Grand Uncle.[17]

When Charles rejoined the 14th Regiment in 1763, it is likely it was in Exeter or Plymouth, England. The regiment was stationed near London in 1764 and on May 7, it was reviewed by King George III at Hyde Park. (The review included the "imitation" of a "Bush Fight against the Indians, to the great Delight of the numerous Spectators.")[18] In 1765, three companies of the regiment were on duty at Windsor and Hampton Court. In May 1766, the regiment marched into village quarters near Hounslow Heath, where it was again reviewed by the King on June 4.[19] That same month the regiment embarked at Portsmouth for North America, where it would be stationed in Halifax, Nova Scotia.

Planning for the actual deployment of the regiment to America began on April 29, 1766—a month after the Stamp Act was repealed—when Secretary at War William Barrington wrote the Secretary of State for the Southern Department, Henry Conway, informing him of the King's orders for the 14th Regiment and the need for transports to America.[20] Captain Fordyce and the rest of the 14th left Southampton, England on their voyage to Nova Scotia about two months later on June 30, 1766.[21] They arrived at Halifax 54 days later on August 23, 1766.[22]

The new home of the 14th Regiment was itself a new settlement in British America. Halifax had been founded just seventeen years earlier in 1749 by Edward Cornwallis, the uncle of General Charles Cornwallis of Revolutionary War fame. Despite the fact Halifax was a newly developed settlement of modest size, British military planners recognized the value of the town and port as a strategically located nexus from which troops and ships could be dispatched to any of their holdings in North America and the Caribbean (West Indies). Consequently, they made it the headquarters of their North American Station in 1758. As such, it was a staging base where military units could be reconstituted and reinforced and where the military were welcome.[23] Halifax was, by design, a safe haven for British troops.

In 1766, there was no serious Indian threat to the town and the threat of Indian attack on the frontiers of the province was nominal. Neither were the colonists threatening rebellion or attacking the civil servants collecting stamp duties or monitoring shipping.[24] A few months before the 14th was deployed to Nova Scotia, reports were published in England that the "Barracks for the Military" in Halifax, were "almost finished in a neat and most commodious manner both for Officers and Men, resembling much those of Chatham, with separate Kitchens and other Conveniences."[25]

Other than Halifax, centrally located on the east coast, the troops in Nova Scotia were stationed in Louisbourg on Cape Breton Island, at the north-eastern end of the province, and various outposts or forts. These included Forts Cumberland, Annapolis Royal, Frederick—at the mouth of St. John's River—and Amherst, near Charlotte Town on what was then called St. John's Island, now Prince Edward.[26] The locations of these towns and forts are noted on the map of Nova Scotia presented in Figure 5.

Although Nova Scotia was not a colony in the sense of the thirteen "original" American colonies, most of the inhabitants of the province were Americans. There had been a very active migration from New England to the province after the ouster of the French settlers (Acadians) in the latter years of the French and Indian War. When the 14th Regiment arrived in 1766, the population of the entire province of Nova Scotia was 13,374 and of these, "the number ranked as 'Americans'" was almost 7,000. It is likely this number did not account for the settlers who had come from New England with their parents a generation earlier, so the number of Americans was probably much greater than the estimated 7,000. Of the 3,022 residents of Halifax in 1766, almost half—1,351—were listed as Americans.[27] In terms of primary occupations, the residents of Nova Scotia were engaged in fishing, farming and forestry.[28] Of course, there were merchants, administrators, teachers, clergy, judges and engineers who provided the province's civil and commercial infrastructure.

Figure 5. *A New Map of Nova Scotia, and Cape Britain.* Thomas Jefferys and Robert Sayer. Map reproduction courtesy of the Norman B. Leventhal Map & Education Center.

The 14th Regiment was on garrison duty in Nova Scotia. Normally, such duty involved guarding a town or some other well-defined zone or region. Under the circumstances in Nova Scotia, that is, relative peace and quiet, guard duty was probably performed as much as a training exercise as a military necessity. So, Nova Scotia served as a training center as well as a staging base.

Garrison duty involved the posting of guards and sending out patrols to augment the posted guards. The governor provided the directions on the actual duties of the guards and those directions were communicated to the guards by an officer designated the Town Major. This was a position of considerable responsibility and General Gage appointed Captain Charles Fordyce Town Major of Halifax in 1767.[29]

Charles' military skills—honed in the Seven Years War—were probably well known, a fact reflected in his assignment as commander of the regiment's prestigious and exclusive grenadier company. His appointment to Town Major was an affirmation of his skill as an administrator and his mature understanding of the military capabilities of the entire regiment. Lieutenant Colonel Dalrymple was confident in these abilities of his twenty-six-year-old captain and he was able to convince the Commander-in-Chief his confidence was well placed.

~

Coincident with this phase of Charles Fordyce's military career was the Parliamentary career of John Murray, 4th Earl of Dunmore. Dunmore had taken his seat in the House of Lords in 1761—the same year Charles enlisted in the army. He would retain his seat in the Lords through 1774, thirteen years. For four of those thirteen years, 1770–1774, he would be in America, first as Governor of New York and then as Governor of Virginia. He would be the last royal governor of Virginia, replaced in 1776 with Virginia's first elected governor, Patrick Henry.

As a member of the House of Lords at this time, he would have had direct access to the individuals framing colonial policy. He would have had access to official intelligence and analysis of the issues at the core of the legislative and political antecedents of the American Revolution. He would have been familiar with the Stamp Act, its repeal a year after it was passed, the Declaratory Act passed to affirm the prerogative of Parliament to tax the colonies at will, and then Townshend's Revenue Acts.

It seems Lord Dunmore was a dutiful but not a devoted Parliamentarian. His record in the House of Lords suggests he was indifferent to the political discord developing over what Parliament called the "tumults in America." Although he witnessed the

Chapter 3: Deployed to Nova Scotia, 1766 - 1768   45

development and progression of a history-making legislative sequence at its source, it seems he was disposed to be involved more as an observer than a participant. Regarding his commitment to either the government or the opposition at this time, biographer William Lowe noted he "had neither a close association with any of the parties led by the great English politicians nor a commitment to the King's friends" and it was "impossible to say how deeply his interest or involvement in politics went."[30] He had "silently" supported the repeal of the Stamp Act in 1766 and his voting record on legislation pertaining to the colonies might be considered impartial if not indifferent.[31]

Two of the Lords with whom he would later be allied, John Russell, the Duke of Bedford, and Granville Leveson-Gower, 2nd Earl Gower, opposed repeal of the Stamp Act. Both Bedford and Gower spoke against repeal as the act made its way through the Lords. Both men signed the rather lengthy "dissents" denouncing the repeal and voted against it.[32] Although associated with these two "hardliners" at this time, biographer Lowe noted Dunmore was in favor of repeal and supported the Rockingham administration's "relatively conciliatory approach toward the colonies."[33]

This display of independence suggests Lord Dunmore was evaluating the issues affecting colonial policy based on a variety of views. And given such independence, it is wrong to characterize him as a puppet or an unbending conservative.* That said, at some point he developed a firm conviction Parliament did have exclusive and supreme authority over the colonies—authority

---

* Such an assessment is corroborated from a remarkable source. It seems Lord Dunmore was an acquaintance of Jeremy Bentham—famous for his "utilitarian" philosophy based on the axiom, "it is the greatest happiness of the greatest number that is the measure of right and wrong." Of Lord Dunmore, Bentham noted, "He was a sort of a liberal; and we used to stimulate one another by talking of the despotism which had been exhibited by the expulsion of the six Methodists at Oxford." (The Methodists had been expelled in 1768 for being "righteous overmuch." *Stamford Mercury*, 17 March 1768, p. 4.) In the same vein, Bentham recalled, "For a Church-of-England man, Dunmore was free of prejudices, and we had many common sympathies." Jeremy Bentham, *The Works of Jeremy Bentham*, Vol. 10, Edinburg: William Tait, 1843, p. 124.

established by the British Constitution and affirmed by the Declaratory Act. He could have developed such a conviction early in life, before entering Parliament, but it is also possible that conviction was aroused and strengthened by his experiences and associations in Parliament. At any rate, this conviction would be applied rigorously in the legislative agendas he would pursue as governor of New York and then Virginia.

Captain Fordyce would have known of Lord Dunmore's association with inveterate proponents of Parliamentary authority, Lord Gower and the Duke of Bedford. His cousins, Lord Cathcart (first cousin once removed) and the Earl of Loudoun (second cousin once removed), served in the House of Lords with Dunmore, Gower and Bedford at this time. In fact, it seems Lord Cathcart was a particular friend Dunmore named as his proxy when he was not able to attend the House of Lords.[34]

In addition to the Parliamentary connections between Charles' relations and the Earl of Dunmore, there were family, personal and business connections as well. The family connection was by marriage. As noted previously, John Fordyce, Charles' brother, married Katherine Maxwell. Katherine's second cousin, Charlotte Stewart, married Lord Dunmore. Thus, by marriage, and in the most liberal connotation of the kinship title, John Fordyce and Lord Dunmore were second cousins.

Lord Charles Cathcart, just noted as Charles' first cousin once removed, had, like Lord Dunmore, served in the 3rd Foot Guards.[35] In his assessment of Dunmore's Parliamentary career, Lowe notes Lord Cathcart "... may have had a hand in Dunmore's introduction to the King's List." The King's List was a "prearranged selection of peers whose election [to the House of Lords] the ministry desired."[36] So Charles' close relative may have been personally involved in securing Lord Dunmore's place in the House of Lords as one of the sixteen representative Scottish peers.

It seems there was also a Fordyce-Dunmore connection involving business dealings associated with the Port Seton glassworks. In 1750, Charles' father, Thomas Fordyce, wrote banker George Innes and reported he needed a loan to repay his share of a debt incurred "for support of the Glassworks." Mr. Fordyce explained to Mr. Innes that Lord Dunmore was among a group of gentlemen who "prevailed with me to join in borrowing £300" for the said support. At the time—1750—Lord Dunmore was John Murray, the 2nd Earl, uncle of the 4th Earl who would be the governor of Virginia twenty years later, but this transaction still suggests a material link between the families.[37]

ം

Lord Dunmore (the 4th Earl) would be the last American Governor to host the 14th Regiment. In addition to this distinction, his association with the 14th would be significant and unique in that he would be the first and only governor to exercise the prerogative of direct military command implied in his appointment as "Governor General of the said Colony and Dominion, and Vice Admiral of the same." But this last assignment would be nine years after the initial assignment to Nova Scotia.

The first American Governor to host the 14th Regiment would be Francis Bernard, Governor of the Province of Massachusetts Bay. His involvement with the 14th in terms of military command would be nominal. Unlike Lord Dunmore, Governor Bernard had no military experience. He was afraid the presence of troops in the province might precipitate an insurrection and, consequently, he hesitated to request military support, even when his government and the King's agents for whom he was responsible were threatened with actual violence.[38] In 1768, the Commissioners of Customs in Massachusetts would make it clear to him they could not enforce the Revenue Acts without risking their lives.[39]

General Thomas Gage would order the 14th to Boston to support Bernard and the Customs Commissioners even though the governor never explicitly applied for such support. Gage's orders would be in response to a directive from the Secretary of State for the Colonies, Lord Hillsborough, who would, in turn, be responding to Bernard's implicit appeals and the explicit appeals of the commissioners regarding the "very alarming State of things in Boston."[40]

CHAPTER 4: UNREST IN BOSTON, 1767 - 1768

The tranquility of service in Halifax would last two years for the 14th Regiment—from August 1766 through September 1768. Arguably, the end of the tranquility was predetermined by Parliamentary legislation evolving as the 14th prepared for their American deployment and enacted just a few months after they arrived in Halifax. The legislation in question, enacted June 29, 1767, came to be known as the Townshend Acts, named for the gentleman who proposed them, Charles Townshend, Chancellor of the Exchequer. As with the Stamp Act, these acts were passed "for making a more certain and adequate provision for defraying the charge of the administration of justice, and the support of civil government, in such provinces where it shall be found necessary; and towards further defraying the expenses of defending, protecting, and securing, the said dominions."[1]

Initially the response to these acts was non-violent although there was no question the acts were seen by the colonists in America as illegal (unconstitutional). This report from an anonymous correspondent for the *Boston Gazette and Country Journal* provides a hint of the suspicion and disaffection engendered by Townshend's Revenue Acts.

> … duties are now to be paid in the Colonies on above one hundred articles of our imports, and if these are established, we may fear that every future session of Parliament will increase the number, until our property is wholly swallowed up. Swarms of new officers are flying over to us, to fatten themselves upon the spoils of trade, and Governor Bernard,* and his junto are exalting at the news of new appointments and increased salaries.[2]

---

*Francis Bernard, Governor of the Province of Massachusetts Bay, 1760 – 1769.

In response to the Townshend Acts, the citizens of Boston resolved on October 28, 1767, "That effectual methods should be taken to prevent the unnecessary importation of European commodities," and "That all prudent and legal measures should be adopted to encourage and produce home manufactures, and to lessen the use of superfluities."[3] These measures would evolve into non-importation pledges and quasi-legal agreements which would be observed very strictly throughout the colonies.[4] The merchants of Boston began publishing a list of their fellow merchants who did not support the non-importation agreement. They determined this to be necessary to gain the "Concurrence of every person on this continent, who has the public welfare at heart, in rendering their base and dangerous designs abortive."[5]

In addition to encouraging home manufactures and promoting a non-importation agreement, the Massachusetts House of Representatives sent a "Circulatory Letter" to the "Speakers of the respective Houses of Representatives and Burgesses on the Continent." The letter was sent February 11, 1768 and in it the Massachusetts Representatives denounced the Townshend Acts as "infringements of their natural constitutional rights."[6] This letter was written just after Wills Hill, the Earl of Hillsborough, was appointed Secretary of State for the Colonies. Lord Hillsborough considered the letter "inflammatory" and an effort by a "desperate Faction to disturb the public Tranquility."[7] The letter would come to be one of the key determinants of the kinds of actions he would take to restore the public tranquility a few months later.

Notwithstanding the confrontational tone of the calls for non-importation agreements and the circular letter from the Massachusetts House of Representatives, these actions demonstrated a respect for law and order and an appreciation of the way moderation could keep strained lines of communication open. Nevertheless, the truce between Parliament's local representatives—the Customs Commissioners—and members the Patriot faction in Boston was uneasy and susceptible to compromise and violation. And in 1768, the Patriots had a number of opportunities to violate the truce by provoking the King's officers, if they were so inclined.

One such opportunity was the celebration of an event for which the Americans took credit, but which could also be considered simply as Parliament's exercise of prerogative. It was an event quite recent and peculiar in Anglo-American history—the repeal of the Stamp Act. As noted previously, the repeal occurred on March 18, 1766 and the Sons of Liberty considered it "a day much to be observed, for the deliverance of a whole country from slavery and misery."[8] The celebration of the repeal had indeed been extravagant and exciting in 1766—on both sides of the Atlantic.[9]

Solemnizing the day as an annual memorial might have been considered an indulgence in patriotic self-righteousness by more dispassionate observers. John Adams made this point in his assessment of another peculiar memorial associated with the Stamp Act—the day citizens rioted in Boston against passage of the act, August 14, 1765. This date was celebrated as the unofficial birthdate of the Sons of Liberty. Of the celebration in 1769, Adams observed, "Otis and [Samuel] Adams are politic in promoting these festivals; for they tinge the minds of the people; they impregnate them with the sentiments of liberty; they render the people fond of their leaders in the cause, and averse and bitter against all opposers."[10]

Be that as it may, the day the Stamp Act was repealed was celebrated annually and in March 1768, some of the citizens unhappy with the new Revenue Acts took advantage of the celebration to vent their displeasure. They did so in the manner common to the era—the hanging of effigies. Of the 1768 celebration in Boston, diarist John Rowe noted, "A considerable Mob of young fellows & negroes [sic] got together this Evening & made great Noise & Hallooing, abt Eight hundred appeared in King St & at Liberty Tree & went to the North End to John Williams the Inspector General, but did him no Damage." Regarding the effigies Rowe added, "There were two Effigies on Liberty Tree this morning marked C. P. & J. W.* but were taken down."[11] It seems there was an honest effort by the townspeople to keep this hallooing from

---

*Commissioner Charles Paxton and Inspector General John Williams

escalating into violence or damage. They considered the effigies a "Piece of Buffoonery...designed to excite Mobs and Riots."[12]

Buffoonery or not, Governor Bernard was not amused. The day after the celebration, he wrote the Earl of Shelburne, then Secretary of State for the Southern Department in America, to apprise him of the "dangerous opposition" to the Commissioners of Customs in Boston, which he had recently observed. He informed the Earl an insurrection was planned for the anniversary of the repeal of the Stamp-Act and "two Persons, Mr. Paxton a Commissioner and Mr. Williams one of the Inspectors General, were mentioned as devoted to the Resentment of the Mob." He told Lord Shelburne, "Early the next Morning the Sheriff came to me to inform me that the Effigies of Mr. Paxton and Mr. Williams were hanging upon Liberty-Tree." He added, "At Council I set forth in strong Terms the Atrociousness of this Insult, the Danger of it's [sic] being followed by actual Violence, and the Necessity there was of providing for the Preservation of the Peace of the Town."[13]

In his dispatch to Secretary Shelburne, Governor Bernard goes on to explain why he has not applied for troops to support the King's government and protect the persons of his officers. He reminds the Earl, "All the King's Governors are directed to take the Advice of the Council in Military Movements; and in this Government where the Governor is in a more peculiar Manner obliged to have the Advice of the Council for almost every Thing he does, it would be dangerous to act in such an important Business without such Advice." And to highlight the precariousness of his predicament he assures Lord Shelburne "...it is in vain to put such a Question to the Council, for, considering the Influence they are under from their being Creatures of the People, and the personal Danger they wou'd be subject to in assisting in the restraining them, it is not probable that the utmost extremity of mischief and danger would induce them to advise such a measure."[14]

The accuracy of his assessment of the futility of having the Council affirm his request for troops was clearly manifest in an exchange between the Governor, his Council and the Massachusetts House of Representatives over the quartering of troops almost a year earlier. On May 18, 1767, Governor Bernard had informed the House of Representatives that Ensign John Dalrymple* of the 14th Regiment of Foot had arrived from Scotland with twenty-seven recruits and needed quarters. The Governor ordered that they should be received into the barracks at Castle William on Castle Island in Boston Harbor, but he also informed the House he had "laid the matter before the Council, and asked their advice concerning the ordering the usual allowances for these men, while they remain in the barracks."[15]

The "usual allowances," sometimes referred to as "necessaries" had been specified in the Quartering Act of 1765 as, "fire, candles, vinegar, and salt, bedding, utensils for dressing their victuals, and small beer or cyder, not exceeding five pints, or half a pint of rum mixed with a quart of water, to each man."[16] In response to the Governor's request for advice concerning these allowances, his Council had told him to ask the House. Three weeks later, on June 16, the House Resolved "that such provision be made for these men, while they remain here, as has been heretofore usually made for his Majesty's regular troops, when occasionally in this province."[17]

The caveat "occasionally," was used very deliberately here. In his biography of Samuel Adams, William Wells alludes to the calculated—if not sinister—tone of the language in the response when he concludes: "This resolution showed that, while the House were disposed to comply with an act of Parliament, they saw and feared the first steps towards establishing an armed force in the Province."[18] The House of Representatives wanted to set the precedent that while troops might have reason to visit Boston on occasion, there was to be no inference such visits should ever be routine or frequent. The fact the Governor's Council refused to address the matter themselves or support the Governor with any

---

*Ensign John Dalrymple (later Captain and a combatant at Great Bridge) was the third cousin of the commander of the 14th Regiment in Nova Scotia at this time, Lieutenant Colonel William Dalrymple. Both men were related to Charles Fordyce. Lieutenant Colonel Dalrymple was his second cousin once removed and Ensign Dalrymple was a third cousin once removed.

substantive advice suggests an appreciation on their part of the unpopularity of the Revenue Acts or enforcement of the same.

The danger of violence Governor Bernard ascribed to the behavior of the mobs intimidating the Commissioners of Customs was not without foundation. He considered Captain Daniel Malcom's 1766 evasion of prosecution for smuggling wine[19] "a violent and riotous resistance to the Custom House officers…."[20] Bernard believed other Massachusetts' merchants and traders condoned or colluded in this resistance. Such complicity was certainly manifest in assessments of the incident published in the local newspapers. In one contemporary report, the men Governor Bernard characterized as violent and riotous were characterized as orderly "as if they were at church."[21]

Despite such reports, the Governor was convinced the celebrations in March 1768 incited rebellion. For him, burning or hanging effigies of the revenue officers was not buffoonery but the sanctioning of evasion and lawlessness—a prelude to the flagrant rejection of the Revenue Acts and the actual violence the Customs officers would suffer later that year.[22]

The Commissioners of the Customs agreed with the Governor, but they also knew he was powerless. In a letter to the Lords Commissioners of the Treasury of March 28, they declared "every Officer who exerts himself in the Execution of his Duty will be exposed to the Resentment of the Populace, without the least probability of receiving any Protection." They concluded that— under the circumstances they described— "we cannot answer for our Security for a day, much less will it be in our power to carry the Revenue Laws into Effect."[23]

Lord Hillsborough agreed with Governor Bernard and the Commissioners. He determined Boston and the Province of Massachusetts Bay to be especially insolent and dangerous in their rejection of the Revenue Acts, their intimidation of the Commissioners of the Customs and in their encouragement of the same by the other provinces. He was particularly annoyed over the "Circular Letter" the Massachusetts Assembly adopted on February 11, 1768. In a letter of April 22, he told Governor Bernard the Massachusetts' circular would "excite an unjustifiable Opposition to the constitutional Authority of Parliament, and to revive those unhappy Divisions and Distractions which have operated so prejudicially to the true Interests of Great Britain and the Colonies." The Secretary insisted Governor Bernard "require of the House of Representatives, in his Majesty's Name, to rescind the Resolution which gave Birth to the circular Letter … and to declare their Disapprobation of, and Dissent to, that rash and hasty Proceeding."[24]

The Massachusetts' Representatives would not budge but Hillsborough did not wait to hear of their defiance. On June 8, 1768—informed by the dispatches of Governor Bernard and the letter from the Commissioners of Customs to the Lords of the Treasury—he wrote General Gage and directed him to,

> … order one regiment, or such force as you shall think necessary, to Boston, to be quartered in that town, and to give every legal assistance to the civil magistrate in the preservation of the public peace, and to the officers of the customs in the execution of the laws of trade and revenue.[25]

It was in response to this order the 14th and 29th Regiments were deployed to Boston but the delays in transmitting and receiving orders occasioned by the eight-weeks-long trans-Atlantic line of communication meant these regiments would not leave Halifax for another three months. In fact, General Gage did not receive Hillsborough's June 8 directive until September 7.[26]

To his credit, Lord Hillsborough appreciated the sensitivity of the mission to Boston. In his letter to General Gage, he was explicit that, "…as this appears to be a service of a delicate nature, and possibly leading to consequences not easily foreseen, I am directed by the King to recommend to you to *make choice of an officer for the command of these troops, upon whose prudence, resolution and integrity you can entirely depend* [emphasis added]." When General Gage replied to Lord Hillsborough's directive on September 7 he informed him, "Lieutenant Colonel Dalrymple of His Majesty's 14th Regiment of Foot, is appointed to command the Troops who are ordered on this Service, an Officer in whose Prudence, Resolution, and Integrity, I have Reason to confide."

General Gage had selected Lieutenant Colonel Dalrymple to coordinate the deployment of troops to Boston before he received Lord Hillsborough's orders. He did so because he was concerned about reports he received later in June of "Disturbances ... at Boston, on occasion of the Seizure of a Vessel."* As a result of those concerns, on June 25—long before he received Lord Hillsborough's directions—he informed Dalrymple, "Should Governor Bernard find Occasion to make Application to you, for the Assistance of his Majesty's Forces, you will immediately move with the Troops under your Command at Halifax, and proceed to Boston."[27]

General Gage's confidence in Lieutenant Colonel Dalrymple's qualifications for this mission was not misplaced. The Commissioners of the Customs at Boston had informed Lieutenant Colonel Dalrymple of the disturbances in Boston in a letter of June 15[28] and on June 23, he provided them this sympathetic, encouraging but measured response,

> My feelings as a Man joined with those of a Servant of the Crown, are deeply affected on this Occasion; and I am very unhappy at not being able to give you instant and effectual relief; but the Board may rely entirely on my performing the Part that

---

* The vessel in question was the *Liberty*, property of one John Hancock. This seizure occurred on June 10, 1768 and devolved into the "*Liberty* Affair," which resulted in undeniable violence toward the Commissioners and their families. In turn, this would result in the Commissioners again requesting protection and a flurry of correspondence between Governor Bernard, Lord Hillsborough, General Gage and the commanders of the British naval and land forces in America to effect that protection. As a result of the *Liberty* Affair, Lord Hillsborough arranged for another two regiments to be sent to America. He notified Governor Bernard "the Troops intended for the Relief in North America in the next Spring, consisting of Two Regiments from Ireland, should be immediately sent over to America and landed at Boston." ("The Earl of Hillsborough to Francis Bernard, Whitehall 30th July 1768, and "The Earl of Hillsborough to Thomas Gage Whitehall July 30th 1768," *The Papers of Francis Bernard*, Vol. 4: 1768, p. 271 and Appendix 12, p. 397.) Colonel John Pomeroy with the 64th and part of the 65th Regiments arrived in Boston in November 1768, about two months after the 14th Regiment. (*The Boston Gazette, and Country Journal*, 21 November 1768, p. 3.) Colonel Alexander Mackay, with the rest of the 65th Regiment, arrived on April 30, 1769. (*The Boston Evening Post*, 1 May 1769, p. 3.)

my Situation enables me to do, which is the holding ready at a Minute's Warning the whole of the Troops under my Command, to act in Obedience to any orders or in compliance with any requisitions given or signified to me by my superiors; and I trust, that, should there be unhappily occasion, the force here is more than sufficient to compel all those who shall dare to resist lawful authority, to act in a manner more becoming good subjects.[29]

General Gage must have sent orders to Lieutenant Colonel Dalrymple to embark his troops for Boston as soon as he received his directions from Lord Hillsborough on September 7, 1768. For Lieutenant Colonel Dalrymple, these orders were the "requisitions given or signified to me by my superiors" he needed to provide what he hoped would be "instant and effectual relief" for the Commissioners of the Customs. The record of the 14th Regiment in Boston supports a conclusion Lieutenant Colonel Dalrymple did a credible job of providing the relief requested, including the "Circumspection in his Conduct, and the strictest Discipline among the Troops" General Gage had "recommended"[30] in response to Lord Hillsborough's concerns over the delicate nature of the service.

CHAPTER 5: DEPLOYED TO BOSTON, 1768 – 1772

The 14th Regiment was ordered to Boston early in September 1768, just over two years after their arrival in North America. They sailed from Halifax for Boston on September 19.[1] Based on the sparse record of their activities at Halifax, and the fact Lieutenant Colonel Dalrymple was prepared to send the whole of the troops under his command to Boston at a minute's warning, it is reasonable to conclude the demands on the 14th in terms of actual military engagements in Nova Scotia had been minimal.[2] Duties performed were predominantly those of training, guard duty and an occasional show of force adequate to dissuade mistrustful Indians and disaffected French settlers from actual hostilities.*

With the request from the Commissioners for protection, both the threat and the proximity to the threat faced by the 14th would change dramatically. Lieutenant Colonel Dalrymple's response to the Commissioners foreshadows some of that drama. He assures them he is deeply affected as a man and a servant of the Crown over what he called in his June 23 letter the "outrageous proceedings" in Boston. He also expresses his confidence in his troops and his conviction the Americans are—and should behave like—

---

*It was difficult to assess the Indian threat. In 1766 Lieutenant Governor Michael Franklin told Lord Shelburne, "We are at perfect peace with the Indians." "Franklin to Shelburne, November 19, 1766, Halifax," Canadian Archives, Nova Scotia and Cape Breton, Original Correspondence (CO 217), C-9130, image 193. In 1768, when General Gage informed Governor William Campbell of Nova Scotia troops would be withdrawn to support Governor Bernard in Boston, Campbell told Lord Hillsborough, "Nothing could happen so prejudicial to the infant Province as the removal of the troops," explaining their withdrawal would expose the thinly inhabited settlements to attacks from the Indians. "Campbell to Hillsborough, September 12, 1768, Halifax," Douglas Brymner, archivist, *Report on Canadian Archives*, Ottawa: S. E. Dawson, 1895, p. 290. Also (CO 217), C-9130, image 1210. Shortly after the 14th and 29th Regiments departed for Boston Indians reportedly attacked Louisburg. *The Boston Evening-Post*, 24 October 1768, p. 2.

the Crown's dependents when he closes his reply with the assurance, "the force here is more than sufficient to compel all those who shall dare to resist lawful authority, to act in a manner more becoming good subjects."

The comparison Lieutenant Colonel Dalrymple made between a force that was "more than sufficient," and subjects who "dare to resist lawful authority," would have been apt for a military commander preparing his troops for a confrontation, regardless of who was to be confronted. It was probably a comparison all the soldiers in the 14th Regiment would have made regarding this assignment. No doubt they were aware of what must have been considered the impudent and belligerent reaction of the colonists to the taxes (duties) and regulations imposed to fund troop deployments and pay civil servants. Taxes and regulations the soldiers understood to be legal and necessary. They could and would confront the rabble and enforce the law.

However, as is the case with many military assignments, a comparison between a lawless rabble and unimpeachable law officers did not account for the nuanced interpretations of lawful and lawless and rights and obligations governing this particular law-enforcement mission. This was a complex mission involving belligerents who were also countrymen, law abiding citizens who were sincere in their conviction their constitutional rights—their human rights—were in jeopardy, commissioners who were sworn to obey and enforce the law regardless of its perceived legitimacy,[3] soldiers who likewise were sworn to defend the King and his government without compunction and Parliamentarians who were obliged to secure the King's borders—borders threatened by "savages," foreign princes and unscrupulous speculators—while balancing budgets with the feudal tools of tariffs and monopolies.

Resolving the disputes engendered by such a variety of conflicting convictions and responsibilities called for sophisticated administration and arbitration policies. Despite such a call, the deployment of the 14th Regiment to Boston would be—in effect—a deliberate first test of the simplistic, authoritarian policy embodied in the Declaratory Act. In all likelihood, none of the parties involved in the disputes appreciated the demands being made on the regiment. One might argue such ignorance was bound to degrade the performance of the unit, but the record does not support such a conclusion. True, the record is in fact rather sparse, but sparse as it is, it supports the conclusion the 14th Foot—while in this awkward and demanding position of enforcing ill-conceived and incomparably unpopular legislation—performed well. They served as a well-disciplined military force and they served with loyalty, resolution, dignity and courage.

෴

Charles probably landed in Boston with the rest of the 14th Regiment, the 29th Regiment and an artillery company of the 59th Regiment on October 1, 1768. Paul Revere—already a leading figure among the dissidents in Boston and bound for even greater notoriety for his famous ride of seven years later—engraved an illustration of the landing of the troops. Figure 6 is a copy of Mr. Revere's print. The caption he provided to his engraving reflects the position taken by the Selectmen of Boston that "The Design of

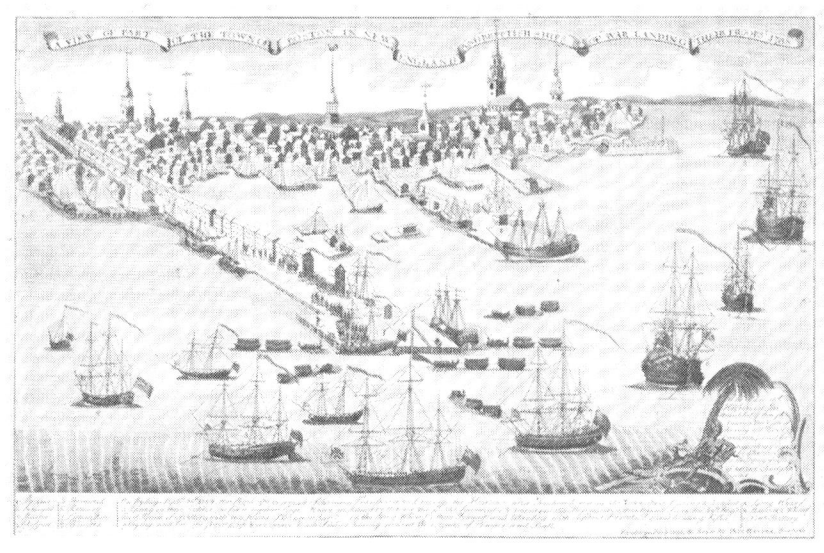

Figure 6. "A View of Part of the Town Boston in New England and Brittish Ships of War Landing Their Troops 1768." Paul Revere, 1770. Map reproduction courtesy of the Norman B. Leventhal Map & Education Center.

these Troops is in every one's Apprehension nothing short of Enforcing by military Power the Execution of Acts of Parliament, in the forming of which the Colonies have not, and cannot have any constitutional Influence. This is one of the greatest Distresses to which a free People can be reduced."[4] This is how Revere described the landing:

> On Friday, Sept. 30th 1768, the Ships of War, armed Schooners, Transports, &c. Came up the Harbor and Anchored round the Town, their Cannon loaded, a Spring on their Cables, as for a regular Siege. At noon on Saturday, Oct. 1st, the fourteenth and twenty-ninth Regiments, a detachment from the 59th Reg[t] and train of artillery with two pieces of cannon, landed on the Long Wharf; then Formed and marched with insolent Parade, Drums beating, Fifes playing and Colors flying, up King Street, each soldier having received sixteen rounds of Powder and Ball.

On coming ashore in Boston on October 1, the 14th Regiment was assigned quarters in what was then downtown Boston. Initially, Lieutenant Colonel Dalrymple planned to quarter his regiment in a public building called the Manufactory House. At the time, the building was occupied by Mr. John Brown and his family. It was Colonel Dalrymple's understanding Governor Bernard and his Council had ordered Mr. Brown to vacate the premises. He sent Lieutenant David Cooper of Captain Fordyce's Company to speak to Mr. Brown and ensure he was complying with the Governor's order. But Mr. Brown refused to comply. Rather than effect an armed takeover on the first day in town, Dalrymple negotiated with the Selectmen to quarter the regiment in two other public buildings, Faneuil Hall and the Townhouse, also known as the Old Court House or Old State House.[5]

Figure 7 is a map of Boston drawn in 1775 at the height of the British presence in the city.[6] This was three years after most of the 14th Regiment left on deployments to St. Vincent in the Caribbean and then to St. Augustine, Florida. But the town changed little between the arrival of the 14th in 1768 and 1775 so the various buildings and locations identified are those that would have been familiar to soldiers in the 14th when they were in town. These include barracks, duty stations, places of worship and business

Chapter 5: Deployed to Boston, 1768 - 1772   61

where soldiers in the 14th Regiment stood guard, drilled, worshiped, exercised and went about their daily routines of eating

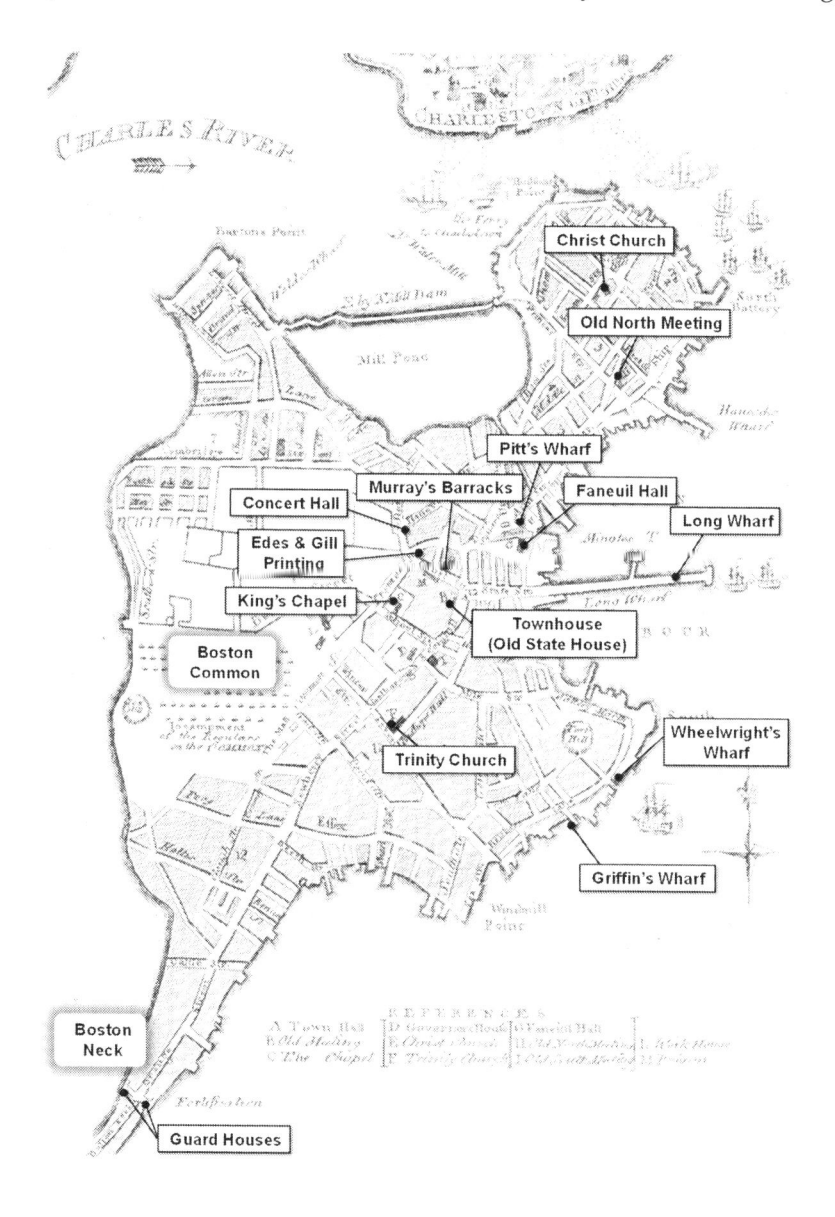

Figure 7. John Norman Map of Boston. Map reproduction courtesy of the Norman B. Leventhal Map & Education Center.

and drinking, washing, equipment maintenance, shopping, socializing and sleeping.

The city was compact. The march from the end of Long Wharf to the Townhouse where some of the 14th was quartered their first night in Boston was about one-half mile. From the Townhouse to Faneuil Hall, where the rest of the regiment was eventually quartered that first night, was a few hundred yards. Murray's Barracks, where the regiment was quartered for most of their stay in Boston was centrally located so the Common and the three Anglican churches would have been within a half-mile walk (Christ Church was about three quarters of a mile distant.) The guard house at the neck would have been one of the posts farthest from the barracks. Given the two guard houses identified in Figure 7 are those to which the men of the 14th were posted in 1768, they were less than two miles from the barracks when monitoring this approach to the city.

୬

In the first complete muster of the 14th Regiment after their arrival in Boston, Charles is identified as the captain of a company of "forty-one effective private men." The muster roll was taken April 24, 1769, about seven months after the regiment arrived. Charles' company was the elite grenadier unit in the regiment. The officers and men are listed in Table 1.

Throughout his service in the 14th Regiment, Charles was affiliated with the grenadiers, most notably as the captain of the single grenadier company in the regiment. Sibbald Scott notes in his *The British Army: Its Origin, Progress, and Equipment*, the grenadiers were introduced to the British army in 1677 as soldiers set apart and trained "in the art of throwing hand grenades." Regarding the grenades Scott adds they, "weighed from three to four pounds each, and three of them were delivered to each man on service; he had also to carry rounds of ammunition for his fuzee [musket], and to take care of his burning match, so that his duties were onerous." Because of the onerous duty, grenadiers were selected based on their height and strength. Given the demands made of the grenadier company, the officers of the company also would have been elite in terms of physical capability, skill, training and experience.

Table 1. Muster Roll of Charles Fordyce's Grenadier Company in the 14th Regiment of Foot, Taken at Boston, April 24, 1769.[7]

NAME	RANK	NAME	RANK
Fordyce, Charles	Captain	Morton, Joshua	Private
Cooper, David	Lieutenant	Martin, Thomas	Private
Ross, Alexander	Lieutenant	Purvis, John	Private
McCrery, Robert‡	Sergeant	Parry, Edward	Private
Phillips, John	Sergeant	Perkins, James	Private
Findlay, Alexander	Corporal	Redfern, Thomas	Private
Taylor, William‡	Corporal	Ricketts, Benjamin	Private
Crocker, William	Drummer	Redmans, Reddy	Private
Almond, William	Private	Riley, John	Private
Ballantine, James‡	Private	Smith, John	Private
Botton, Edward	Private	Smith, Thomas	Private
Carr, John	Private	Stokes, John	Private
Confield, Pierce	Private	Stokes, William	Private
Druckland, William	Private	Swindon, James	Private
Easterly, William†	Private	Simpson, George	Private
Entwistle, Edmund	Private	Stevenson, Jonathan	Private
Elliott, Joseph	Private	Throop, Thomas	Private
Fairchild, James	Private	Thornley, Thomas‡	Private
Greenjud, Henry	Private	Unwin, William	Private
Glossop, Abraham	Private	Watkinson, Robert	Private
Gretton, William	Private	Wilson, Thomas	Private
Hudson, James	Private	West, Thomas	Private
Hale, Samuel	Private	Woods, Robert	Private
Jackson, Francis	Private	Wreyton, Henry	Private
King, William	Private	Woolhouse, John	Private
Lake, William	Private		

Danks, John	Private	Died, 26 April 1768
Cameron, John	Private	Deserted, 22 Oct 1768
Reynolds, Edward	Private	Deserted, 22 Oct 1768
Lane, Thomas	Private	Entered, 10 Mar 1769

NOTES: †Party [i.e., special assignment], ‡Sick

With few exceptions, hand grenades were not in use by the time Charles entered the service, but the grenadiers remained in each regiment as a distinctive unit of tall, strong soldiers with the "privilege of forming the right flank of their battalions, and being the stoutest men were the first brought forward for perilous assaults." Another student of the organization of the British army called the grenadiers, "the flower of each regiment."[8] An illustration depicting a grenadier of the 1st Foot Guards in 1745 is presented in Figure 8.

Lieutenant Colonel William Dalrymple of the 14th Regiment was assigned overall command of the military force that landed in Boston on October 1, 1768. He would relinquish command to Brigadier General John Pomeroy, commander of the 64th Regiment on December 2, 1768. At the same time, Charles was appointed Brigade Major.[9] General Pomeroy would in turn relinquish command of the troops in Boston to Major General Alexander Mackay, Colonel of the 65th Regiment, when he arrived in April, 1769.[10] Charles would continue to serve as Brigade Major under Major General Mackay. Mackay returned to England in August 1769, at which time command devolved back to Lieutenant Colonel Dalrymple. Here again, Charles continued as Brigade Major.[11]

Figure 8. Grenaidier of HM 1st Regiment of Foot Guards, 1745. Sibbald David Scott, *The British Army: Its Origin, Progress, and Equipment*, Vol. 2, London: Cassell, Petter, Galpin, 1868, p. 306. Huntington Library, San Marino, California.

As noted previously, Charles had been appointed Town Major of the forces in

Halifax in 1767. There was considerable overlap in the duties of Town Major and Brigade Major. Both were responsible for the routine operations of the brigade or any smaller detachment that might be assigned to a particular town. Routine duties included daily and weekly accounting for the forces in terms of numbers, readiness and capability, parading of the force and assignments of guards and detachments. Most of the orders for the various duties performed at a given garrison or town were issued by the Brigade Major.[12] One duty Charles performed as Brigade Major was recorded in the Boston newspapers. That duty was to locate, apprehend and, as directed by the commander in Boston, pardon deserters. In performing that duty, Charles placed advertisements in the *The Boston Evening Post*, *The Boston Gazette and Country Journal* and *The Massachusetts Gazette* to inform deserters of General Mackay's free pardon.[13]

Charles was also involved in activities other than military duty during his stay in Boston. On March 15, 1769, a few months after he arrived in Boston, he was among the guests at a dinner-dance which seems to have been hosted by Massachusetts' Governor Francis Bernard. Of this occasion Mr. John Rowe, one of Boston's prominent citizens, noted in his diary, "Spent the evening at the assembly with the Governour, Commodore, General, Colo. Kerr [Carr], Colo. Lesly [Alexander Leslie], Major Furlong, Major Fleming, Major Fordyce, a great number of officers of the navy and army and gentlemen and ladies of the town … was a brilliant assembly and very good dancing."[14]

That Charles and other officers of the army and navy could enjoy the company of gentlemen and ladies of the town at a dance might seem unlikely considering the circumstances. That is, the officers were in town to enforce legislation some citizens reasoned equivalent to enslavement. But it seems the civil servants (tax commissioners appointed to collect the duties associated with the Revenue Acts) had anticipated the possibility hatred of Townshend's duties might engender personal animosities. They reasoned dances and balls—popular in Britain and New England—would be one way to help dispel those animosities. It is likely they hoped these social interactions would foster a broad assimilation and, in turn, lead to more temperate views of British administrative policies in general. In a letter to her friend Elizabeth Lightbody of February 1768, Ann Hulton, sister of Commissioner of Customs Henry Hulton, noted, "The Commissioners began an Assembly at Boston in order to wear off the prejudice of the people and to cultivate their Acquaintance." The assembly in question seems to have been a forum promoting the high-society balls and dinners so fashionable at the time. Ms. Hulton, in London but soon to depart for America, would have received her intelligence from her brother who had arrived in Boston on November 7, 1767, almost a year before the 14th Regiment.

Ms. Hulton joined her brother in Boston in 1769, a few months after the 14th Regiment was posted there. In another letter to Ms. Lightbody shortly after her arrival, she noted her enjoyment of concerts and dances in the city. She told her correspondent there was a concert every other week and added, "Here is a very good Assembly set up since we came, the best there is in all America they say, about sixty couple dance every night once a fortnight."[15]

The Hultons took up residence in the estate once owned by Jeremy Gridley; lawyer, educator, Attorney General of Massachusetts and former Grand Master of St. Andrew's Lodge of Freemasons. The property was in Brookline, Massachusetts, just west of Boston. Their home was a popular destination of "Parties of British officers," and according to one historian, the officers "rode through the town, to and from Boston, attired in uniforms, with nodding plumes and gay trappings."[16] Since Mr. Hulton served as Commissioner during the time the 14th Regiment was in Boston, it is reasonable to speculate officers of the 14th, including Charles Fordyce, were among the guests at his country seat—arriving in uniform with nodding plumes and gay trappings.

Concerts were also popular in Boston and would have afforded officers like Charles entertainment as well as a means of socializing. By the time the 14th Regiment arrived in Halifax in 1766, Boston had an active association of "subscribers" who attended monthly concerts at the "Concert Hall in Queen Street" during an eight-month season. Mr. Stephen Deblois arranged these concerts and advertised them in the local newspapers.[17]

Chapter 5: Deployed to Boston, 1768 - 1772   67

"Officers of the army," meaning officers of the 14th, 29th, 59th and 64th Regiments in Boston, are mentioned in the "Journal of The Times"—a feature introduced in the *Boston Evening Post* after the troops arrived—in connection with a concert Mr. Deblois held on January 25, 1769. Mention of the officers was sarcastic and they were accused of turning the concert "topsy turvy." However, it seems "proper concessions" were made to Mr. Deblois and on February 16 the "Journal" announced the concert hall was "again opened to all who have, or may commence subscribers to such musical entertainments." Evidently this included the soldiers because the announcement provided the assurance, "General Pomeroy, has engaged that the officers of his core [sic, corps], shall for the future behave with decency, and agreeable to the regulations of such assemblies."[18] These "Journal" entries clearly establish the involvement of British officers in the more sophisticated entertainments offered in the city.

At some point during the stay in Boston, Charles took on the role of mentoring a young man interested in military science. A few years prior to the arrival of the 14th, a well-to-do judge in North Carolina, Maurice Moore, sent his son to Boston for his education. Some time after he was settled in town, the 14th was deployed to Boston and the young man, Alfred, "attracted the notice of a Captain Fordyce, a man of fine taste and acquirements." Evidently Captain Fordyce was very impressed with young Moore and offered "to procure him an Ensigncy in the army." Moore declined but "under the instructions of his friend, he learnt the elements of military science, and furnished himself with a variety of knowledge which highly qualified him for that stormy period in which he was destined to live."[19]

Moore was a good student. When he returned home to North Carolina in 1775, "he was appointed a captain in the First North Carolina Regiment of Continentals, commanded by his uncle, James Moore, and he served in the brilliant campaign that ended in the disastrous defeat of the Highlanders at Moore's Creek Bridge" on February 27, 1776.[20] This achievement suggests Moore was well versed in the elements of military science, a combination of knowledge and skill that likely involved a considerable amount of training. Given this likelihood, and the fact Charles was his instructor and friend, it is reasonable to conclude these men—and perhaps some of their associates—spent hours together.

At the same time Charles was introducing Alfred Moore to the elements of military science, it is possible he was engaging Captain William Heath of the Massachusetts Militia in discussions of the same topic at a more advanced level. Heath had been appointed lieutenant of the Ancient and Honorable Artillery Company of Massachusetts in 1768 and he was captain of the company in 1770. He was also the commander of the Suffolk County Militia Regiment. In August 1776, as the British and Americans maneuvered for the first major campaign of the Revolutionary War, Heath would be promoted to Major General in the Continental Army.

A possible personal connection between General Heath and Charles may be inferred from the entry Heath made in his journal when he received the news of Fordyce's death at the Battle of Great Bridge in December 1775. Of this event, he chronicled there was "an action at Norfolk in Virginia, between Dunmore's army and the Virginians, to the advantage of the latter. Fifty of the regular troops were said to have been killed and wounded; among the former was Capt. Fordyce, of the 14th British regiment, *an active and good officer* [emphasis added]."[21] Heath's commending Captain Fordyce as an active and good officer suggests he knew him well, respected him and admired him.

Heath and Fordyce could have been introduced at some of the previously described social events organized to "wear off the prejudice of the people and to cultivate their Acquaintance." For example, in his diary entry for June 5, 1769, John Rowe noted he "Dined at Fanewill [sic, Faneuil Hall] with the Govern' & Council & the Artillery Company." The Artillery Company in question was Heath's Ancient and Honorable Artillery Company of Massachusetts, a fraternity of sorts as well as a genuine militia unit of legitimate military worth. Since Lieutenant Heath was a prominent member of the Artillery Company at this time, it is reasonable to conclude he was present. Mr. Rowe closes his journal entry for that day noting he "Spent the evening at the Concert Hall with a very Brilliant company of Gentlemen & Ladies—a fine

Ball, excellent Musick & a good large Plumb Cake."[22] Although there is no mention of British officers in the brilliant company, such gentlemen—in particular Charles Fordyce—had been included in the "brilliant assembly" Mr. Rowe described in his diary entry for March 15, so both Charles and Lieutenant Heath might have attended this ball.

One of Heath's biographers observed "A strong private attachment grew up between Governor Bernard and Captain Heath."[23] Since Governor Bernard was considered an accomplice of the British Army and generally scorned by the Patriot faction in Massachusetts, such an attachment suggests Heath was a man of integrity and open to differing opinions. The kind of man who would put his interest in military science above his unease over the revenue measures and, if offered the opportunity to engage an expert such as Captain Fordyce, take it. In fact, it may be argued, a prudent militia officer would be eager to engage a military expert such as Captain Fordyce *because* of his unease over the revenue measures. In any event, such eagerness, coupled with Heath's testimony Captain Fordyce was an active and good officer, suggest he and Fordyce were not only acquainted, but shared their professional knowledge and experiences. The possibility of such an alliance between two professionals could have promoted the development of a broader alliance that included any of the British and American officers passionate about their craft.

Despite the best efforts of men like John Rowe and William Heath—both ardent Patriots—to engage the British officers and facilitate their assimilation into Boston society, tensions between the soldiers and townspeople mounted. True assimilation was futile as another 19th-Century British historian, George Trevelyan, highlighted in this assessment of the alienation between soldier and citizen.

> If they had been a legion of angels under Gabriel and Michael they would have been just as much, and as little, beloved in Fish Street, or in Battery Marsh. Their good qualities were denied or travestied, their faults spied out and magnified. Men who during Pitt's war [French and Indian War] never tired of standing treat with soldiers, now talked of them as idle drunkards. If they

civilly passed the time of day to a woman, she drew herself aside with a shudder. The very colour of the cloth in which, in order that America might be safe and great, Englishmen had struggled through the surf at Louisburg, and clambered up the heights of Abraham, was made for them a by-word* and a reproach.[24]

Under these circumstances, it is likely Charles' duties would have included pacifying the ire of offended, insulted and, in some cases, injured townspeople or the city administrators—selectmen and judges—who represented them. One of the notable instances of such duty was an "affair" which occurred between one of Charles' grenadiers, Private John Riley, and a Boston butcher, Jonathan Winship. Riley was accused of assaulting Winship during an altercation of July 14, 1769. He was arrested and ordered to pay a fine. The fine—thirteen shillings—was excessive and when Captain Fordyce was apprised of the proceedings he asked his Lieutenant, Alexander Ross, to intercede on Riley's behalf.

In a deposition he made regarding the affair months after it occurred, Captain Fordyce told Justice James Murray he asked Lieutenant Ross to "go to the justice and represent how impossible it was for a soldier to pay such a sum and intercede for a remission of the fine, which he imagined would be granted having been assured by several soldiers who were present when the quarrel happened, that Riley had bore a great deal of abuse and ill language from the butcher before he struck him." Ross' intercession proved ineffectual. Unable to pay, Riley was ordered to be incarcerated but escaped in a confused encounter of the detachment of soldiers with Riley and a large group of excited onlookers.

As a result of this escape, Lieutenant Ross was ordered back to court and Captain Fordyce accompanied him. Of this proceeding, Captain Fordyce observed, "a very great degree of partiality in the proceedings of the justices in encouraging the inhabitants in their abuse of the soldiers, and the justices themselves often loading the

---

* Of the Accession Day celebration of 1768, the "Journal of the Times" included the observation, "we might now behold American grievances *red dressed.*" *The Boston Evening Post,* 26 December 1768, p. 2. British soldiers were called "Lobster scoundrel" and "Bloody back" in depositions made after the Boston Massacre.

men at their bar in particular and the army in general with the most gross and unwarrantable abuse." He "addressed himself to the bench to speak in favor of the soldiers," but "was instantly in a very preemptory and haughty manner ask [sic] by the said Justice Richard Dana if he was counsel for these people meaning the soldiers and immediately ordered to be silent."[25]

Determining who was at fault in these fights between soldiers and citizens is impossible. Likewise, it is not possible to determine if the judges were loading the soldiers with gross and unwarrantable abuse or even if Captain Fordyce was ordered to be silent in a preemptory and haughty manner. That said, this record does affirm Charles' support of his men. In this trying situation, it seems he was a patient, composed, encouraging advocate.

The greatest test the soldiers of the 14th and 29th Regiments faced in Boston was the escalation of the brick-throwing, bat-swinging, bayonet-wielding tussles into the shooting and killing of the evening of March 5, 1770. On that occasion, soldiers of the 29th Regiment sent to defend a sentry surrounded by a mob at the Old State House fired on the mob and killed five men. Named the "Boston Massacre" by the Patriots, it was indeed a terrible tragedy. However, in his summary account of the event, Governor Thomas Hutchinson credited the "principle persons of both parties," for their part in keeping what he called an "unhappy disturbance" from becoming a genuine massacre. As he put it, they, "interposed their authority and influence to prevent further mischief."[26] Hutchinson named the principle persons in the military party as the commanding officers of the two regiments—Lieutenant Colonel Carr of the 29th and Lieutenant Colonel Dalrymple of the 14th. Based on the depositions of the citizens and soldiers involved, it seems Governor Hutchinson's commendation of the principle persons of both parties on this occasion was warranted. A much more extensive riot could have ensued had not all the officers interposed their authority to prevent further mischief.

After the massacre, the soldiers were relocated from barracks in Boston proper to the barracks on Castle Island in the harbor. This move was in direct response to the demands of the Selectmen of Boston but it did involve tense negotiations, and required a survey of the facilities and refurbishment of the barracks on the island as well as new construction.[27] Castle Island and the fort at Castle William on the island were occupied by provincial troops when the 29th and 14th were ordered there and it took months before the transition from a provincial garrison to His Majesty's garrison was complete. Figure 9 provides an overview of the geographical relationship between Castle Island and Boston.

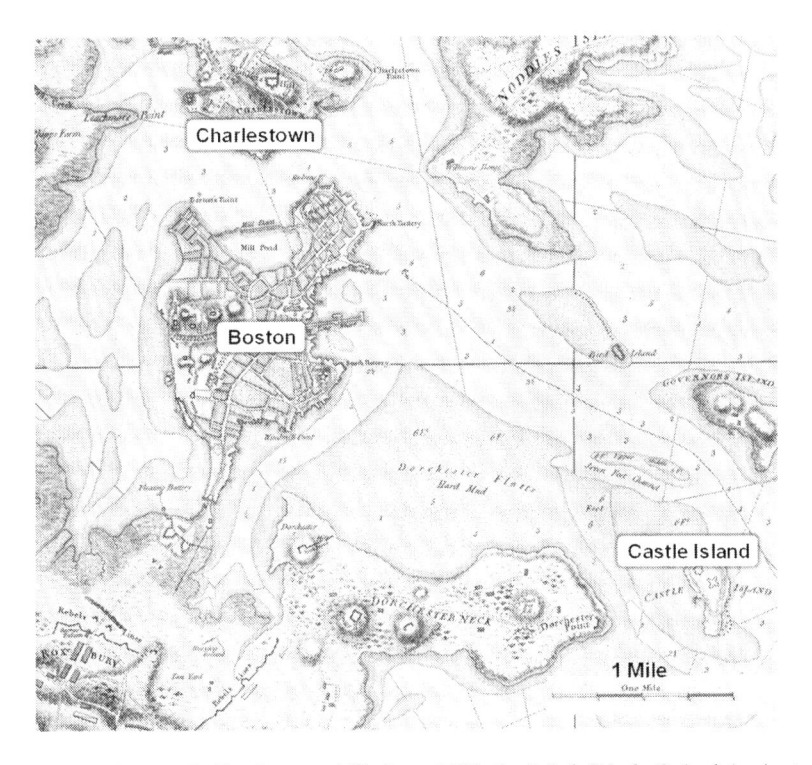

Figure 9. *Boston, Its Environs and Harbour, With the Rebels Works Raised Against That Town in 1775.* Sir. Thomas Hyde Page. Map reproduction courtesy of the Norman B. Leventhal Map & Education Center.

Charles was involved in this transition in his role as Brigade Major. Of the transition, Governor Hutchinson noted in his journal, "About the middle of Aug. [1770] Gen. Gage wrote desiring me to consider of the best way of possessing the King's troops of Castle William, & with-drawing the provincial garrison if necessary." In response to that letter Governor Hutchinson met with Colonel Dalrymple on September 9 and agreed to send General Gage their plans for the move. They "proposed Major Fordyce should set out the next morning"[28] with their plan. Evidently Governor Hutchinson sent word to Captain John Phillips, commander of the provincial garrison, at this same time informing him of the orders to evacuate the fort. Captain Phillips relinquished command to Lieutenant Colonel Dalrymple and the "Detachment of the regular Troops now upon the Island" on September 10.[29]

It seems the shock of the Boston Massacre coupled with the relocation of the regular troops ushered in a period of relative calm in Boston. The report of the verdict of "not guilty" in the trial of Captain Preston, who had commanded the detachment of the 29th Regiment involved in the shootings of March 5, was published in the November 5 edition of the *The Boston Gazette and Country Journal*.[30] Given the enmity engendered by the alleged massacre, Preston's acquittal was a victory for peace and justice. It must have been an encouragement to the soldiers of the 14th and 29th Regiments relegated to the Spartan accommodations on Castle Island.

֍

While in Boston, and particularly during the time spent on Castle Island, Captain Fordyce and the 14th Regiment might have been diverted by news of the assignment of the Earl of Dunmore to the influential post of the Governor of New York and his subsequent reassignment to the Governorship of Virginia less than a year later. As noted in Chapter 3, it is likely Charles knew of Lord Dunmore's link to the Bedford party in the House of Lords—the party in favor of the strict enforcement of the Stamp Act of 1765 and adamantly opposed to its repeal in 1766.

Lord Dunmore's debut in the Boston press was probably the February 5, 1770 announcement in *The Boston Gazette and Country Journal*, he had been appointed Governor of New York.[31] The date of the appointment was December 23, 1769. Dunmore would not arrive in New York for months, but shortly after his appointment was announced, a letter from a correspondent in London was published in Massachusetts commending him as having the "Character of being a good temper'd honest man; a Soldier, brave and generous."[32] In this same paper, the link between Governor Dunmore and the Earl Gower was published with the news "The Lady of the Earl of Dunmore our Governor, is sister to Lady Gower."

This news of Lord Dunmore's appointment to Governor of New York probably would have been reassuring to the Revenue Commissioners and the military in that he had a reputation—or he was linked closely to a party that had a reputation—as a strong proponent of the right of Parliament to tax the colonies and enforce the revenue laws with whatever force might be required. But four days after the curt but agreeable introduction of the new governor, five Bostonians were killed in front of the Old State House by soldiers of the 29th Regiment—the Boston Massacre. Naturally this news eclipsed any news outside of New England and no more was heard of New York's new governor for months.

In October, shortly after the 14th finally was quartered on Castle Island and in command of Castle William, Boston papers published the news of Lord Dunmore's being ready to sail from England. The new Governor arrived in New York on October 18, over eight months after the report of his appointment. His arrival amidst "repeated loud huzzas" was noted in a brief account published in Boston on October 29, 1770.[33]

These reports were, more-or-less, public service announcements of a change of command. Another such report was published a few weeks after the announcement of Lord Dunmore's arrival. It was a report that might have been considered unremarkable by the men of the 14th Regiment but it was, in fact, news that would have far reaching consequences for them. It was the announcement in the form of an aside in a personal letter of the death of Lord Botetourt, Governor of Virginia.[34] Lord Botetourt died in Williamsburg on October 15, 1770, three days before Lord Dunmore arrived in New York. Although no one would have predicted it at the time, Dunmore soon would be reassigned to take

Botetourt's place as Governor of Virginia.[35] The reassignment would be announced in February 1771. He would be in office as Governor of Virginia in 1775 when Captain Charles Fordyce's detachment of the 14th Regiment—then at St. Augustine, Florida—was ordered to Virginia.

Before Lord Dunmore was reassigned to Virginia, Americans from New England to Virginia, as well as the British soldiers on Castle Island, would come to know him as a loyal and ardent representative of the British political faction promoting the authority of the King and Parliament in the colonies. On December 13, 1770, in his first speech to the General Assembly of New York, he advised the legislature he was "peculiarly fortunate in having been appointed to the command of this Province, whose example has been the happy means of renewing that mutual intercourse between the Mother Country & her Colonies, which is so much the interest of both to preserve uninterrupted." To the uninformed, this might have seemed like an innocuous compliment but to the editors of the *Boston Evening Post*—who no doubt considered themselves well informed—it plainly referred "to the part taken by the merchants and traders of New York towards vacating the non-importation agreement, and breaking that union among the Colonies in this as well as other very important points"—behavior the Boston editors considered "base and odious."[36]

A month later, in a message to the General Assembly on January 13, 1771, Governor Dunmore explained he was not at liberty to accept the salary voted to him as Governor since he was paid out of his Majesty's treasury.[37] This too might seem to be innocuous and even favorable to the citizens of New York but it was another instance of Lord Dunmore's adherence to the Revenue Act of 1767—the first of the Townshend Acts—calling for import duties (taxes) in America for "defraying the charge of the administration of justice, and the support of civil government." So, in not accepting a salary from the Assembly, Governor Dunmore was honoring and implementing the Townshend Acts.

The Patriot disdain for this particular element of the Revenue Act is easily inferred from the rhetorical question of an anonymous pundit, "Brutus," writing to *The Boston Gazette and Country Journal*, a few days after Governor Dunmore refused a salary from the province. Brutus asked, "… whether a governor appointed by the King and amply subsisted by him, without the least dependence on the people, would not be an absolute despot, having a power vested in him without a check?"[38]

The men of the 14th Regiment had no way of knowing these reports providing insights into the character and politics of Lord Dunmore could be of particular value to them. To the extent they did develop a dossier on the governor, he must have rated rather highly as a proponent of British policy, the military and the British government. But while Governor Dunmore was making his reputation, the men of the 14th were getting news of actual confrontations between British colonizers and distraught colonials that might have prompted them to contemplate a new and rather exotic deployment thousands of miles from Boston.

It is likely the officers of the regiment had access to British newspapers—albeit six weeks after they were published. That said, they would have read accounts of unrest in the West-Indian islands Britain appropriated from France with the treaty concluding the Seven Years War. In September of 1770, news the "Mountaineer Indians of St. Vincent's grow daily more formidable to the English settlers on the Sea Coasts making frequent excursions from their Island Fortresses upon the low Ground Plantations, and doing much Damage," was published in the *Manchester Mercury*.[39] Throughout 1771, the productivity and economic worth of St. Vincent would be reported with regularity but at the end of the year, another correspondent cautioned, "The daring insolence of the Carrabees daily increases, and renders the tenure of property here uncertain."[40] Given the relative quiet in Boston, this was news of portent to the commanders of the military units deployed to curb such insolence.

CHAPTER 6: DEPLOYED TO ST. VINCENT, THE CARIB WAR, 1772 -1773

In addition to the enormous territory in North America ceded to the British after their victory in the French and Indian War, the French relinquished control of their Caribbean territories as well. These territories included the islands of Grenada and the Grenadines, St. Vincent, Dominica and Tobago. British businessmen and bureaucrats turned their attention to the commercial value of these territories as soon as the treaty ending the war was signed in 1763.[1] As usual, the commercial focus placed a premium on land and infrastructure with little appreciation for the rights or expectations of the inhabitants.

In 1764, a British military officer stationed on St. Vincent provided an unofficial assessment of the status of the island, including an unflattering and prejudicial evaluation of the natives. He noted the French colonists had not planted "sugars," because of "the continual dread they are under of being insulted and plundered by the savages, or the Carribees." Of these natives he noted,

> Their numbers are computed 2000, or 2500, including men, women, and children; but they are a rascally crew, which it were well to clear the island of, by sending them to the coast of Spain. They go naked, are armed with bows and arrows, and cutlasses; and are by nature cruel and cowardly. They are so fearful of any military appearance that since my arrival here they have not shewn themselves in bodies; alleged they are frightened at the red coat; they have even promised to be quiet; but there is no trusting to their word.[2]

He further observed these savages— "restless and turbulent people" —inhabited the mountains in the western part of the island which were "undoubtedly the finest part of the island." It seems such amateur assessments, along with an implicit faith in his Majesty's beneficent intensions, provided the foundation of

British policy toward the inhabitants of the newly acquired West Indian territories.

On March 26, 1764, King George III issued a proclamation for a survey of the islands of Grenada, the Grenadines, Dominica, St. Vincent and Tobago, in order to lay out plantations and facilitate the growth of sugar, coffee, cocoa, cotton, "or other articles of beneficial culture." This survey was proclaimed in response to considerations of "the great Benefit which will arise to the Commerce of Our Kingdoms and the Interests of Our Subjects, from the speedy Settlement of our Islands."[3]

In January of 1765, a "public notice" was published providing additional details of the proposed survey and sale of land in the West Indian islands. The notice included the provision that the "native Caribbees of St. Vincent" would continue undisturbed in their possession of their "cottages and grounds." Sale of the lands on St. Vincent was set for May 28, 1766.[4]

At the end of the year—November of 1765—the King's commissioners provided the public with still more details regarding the land to be sold on St. Vincent. According to this notice, the lands available included property claimed by the Caribs, namely the mountainous region of Morne Agarou [Garou] and the coastal region of Chateau Bellair.[5] At this point, however, the commissioners were told to await further instructions before surveying land inhabited by or claimed by the Caribs. Those further instructions, authorizing a survey of the land claimed by the Caribs, were provided at the close of the year 1767. On January 18, 1768, the British Secretary of State for the Southern Department, William Petty, 2nd Earl of Shelburne, notified the Governor of the British West Indian territories, Robert Melville, the sale of the lands inhabited by the Caribs had been authorized and that he should "give every support and assistance to the commissioners in the execution of their instructions."[6]

Thus was the stage set for a confrontation between the Caribs and official Britain—embodied in the survey teams sent out to divide the land on St. Vincent in response to the King's proclamation. Inasmuch as the Caribs considered themselves "perfectly independent," and did not "acknowledge the sovereignty of any prince"—an assessment Lieutenant Governor Ulysses Fitzmaurice made of them in 1769[7]—this confrontation and the subsequent war with the Caribs had much in common with the war that would develop between Great Britain and America a few years later.

By 1769 the Caribs had—in effect—revolted at the prospect of losing their land and liberty, a prospect made clear to them by the presence of survey teams guarded by British soldiers. On May 1, 1769, Commissioner William Young informed Harry Alexander, President of the Island of St. Vincent, "…the Caribbs have expressed great uneasiness and dissatisfaction at the endeavours of the commissioners to carry out the King's instructions for the survey and disposal of the lands in the island."[8] The Caribs had, in fact, stopped the King's survey party at the Jambou River well before that party was half way up the east coast from Kingstown.[9]

In July 1769 the Commissioners for the Sale of Lands told the Commissioners for Trade and Plantations, "…it will be impossible, without imminent danger to the colony [St. Vincent] to complete any settlements … without a force sufficient to restrain and awe them [the Black Caribs] into obedience."[10] Two weeks later the Secretary of State for the Colonies, Lord Hillsborough, suggested to Lieutenant Governor Fitzmaurice he apply to the Commander-in-Chief of the British forces in North America, Lieutenant General Thomas Gage, for troops, "if these savages should continue in their hostility," and you cannot "reduce them to a proper submission to his Majesty" with the force collected from the other islands.[11] Evidently Lord Hillsborough informed General Gage of the possibility troops would be needed in St. Vincent at the same time. On October 7, General Gage informed the Secretary he would send the troops as soon as they were requested.[12]

Fitzmaurice recognized the need for more troops although he told Lord Hillsborough in February 1770 he had not applied to General Gage.[13] But a month later the Board of Trade informed the King it would be impossible without a considerable military force to induce the Caribs to submit to the measures ordered for the settlement of St. Vincent.[14] In October 1771, the Commissioners for the Sale of Lands reported they were convinced "all treaty and negation" would be fruitless and that obliging the Caribs to submit to his Majesty's government would require "a sufficient force to terrify them into obedience."[15] These appeals finally prompted the King to action. On April 16, 1772, Secretary Hillsborough informed the Lords of the Admiralty the King had directed General Gage to send a force from North America to the island of St. Vincent, to reduce the black Caribs of that island to a due submission of his Majesty's authority and government.[16]

Two days after he wrote the Lords of the Admiralty, Lord Hillsborough wrote General Gage to apprise him of the King's pleasure and advised him "to send to St. Vincent's two complete regiments of the troops under your command." He also noted the success of the "very important service" would "depend in a great measure upon the discretion and ability of the officer who will have from seniority the command of the whole force to be employed." In closing, Secretary Hillsborough acknowledged the risks associated with the mission noting, "the regiment to be sent to St. Vincent's be supplied with every thing you shall think the nature of the service may require, and may contribute to their comfort and convenience in so unhealthy a climate."[17]

In 1768, when General Gage had been instructed to be careful to select an officer "upon whose prudence, resolution and integrity you can entirely depend" to quell the disturbances in Boston, he picked Lieutenant Colonel Dalrymple of the 14th Regiment for the task. Here again, he resorted to Lieutenant Colonel Dalrymple—still in command of the troops in Boston—as the officer of "discretion and ability" to command the force performing the "very important service" in St. Vincent. Dalrymple would be promoted to the local rank of Major General to command the combined force sent to St. Vincent.[18]

On June 29, 1772, Gage told Secretary of War Barrington the regiments he ordered to St. Vincent were Lieutenant Colonel Dalrymple's 14th Regiment, then at Castle William in Boston Harbor, and the 31st Regiment from St. Augustine, Florida. According to General Gage, the regiments were supplied with camp equipment, ammunition, entrenching tools and six-months' provision "so that they will be in a Situation to pursue any Operations Governor

Lyborne has resolved upon against the Charibs, as soon as they join him." The General took Lord Hillsborough's warning of an unhealthy climate seriously. He told Secretary Barrington he had "taken into Consideration the Health of the troops," and had "ordered out Doctor Anderson, Mate of the General Hospital, with Medicines, Refreshments and Necessaries proper for establishing of a General Hospital at St. Vincent."[19]

It seems the redeployment of the 14th at this time was of general interest although the looming conflict with the Caribs was not. General Gage determined to keep the destination of the 14th a secret to the public until after they sailed from Boston.[20] On August 3, 1772, the *Boston Gazette and Country Journal* reported, "On Monday last [July 27] Colonel Dalrymple, with the whole of the 14th Regiment under his command, having embarked on board the transports lately arrived here from New York, sailed from this place with a fair wind." In this same edition, the deployment of twelve transports from New York to take two regiments to a rendezvous at Barbados was reported, but the report ended with the postscript their design was secret.[21] No mention was made of Colonel Dalrymple's Regiment being sent to St. Vincent at this time even though a report in the previous edition of the same newspaper provided a rather detailed summary of the unfolding conflict there and the news two regiments "from North America" were being dispatched to the island.[22]

In a letter of September 12, 1772, Governor William L. Leyborne of the British West Indies informed the Secretary of State, the Earl of Hillsborough, of the arrival of the "14th Regiment under Lieutenant Colonel Dalrymple from Boston" at St. Vincent.[23] Lieutenant Colonel Dalrymple notified Lord Barrington he arrived at St. Vincent with the 14th Regiment on August 30.[24] Given they departed Boston on July 27, they were thirty-five days in transit.

Governor Leyborne reviewed the 14th at Fort Tyrrel, St. Vincent, on September 18, 1772. After the review, he wrote Secretary Barrington and reported his satisfaction "at seeing this fine Body of Men, so completely Disciplined."[25] At this time, the strength of the regiment was 18 officers (not including Major General Dalrymple), 3 staff (quarter master, surgeon and mate), 30 sergeants and drummers and 361 rank and file, which included recruiters and soldiers on furloughs for a total of 412.

Details of the Summary Return from which these numbers are drawn are presented in Table 2 with the names of the officers present. The report was prepared by Major Furlong. In preparing the report, he did not list the officers present by name. However, he does name all the absent officers. So the names listed in Table 2 were determined by a process of elimination. That is, the names listed are those remaining when the names of the absent officers are eliminated from the *Army List* for the year of the report, 1772. Since the list in the table was developed by this process of elimination, it should not be considered authoritative.

Table 2. Summary Return of the 14th Regiment at Fort Tyrrel, St. Vincent, September 18, 1772.[26]

RANK	NUMBER	NAMES	
Major	1	Jonathan Furlong	
Captains	4	William Blackett Charles Fordyce Brabazon O'Hara	Edmund Mason John Stanton[†]
Lieutenants	8	John Batut William Browne David Cooper Edward Gower	William Napier Alexander Ross Cornelius Smelt[◊] James Urquhart
Ensigns	5	Peter Burnett Henry Hallwood Henry Kelvington	Hill Wallace Francis Wilkie
Quarter Master	1	Peter Burnett	
Surgeon	1	Charles Hall	
Surgeon's Mate	1	John Weir	
Sergeants	19		
Drummers and Fifers	11		
Rank and File	361		
Fit for Duty	338		
Sick in Barracks	7		
Sick in Hospital	5		
Recruiting	3		
On Furlough	8		
TOTAL ALL RANKS*	412		

NOTES

*Quarter master not included since he is counted in the number of officers. Major General Dalrymple not included.
[†]Captain O'Hara died of disease on October 5, 1772. Captain Stanton replaced him on December 22. *Commission Book*, 1772-1776, WO 25/32, p. 57.
[◊]King's leave.

Chapter 6: Deployed to St. Vincent, the Carib War, 1772 - 1773

The company of grenadiers, commanded by Charles Fordyce, included 1 captain, 1 lieutenant, 2 sergeants, 3 drummers/fifers and 39 rank-and-file, including 2 sick.[27] The men in Captain Fordyce's Company at this time are listed in Table 3. This list is from a complete muster of the regiment as they prepared to leave Castle William (Boston) for St. Vincent.

Table 3. Muster Roll of Charles Fordyce's Grenadier Company in the 14th Regiment of Foot, Castle William (Boston), May 15, 1772.[28]

NAME	RANK	NAME	RANK
Fordyce, Charles	Captain	Lockett, John	Private
Cooper, David	Lieutenant	Morton, Joshua	Private
Ross, Alexander◊	Lieutenant	Milsom, William‡	Private
Mills, Benjamin	Sergeant	Purvis, John	Private
Phillips, John	Sergeant	Parry, Edward†	Private
Elliot, Joseph	Corporal	Perkins, James	Private
Bollen, Edward	Corporal	Redfern, Thomas	Private
Heal, Samuel	Corporal	Ricketts, Benjamin	Private
Crocker, William	Drummer	Redmans, Ready	Private
Morris, John	Fifer	Riley, John	Private
Coleman, William	Fifer	Stokes, William	Private
Almond, William	Private	Stokes, John	Private
Brison, James	Private	Smith, Thomas	Private
Carr, John†	Private	Simpson, George	Private
Druckland, William	Private	Throop, Thomas	Private
Easterly, William†	Private	Tayler, William*	Private
Entwistle, Edmund	Private	Townshend, John	Private
Fairchild, James†	Private	Unwin, William†	Private
Glossop, Abraham‡	Private	West, Thomas	Private
Greaten, William	Private	Watkinson, Robert	Private
Hudson, James†	Private	Stevenson, Jonathan	Private
Holam, William†	Private	Wilson, Thomas	Private
Jackson, Francis	Private	Wreyton, Henry	Private
King, William	Private		

NOTES: ◊King's leave, †Duty, ‡Sick, *On furlough

All the officers listed in Table 3 are the same as those listed in the roll of three years earlier when the company arrived in Boston.

Sergeant Benjamin Mills has replaced Sergeant Robert McCrery. The corporals listed are all new, but they are all men who were privates in the roll of 1769. Two fifers have been added to the 1772 roll. Of the 36 privates listed, six are new. Captain Fordyce notes on the roll that of the 47 men listed, 12 were absent so the total number of effective men was 35. In the 1769 roll he listed a total of 52 men, five of whom were absent, leaving a total of 47 effective men. So the total number of men in the company in 1772 was five less than in 1769 and the number of effective men had been reduced by twelve, from 47 to 35.

※

St. Vincent Island is eighteen miles long and eleven miles wide. It lies about 13 degrees north of the equator and the climate is tropical. The 13-degree latitude puts it in line with the Philippines and Viet Nam in Asia and Gambia in Africa. The temperature is almost constant throughout the year with highs in the mid to high 80°F (27°C) and lows in the mid to high 70°F (21°C). Of the geography and potential for agriculture, a visitor in 1764 observed, "It abounds with the finest Rivers, the best of Water, and plenty of excellent Fish. The Soil is Virgin Earth, and of the fittest Kind for growing of Sugar, Coffee, Cocoa, and all Sorts of Produce."[29] The island was thickly forested, but some areas were well situated for cultivation. Figure 10 is a map of St. Vincent[30] providing additional details of the geography and notes regarding the locations and features related to the campaign.

At the time of the expedition against the Caribs, the most serious concern of military planners devising a campaign to the West Indies was the prospect of tropical diseases. By the 18th century, the threat of disease in the tropics was well established, and the initial reports of the activities of the 14th Regiment in the expedition to St. Vincent certainly bore testimony to the seriousness of the threat. During the campaign one reporter observed, "The climate of St. Vincent's is so unhealthy, that as soon as English horses, cows, sheep, &c. are landed upon the island, they begin to lose their flesh and vigour, and generally die in about twelve months."[31] And it seems the climate was equally bad for English

Chapter 6: Deployed to St. Vincent, the Carib War, 1772 - 1773   85

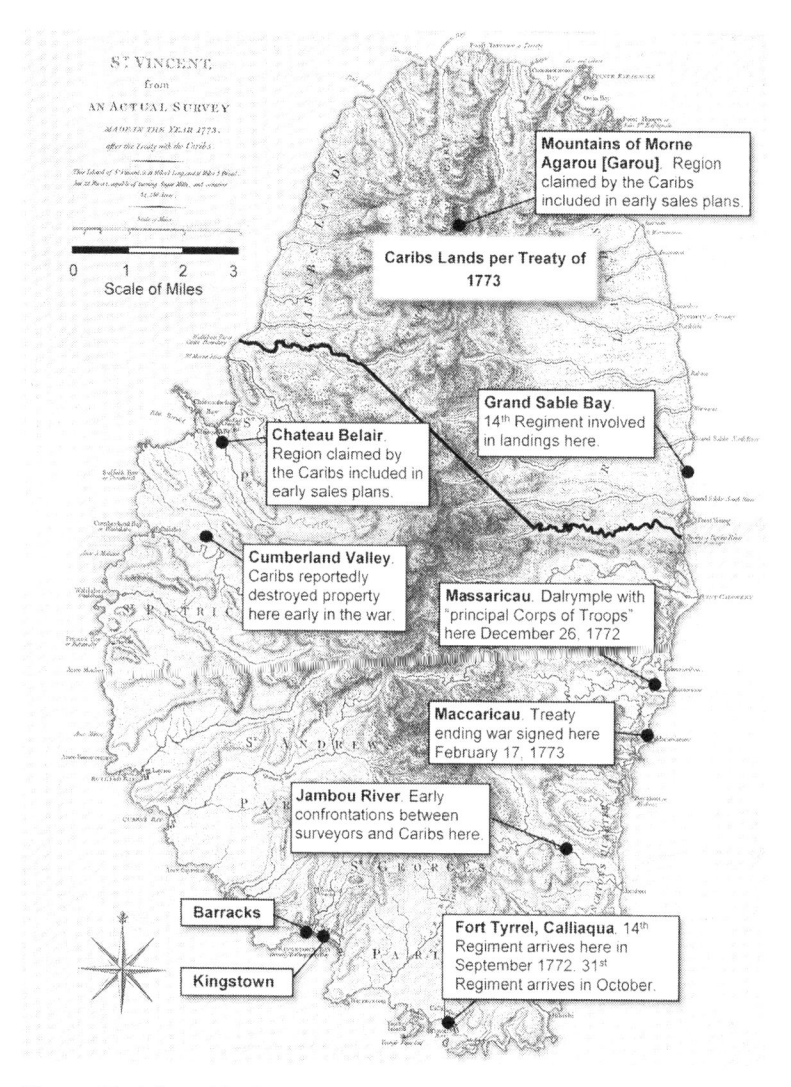

Figure 10. Map of St. Vincent with Locations Associated with the Carib War of 1772-1773. Thomas Jefferys. Map reproduction courtesy of the Norman B. Leventhal Map & Education Center.

men. In November, a report of deaths due to illness was published in Boston. The reporter observed, "… the troops began to be sickly. Not only Captain Brabazon O'Hara, of the 14th regiment, died there, but seven or eight soldiers of that regiment."[32] In a report published December 31, 1772, Captain O'Hara's death is given as October 5,[33] so he died about a month after the 14th arrived in St. Vincent. According to another early report of the impact of disease on the operation in St. Vincent, "no less than one half of the fourteenth regiment, that were ordered out to that inhospitable region, have died of the climate, without having ever seen the face of their formidable enemy."[34] This was an exaggeration, but deaths due to disease would outnumber combat deaths. Thirty-seven men in the 14th Regiment died on St. Vincent and the ratio of those who died from disease to combat deaths was 26 to 11.[35]

Actual combat was limited to skirmishes. The skirmishing was an element of what is known today as asymmetric warfare. This was the kind of warfare the deadly climate and rugged terrain afforded the Caribs, who were inured to both.

During debates on the expedition in the House of Commons, General Cyrus Trapaud, commander of the 70th Regiment at St. Vincent, read a letter into the record that addressed the kind of action involved in the asymmetrical warfare. According to the letter, the Caribs "act with great caution, and the woods are so thick, that they Knock our men down, with the greatest security to themselves, as it is impossible we can see them. We have only been able to penetrate four miles into the country."[36]

A "gentleman in St. Vincent's" wrote his friend in London, the Caribs "frequently make sallies from among the rocks in very formidable bodies, and by that means destroy several of our soldiers, who are continually exposed to the fire of the savages from the advantageous posts they take, such as skulking behind trees, &c."[37] After almost two months on the island, an officer in the 14th Regiment reported they had "advanced about 10 miles into the Caribs' country." But he noted the Caribs were taking advantage of the terrain to slow the British advance. He informed his correspondent, "I imagine our stay here will be longer than we first expected; for tho' these blacks dare not fight us fairly, yet they give trouble by ambushing us, for which they have an excellent opportunity; the country is naturally strong being very mountainous and woody."[38]

Regarding the extent of the asymmetry associated with this kind of warfare, another reporter summarized,

> The woods in which the savages reside at St Vincent's are so impenetrable to our soldiers, that though the force of the former is very small, it can act with great vigour; whereas, large as the force of the latter is (comparatively considered), it can act only by accident: therefore, as the numbers of the dead or dying, by the diseases of the country, are naturally proportioned to the number of the troops, the Caribbees, like Maximns*, are enabled to conquer by delay; and, barbarous as they are, have sense enough to let the seasons (unless where they have a certain advantage) make away with the enemy.[39]

Despite the disadvantages of climate, terrain, and asymmetric combat, Major General Dalrymple persevered with the campaign. On November 20, 1772, an officer on one of the ships in in Kingston Road observed, "… we appear now to be in earnest. Major [Alexander] Mackenzie [of the 31st Regiment] is supposed to have landed yesterday with 100 soldiers and some blacks at Grand Sable Bay, which is in the heart of their country; and Colonel Dalrymple with the body of the army is advancing from this side of the Island with an intention to join the others."[40] On December 26, Dalrymple reported to Lord Barrington, "… the principal Corps of Troops are arrived at a place called Massiricau being the utmost extent of the road formerly marked out by the King's Surveyors, from thence to the Corps posted at *Grande Sable* may be near six Miles, I hope to effect a junction soon."[41] In a letter of January 14, 1773, Major Mackenzie told his correspondent, "I am still working the way to accomplish a Junction with General Dalrymple's Army."[42] Evidently Mackenzie and Dalrymple did effect the pincer maneuver that seemed to constitute the main campaign against the Caribs and it was successful. The military victory, coupled with what could be considered generous concessions offered the Caribs for their cooperation in a peaceful settlement, ended the conflict.[43] The treaty ending the war was signed in Maccaricau on February 17, 1773.

---

* Quintus Fabius Maximus Verrucosus. Roman military commander famous for his cautious delaying tactics.

A week later, Major General Dalrymple reported the results of the campaign to Lord Dartmouth. In the introduction to his report, Dalrymple asked the Secretary to "lay before His Majesty the activity, bravery and patience of the troops employed on this service."[44] He included the following summary of the casualties incurred during the expedition and this information was published in the *London Gazette* in April.

> Major-general Dalrymple transmits the following returns of the loss sustained by his majesty's troops, and highly commends their activity, bravery, and patience, in the course of this difficult and fatiguing service.
>
> Return of the casualties of the several regiments in St Vincent's, from the time of their taking the field against the Caribbee Indians, in September 1772, to the conclusion of the campaign the 20th of February 1773.
>
> Killed, 1 lieutenant-colonel, 3 subalterns, 3 serjeants, 65 rank and file; total, 72.—Wounded, 1 captain, 1 subaltern, 8 serjeants, 73 rank and file; total, 83.—Deceased, 1 captain, 1 subaltern, 8 serjeants, 100 rank and file; total, 110.—Deserted, 4 rank and file; total, 4.—Sick, 1 lieutenant-colonel, 5 captains, 12 subalterns, 16 serjeants, 394 rank and file; total, 428.
>
> Killed, lieutenant-colonel [Ralph] Walsh, of the 31st regiment, lieutenant [Nicholas] Darrah of the 70th, lieutenant [Edward] Gower of the 14th, ensign Mackay of the 14th [possibly Ensign George Mackay of the 68th Regiment]—Deceased, captain O'Hara of the 14th, ensign [Samuel] Bruce of the 70th—Wounded captain [John] Stanton, of the 14th; lieutenant [William] Brown of the 14th.[45]

Curiously, the death of Charles Fordyce of the 14th Regiment was reported in several newspapers throughout England at about the same time Major General Dalrymple's report was published. The report regarding Fordyce was cryptic. The single sentence in the *Bath Chronicle and Weekly Gazette* was: "Letters from St. Vincent's bring an account of Capt. Fordyce, of the 14th regiment, being killed in a Skirmish with the Caribbs."[46] The curious aspects of the report are that it was published just a month before Major General Dalrymple's official report, it was not corroborated by

Dalrymple's report and it was in fact, false. There had been reports of unnamed officers being killed in the Carib War[47] but there seems to be no particular reason why Charles Fordyce would have been associated with any of those deaths. The report was never retracted and to some extent it may account for Charles' anonymity. As noted previously, Charles is listed as "unconnected" and as having "died in St. Vincent's, November, 1772, in a skirmish with the Caribs," in Alexander Dingwall Fordyce's rather comprehensive genealogy of 1885, *Family Record of the Name of Dingwall Fordyce in Aberdeenshire*.

※

The war against the Caribs had been unpopular on the British home front. A good example of the extent of the war's unpopularity was an open letter to Secretary Dartmouth from a correspondent pen-named "Probus." The letter was published on the first page of *Caledonian Mercury* of December 7, 1772. Probus voiced the concern of many Englishmen that the war had been instigated by "a few mercenary traders and purchasers of lands on the island." He also asserted Lord Hillsborough's plan to reduce the black Caribs of that island to a due submission of his Majesty's authority and government was "barbarous."[48] In Parliamentary debates on the expedition in February 1773, one member put forth a motion characterizing the action as "repugnant to the known humanity of his Majesty's temper, disgraceful to his Majesty's arms, and dishonorable to the character of the British nation."[49] The motion failed, but it did serve as an indictment of the parochial, uncoordinated, inadequate and ineffectual analysis and planning involved in committing Britain's well-qualified, conscientious and loyal military forces in support of the "national interest." Naturally such disparagement and confusion was discouraging to the troops. Under these circumstances they must have been eager to quit the island as soon as the campaign ended, and they did. Within a month of the signing of the treaty with the Caribs, Major General Dalrymple left for London and the 14th sailed for St. Augustine under the command of Major Jonathan Furlong.[50]

CHAPTER 7: DEPLOYED TO ST. AUGUSTINE, FLORIDA, 1773 - 1775

When Lord Hillsborough sent General Gage instructions to send two complete regiments to St. Vincent, he also informed him "it was his majesty's intention these regiments should return to North America so soon as the service is completed." In apprising Secretary of War Barrington the two regiments he was sending to St. Vincent were the 14th and the 31st, General Gage acknowledged the instructions for the return of the regiments to North America and noted, "As it is his Majesty's Pleasure, that the two Regiments should return to North America, when the service they are going upon is completed; I mean, on their Return, to order them to other Places than where they were before stationed, and to direct the 14th to repair to St. Augustine, [Florida] and the 31st to Halifax."[1]

After the peace treaty with the Caribs was signed in February, General Gage, true to his plan, ordered most of the 14th Regiment to St. Augustine. In a letter of May 5, 1773, he told Lord Dartmouth he believed the 14th had arrived in St. Augustine since they sailed from St. Vincent about the middle of March.[2]

Florida had been a Spanish colony prior to 1763 when Spain ceded it to Great Britain in exchange for Havana, which the British had captured in the closing months of the Seven Years War. St. Augustine was the capital of Spanish Florida when the British took possession of the province. At the time, 1763, the Spanish population of St. Augustine was estimated to be 3,046.[3] In 1766, three years after the British takeover, William Stork published one of the earliest assessments of the British holdings in East Florida. His survey was based on a journal kept by John Bartram, an American naturalist King George III had commissioned to explore Britain's new Florida provinces as a royal botanist. With Bartram as his authority, Stork described St. Augustine as,

... an oblong square, the streets are regularly laid out, and intersect each other at right angles, they are built narrow on purpose to afford shade. The town is above half a mile in length, regularly fortified with bastions, half bastions, and a ditch; besides these works it has another fort of fortification, very singular, but well adapted against the Indians, an enemy the Spaniards had most to fear: it consists of several rows of palmetto trees, planted very close along the ditch, up to the parapet; their pointed leaves are so many *chevaux de frieze*, that make it entirely impenetrable; the two southern bastions are built of stone. In the middle of the town is a spacious square called the parade, open towards the harbour: at the bottom of this square is the governors house, the apartments of which are spacious and suited to the climate, with high windows, a balcony in front, and galleries on both sides; to the back part of the house is joined a tower, called in America a look-out, from which there is an extensive prospect towards the sea, as well as inland. There are two churches within the walls of the town, the parish church a plain building, and another belonging to the convent of Franciscan friars, which is converted into barracks for the garrison. The houses are built of free-stone, commonly two stories high, two rooms upon a floor, with large windows and balconies: before the entry of most of the houses runs a portico of stone arches; the roofs are commonly flat. The Spaniards consulted conveniency more than taste in their buildings; the number of houses in the town, and within the lines, when the Spaniards left it, was above 900; many of them, especially in the suburbs, being built of wood, are now gone to decay.[4]

Mr. Stork also included a brief assessment of the demographics of the town in his survey and determined, "The inhabitants were of all colours, white, negroes mulattos, Indians, &c. at the evacuation of St. Augustine, amounted to 5,700, including the garrison of 2,500 men." Since his estimate of the population includes Negroes mulattos, Indians, &c., it is naturally greater than the 3,046 Spanish residents counted by the Spanish Governor. According to another census and survey of trades in the region,

> The number of inhabitants in East Florida from 1763 to 1771, besides [Andrew] Turnbull's colony [New Smyrna], are recorded as two hundred and eighty-eight householders and women, one hundred and forty-four of these householders being married. Among this number we find that there are thirty-one store-keepers, three haberdashers, fifteen inn-keepers, forty-five artificers and mechanics, one hundred and ten planters, eleven overseers, twelve draftsmen in the employ of the government, six cow-keepers, and four hunters.[5]

Regarding the constituents of the military establishment at the garrison at St. Augustine and the kinds of duty the soldiers might perform, 20th Century historian Charles Mowat provides this rather comprehensive summary. The locations named in this summary are identified on the map in Figure 11.[6]

> St. Augustine was from the start one of the military stations, and in normal times had an establishment consisting of one regiment of infantry, a company of the Royal Regiment of Artillery, members of the "civil branch" of the ordnance, specifically a surgeon, an ordnance barrack master, a storekeeper, a "clerk of the survey and cheque," an extra clerk, carpenters and a blacksmith, one or two engineers of the corps of engineers, and the garrison staff consisting of the surgeon of the garrison hospital and his mates, the fort adjutant and barrack master, the chaplain (an absentee in this case) and the commissary for stores and provisions. Owing to the high proportion of absentees among both the officers and men, the regiment's strength in St. Augustine was usually only about two hundred; in addition, one of its companies was usually stationed at New Providence, and small detachments were maintained at the outposts in the province itself, Apalache, Picolata, Mosa, Matanzas, the lookout on Anastasia Island, and New Smyrna. The first five of these outposts were all inherited from the Spaniards. Mosa, a redoubt of turf on marshy ground two miles north of town, was manned by a sergeant and twelve men until dismantled in 1775. Matanzas, a coquina tower,* which is still standing, lay about fourteen miles to the south on

---

* A watch tower constructed of coquina, a sedimentary rock composed of seashells or coral.

Chapter 7: Deployed to St. Augustine, Florida, 1773 - 1775   93

a marshy island commanding the southern entrance to the Matanzas River and had a guard of some half-dozen men. Picolata, another coquina tower, had a guard of eight until abandoned in 1769. The lookout was not armed and was manned by two privates and an artilleryman. At New Smyrna there was no fort, but a guard of some twenty men was kept there after the riot in 1768. Apalache, the most desolate outpost, and nearly two hundred miles from St. Augustine, was manned by a company and a few supernumeraries. It suffered much from sickness, inadequate food and water supply, and the difficulty of provisioning it, and was abandoned in 1769 after being seriously damaged in a hurricane in October, 1767.[7]

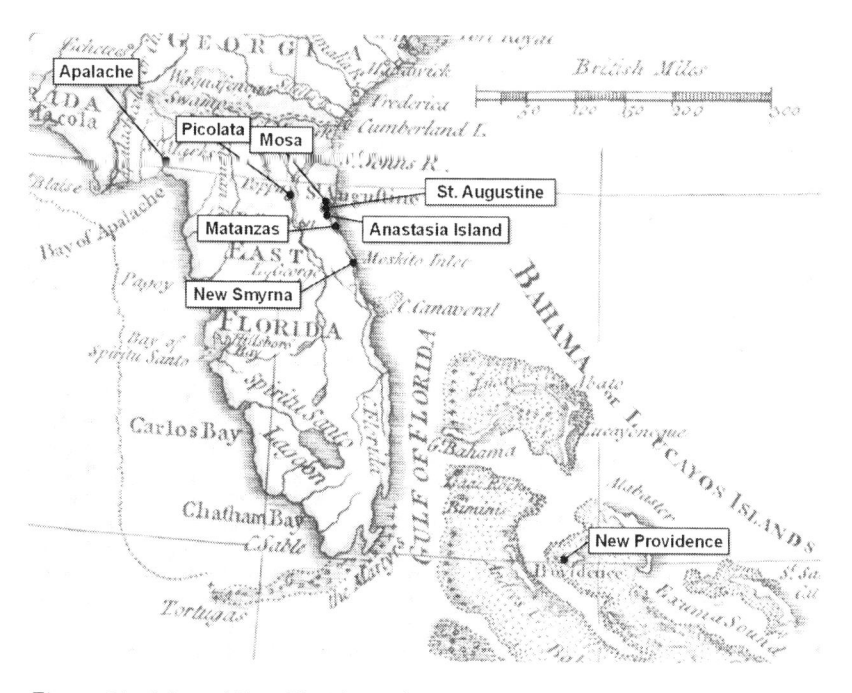

Figure 11. Map of East Florida with Locations Manned by British Soldiers Assigned Duty at St. Augustine. *A New Map of the United States of North America*. Samuel Dunn, Jonathan Carver, Robert Sayer and John Bennett. Map reproduction courtesy of the Norman B. Leventhal Map & Education Center.

According to this assessment, guard duty constituted much of the service performed by the troops at St. Augustine. This conclusion is also supported by a report of the "Detail of the Guards" submitted by Lieutenant Colonel Edward Maxwell of the 21st Regiment when that unit was deployed to St. Augustine in 1770. According to Maxwell, a total of 69 guards were posted as delineated in Table 4.

Table 4. Detail of the Guards for the 21st Regiment of Foot at St. Augustine, February 1, 1770.[8]

DUTY	SERGEANTS	CORPORALS	DRUMMERS	PRIVATES
Fort Guard	1	1	1	16
Barrack Guard	1	1	1	14
Town Guard	1	2		21
Camp Guard				4
Orderly Men	1			4
Total	4	4	2	59

If the requirement for guarding the locations specified was for 24 hours a day, seven days a week, the minimum number of guards required for the duty listed in Table 4 would be 138 men assuming the men worked twelve-hour shifts. Accounting for sickness and the likelihood guards would need more than twelve hours off per day for sleeping, eating, maintaining their equipment and their psychological wellbeing, it would not be unreasonable to employ three men to provide 24/7 coverage for any single duty requirement. Given this likelihood, the number of men required to provide the guard specified in Table 4 would be 207.

By the time the 14th Regiment arrived, living conditions had been improved by the construction of a new barracks described in Mr. Mowat's history as an "E-shaped building girt with piazzas and adorned with a cupola and a large weather cock."[9]

The British divided Florida into two separate provinces, West Florida on the Gulf of Mexico (the "pan-handle" of today's Florida) and East Florida on the Atlantic Ocean. In 1773, the Lieutenant Governor of the province of East Florida was John Moultrie.

He had been appointed to this position in 1771 when James Grant was Governor. Since Governor Grant took a leave of absence in May 1771, Moultrie was acting Governor for the first year the 14th was in St. Augustine. On March 9, 1774, Patrick Tonyn was sworn in as Governor of East Florida, a position he would hold during the remainder of the time the 14th was stationed there.

Governor Grant had a reputation for hospitality which included the entertainment of the soldiers stationed in St. Augustine. Grant was a bachelor, so he called on Eleanor Moultrie, wife of the Lieutenant Governor, to act as hostess. According to Mowat,

> The tedium of life in such a remote outpost was somewhat relieved by the generous hospitality of the bachelor governor, Grant, and by balls and assemblies at which the lieutenant governor's lady took first place in an order of precedence which was rigidly insisted on. The brief stay in town of General Haldimand, in command of the Southern Brigade, provided the occasion, perhaps, for a good deal of entertaining, and later, in 1771, the presence of the "Music" or military band of the major of brigade made it, by Grant's account, "the gayest Place in America, nothing but Balls, Assemblies and Concerts."[10]

The Governor's assessment was corroborated in a report Lieutenant Colonel Maxwell sent General Haldimand in April 1771. In the report, Maxwell noted, "We have every week alternately a Concert or an Assembly, there have been besides some private Hops, and constantly dancing after the Concert is over."[11]

As just noted, John Moultrie was acting Governor when the 14th arrived and since the gaiety of St. Augustine seems to have been promoted by his predecessor, Governor Grant, the regiment may have endured some degree of tedium in their remote outpost. That said, to the extent the hospitality was due to Mrs. Moultrie, her continued presence could have encouraged some vestige of the hospitality attributed to the former Governor.*

---

*Surveyors of life in Florida and St. Augustine at this time produced assessments of the town and its inhabitants which varied greatly. Some of the variation seems to be related to the particular governor but some is more difficult to explain,

On April 28, 1773, Lieutenant Colonel Maurice Carr, at St. Augustine with the 29th Regiment, notified Major General Frederick Haldimand, *pro tempore* Commander-in-Chief of the British forces in North America (General Gage was on leave in England), "that Major Furlong and the 14th Regiment are all landed safe, and much better in health, than I expected to have met them. They have but 34 on the sick list, and none of them in any dangerous Disorders."[12] The 14th left Boston for St. Vincent on July 27, 1772 and arrived there on September 3. So if they arrived at St. Augustine on April 28, 1773—possibly a few days earlier—their total deployment associated with the Carib War was nine months. They were probably on the island for a little over seven months.

About six weeks after the 14th landed at St. Augustine, Lieutenant Colonel Carr informed General Haldimand he had ordered "a company of the 14th Regiment to be ready to embark for [New] Providence to relieve Captain [John] Corrance's Company."[13] New Providence was an island in the Bahamas, an archipelago which Governor Thomas Shirley described as islands of extraordinary importance, "particularly from their situation."[14] The situation in question was the strategic location as the northern most island group in the West Indies and the best location from which to monitor shipping from the West Indies to North America.

Duty in New Providence could have involved some enforcement support for Commissioners executing the Revenue Acts and intelligence gathering for the British military commanders in America and Great Britain. Captain William Blackett's company was chosen for this assignment.

---

although neglect in the semi-tropical climate of Florida can account for extensive changes to structures in a single season. An example of the variation is found in comparing the surveys of Captain Bernard Romans and Dr. William Stork, already referenced. Captain Romans visited St. Augustine a few years after Stork and disputed Dr. Stork's evaluations of the construction of some of the buildings. He also claimed the population consisted of outcasts, a state to which "their ill form of government does not a little contribute." He quoted a correspondent of his who claimed in 1774 the town had become a "heap of ruins." Bernard Romans, *A Concise Natural History of East and West Florida*, New York printed: Sold by R. Aitken, 1776, p. 264.

Chapter 7: Deployed to St. Augustine, Florida, 1773 - 1775   97

On October 1, Blackett reported to General Haldimand from New Providence the deaths of two of his officers, Lieutenant Daniel Mattear and Ensign Henry Hallwood. He attributed these losses to "the sickness under which we have suffered."[15] It seems the deployment of Blackett's detachment to New Providence also left the 14th in St. Augustine undermanned. Later in October Major Furlong reported from St. Augustine on the "weakness of the 14th Regiment." He noted "I find the duty on the men (for a continuance) to be rather hard; for since the Relieving of the different posts, which was occupied by the 29th Regiment, they have but one, and sometimes two nights in bed."[16] Captain Fordyce and his grenadier company would have been among the men performing the "rather hard" duty.

Lieutenant Colonel Carr was aware of the difficult working and living conditions in St. Augustine. In September 1773, he and his 29th Regiment were leaving St. Augustine for England, but before they left, he was obliged to obey one last order, namely, providing "volunteers"* from the 29th to remain in St. Augustine to reinforce the newly arrived 14th.[17] Lieutenant Colonel Carr informed General Haldimand, "I read the orders to the regiment for them to turn out volunteers for the 14th Regiment and used my endeavors to encourage them, But could get no more to turn out than nine men, I imagine on account of the regiment being going home, And this being so poor a place for a soldier to live in."[18]

With the departure of Lieutenant Colonel Carr, Major Furlong of the 14th Regiment was in command of the forces at St. Augustine and the province of East Florida. But shortly after taking command, he took a leave of absence to visit New York and Philadelphia. At this time, December 1773, Charles Fordyce took the

---

*"When a regiment in America, or in fact on any foreign station, had become much reduced in strength, it was customary to draft (i.e., to transfer) the remaining privates into some other regiment whose ranks needed replenishment. The first regiment would thus be reduced to a mere skeleton, consisting of the commissioned and non-commissioned officers and the drummers. These would be sent home to fill up the cadre by recruiting." Edward Ely Curtis, *The Organization of the British Army in the American Revolution*, Vol. 19, New Haven: Yale University Press, 1926, p. 77.

command. On December 17, in a report to General Haldimand, Captain Fordyce acknowledged "the command of His Majesty's Troops in this province devolves to me." In this first report as the local commander, he informed Haldimand of the death of one of his officers, Ensign Thomas Scrimshire. He also noted he replaced the adjutant, Mr. John Roberts of the 29th Regiment, with Lieutenant John Batut of the 14th. Fordyce recommended Lieutenant Batut, who would serve with him at the Battle of Great Bridge, "as a deserving and experienced officer."[19]

When he took command, Captain Fordyce submitted a report on the "State of His Majesty's Forces in the Province of East Florida," to General Haldimand. He submitted two reports, one in January and another in February 1774. In the February report, he notes there has been no change in the status of the forces from the previous month. Charles' reports include all the officers in the regiment and all the rank and file at St. Augustine and those detached to New Providence. It seems these are the first complete status-of-forces reports made for the 14th since September of 1772 when the regiment arrived at St. Vincent.

According to the reports, the force at St. Augustine included three captains, five lieutenants and five ensigns. There were seventeen sergeants, ten drummers and fifers and 213 rank and file fit for duty. Captain Fordyce notes that Captain Blackett and 42 rank and file are "on command." This would have been the detachment at New Providence. The total force Captain Fordyce enumerated was 324, including those absent, on command, recruiting, on furlough and sick.[20] When the regiment arrived at St. Vincent sixteen months earlier, the total of the State of Forces was 412. Thus, there had been a loss of 89, or about 21%, between the arrival at St. Vincent on September 18, 1772 and Captain Fordyce's report from St. Augustine of February 1, 1774.

In his reports, Captain Fordyce lists the number of officers present but not their names. This was consistent with the way the report at St. Vincent had been prepared. However, he identifies all the absent officers by name, as did Major Furlong when he prepared the report at St. Vincent. The Summary Return for the 14th Regiment is presented in Table 5 with the names of the officers

Chapter 7: Deployed to St. Augustine, Florida, 1773 - 1775

present. The names listed were determined in the same way as was done in summarizing the report submitted at St. Vincent— the names of the officers present are those remaining when the names of the absent officers are eliminated from the *Army List* for the year of the report, in this case, 1774. The same caveat applies to this list as was applied to that of the St. Vincent summary report, namely, the list should not be considered authoritative since it was developed by a process of elimination.

Table 5. Summary Return of the 14th Regiment at St. Augustine, Florida, February 1, 1774.

RANK	NUMBER	NAMES
Captains	3	Charles Fordyce Samuel Leslie James Urquhart
Lieutenants	5	David Cooper Alexander Ross William Browne John Batut William Napier
Ensigns	5	Hill Wallace Peter Henry Leslie Peter Burnett Thomas Hayter Thomas Wools
Adjutant	1	David Cooper
Quarter Master	1	Peter Burnett
Surgeon	1	Charles Hall
Chaplin	1	John Forbes, Acting
Sergeants	17	
Drummers and Fifers	10	
Rank and File	282	
Fit for Duty	213	
Sick in Barracks	16	
On Command	42	
Recruiting	1	
On Furlough	10	
TOTAL ALL RANKS*	324	

*Adjutant and quarter master are not included since they are counted in the number of officers. Evidently there was a contingent of rank and file at Boston at this time and they may not be included here or in the return from St. Vincent.

Although the status-of-forces report suggests the regiment is at or near a fully functional state, the pertinent numbers for performing the service at St. Augustine and later in Virginia are the numbers of rank and file fit for duty, 213, and the number of officers, thirteen. These numbers are little over half of the allowance for a complete regiment of about 400 rank and file (privates and corporals) and some twenty-seven officers.[21]

༄

Charles' second report to General Haldimand reflected the normal routine of garrison life at St. Augustine. This report, dated January 9, 1774, contained the results of an inventory he had taken of items in the "Provision Stores." Many of the items had been damaged and he was dutifully informing the general of his conclusion it would be cost effective to repair the provision storehouses.[22] Captain Fordyce's regard for government property was an elementary but clear manifestation of the conscientious leadership vital to effective command, especially on remote assignments.

But just a month later, the routine was interrupted by an alleged Indian attack in neighboring Georgia. Fordyce wrote General Haldimand on February 6 to inform him Lieutenant Governor Moultrie "was under some apprehensions for the safety of this Province." Moultrie had directed Fordyce to reinforce the detachment at Smyrna and occupy some additional posts on the St. John's River. Charles was concerned about the limited number of men and the small quantity of gunpowder available, but he assured General Haldimand he "instantly ordered" the requested reinforcement.[23] About five weeks later, he received word from General Haldimand he should proceed with the proposed reinforcements. He replied to the general he was "extremely sorry to find that you think it necessary to make the Detachments," and expressed his concern over the dangers of detaching "small parties at so great a distance as will render it very difficult to have any communication with them, and almost impossible to afford them assistance in case of their being hard pressed by the enemy." In addition to the vulnerability of the detachments, Captain Fordyce reminded the general of "how very few our numbers will be here when weakened by these Detachments." He pointed out, "the duty is already very hard upon the Men, but when forty are struck off it will be impossible to mount the same Guards." He then provided an assessment of the Details of Guards for which he was then responsible, namely, Hospital Guards, Fort Guards, Barracks Guards and the Town Guard.[24]

Based on these exchanges, one might characterize Charles as a rather impertinent junior officer making excuses for his men. But the dissecting of the 14th Regiment would prove fatal in the months to come. Fordyce was, in fact, demonstrating a studied appreciation of fitness of his unit for the various services required of them. He was certainly demonstrating an appreciation of the needs his men had for sleep and gunpowder as well as the particular need for a reserve when the only force available for a particular outpost was the minimum allowed by military standards.

Two days after Charles wrote General Haldimand addressing what he considered the ill-advised posting of small detachments of the 14th, he was able to report on what seemed to be signs of a peaceful resolution to the uprising. On February 17, 1774, he notified the general "Everything is at present perfectly quiet, several Creek families have been here lately and seemed seem well disposed, one of them is sent into the Nation by Mr. Moultrie with a talk." He had also heard from the officer at Smyrna who reported "everything was peaceable in that part of the country." In this same report he added a request of General Haldimand, which can be construed as another demonstration of his conscientious appreciation of a commander's role in times of crisis. He had been forced by the Lieutenant Governor into a reactive mode which he saw as putting his beleaguered men as well as any mission they were called on to perform at risk. He saw the need to address the ultimate conflict that might ensue from a sizeable uprising, namely an attack on East Florida, which would be an attack on St. Augustine. He could see the piecemeal deployment of his regiment was nothing less than the enemy's successful dilution of any effective concentration of forces he might otherwise present. He put the proposition of planning for such an attack directly to General

Haldimand noting, "I shall esteem myself most exceedingly obliged to your Excellency if you will be pleased as soon as possible to favor me with Instructions for my Conduct in case these people should commit hostilities in this province."[25]

On March 14, General Haldimand replied to Charles' letters of January and February and provided the guidance requested—although rather more diplomatic and military. He told Charles, "I would have been sorry if you had conceived yourself authorized to refuse him [i.e., Lieutenant Governor Moultrie's request for troops], at the same time you will be pleased to observe that tho it is proper to protect the Province and follow the Governor's directions in that respect, yet you are not in any case whatever to act in the offensive and if the circumstances shou'd require it you shall receive the instructions that may be necessary for that purpose, I have reason to hope that the present disturbances with the Indians will be settled soon and must desire you would instruct those officers who are detached to act with all the caution possible and to avoid every proceeding that may give them any offense."[26]

By mid-March, Charles was able to report to General Haldimand the crisis of an Indian insurrection had been averted. Lieutenant Governor Moultrie had received "the strongest assurances" of the pacific intentions of the Creeks, a number of whom—"as well disposed and friendly as possible"—had visited St. Augustine and disavowed "having had any share in or knowledge of the Hostilities Committed in the Province of Georgia." He added Governor Tonyn had arrived and intended to hold a congress with the Creeks as soon as it could be arranged.[27]

Evidently Major Furlong returned to St. Augustine and resumed his position as local commander of the 14th–replacing Charles—sometime in the fall of 1774. It seems he was ending his leave of absence earlier than originally planned. General Gage noted with some surprise in a letter to Secretary of War Barrington of October 3, 1774, that Major Furlong had "set out sometime since for St. Augustine in order to join the regiment."

During his tenure as commander of the British forces in St. Augustine, Charles oversaw a force of modest size. According to a return submitted by Patrick Tonyn when he took over as Governor on March 1, 1774, the 14th mustered 17 officers, 57 non-commissioned officers and drummers and 207 privates for a total strength of 281.[28] Given the new governor did not count that part of the regiment at New Providence, this summary was essentially the same as Charles had reported the month before.

Charles' circumspect management of this modest force during what turned out to be an overblown threat of an Indian uprising was the high point of his tour in St. Augustine. In his handling of this situation, he proved himself a capable administrator and leader. Although no longer commander of the garrison after Major Furlong returned, Charles continued to serve in St. Augustine for the remainder of 1774 and most of 1775.

∽

Charles' tours to St. Vincent and St. Augustine coincided with the years of undeclared rebellion in the colonies pursuant to passage of the Townshend Acts, the concerted attempts to enforce those acts, the passage of the Tea Act and the renewed emphasis on enforcement of the Navigation Acts.

Shortly after orders were formulated to send the 14th to St. Vincent, one of the more violent attacks on His Majesty's property during the lead up to the war occurred off the coast of Rhode Island. On June 9, 1772, the British customs schooner *Gaspee*, enforcing the Navigation Acts, ran aground chasing the packet *Hannah*, thought to be smuggling goods between Newport and Providence, Rhode Island. In command of the *Gaspee* was Lieutenant William Dudingston. The maritime laws against smuggling, which the *Gaspee* was attempting to enforce, had been in place in one form or another for decades, but Dudingston was thought by the colonists to be exceeding his authority. While the *Gaspee* was grounded, the Sons of Liberty burned it and in the melee Lieutenant Dudingston was shot and wounded. When the British tried to apprehend and prosecute the perpetrators the local citizens and courts were so evasive and obstinate the case had to be dropped. In a letter to the Governor of Rhode Island—published in *The Boston Gazette and Country Journal*—Lord Dartmouth noted the incident was considered "High Treason, viz., levying war against the King."[29]

A little over a month after the incident and while it was still front-page news, the 14th Regiment had sailed for St. Vincent. The *Gaspee* Affair would remain in the news the entire time the 14th was in St. Vincent.[30] It was indeed a harbinger of an escalation in lawlessness that would culminate in the bloodshed at Lexington and Concord on April 19, 1775.

As had been the case at their other North-American duty stations, it is likely the 14th Regiment had access to newspapers while stationed in St. Augustine. American newspapers would have included those brought by ship from Boston, Philadelphia, Williamsburg, Charleston and Savannah.

Some of the first reports they would have read in 1774 would have been those of the dumping of tea in Boston Harbor on December 16, 1773 (the day before Charles took command of the garrison in St. Augustine). This event was reported immediately in Boston and in the January 6, 1774 edition of Purdie and Dixon's *Virginia Gazette*.[31] The news could have reached St. Augustine later that month and with that news the men of the 14th would read of "The unanimity, spirit, and zeal, which have heretofore animated all the Colonies, from Boston to South Carolina, have been so eminently displayed in the opposition to the pernicious project of the East India Company in sending tea to America, while it remains subject to a duty."[32]

The Boston Tea Party and subsequent Boston Port Act would be the catalysts that ultimately precipitated the outbreak of war between the American colonies and Great Britain. These events secured for New England its place as the center of attention for the British ministers grappling with some means—as the King put it—to reduce his Rebellious Subjects to Obedience.

After the men of the 14th Regiment received weeks-old newspapers from Boston, Charlestown and Williamsburg reporting the dumping of tea in Boston Harbor, they would have read of the Indian uprising in Georgia which had alarmed Lieutenant Governor Moultrie and provoked a call to arms in St. Augustine.[33] By May, the Boston Port Act—passed in response to the Boston Tea Party—was making news in Boston and Williamsburg and the troops at St. Augustine would have learned of that legislation and some of the furor it was inciting at about the same time. Specifically, they would have read of the resolution of the Virginia House of Burgesses calling for a day of fasting and prayer in response to "the hostile invasion of the city of Boston"[34] and of Governor Dunmore dissolving the House in response to that resolution. Given the snippets of news they had received of Lord Dunmore's behavior while Governor of New York, his dissolution of the Virginia Assembly was probably no surprise. After the legislature was dissolved, they would have read of county after county in Virginia resolving support for Boston.

It is likely these resolves reinforced any feelings the soldiers might have had for the Virginians as ungrateful delinquents. The resolve of one of the first counties to speak out, Chesterfield, presented here, was a model of the unprecedented level of contempt for the British administration that had evolved in Virginia.

> Resolved, That the Act of the British Parliament for depriving the inhabitants of the town of Boston, in our sister Colony of the Massachusetts Bay, of their lawful trade, as also the Bills brought into the House of Commons of Great Britain, one of which Bills is entitled, "A Bill for the impartial administration of justice in the cases of persons questioned for any act done by them in the execution of the law, or for the suppression of riots or tumults in the Province of the Massachusetts Bay, in New England," are unjust, arbitrary, and unconstitutional; and although levelled particularly against one of our first Colonies, yet ought to be resented with the same indignation by this, and every Colony, as if all of them were included in the said Act and Bills.[35]

As summer gave way to fall, the soldiers would read the "Brief Enumeration of American Grievances" —which was not so brief, and included a number of aspersions directed at the military.[36] They would read alarmist accounts of General Gage's removing the gunpowder from the magazine in Cambridge.[37] In the first months of 1775, they would learn that the "Freeholders and other inhabitants of the town of Boston," had informed Governor

Hutchinson the "seizing of powder in the magazine at Cambridge ... and many other acts which could not leave any doubt in the minds of the people of the General's intension [sic] to employ military force against the province, at length roused the people to think of defending themselves and their property by arms."[38] They would read of the meeting of the first Continental Congress and of the Articles of Association promulgated by that body. Articles calling for repeal of "several late, cruel, and oppressive acts" said to be threating "destruction to the lives liberty, and property of his majesty's subjects, in North-America." By late 1774 or early 1775 they would learn of Secretary Dartmouth's letter to the governors prohibiting the importation of gun powder to the colonies.[39] In short, they would read a steady stream of reports of treason, threats and counter threats, calls to arms, accusations of enslavement, claims of violences, rapine, impending destruction, aggression, intimidation and all manner of contumely directed at British soldiers.

The disaffection underlying this avalanche of invectives would soon lead to bloodshed and a redeployment of Captain Fordyce and the 14th Regiment from St. Augustine to Virginia. The redeployment would be in reaction to Governor Dunmore's perception of a clear and present danger to his person and his government resulting from his removal of the gunpowder from the provincial magazine in Williamsburg on April 20, 1775. Known as the Gunpowder Incident, it would so incite the Virginians the Governor would be forced to flee the capital and take refuge on a British ship in the York River. At the same time, he would apply to General Thomas Gage for "immediate Assistance."[40] Of course, this application was reactionary—it was not part of a well-developed strategy or an adequate understanding of the broader threat he faced or the threat the 14th Regiment would encounter.

CHAPTER 8: LORD DUNMORE AND THE "SPIRIT OF FACTION"

To the extent any individual may be credited with, or blamed for, a particular event in history, John Murray, 4th Earl of Dunmore, is the most likely candidate to receive credit or blame for the Battle of Great Bridge. He was the Governor of Virginia when the battle occurred. He admitted to instigating the battle. In explaining his actions to the British Secretary of State, Lord Dartmouth, he focused on the military situation—the fact he needed to keep the lines of communication open to a Loyalist enclave he had established in Princess Ann and Norfolk Counties, the fact he was surrounded, the fact he expected the Patriots to be reinforced within days if not hours.[1] A factual and compelling explanation, but incomplete and misleading. It did not address the cause of his predicament, which was, in fact, the cause of the battle. That cause was a clash of convictions over principles of authority and, in particular, the commitment of the Virginians to their convictions—their "spirit of faction." Lord Dunmore would acknowledge the clash but consistently underestimate the Virginians' commitment to their principles. In his report to Lord Dartmouth, he endeavored to put a positive spin on a military embarrassment. His underestimation of the spirit of faction—the miscalculation underlying the embarrassment—would never be addressed.

Governor Dunmore was, at least to some extent, obligated to report the confrontation at Great Bridge—a military operation—in military terms. As governor, it was his responsibility to ensure British law was, in the language of the time, "carried into due execution." His role was to execute policy, not make it. His official title—Lieutenant and Governor General of the Colony and Dominion of Virginia, and Vice Admiral of the same—reflected that role. The rank of vice admiral was a "local rank"—only valid in Virginia—but it meant he was the *de facto* Commander-in-Chief of

British forces assigned to the colony. In addition to the King's assignment of such authority, he was vested by the Virginia Assembly with authority to make provisions against invasions and insurrections[2] (authority implicitly associated with military actions required to stop invading Indians or rebellious slaves). Under these circumstances, his report of the Battle of Great Bridge was simply the after-action summary of the military commander.

Governor Dunmore was, in fact, trained as an infantry officer. He served in the 3rd Foot Guards between 1749 and 1758, first as an ensign and finally as a captain. When he entered the service as a nineteen-year-old ensign in 1749, his uncle, John Murray the 2nd Earl Dunmore, was colonel-commandant of his regiment.[3] Figure 12 is a copy of Joshua Reynolds' portrait of Lord Dunmore in the Highland Dress of a captain in the 3rd Foot Guards.

According to the regimental history of the 3rd Guards, Lord Dunmore's enlistment coincided with a time of "home service" when the regiment was not "engaged in any transaction of importance."[4] That said, the 3rd did take part in raids on the coast of France at this time as part of the ongoing Seven Years War. Perhaps it is accurate to say these raids were of little importance, but Dunmore took part in them and the experience would have added to his modest but valid military

Figure 12. John Murray, 4th Earl Dunmore, Wearing the Highland Dress of the 3rd Regiment of Foot Guards. Joshua Reynolds. National Galleries of Scotland. Used by permission.

resume.[5] However, his combat experience was limited. Given the way the 3rd was employed during the time he served, it is unlikely he ever commanded troops in battle or was ever in a battle.

In addition to his personal service, Governor Dunmore was from a family of military professionals. His grandfather, Charles Murray—the 1st Earl—was a general in the army. Five of the 1st Earl's seven sons were military men, three of whom, John (2nd Earl), Robert and Thomas, also achieved the rank of general.[6] Son William, Governor Dunmore's father, became the 3rd Earl after the death of his brother John. William was also a military officer although not distinguished with the rank of general.

With this heritage and his own service, it seems Governor Dunmore acquired a taste for military command. Other than the fiasco of Great Bridge, one might argue he demonstrated some skill as a commander. Slightly over a year before the Battle of Great Bridge, he had organized a campaign against the Shawnee Indians on the frontiers of Virginia and Pennsylvania. Known as Dunmore's War, the action was considered a success—at least at the time.* The Virginia militia officers involved in the campaign resolved they entertained "the greatest respect for his Excellency the Right Hon. Lord Dunmore, who commanded the expedition against the Shawnese, and who, we are confident underwent the great fatigue of this singular campaign from no other motive than the true interest of his country."[7] In December of 1774, the Virginia Council congratulated the Governor on his safe return from the "Fatigues and Dangers of a troublesome Expedition," noting his "vigorous

---

* After the attack at Lexington and Concord on April 19, 1775 and Lord Dunmore's confiscation of the gunpowder in the provincial magazine in Williamsburg on April 20, 1775, he was accused of starting the war with the Shawnee. *Virginia Gazette*, Purdie, Oct. 27, 1775, p. 2. See also: Clarence W. Alvord, "Virginia and the West, an Interpretation," *The Mississippi Valley Historical Review*, Vol. 3 (June 1916), pp. 26, 27; Reuben Gold Thwaites, *Documentary History of Dunmore's War*, Madison: Wisconsin Historical Society, 1905, p. xxiv and Virgil Anson Lewis, *History of the Battle of Point Pleasant*, Charleston, West Virginia: The Tribune Printing Company, 1909, pp. 84-94. One of the most critical of Dunmore's biographers was George Bancroft, in: George Bancroft, *History of the United States*, Vol. 7, Boston: Little, Brown and Company, 1858, p. 161 ff. (Chapter 15).

Opposition to the Incursions and Ravages of an Indian Enemy hath effectually prevented the Desolation of a growing back country, and the Horrors of human Carnage."[8]

Governor Dunmore was a staunch advocate of a Southern campaign[9] to defeat what he termed "the rebels" as soon as hostilities erupted in April 1775. In June, he wrote the commander of Britain's North American Station, Admiral Samuel Graves, explaining the key role Virginia could play in such a campaign. In his letter he noted, "… the keeping of these considerable Countries lying upon the great Rivers which empty into the Bay of Chesapeake in awe cannot but contribute much to the Success of the General Plan for enforcing the Authority of Government in the Colonies."[10]

In fact, he was confident enough of the way a Virginia-based campaign could bring all the King's rebellious subjects to obedience he took the initiative to plan such an operation. With one of his military confidants, Lieutenant Colonel John Connolly, he developed a rather comprehensive strategy to take advantage of Virginia's location as a gate controlling the communication between the Northern and Southern colonies.[11] Connolly believed the plan would, "promote the success of his Majesty's arms, and the like happy effects universally."[12] Governor Dunmore apprised General Gage of the plan in a letter of September 15, 1775 and Gage seemed to think the plan had merit. He told Lord Dartmouth of Dunmore's "project" to "make a Diversion on the Frontiers of Pennsylvania and Virginia," concluding, "If his Lordship is able to make a stand at the same time in the lower parts of the Country the Project will be of great use, and I will do all I can to promote it's [sic] success."[13] The plan was thwarted before it could be set in motion when Connolly and two co-conspirators were captured in Maryland in November.[14] Nevertheless, the plan demonstrated Dunmore's initiative and vision as a military strategist.

Arguably Lord Dunmore was again demonstrating initiative and vision as he maneuvered to establish a stronghold in Princess Ann and Norfolk Counties after his rather humiliating flight from Williamsburg following the Gunpowder Incident. His assessment the more "well disposed" citizens resided in this region was correct and control of Norfolk would provide the terminus he needed for open communication with General Gage in Boston as well as the ministry in Great Britain. But while the maneuvering seems to have demonstrated commendable military judgment, his overall plan was flawed by a failure of military judgment. This failure was his implicit endorsement of the proposition espoused by many of the British commanders that the Americans were inept and reluctant soldiers.

Over-rating the British regulars and under-rating the American citizen soldier was not universal among British planners, but it was common. Not long before the rout of the British at Lexington and Concord and the determined defense at Bunker Hill, British Marine, Major John Pitcairn, reported, "When this army [the British Army] is ordered to act against them, they will soon be convinced that they are very insignificant when opposed to regular troops."[15] The two ranking commanders of the British force in Virginia were also proponents of the proposition Americans were inexpert soldiers. Just before the Battle of Great Bridge, Naval Captain Matthew Squire of HMS *Otter* informed his commander, Admiral Graves, "I have great reason to suppose, & hope from their being such Cowards, and Cold weather coming on, that they will return to their respective homes, & we shall be quiet the remainder of the Winter."[16] In his report of successful raids after the arrival of the 14th Regiment, Captain Samuel Leslie, ranking officer of the land force in Virginia, told General Howe, "at least seventy seven pieces of ordinance taken & destroyed since my Detachment arrived here without the smallest opposition, which is a proof that it would not require a very large force to subdue this Colony."[17] One of the most scornful assessments of the character of the American soldier was made by a gentleman who was evidently a British naval officer aboard the *Otter*, Beesly Joel. In a letter of October 1775, he told his correspondent, "Forgive me, my friend, if I cannot forbear Laughing, at the false opinion you have of the Courage of the Americans, mere Poltroons, I assure you, not a single grain of that spirit, so conspicuous in the Character of an Englishman."[18]

Assessing American soldiers as lacking in spirit and inept or reluctant to fight meant American manpower advantages were discounted and the correlation of forces favored the British even when they were outnumbered. Governor Dunmore's endorsement of this dubious proposition was of course dubious in itself. So inasmuch as this endorsement—and the plan that evolved from it—were his "military" contribution, his role in the battle from a military standpoint must be rated as detrimental.

But while this military contribution—such as it was—provides some explanation for why the battle at Great Bridge was fought, it provides a better explanation for why it was lost. As postulated at the beginning of this chapter, Governor Dunmore's role in instigating the battle is better understood in terms of a spirited clash of convictions over principles of authority.

At some point, Lord Dunmore committed himself to the Declaratory Act principle the King and Parliament had "...full power and authority to make laws and statutes of sufficient force to bind the colonies, and his Majesty's subjects in them, in all cases whatsoever." The Virginians—in diametric opposition—were committed to the principle "the General Assembly of this Colony have the only and exclusive Right and Power to lay Taxes and Impositions upon the inhabitants of this Colony."[19] Arguably the clash over these principles was the underlying cause of the Battle of Great Bridge (and, for that matter, the Revolutionary War). However, as is often the case in war, the proximate cause of the battle would be less esoteric than a principle of governance. The proximate cause would be the Virginians' commitment to their principle. More to the point, the proximate cause of the battle would be Governor Dunmore's underestimation* of the Virginians'

---

* Lord Dunmore was not the only one who failed to appreciate the strength of the Virginians' commitment. When he apprised moderate Lord Dartmouth of the commotion, threats and disobedience ensuing his confiscation of the gunpowder at Williamsburg, Dartmouth responded, "The Madness of the People of Virginia exceeds all bounds, & leaves no room for any other Consideration than that of the means of suppressing by the most vigorous efforts a Rebellion which … threatens to overturn the Constitution." "Lord Dartmouth to Lord Dunmore, Whitehall 5th July 1775," NDAR 1:1311-1313.

commitment and the spirit of faction engendered by that commitment.

To his credit, Governor Dunmore did acknowledge the determined resolution of the Burgesses of Virginia to deny and oppose the authority of Parliament when he dissolved that House in 1774 over their denouncement of the Boston Port Act[20]—an instance of the clash of convictions. It seems he was alarmed at the language in the Burgesses' Resolution predicting "heavy Calamity" and "Destruction to our civil Rights, and the Evils of civil War." He told Lord Dartmouth he was concerned this action by an "undutiful part of the legislature of Virginia," could "inflame the whole country."[21] After the bungled Gunpowder Incident a year later, he would—by Proclamation—describe this resolution to oppose the authority of Parliament a "spirit of faction" to be suppressed.[22]

Although it seems Governor Dunmore was affronted by the spirit of faction he observed after the Gunpowder Incident, the presence of that spirit in Virginia should have come as no surprise. It had been quite conspicuous for years. Lieutenant Governor Robert Dinwiddie had noted it in 1754.[23] It was the spirit manifested with such fervor when the Stamp Act was passed in 1765—when the Burgesses resolved, "The General Assembly of this Colony have the only and exclusive Right and Power to lay Taxes and Impositions upon the inhabitants of this Colony." In response to this resolve, then Governor Francis Fauquier had dissolved the assembly and characterized the proceedings as a "rash heat," a condition that could have been construed as a spirit of faction or certainly a condition foretelling such a spirit.[24]

Four years later, after passage of the Townshend Acts in 1767, the Virginia Assembly reiterated the principles of their earlier Resolutions, declaring in 1769 "the sole Right of imposing Taxes on the Inhabitants of this his Majesty's Colony and Dominion of Virginia, is now, and ever hath been, legally and constitutionally vested in the House of Burgesses."[25] Norborne Berkley, Baron Botetourt, was Governor of Virginia at the time. As his predecessor, Governor Fauquier, had done in 1765, Botetourt dissolved the Burgesses, informing them he had "heard of your Resolves, and auger ill of their Effect."[26] The fact the Burgesses determined to publish Resolutions that augured ill suggests the spirit of faction they had manifest during the Stamp Act crisis had not abated.

The Burgesses' Resolutions, so patently contrary to the mandates of the Stamp Act, Declaratory Act and Townshend Acts, were never rescinded. This meant—in effect—the spirit of faction had been institutionalized. This spirit, this institution, would have influenced every discussion and display of authority in Virginia after 1765. Lord Dunmore would have been wary of any suspected recourse to the Resolutions by the legislators. Under the circumstances, such vigilance would have been instinctive, but— given the Virginians' record—futile. As soon as the Boston Port Act was passed in 1774, the Burgesses again reiterated the principles embodied in their well-established Resolves. They denounced the act as a threat to their civil rights and injurious of American rights.

As had been the case when the Assembly denounced the Stamp Act and Townshend Acts, the governor, now Lord Dunmore, dissolved the Burgesses. His report of the episode to Secretary Dartmouth included an implicit acknowledgement of the way the faction between the Burgesses and Parliament had been institutionalized, but consistent with his tendency to discount the commitment of the Virginians, it seems he considered this institution more annoying than threatening. He told Lord Dartmouth with a patronizing tone the Port Act "induced the house of burgesses again, on this occasion, to declare, what they are fond of having it thought always originates with them, a determined resolution to deny and oppose the authority of parliament."[27] With such an assessment, Lord Dunmore was relegating the Burgesses' declaration of their principle of self-governance to a prideful indulgence instead of respecting it as a principle the Virginians held sacred.

༄

Lord Dunmore was born John Murray in Scotland in about 1730. His parents were William Murray and Catherine Murray. William and Catherine were first cousins. Their fathers were brothers, both sons of John Murray, the 1st Marquis of Atholl, and his wife, Lady Amelia Anne Sophia Stanley. John was the oldest of five children born to William and Catherine. During the Jacobite

Rebellion in Scotland in 1745, both William and his then fifteen-year-old son, John, supported the Jacobites and William was imprisoned in 1746 for treason. He pleaded guilty and was pardoned by King George II—an instance of deference to the Murray family at the highest levels of court that could have made a lasting impression on teen-aged John.

As noted previously, John joined the 3rd Foot Guards in 1749 as a nineteen-year old ensign. Three years later, in 1752, his uncle, the 2nd Earl and also commander of the 3rd Guards, died and William inherited the title of 3rd Earl Dunmore. William died four years later in 1756 and John, then 26 years old, inherited the earldom, becoming the 4th Earl of Dunmore while serving as a captain in the 3rd Foot Guards.

At this time, the new Earl had seven years of military service and he would continue to serve for two more years. As noted earlier, little, if any of his service involved combat. He had not advanced rapidly—he was in the regiment five years before his promotion to lieutenant[28]—but the fact he remained in the army after inheriting the earldom suggests he found military service agreeable. One biographer alludes to the possibility he had aspirations of "martial glory" –noting he had requested service in Germany during the Seven Years War.[29] His request was denied, and martial glory is absent from his resume. Even so, his service would qualify him as a military professional of more than usual accomplishment when later considered for a post as governor in America.

Lord Dunmore married his first cousin, once removed, Lady Charlotte Stewart, on February 21, 1759, shortly after he resigned his commission in the 3rd Foot Guards. Lady Charlotte had two siblings who would exercise considerable influence in Lord Dunmore's political career and his eventual appointments to the governorship of New York then Virginia. Her younger sister, Lady Susanna, would marry a well-respected and influential English peer, Granville Leveson-Gower, 2nd Earl Gower. Her brother was Scottish peer John Stewart, the 7th Earl of Galloway, styled Viscount Garlies during the time he served in Parliament.

Lord Garlies was a devotee of John Russell, the Duke of Bedford. Bedford led the conservative political party known as the

Bedford Whigs. This Parliamentary faction took a hard line on colonial affairs, insisting colonial assemblies and merchants comply with any and all of Parliament's dictates. Garlies was active politically so he would have probably taken some pains to make sure his brother-in-law and Lord Bedford were introduced when Dunmore entered Parliament in 1761. The connection to Bedford would be reinforced in 1768 when Lord Dunmore's sister-in-law, Lady Susanna, married Bedford's protégé and brother-in-law, the Earl Gower. Gower would assume control of the Bedford faction when the Duke of Bedford died in 1771.

Lord Dunmore was elected one of sixteen Scottish peers on May 5, 1761 when he was 31 years old. As a member of the House of Lords at this time, he would have been involved in evaluating and enacting the legislation Parliament would consider in their efforts to pay for the recent war and secure their new, expansive borders. In particular, he would have witnessed the development and passage of the Stamp Act in 1765 and its repeal a year later. Likewise, he would have witnessed the development and passage of the Declaratory Act, which was introduced while repeal of the Stamp Act was under consideration in 1766. In 1767 and 1768 he would have witnessed the debates and negotiations associated with Townshend's Revenue Acts.

As a party to this legislative sequence, he would have had access to a comprehensive collection of newspaper articles, official correspondence, journals and personal anecdotes brought before Parliament to inform the debates on these bills, which were already arousing a spirit of faction.[30] It is reasonable to speculate that, in evaluating that collection, he would have formed opinions about the political and personal nature of the belligerents in the disputes over Parliamentary authority. In particular, he might have formed several opinions of the nature of Virginians. They were quite prominent in the news after publishing their notorious "Resolves"[31] in response to the Stamp Act. These Resolves might have led Lord Dunmore to surmise the Virginians were jealous of their sovereignty and disposed to challenge perceived encroachments on their sovereignty quickly and forcefully. This legislative gambit also may have suggested to the young Lord the Virginians were—in language that would be used in later indictments—refractory.

He might have formed an opinion the Virginians were naturally quarrelsome based on an assessment Virginia Governor Francis Fauquier presented in a letter to Lord Halifax, Secretary of State for the Southern Department, a few weeks after the Resolves were passed. In that letter Fauquier observed "the general dissatisfaction at the duties laid by the Stamp Act" and the way "the private distress which every man feels … breaks out and shows itself upon every trifling occasion."[32] He might have formed the opinion the Virginians were, by nature, impudent based on another of Governor Fauquier's assessments. In a letter to the Lords of Trade, Fauquier described the Virginians who spirited the Resolves through the House of Burgesses as "young, hot, and giddy."[33]

After the Stamp Act was repealed in 1766, the Lords of Trade turned their attention to concerns over the development of "manufactory" capabilities in the colonies. Regarding the Virginians, Fauquier assured the Lords such developments were never a serious threat to British hegemony since "the nature of the people is such that they are too indolent to engage in manufactures or work of any kind."[34] How such an assessment might have influenced then 36-year-old Lord Dunmore is unknown, but his own assessment of the Virginians regarding their industry after he took over as Governor of the province suggests it did. In 1774, when evaluating Virginia's non-importation resolves, he told Lord Dartmouth, "As to manufacturing for themselves, the people of Virginia are very far from being naturally industrious."[35]

To the extent Lord Dunmore had ever formed any unflattering or prejudicial opinions of the Virginians—whether based on experience, aristocratic prerogative or personal ethos—they could have contributed to and amplified the spirit of faction he observed in 1774 and 1775. Such opinions also would have hampered attempts to mollify the spirit. They could have biased and discredited any assessments Lord Dunmore might have conducted to gain an appreciation of the magnitude of the spirit of faction he observed.

Another factor that seems to have contributed to Lord Dunmore's failure to appreciate the magnitude of the spirit of faction was his hope many in Virginia were "well-disposed" to the government. After the Gunpowder Incident, he told Secretary Dartmouth he had been "Strongly Solicited by a great Number of Gentlemen well disposed to His Majesty's Government to Erect the King's Standard, and that they (and thousands more they are persuaded) would flock to it immediately."[36] Earlier he had expressed his hopes control of the Burgesses by those he called the "undutiful part of the legislature of Virginia," was by a slim margin. When apprising Lord Dartmouth of the dissolution of the Burgesses over their Port Act Resolution, he told the Secretary, "I have heard from many of the dissolved members, and I hope it is true, that the house in general ... did not advert to the whole force of the terms in which the order ... [was] conceived," and speculated if the proceedings had not been so hasty, "it is believed a strong opposition would have been made to it, and ... it might have met a different fate."[37]

Arguably, some proceedings of the House of Burgesses supported Lord Dunmore's hopes. The House had been split over the Virginia Resolves in 1765 and some members were indignant at what they considered Patrick Henry's near treasonable behavior during the debates on the Resolves. Peyton Randolph—then Speaker of the House and later president of the Continental Congress—is said to have exclaimed he would have given one hundred guineas for a single vote to defeat Henry.[38] Governor Fauquier noted Speaker Randolph's strong opposition in the report of the incident he submitted to the Lords of Trade. At the same time, Fauquier expressed his hope the Resolves did not reflect "the sense of the colony," –the same hope Lord Dunmore later embraced.

This hope was shared by many in Parliament and the ministry, in particular Lord Dartmouth. Even after the near-bloodshed of the Gunpowder Incident, Dartmouth encouraged Lord Dunmore "There is still some room to hope that the Colonies to the Southward may not proceed to the same lengths with those of New England."[39] In another letter to the Governor a week later, Dartmouth noted "The Support your Lordship met with from the Gentlemen of the Council … does them much honor, and I think it affords good ground to hope, that Men of Spirit and property will at length be awakened to a sense of their Situation."[40]

Nevertheless, even though Speaker Randolph had supported Governor Fauquier on matters of procedure and propriety in 1765 and Governor Dunmore had the support of "Gentlemen of the Council" in 1775, the hope in a "strong opposition" to Virginia's Resolves or the hope Virginia would not proceed to the same lengths as New England, was vain. To the extent Governor Dunmore was influenced by such hope in estimating the magnitude and danger of the divide between his convictions and the Virginians, he would have underestimated the magnitude and danger.

Lord Dunmore's failure to appreciate the magnitude of the spirit of faction fomenting in 1774 and 1775 has been posited as the proximate cause of the Battle of Great Bridge, but such a failure would have been obviated by his rejection of the Declaratory Act principles in the first place. It seems this had been a possibility. As noted in Chapter 3, biographer Lowe concluded Dunmore's early record in the House of Lords suggested he had taken a "relatively conciliatory approach toward the colonies." But fatefully, his commitment to such an approach was subject to fiscal constraints. He was persuaded to abandon the conciliatory approach and commit to a hardline Declaratory Act approach sometime between 1767 and 1769, when financial pressures moved him to consider a foreign-service assignment as a means of supplementing his income.[41] This consideration coincided with the 1768 marriage of his sister-in-law to Lord Gower, a man who could help secure such an assignment. In addition to his connections to the Duke of Bedford, Gower was one of the wealthiest men in Great Britain and Lord President of the Council, a post which provided direct access to the King and the highest-ranking members of Parliament. Little over a year after Lady Susanna married Lord Gower—and with the concurrence of the Bedford faction—Dunmore was appointed Governor of New York.

An obligation to support the Bedford position of taking a firmer line with the colonies[42]—the line established in the Declaratory

Act—would have been implicit in his appointment as governor.* In practice, this firmer line would mean insisting on the exclusive power and authority of the King and Parliament regarding colonial affairs and curtailing any colonial aspirations of sovereignty. And if, despite his record as a moderate, his own political inclinations were actually in line with the principles embodied in the Declaratory Act, his interest in promoting those principles would have been redoubled by his new family alliance with a proponent of the act like Lord Gower.

Lord Dunmore was appointed Governor of Virginia less than a year after he arrived in New York. Evidently, Lord Gower promoted and facilitated this appointment. Dunmore found the administration of New York agreeable and he was also able to augment his income there with fees associated with land patents. Under the circumstances, he did not want to leave, even with his brother-in-law's encouragement. It seems he was finally persuaded to go under considerable duress. He arrived in Virginia in September 1771.[43] As Governor of that province, he would maintain his commitment to the principles delineated in the Declaratory Act although he did exercise conciliatory discretion in some early legislative negotiations.[44]

∽

The Virginians knew of Gower's hardline position. It would have been well known throughout the colonies. Because of their loyalty to the King and his ministers at this time, British historian William Lecky concluded the Bedford faction—along with any others determined to be the "King's friends"—"were very naturally

---

* British historian George Trevelyan observed governors were appointed because they "had done a good turn to a Minister, and for whom a post had to be found." As a result, he claimed "the personages upon whose reports Lord Hillsborough and Lord Dartmouth had to depend for forming their notions of the American population, and in accordance with whose suggestions the course taken at an emergency by the British Cabinet was necessarily shaped, were in many cases utterly unworthy of their trust." George Trevelyan, *The American Revolution*, Vol. 1, pp. 14, 15. Trevelyan's assessment seems harsh in Governor Dunmore's case but it highlights the way good turns, and the prospect of good turns associated with family alliances, could compromise policy and planning.

regarded by the Americans as their most rancorous enemies."[45] Their vote against the repeal of the Stamp Act was reported in Purdie and Dixon's *Virginia Gazette* of May 19, 1768. Earlier that year, Bedford had moved to have what he considered a particularly inflammatory edition of the *Boston Gazette* read in the House of Lords to expose what he considered the treasonous and rebellious attitudes of the Massachusetts Bay Colony. This move by Bedford was also reported in the *Virginia Gazette* along with other reports of his polices contrary to the interests of the Colonies.[46] When the Port of Boston was closed and Lord North was quoted in the *Virginia Gazette* as declaring "the punishment of Boston was intended as an example to all the other colonies," the reporter claimed, "This you may be assured is the language of every ministerial man,"[47] which would have included the Earl Gower. A year later Gower's avowal of the "settled intensions of the government of compelling the Americans to the immediate obedience of the legislature of the mother country," was published in Purdie's *Virginia Gazette*.[48] To the extent Lord Dunmore was considered a political ally of Gower and the Bedford faction, he too would have been characterized as a proponent of Parliament's absolute authority.

Even if the Virginians did not presume Lord Dunmore was politically allied with Gower and Bedford, it is likely they were aware of the firm line he had drawn respecting the colonies' legal obligation to defer to British authority. They would have been made aware of his position by following his legislative agenda in New York. Another edition of the *Virginia Gazette* that included the announcement of his selection for the post of Governor also included the report of his passing an Act making "further provision of two thousand pounds for furnishing his Majesty's troops quartered in the Colony with necessaries."[49] This act enforced the provisions of the Restraining Act, which Parliament passed to force New Yorkers to comply with the Quartering Act of 1765.

Despite the Virginians' awareness of the personal relationship between their new Governor and Lord Gower, their mindfulness of Gower's hardline position on Parliamentary authority and Lord Dunmore's enforcement of the Quartering Act in New York, it seems they held any spirit of faction they may have harbored in check when receiving him as Governor of Virginia in 1771. Upon his arrival, he was greeted with all the pleasantries and ceremony the Colony could afford. The report of his being appointed Governor in the March 7, 1771 editions of the *Virginia Gazette* made no mention of any of his alignments or ties—political or family— his record in Parliament or his record as Governor of New York.[50] When he arrived in Williamsburg on September 25, 1771, Purdie and Dixon reported, "In the evening there were Illuminations, &c., as a Testimony of our Joy at his Excellency's safe Arrival, and Gratitude to his Majesty for appointing a Nobleman of his Abilities and good Character to preside over us."[51]

But gracious as these expressions of joy and gratitude were, they were also perfunctory. The previous Governor, Lord Botetourt, had been welcomed with exactly the same expressions when he arrived in 1768.[52] The Virginians were well aware of Lord Dunmore's reluctance to accept his appointment as their Governor in the first place.[53] Even though this reluctance had more to do with personal inconvenience than political differences, it could have aroused suspicion and mistrust—components of the spirit of faction. For Virginians, it is likely Dunmore's reluctance was interpreted as indifference if not arrogance, either of which boded a predisposition to devalue their affairs. They would have been particularly sensitive to the way such a predisposition might lead to disagreements between executive and legislature involving their long-standing Resolves, which they knew to be contrary to the British ministry's edict regarding Parliamentary authority.

In his first responses to the welcomes of his constituents, he made awkward references to the slight of evading the assignment to Virginia. He told the President and Professors of the College of William and Mary, "though I must acknowledge the Desire I had of remaining in New York, from the sincere Affection I had received, and ever shall retain, for a Province the People whereof had manifested so earnest an Inclination to make my Administration easy to me, and my Residence among them agreeable, I shall, nevertheless, exert my utmost abilities to conciliate the Affection of the Colony which I now have the Honor to preside over." An explanation insinuating a desire for amiable association, but one some might construe as prejudicial to the hospitality, sincerity and agreeability of Virginians.[54]

When it came to encroachments on their sovereignty—actual or perceived—Virginians were not agreeable. As noted previously, Lord Dunmore might have formed an opinion regarding this characteristic when serving in the House of Lords and introduced to the widely acclaimed Virginia Resolves. These provided indisputable evidence there was a vocal and influential element of the Virginia Assembly determined to assert Virginia's sovereignty and deny and oppose the authority of Parliament.

Lord Dunmore was also aware of another subtler instance of Virginia's assertion of sovereignty. This was in their evasion of the Proclamation of 1763 regulating trade with the Indians and access to the Indian lands won in the French and Indian War. On September 26, 1771, the day after his arrival in Williamsburg, he issued a Proclamation making "void, and of none effect" the Virginia Assembly's "Act for Appointing Commissioners to Meet with Commissioners Who Are or May Be Appointed by the Legislatures of The Neighboring Colonies, to Form and Agree upon a General Plan for the Regulation of Indian Trade."* According to John Pendleton Kennedy, Virginia's first State Librarian, this action alone resulted in "much dissatisfaction."[55]

As speculated for Lord Dunmore's slight of the Virginians in his evasion of the assignment to the colony, his executive reprimand of the Virginia Assembly the day after he arrived suggests the suspicion and mistrust underlying a spirit of faction were present when the new governor took office or sown when the new legislature convened. This despite the obsequious protestations to the contrary manifest in official courtesies.

---

* Evidently this Act was considered a violation of the stipulation in the Proclamation of 1763 that "Trade with the said Indians shall be free and open to all our Subjects whatever, provided that every Person who may incline to Trade with the said Indians do take out a License for carrying on such Trade from the Governor or Commander in Chief of any of Our Colonies and ... observe such Regulations ... by ourselves or by our Commissaries to be appointed for this Purpose, to direct and appoint for the Benefit of the said Trade."

Under the circumstances, there was probably little surprise when Parliament passed the law closing the Port of Boston on March 31, 1774—two and a half years after Lord Dunmore arrived in Virginia—the House of Burgesses responded by calling it a "hostile invasion of the City of Boston," and passing a resolution setting aside a day of prayer and fasting as a show of solidarity with the city.[56] Likewise, there was little surprise Governor Dunmore considered this resolution unacceptably sympathetic of what he considered open rebellion in Boston—a flagrant breach of Declaratory Act mandates—and dissolved the House of Burgesses on May 26. He insisted their Resolves necessitated the dissolution since they were "conceived in such Terms as reflect highly upon his Majesty and the Parliament of Great Britain"[57]— an indirect but unmistakable acknowledgement of the faction between mother country and colony.

In one of the more strident displays of unity and resolve in the lead up to the clashes of April 1775 (the shots fired at Lexington and Concord and the Gunpowder Incident in Virginia), almost every county in Virginia would publicly announce their support for the Burgesses, their approval of the proposed general congress (the Burgesses made this proposal the day after they were dissolved), their concern over their loss of constitutional rights and their insistence the cause of Boston was the cause of every colony in America.[58] These announcements were very spirited. The "freeholders, merchants and other inhabitants of the county of Prince William" resolved, "... any act of parliament, levying a tax to be collected in America, depriving the people of their property, or prohibiting them from trading with one another, is subversive of our natural rights, and contrary to the first principles of our constitution."[59] In some cases, as in Fairfax County, the announcements were soon followed by the establishment of "independent companies of volunteers" to "defend to the utmost of our power ... the just right and privileges of our country."[60]

It seems the governor could only have regarded such announcements as confrontational and that is how the county committees that published them wanted them to be regarded. In any event, the announcements and establishment of companies of volunteers to defend their just rights and privileges were explicit pronouncements the divide between the convictions of governor and citizens, mother country and colony, was wide and dangerous. These announcements gave notice that resistance to any additional dictates the Virginians considered repressive and unconstitutional could now include the option of military force.

When these announcements were published in the summer of 1774, Governor Dunmore was on his expedition to quell the Indian disturbances on the borders of Virginia and Pennsylvania. He made no official acknowledgement of them. In his defense, these announcements of support for the Burgesses and the Continental Congress and the establishment of independent companies would coincide with publications of effusive expressions of gratitude for his leadership in resolving the Indian crisis. Of course, this coincidence was accidental. If Governor Dunmore were beguiled into believing these expressions of gratitude outweighed the rancor engendered by his dissolution of the Burgesses, such a notion would have been short-lived. Beguiled or not, it seems he ignored these resolutions and missed one of the last opportunities he would have to gain an appreciation of the breadth and danger of the divide between the Virginians' convictions—their interpretation of the constitution—and his.

❧

The Association of 1774—instituted by the Burgess when that House was dissolved—evolved into the Virginia Conventions. These Conventions and later the Virginia Assembly formed the legislative and executive branches of an independent state government that allied itself with the general or Continental Congress. These changes marked the end of cooperation between the legislative and executive branches of the government of Virginia and the beginning of a formal, material and permanent faction.

Governor Dunmore was alert to the threat this independent government—this faction—posed to his administration. A few days after he dissolved the Burgesses, he included their call for a general congress among the "violent measures" the Burgesses were considering. He admitted to Secretary Dartmouth he was apprehensive "the prudent views and the regard for justice and equity, as well as loyalty and affection ... will avail little against the turbulence and prejudice which prevails throughout the country."[61] In December of 1774, he would tell Lord Dartmouth, "I can assure your lordship, that I have discovered no instance where the interposition of government, in the feeble state to which it is reduced, could serve any other purpose than to suffer the disgrace of a disappointment, and thereby afford matter of great exultation to its enemies, and increase their influence over the minds of the people."[62] However, in spite of these gloomy assessments, it seems the Governor maintained a degree of optimism regarding the prognosis for the enfeebled government—optimism based at least in part on his underestimation of the Virginians' military capability as well as the intensity of the spirit of faction.

In his December letter to Secretary Dartmouth, he assessed the most serious threat posed by the new government to be their abetting the "lawless mob" enforcing the Articles of Association promulgated by Congress. But he reasoned further, "... every step which has been taken by these infatuated people, must inevitably defeat its own purpose." This labeling of the Virginians as infatuated people and a lawless mob underscored Governor Dunmore's dismissive attitude of their declaration to "defend to the utmost of our power ... the just right and privileges of our country." One might argue such a flippant assessment was an outburst of aristocratic arrogance,* behavior bound to make any disagreement adversarial and confound further objective assessment of the genuine claims and capabilities of either party. Arrogant or

---

* Arrogance is an epithet often glibly ascribed to aristocrats but in this case it may be apt. Another letter from Lord Dunmore to Lord Dartmouth shortly after the Gunpowder Incident supports a claim he suffered from this character defect on occasion. In describing the reaction of the Williamsburg magistrates to the incident and their request for an explanation, he tells Lord Dartmouth he received "... an address in reality milder in terms, than I expected, but still from the manner in which it was presented can be deemed, if not a treasonable proceeding at least nothing less than one of the highest insults, that could be offered to the authority of his Majesty's Governor." *Journals of the House of Burgesses of Virginia 1773 – 1776*, 1905, pp. xvii – xviii.

not, it was behavior that again underscored a lack of appreciation of the capability, resolve and determination of the Virginians to assert and defend their sovereignty.

The faction between governor and legislature led to the Second Virginia Convention's revival of the Virginia Militia Act in March 1775—the most dramatic assertion of sovereignty the Virginians would make prior to enacting the ordinance to raise a provincial army in August of 1775. It was at the March Convention, and in support of the Militia Act, Patrick Henry is said to have articulated what came to be the battle cry of democratic movements to this day, "Give me liberty or give me death." A month later, on April 20, Governor Dunmore would confiscate the gunpowder and arms in the magazine at Williamsburg—an action he would later admit he took in response to the revival of the Militia Act.[63] But even though he explicitly acknowledged the spirit of faction and the "rage & violence ... of these People," after his gunpowder foray, he also concluded "these People" were "*pretending* to contend for Liberty [emphasis added]"[64] –once more discounting the sincerity and fervor of the Virginians' devotion to their sovereignty—sovereignty they insisted was constitutionally established and guaranteed.

Time and again Lord Dunmore was presented with opportunities to acknowledge and address the opposing views of the British ministry (which he represented) and the colonial assemblies regarding constitutional authority. He never did. Ultimately his intransigence regarding this definitive component of governance engendered an insuperable spirit of faction among the Virginians. Lord Dunmore did acknowledge this spirit but he never would have characterized it as insuperable. In fact, he determined it was his job to suppress it. One of the actions he would take in the performance of that job would be the assault on the rebel fortifications at Great Bridge on December 9, 1775.

CHAPTER 9: DEPLOYED TO VIRGINIA, 1775

It seems Governor Dunmore was honestly surprised and frightened by what he described as the threats, ferment, commotion, insults, alarm, rebellion, vengeance, assaults, rage, fury and danger occasioned by his taking the gunpowder from the magazine at Williamsburg to one of His Majesty's ships in the York River. His reaction to the commotion was to request military support from the British commanders in America and the British ministry. He told Lord Dartmouth he had word that 2000 armed men were on the way to Williamsburg to "assault my house, & spare neither me, nor any person adhering to me." He added the obvious justification for his request, namely, he needed the detachment to "protect me & those Officers of Government who would choose to attend me."[1]

Thus, it was what Governor Dunmore considered a combative, rebellious Patriot reaction to his attempt to disarm them that precipitated the deployment of the 14th Regiment to the province. As noted above, the Governor justified the request and subsequent deployment of the 14th in terms of his need for protection. However, it seems he hoped to use the force for more than protection from the outset of the unfolding insurrection, although his initial requests do not suggest a plan that included an aggressive offensive.

The initial requests for help were in the form of letters to Admiral Graves and General Gage. In the letter to Admiral Graves on May 1, 1775—ten days after he had confiscated the gunpowder—the Governor explained, "The people of this Colony are taking up arms in all parts of it, and every species of violence is threatened to be executed upon me unless I restore some gunpowder which I removed on board the 'Fowey.'" He appealed to the Admiral for one of the large ships of war under his command, explaining, "Such a Ship having so considerable a body of Men Onboard, as the Rivers here have, even very high up, great depth of Water, would strike Awe over the whole Country, and a small Post Onshore under the Protection of the Guns of such a Ship would maintain itself against all the efforts which are in the power of an undisciplined Multitude to make."[2]

That same day Governor Dunmore wrote General Gage to inform him, "The Inhabitants of most of the Counties of this Colony are in Commotion, and a Body of two Thousand Men are now Actually preparing to March to the Assault of my House, defended only by my self and the Persons belonging to my Family." He then applied to the General "for such immediate Assistance, as the Circumstances of the Affairs in which you are yourself engaged, and your Orders and Instructions may permit you to Afford me." He assured the General—probably based on his conscientious but incorrect military assessment of his situation— "Two or Three Hundred Men or even one Hundred would probably prevent my being driven out of the Government, and enable me to Maintain an Entrenched Post on the Bank of one of the Rivers under the Protection of the Guns of a Man of War." In addition to maintaining an entrenched post, the Governor suggested such a display might encourage the well affected of the country to rally to the King's standard, which reinforcement would enable him "to make head against the Insurgents."[3]

Admiral Graves was the first to respond to Governor Dunmore's requests. By May 9, the *Otter*, a sixteen-gun sloop (corvette) with a crew of 100, was ordered to Virginia from Boston.[4] Admiral Graves informed Lord Dunmore of this response in a letter of May 20. On May 23, Captain Matthew Squire of the *Otter* weighed anchor at Boston and started the voyage to Virginia. Seventeen days later, on June 9, 1775, the *Otter* was moored in the York River at Yorktown. Editor Purdie reported the arrival in his edition of the *Virginia Gazette* for that same day.[5]

In a letter of June 17 (the day Generals Gage and Howe attacked the Patriots at Bunker Hill), Governor Dunmore reported the arrival of Captain Squire and the *Otter* to Admiral Graves. He told the Admiral of his status as a refugee on the *Fowey* (he had been there since June 7) and noted he planned to "remain in this Situation until I receive Instructions from His Majesty." In this same letter, he also alluded to what today may be referred to as "mission creep," for the forces he had requested. He told Graves, "… the keeping of these considerable Countries lying upon the great Rivers which empty into the Bay of Chesapeake in awe cannot but contribute much to the Success of the General Plan for enforcing the Authority of Government in the Colonies."[6] The Governor's interest in growing the mission from self-protection to a general plan for enforcing authority in the colonies reveals his interest in making Virginia the base of a Southern campaign, an interest more in keeping with the aggressive posture he would take at Great Bridge.

In July, Governor Dunmore left Yorktown and sailed with his naval force, *Fowey*, *Mercury* and *Otter*, for Portsmouth on the Elizabeth River, about 45 miles away. There he established a more permanent base of operations.[7] This move to Portsmouth would have occurred after July 14 since the 24-gun *Mercury*—sent in relief of the *Fowey*—arrived at Yorktown on that date.[8]

The move to Portsmouth may have been occasioned by another furor over the magazine in Williamsburg. It still contained arms and gunpowder and the "keeper"—appointed by Dunmore—rigged a booby trap to protect these remaining government assets. Two men were wounded attempting to burglarize the magazine and Governor Dunmore was blamed for engineering the "diabolical invention." In a letter to Lord Dartmouth of June 25, he noted, "the Cry among the People was for Vengeance."[9] In a postscript to the same letter he told the Secretary, "Guards likewise Continually mount at the Town of York opposite to which the Men of War lie, and thro'out the whole Country the greatest attention is paid to these Military preparations and an universal appearance of War."[10] It is also possible Governor Dunmore and his naval advisors appreciated the better access to the Chesapeake Bay an anchorage at Portsmouth or Norfolk afforded. These communities were also very active trading centers with reputations for supporting agreeable intercourse with Great Britain both commercially and politically.[11]

Regardless of why he moved, the move was portentous in that both Portsmouth and neighboring Norfolk, just across the river, had two sources of supply, the sea line of communication through the Chesapeake Bay and the land line of communication over the Great Road, which was vulnerable to disruption at Great Bridge. The sea line of communication was effectively under British control because of their naval presence—small but entirely adequate since Virginia had no naval capability. Given the accelerating hostilities, controlling the vulnerable land line of communication became Governor Dunmore's most urgent concern.

Figure 13[12] is a stylized map of the locations of these lines of communication as well as the key towns in the Chesapeake Bay area in Virginia where both the Patriot and King's forces served in 1775.

Figure 13. Stylized Map of Chesapeake Bay Area with Nominal Lines of Communication. Borders of Norfolk and Princess Anne Counties are also included.

The same day Governor Dunmore wrote Admiral Graves telling him the *Otter* had arrived—June 17—Captain George Montague of the *Fowey* also wrote the Admiral to tell him he planned to send a sloop and a schooner to St. Augustine to pick up the troops of the 14th Regiment General Gage had authorized Governor Dunmore. The sloop *Betsey* left Yorktown for St. Augustine on June 28[13] and on July 31—just over a month later—*Betsey* was back in Virginia—at Norfolk—with the first contingent of the 14th Regiment. The arrival of this contingent was reported in all three editions of the *Virginia Gazette* published in Williamsburg but with the sloop identified as a "sloop tender" instead of the *Betsey*. In addition to this unusual designation of the transport, the *Gazette* articles included these details.

> On Monday last [July 31] arrived here from St. Augustine about sixty soldiers, on board the sloop tender, some time since belonging to Mr. Bowdine, of the eastern shore. These, with about forty more, which are hourly expected, are to compose a bodyguard for his Excellency the Governor, at his intended place of residence, on board the ship William. The troops above mentioned are under the command of a Captain and two Lieutenants: the Ensign, it is said, is on his way over land.[14]

On August 2, Governor Dunmore informed Lord Dartmouth the troops arrived "last night." He estimated their number to be about seventy.[15]

This detachment was commanded by Captain Samuel Leslie, the second ranking captain of the regiment. William Blackett was first in the list of the eight captains in the regiment at this time but he was still with his detachment in New Providence. On August 20, Captain Leslie wrote General Gage and informed him "I arrived here the 31st of July with a Detachment under my command of the 14th Regiment consisting of two Lieutenants, three Serjeants, three Corporals, one Drummer, & Sixty private men." Based on this return, the strength of the detachment was seventy men—the same number Governor Dunmore had reported to Lord Dartmouth.

Regarding the initial disposition of the detachment in Virginia Captain Leslie noted, "We have been hitherto divided on board two Men of war a Ship that Lord Dunmore has fitted up for himself, and a small sloop; but his Lordship says he will do better for us and have us more together as soon as it is in his power." The Captain also had current information regarding the remainder of the 14th at New Providence and St. Augustine. Of these two detachments he observed, "We daily expect Capt. Blackett's Company from [New] Providence, and Lord Dunmore says he will send to St Augustine for the remainder of the Regiment there as soon as he can procure Vessels for that purpose."[16]

Although Captain Leslie may have been waiting for the detachments from New Providence and St. Augustine, the next contingent of the 14th Regiment to arrive in Virginia was a group of seven officers from Boston. According to Dixon and Hunter's *Virginia Gazette* of August 12, a brig from Norfolk that had taken a cargo of provisions to Boston returned on August 9 "having on board seven officers of the regular army." Purdie noted these officers were sent by General Gage "to assist lord Dunmore in his operations against this colony." In his *Gazette* of two weeks later, Purdie published news he had received regarding the ranks of the officers. There were two captains, one lieutenant, three ensigns and a surgeon.[17]

It is likely three of these officers were Captains David Cooper and John Dalrymple and Lieutenant Andrew Laurie. That Captain Dalrymple and Lieutenant Laurie were aboard the ship from Boston is supported by intelligence in a letter from socialite Katherine Leslie Hunter to a friend in Glasgow, Scotland. In that letter, she notes Captain Dalrymple and Lieutenant Laurie had arrived in Gosport, and she informs her correspondent these men had come from Boston.[18] It is possible Captain David Cooper was with Dalrymple and Laurie since Major Furlong noted in an October 5 letter to General Gage that Captain Cooper was in Boston in July.[19] Based on Major Furlong's listing of Ensigns James Boyes, Charles Ogle and James Lindsay as "Not yet joined," in the Monthly Return for August 1, it is possible they were also in this August 12 contingent of seven officers from Boston. The surgeon mentioned in Purdie's August 25 report was surgeon's mate John Weir.[20]

The third contingent of the 14th to arrive was that of Captain William Blackett's from New Providence. Purdie reported the arrival at Norfolk of twenty to thirty effective men from St. Augustine in his September 15 edition of the *Virginia Gazette*.[21] This was no doubt Blackett's detachment from New Providence, not St. Augustine. It would be another six weeks before the detachment from St. Augustine—under the command of Captain Fordyce—would leave that station.

In the August 1, 1775 "Monthly Return of His Majesty's Forces in the Province of East Florida," Major Furlong noted that 91 men of the 14th Regiment were "on command at Williamsburg, Va."[22] He was referring to that portion of the 14th detached to Virginia but, in fact, still onboard the transports off Norfolk. This 91-man detachment would have included Captain Leslie's initial contingent of seventy men plus a twenty-one-man contingent under Captain Blackett from New Providence, but it seems it did not include the seven officers from Boston. Major Furlong noted the 91-man detachment consisted of two captains, two lieutenants, one ensign, four sergeants, one drummer and 81 rank and file. Evidently the rank and file listed in this return included corporals as well as privates. This same force would be listed in the September 1 "Return."

Since Captain Leslie's initial detachment of seventy men consisted of one captain, two lieutenants, three sergeants, one drummer and sixty-three rank and file (includes the three corporals and sixty privates as listed in Leslie's letter to General Gage), the twenty-one-man detachment from New Providence must have been comprised of one captain, one sergeant and nineteen rank and file. In the August 1 Return, Major Furlong named the officers in Virginia as Captain Blackett, Captain Leslie, Lieutenant Batut, Lieutenant Napier, Lieutenant Leslie and Ensign Wools. The naming of three lieutenants—Batut, Napier and Leslie—in the Return is a source of some confusion since Furlong notes only two lieutenants in the "distribution" section of the same Return. In the next month's Return—that for September 1, 1775—Lieutenant Napier is not included in the list of officers in Virginia, so it seems his inclusion in the list of September was a mistake.[23]

Captain Leslie submitted a Monthly Return for the 14th Regiment at Gosport, Virginia on October 1.[24] In the Return—which included the seven officers from Boston—he listed four captains, three lieutenants, four ensigns, one adjutant, one surgeon's mate, four sergeants, four corporals, one drummer and seventy-nine privates for a total of 101 officers and men. This is ten more soldiers than Major Furlong listed in his September Return so it seems that in addition to the seven officers from Boston, three enlisted men or non-commissioned officers had also joined Captain Leslie's detachment by October 1. These three men could have accompanied the seven officers from Boston.

Table 6 is a list of the officers and men available to Governor Dunmore on October 1. The list is based on Major Furlong's Returns for August and September, Captain Leslie's Return for October, his letters to Generals Gage and Howe addressing the activities of the 14th Regiment in October[25] and reports in the *Virginia Gazette* of seven officers arriving from Boston.

The force listed in Table 6 is quite modest, 101 soldiers in all, but in terms of "regulars," that is, professional soldiers, it exceeded any force Virginia could field at the time.

The Third Virginia Convention authorized the recruiting and training of a professional army in legislation passed on August 21, three weeks after the Captain Leslie's initial contingent of British regulars landed at Norfolk. The legislation, "An Ordinance for Raising and Embodying a Sufficient Force for the Defense and Protection of This Colony," provided for raising

> ... two regiments complete, to consist of one thousand and twenty privates, rank and file: five hundred and forty four of whom to be the first regiment, under the command of a colonel, lieutenant-colonel, and a major, eight captains, sixteen lieutenants, eight ensigns, twenty four sergeants, eight drummers, and eight fifers, and the second regiment to consist of four hundred and seventy-six.[26]

Three days later, on August 24, the Convention passed legislation authorizing a Committee of Safety to, "... superintend, direct and appoint stations, marches, and encampments, for the regular forces to be raised, so that they may be on all emergencies employed for the more effectual assistance and defence [sic] of any part of the country most exposed to danger."[27]

Table 6. Summary Return of the 14th Regiment at Gosport, Virginia, October 1, 1775.

RANK	NUMBER	NAMES
Captains	4	William Blackett Samuel Leslie David Cooper John Dalrymple
Lieutenants	3	John Batut Peter Henry Leslie Andrew Laurie
Ensigns	4	Thomas Appleford Wools James Boyes Charles Ogle James Lindsay
Adjutant	1	Lt. Cornelius Smelt
Surgeon's mate	1	John Weir
Sergeants	4	
Corporals	4	
Drummers	1	
Privates	79	
TOTAL	101	

Recruiters anticipated the legislation authorizing the professional army, so recruits and county militia units had been arriving in Williamsburg since July. The various counties had been training their militia units with more rigor since the Second Virginia Convention resolved on March 24 to "… put in execution the militia law passed in the year 1738, entitled 'An act for the better regulating of the militia.'" This was a resolution wherein the Convention "… recommended to the inhabitants of the several counties of this colony that they form one or more volunteer companies of infantry and troops of horse, in each county, and to be in constant training and readiness to act on any emergency."[28] Although this March resolution advanced the timeline for training and equipping the professional army, trained and equipped regulars would not be available to the Committee of Safety until October.

The fact the Virginians were still training and equipping their regular army in the summer and fall of 1775[29] gave Governor Dunmore a significant advantage in initiating military operations in the colony even though his military force was modest. He had already put the small naval force Admiral Graves provided in June to use committing what editors Dixon and Hunter characterized as "infernal depredations in the rivers, and on the coast."[30] With the arrival of the contingents of Captains Leslie and Blackett and the officers from Boston, Governor Dunmore took the initiative and opened what was, in effect, a campaign to disarm the Patriots in Princess Ann and Norfolk Counties.* By October 22, he could provide Lord Dartmouth a rather glowing account of his exploits. He reported,

> On the 15th Instant [October], I landed with between 70 and 80 Men (which was all we could Spare to take with us) some little distance from this in the Night, and Marched about a Mile and a half up the Country, where we destroyed 17 pieces of Ordinance and brought off two more, that the Rebels had carried from the Town of Norfolk, and concealed there. On the 17th we landed again about eight Miles from this and Marched between two and three Miles up the Country where I had information of a Number of more Guns, and here they had collected about 200

---

* One might argue Governor Dunmore's first use of his newly acquired army was rather petty. On September 30, he sent sixteen of his troops ashore in Norfolk to confiscate the printing press of Mr. John Holt, publisher of what he considered the incendiary *Virginia Gazette or the Norfolk Intelligencer*. In justifying the action, he told Lord Dartmouth "The Public prints ... has for some time past been wholelly [sic] employed in exciting, in the minds of all Ranks of People the Spirit of Sedition and Rebellion by the grosest [sic] misrepresentation of facts, both public and private." "Lord Dunmore to Lord Dartmouth, the Ship *William* by Norfolk, Virginia 5th October 1775," NDAR 2:316, 317. The action was no doubt related to a feud between Mr. Holt and Captain Squire of the *Otter*. The entire affair was reported with sarcasm and disdain in the other Virginia newspapers. *Virginia Gazette*, Purdie, Sept. 15, 1775, p. 3, Oct. 6, 1775 (supplement), p. 2, October 20, 1775, p. 2 and *Virginia Gazette*, Dixon and Hunter, October 7, 1775, p. 3.

of their Shirt men,* who all fled to the Woods, and at this place we found some Small Arms and Ammunition, but could not find the Guns. On the 19th we landed again and Marched about two Miles up the Country, and there destroyed Ten Guns, and brought off Six. On the 20th we landed again and brought off Six more Guns, and Yesterday we landed again and brought off Ten Guns and Two Cohorns [portable mortar], and between fifty and Sixty small Arms and a great quantity of Ball of all Sorts and Sizes, which I believe is all the Military Stores in this Neighborhood that could be of any Service to the Rebels.[31]

Captain Leslie reported on these same activities in a letter to General Howe. He summarized, "Many great guns, small-arms, and other implements of war, have been taken since by small parties; so that there has been, in all, at least seventy-seven pieces of ordnance taken and destroyed since my detachment arrived."[32]

Captain Fordyce had arrived with the fourth detachment of the 14th Regiment just as this campaign ended and two days (three in some records) before Governor Dunmore sent his summary report. In a letter to Captain James Urquhart, who was with a large detachment the 14th Regiment still in Boston,[33] Captain Fordyce explained he had embarked at St. Augustine for Virginia in early October, "with all the Grenadiers, and as many men from the battalion as made up a detachment of sixty, including non-commissions." Regarding the voyage he noted, "We sailed the 7th of October, and got here the 20th." "Here" was Gosport, Virginia, the small port on the Elizabeth River just above Portsmouth where Governor Dunmore had established his headquarters.[34]

In the same letter to General Howe summarizing the raids conducted in October, Captain Leslie reported, "Captain Fordyce, with Lieutenants Napier and Wallace, three Sergeants, three Corporals, two Drummers, and fifty-five private men, arrived here from St. Augustine the 20th [of October], from whence he brought

---

* Most of the soldiers in Virginia's army at this time did not have the more colorful and complete uniform later prescribed for Continental soldiers. Instead they wore "hunting shirts," which were open-front garments of osnaburg (a course linen fabric) with distinctive fringes at the seams. The soldiers wearing these shirts were called shirtmen.

some ammunition, bedding, and provisions."[35] Based on this list, the total number of men in Fordyce's detachment was sixty-six.*

On October 14, a week before Captain Fordyce arrived, Captain Blackett died. He had been in Virginia about five weeks. It is likely he was the victim of a tropical fever contracted in New Providence or possibly St. Vincent.[36] With this loss, the total of the four detachments of troops from the 14th Regiment was 163. This included Captain Leslie's initial detachment of seventy, the seven officers from Boston (six commissioned officers and a surgeon's mate), the remainder of Captain Blackett's detachment—twenty soldiers—and Captain Fordyce's detachment of sixty-six.

Some time prior to Captain Fordyce's arrival, an additional twelve men were added to the British force. Some of these men might have accompanied the ensign reported as traveling over land or, as speculated earlier, it is possible three of the twelve accompanied the seven officers from Boston. With these additional men and Captain Fordyce's detachment, Governor Dunmore's army of regulars stood at 175. It was this this force Captain Leslie listed in the "Monthly Return of a Detachment of His Majesty's Fourteenth Regiment of Infantry," for November.[37] He submitted this report as the senior officer in command of the 14th Regiment in Virginia. Command had devolved to him after the death of Captain Blackett. At 175, Dunmore's detachment of regulars was considerably less than the "two or three hundred" he had requested almost six months earlier, but it was close to twice as many as were mustered in the force he commanded during the successful disarmament campaign he had just completed.

The last Return Captain Leslie made for the troops under his command in Virginia was made at Norfolk on December 1, eight days before the Battle of Great Bridge. This Return was identical to that of November 1 with the exception of the death of one private. Thus, the maximum number of British troops of the 14th Regiment available on December 9, the day of the battle, was 174.

---

* There are discrepancies in the various "Returns." Captain Fordyce told Captain Urquhart he had sixty men and three officers for a total of sixty-three soldiers—three less than the sixty-six man detachment reported by Captain Leslie.

Dunmore's force as of December 1 is presented in Table 7. This force, augmented with those marines and seamen from the *Otter*, *William* and *Mercury* who could be spared (probably about thirty based on the way these forces had been used previously[38]), would be the regulars available to Governor Dunmore at the Battle of Great Bridge.

According to his report to Lord Dartmouth of October 22, Governor Dunmore had effectively disarmed the two lower counties of Virginia by October 21—the day after Captain Fordyce arrived. And with his modest flotilla, he controlled the Chesapeake Bay. It seems these developments—in particular the disarming of Princess Ann and Norfolk Counties and the arrival of sixty-six more regulars—roused the Committee of Safety to action.

Table 7. Summary Return of the 14th Regiment at Gosport, Virginia, December 1, 1775.

RANK	NUMBER	NAMES
Captains	4	Samuel Leslie Charles Fordyce David Cooper John Dalrymple
Lieutenants	5	John Batut William Napier Hill Wallace Peter Henry Leslie Andrew Laurie
Ensigns	4	Thomas Appleford Wools James Boyes Charles Ogle James Lindsay
Adjutant	1	Lt. Cornelius Smelt
Surgeon's Mate	1	John Weir
Sergeants	9	
Corporals	14	
Drummers	3	
Privates	133	
TOTAL	174	

On October 21, the Committee informed Patrick Henry, Commander-in-Chief of the Virginia forces and Colonel of the 1st Virginia Regiment, they were "inclined at present, if the state of the forces will admit of it," to send the 2nd Regiment, ninety riflemen of the Culpeper Battalion and two companies of Minutemen to Norfolk.[39] They provided no explanation for their inclination but the timing of the announcement is consistent with their recognition of the seriousness of Governor Dunmore's disarmament campaign and their awareness more regulars were on the way. Editor Purdie noted in his *Virginia Gazette* of October 20, "Yesterday the Committee of Safety received advice, by express, that two vessels had arrived in Hampton road with a reinforcement of soldiers for Lord Dunmore, said to amount to about 200 men. They are the troops which his lordship sent for to St. Augustine."[40] Two hundred was an exaggeration. The troops in question were Captain Fordyce's detachment of sixty-six soldiers.

Four days later, on October 24, the Committee of Safety deliberated on "the present state of Norfolk & the situation of the inhabitants of the adjacent Counties." They also reviewed the state of their unproven army. Evidently, they determined the two new regiments were ready for action. They resolved the 2nd Virginia Regiment and the Culpeper Battalion of minutemen "ought to March to the Neighborhood of Norfolk or Portsmouth & after reconnoitering the Ground & examining all necessary circumstances ... form an encampment at such a place as ... shall seem most convenient & secure the same in the best manner."[41] The same day the Committee issued orders to Colonel Woodford, commander of the 2nd Virginia, to "... march towards Norfolk; and when you have informed yourself of all necessary circumstances ... fix on an encampment, having regard among other things, to the convenience of winter quarters, which the approaching season makes necessary." Regarding his specific military assignment, the Committee ordered him to "use your best endeavors for protecting and defending the persons and properties of all friends of the cause of America."

Woodford was given plenty of discretion. The Committee told him to "be attentive to the force and motion of the enemy, and act offensively or defensively, as your prudence may direct." More to the point regarding the action that unfolded at Great Bridge, the Committee was clear he was to use every means in his power "for stopping all communication of intelligence and supplies of provisions, to the enemies of America in Norfolk or Portsmouth, and suffer no persons to pass and repass thither, whom, upon examination, you shall suspect to be inimical."[42]

The forces ordered to Norfolk under Colonel Woodford's command would not be consolidated into a single corps until December. When that consolidation occurred, Woodford would have at his disposal all the troops assigned him by the Committee of Safety on October 24. That order of battle is presented in Table 8. This was the army confronting Dunmore's 174 regulars, Loyalist volunteers and fledgling Ethiopian Regiment on December 9.

According to the data in Table 8, Woodford was in command of some 717 Virginia troops and 180 troops from North Carolina for a total of 897, although not all of this total were "Fit for Duty."

The 2nd Virginia Regiment and Culpeper Minutemen left Williamsburg on November 7.[43] Shortly thereafter, Governor Dunmore received intelligence that another Patriot force was on the move. He was told "a hundred and twenty or thirty North Carolina Rebels had marched into this Colony, to a place Called the Great Bridge, … a very Strong Post, in order to join some of ours [i.e., Virginia rebels—Princess Ann County militia] assembled not far from thence." This rendezvous the Governor "was determined not to Suffer."[44]

On the evening of November 14, he took all the 14th Regiment "able to do duty"—109 of the rank and file—and traveled by boat to Great Bridge to confront the North Carolinians and militia. He arrived to discover the report of a rendezvous was incorrect but learned some two or three hundred rebels had assembled at Kemp's Landing, a village about ten miles north-east of Great Bridge. He marched his force to Kemp's on November 15 and engaged the unsuspecting militia.

This was the Battle of Kemp's Landing, a one-sided skirmish, the main action of which involved the grenadiers chasing the rebels into the woods. In his report of the engagement to Lord

Dartmouth, Dunmore admitted the skirmish was trifling—one grenadier was wounded—but he also noted the zeal the success engendered among the people for His Majesty's Service "when unawed by the opposite party." He told Dartmouth that, as a result of this "strong manifestation," he was "determined to run all risques [sic] for their support."[45]

Table 8. "A General Return of the Forces Under Collo: Woodford at the Great Bridge, Decr. 10th 1775."[46]

		CORPS			
COMPONENT		2. Virga. Regimt.	1. Bat. of Min. Men.	Carolina Forces	TOTAL
Field Officers	Collos.	1			1
	Lt. Colls.	1	1	1	3
	Majrs.	1	1	1	3
Comd. Officers	Capts.	6	5	5	16
	Lieuts.	11	5	4	20
	Ensing.	6	5	3	14
Staff Officers	Adjts.	1	1		2
	Chaplins	1			1
	Surgeons	1	1		2
	Surgns. Mates	2	1		3
	Q. Master	1	1		2
Non. Comd. Officers	Sergts. Majr.	1	1		2
	Q. Master Serjt.	1			1
	Serjts.	18	8	9	35
	Drum. Majrs.	1			1
	Fifers	4		2	6
	Drums.	6	4	3	13
Rank and File	Fit for Duty	237	254	179	760
	Sick	51	12		63
	On Com[d]	6	9		15
	Baumen	3	5		8
	Confined	4			4
	Dead	1		1	2
	Deserted	6			6
	Recruted	14			14
	Camp C. men	18	7		25
Total	Total Strength of Corps.	430	287	180	897

Governor Dunmore quickly translated his military victory at Kemp's Landing into a referendum affirming the King's authority. Loyalist John Brown provided this description of the excitement engendered in a letter to his brother William who was in London,

> ...we arrived at Kemps in triumph where the Gov's Proclamation was Published and dispersed throughout the Country. The kings standard was hoisted. The day after The whole Country flocked to it took Oath of Allegiance* abjuring all committees & Conventions and declaring their readyness to defend his Majesty's Crown & dignity whenever called upon by his Excellency for that purpose.[47]

The publication of the Governor's Proclamation referenced above did coincide with the victory at Kemp's Landing but it seems it may have been published at this time because Governor Dunmore had word of the rebel troops having crossed the James River on their way to Norfolk. This would have been Woodford's force and, as already noted, Woodford left Williamsburg on November 7. By November 17—two days after the battle at Kemp's Landing—he had crossed the river.[48] According to William Curle, a Patriot in Portsmouth at the time, Governor Dunmore had "declared that as soon as he certainly knew of the Colony Troops having cross'd the James River" on the march to Norfolk, "he would issue his proclamation declaring them Enemies to the Government."[49]

This was indeed the case. The official date of the Proclamation was November 7—the day colonel Woodford left Williamsburg.

---

* Oath of Allegiance: Whereas a set of factious men, under the names of Committees, Conventions, and Congresses, have violently, under various pretences, usurped the legislative and executive powers of Government, and are thereby endeavouring to overturn our happy Constitution, and have incurred the guilt of actual rebellion against our most gracious Sovereign, I, A B, do therefore abjure all their authority, and solemnly promise, in the presence of Almighty God, to bear faith and true allegiance to his sacred Majesty George III, and will, to the utmost of my power and ability, support, maintain, and defend his crown and dignity, against all traitorous attempts and conspiracies whatsoever. So help me God. "Oath taken by the Inhabitants of Princess Anne County," Published in *Virginia Gazette*, Dixon and Hunter, December 2, 1775, p. 3.

In fact, Governor Dunmore was explicit in the Proclamation it was the "army now on its march to attack his majesty's troops, and destroy the well disposed subjects of this colony" that prompted the Proclamation. That said, Governor Dunmore did wait until he observed the "good effects" of the victory at Kemp's Landing before he ordered the Proclamation to be published,[50] so Mr. Brown's report it was "published and dispersed" immediately after the battle, was correct. The Proclamation would not be printed in any of the editions of the *Virginia Gazette* until November 23.[51]

࿇

It is likely Charles Fordyce's first action in Virginia was the nominal combat at Kemp's Landing. He told Captain Urquhart in his letter of December 1, "…we have had a little brush with the Rebels, who behaved in a most dastardly manner. [Private Thomas] Redfern was the only man hurt; he received a shot in the kneepan, which will render him unfit for service." This "little brush" was the Battle of Kemp's Landing. Private Redfern, one of Fordyce's grenadiers, was the single British casualty mentioned in Governor Dunmore's account of the action. By dastardly behavior, Captain Fordyce was probably referring to the way the militia might resort to ambush and guerrilla tactics.

The fact Charles describes the action at Kemp's Landing as a "little brush," suggests the level of actual military activity in the lead up to the Battle of Great Bridge was rather low. The action at Kemp's was the closest thing to combat the men of the 14th Regiment would experience prior to Great Bridge, so if it were a little brush then Charles and his men may have had some discretionary time to get acquainted with their hosts and their environs.

In his letter to Captain Urquhart, he does mention the construction of the fort at Great Bridge and "throwing up some intrenchments," around Norfolk. But other than the action at Kemp's and skirmishing at the new fort, it seems November was a period of respite for the men of the 14th. In any case, it is evident Charles had a little free time and he spent some of it visiting the family of a gentleman who may have been an old friend. The family was that of Captain James Maxwell and his wife Helen Calvert.

Captain Maxwell, born in Northumberland County, England and formerly of the British Navy, was in the shipping business and he and his wife had a home in Norfolk. Mrs. Maxwell wrote a *Memoir* after the Revolutionary War in which she included a brief account of time spent with Captain Fordyce. She recalled, "He was very intimate with Mr. Maxwell and had been at our house in Norfolk. He was not handsome, but very genteel, and I remember seeing him one day turn over Mr. M's Music, of which he was very fond, and humming some of the tunes."[52]

The "intimate" relationship between Captain Fordyce and Captain Maxwell may have developed years earlier. In her *Memoir*, Mrs. Maxwell notes she met her husband, James Maxwell, when he arrived in Norfolk as the sailing master on HMS *Launceston* commanded by Captain John Gell. Maxwell had been assigned to the *Launceston* in 1766 when it sailed from England to North America. It was stationed in Nova Scotia and Virginia in 1766 and 1767.[53] Back in Nova Scotia in 1768, *Launceston* was assigned the task of transporting the 14th Regiment from Halifax to Boston in September of that year.[54] Two months later the ship was back in Virginia. Purdie and Dixon reported its arrival at Hampton Roads on December 1, 1768.[55]

James Maxwell and Helen Calvert had been married in Norfolk County, Virginia on April 6, 1767.[56] He was reportedly on his way to Barbados in command of his own ship, the *Two Sisters*, in August 1768.[57] These circumstances imply he had been relieved of his duties on the *Launceston* by the time the 14th was transported to Boston. However, the fact he served in Nova Scotia in 1766 and 1767 and the fact Charles Fordyce had been appointed Town Major of Halifax in 1767 support a conclusion some rapport between these two officers developed and was, in fact, likely.

Such an opportunity to develop camaraderie in 1767 helps explain the intimacy of these two men in 1775 but Mrs. Maxwell makes references in her *Memoir* that suggest yet another possible link between Charles Fordyce and Captain Maxwell—a link associated with the marriage of Charles' older brother John Fordyce to Katherine Maxwell and the marriage of Katherine's sister, Jane Maxwell to Alexander Gordon, the 4th Duke of Gordon.

In her *Memoir*, Mrs. Maxwell notes that, in addition to the officer who would become her husband, James Maxwell, Captain Gell "had thirty-two midshipmen on board [the *Launceston*], mostly boys and lads of good families, and several of them sprigs of nobility."[58] Of these, she makes particular note that Midshipman George Gordon, younger brother of the Duke of Gordon, was a guest in her home.

The Duke of Gordon was Katherine Fordyce's brother-in-law. Thus, by marriage, John Fordyce (Katherine's husband) had an indirect but legitimate family tie to both Midshipman Gordon and the Duke, a tie that would have put his brother, Captain Charles Fordyce, and Midshipman Gordon on speaking terms. Depending on whether or not Captain Maxwell was related to the Maxwell sisters—a distinct possibility since both families were from the Borders region of Scotland and England—the relationship between George Gordon, Captain Maxwell and Charles Fordyce might have included two additional "in-law" dimensions. That is, John Fordyce could have been "related" to Captain Maxwell like he was to George Gordon, and Captain Maxwell could have had an in-law relationship with George Gordon as well as John Fordyce. These relationships would have provided an ample foundation for Charles, Captain Maxwell and Midshipman Gordon to be acquainted, especially since all three were associated with Captain Gell and the *Launceston* between 1766 and 1768.

That Charles would have time to enjoy the hospitality of Captain and Mrs. Maxwell may seem implausible considering the heightened tensions resulting from the presence of the British navy and army, Governor Dunmore's raids, his victory at Kemp's Landing and his Proclamation and Oath of Allegiance associated with that victory.[59] But it seems Charles was not the only officer in the 14th Regiment socializing with the locals in and around Norfolk. In another letter to Glasgow, Katherine Leslie Hunter claimed that none other than Captain Samuel Leslie had made romantic overtures. Ms. Hunter may have been deluded, but she confided to her friend, "I am Styled the Governess of the fleet &

Army … & have the Major of the Regiment Here (of my own Name Leslie) [Captain Samuel Leslie] willing to Sell out, & retire me to Sweet Frankfield! If I'll Consent to be His." And Ms. Hunter also had intelligence of activities performed by Captain Fordyce's company other than raids and entrenching. She informed her correspondent his grenadiers were "muster'd twice a Day, just before our windows with a Band of Musick."[60]

CHAPTER 10: THE BATTLE OF GREAT BRIDGE

Governor Dunmore's strategy to address the "unhappy ferment" ensuing his confiscation of the gunpowder in Williamsburg involved two goals. The primary goal was to "keep the Country in some Awe of Government."[1] Directly related to that goal was the goal of securing a "place of refuge" for those who "willingly have espoused His Majesty's interest."[2]

Prior to the Proclamation of November 7, he had concentrated his efforts for achieving his goals on acquiring men and material directly from the British ministry and awaiting "Instructions from His Majesty." He told Lord Dartmouth he expected him, i.e., the ministry, to see to it he was put in a "Situation of Safety."[3] These efforts resulted in rather meager concessions of ships and soldiers doled out over months. His requests for naval and army units had been met with Captain Squire's flotilla of the *Otter*, *William* and *Mercury* and Captain Leslie's detachment of the 14th Regiment. In July, Lord Dartmouth had promised the Governor "2000 Stand of Arms and Ammunition in proportion," but by November none of the promised supplies had been delivered.

With his November 7 Proclamation, Governor Dunmore reluctantly accepted the fact that further help from the ministry was unlikely. Shortly after the Proclamation was published he told General Howe, "Since the 19th of May last I have not received a single line from any one in administration…. I am therefore determined to go on doing the best of *my power* for his majesty's service [emphasis added]."[4] He informed Lord Dartmouth of his Proclamation in a letter of December 6 and asserted with a degree of petulance, "I am equipping a fleet, raising an Army and all this without any order from your Lordship, or any other person."[5] He was no longer awaiting instructions from His Majesty.

Lord Dunmore did not know it, but the ministry had responded to his pleas. The store ship *Maria* left Spithead on August 24 with the arms and ammunition Lord Dartmouth had promised.[6] When the Battle at Kemp's Landing was fought and his Proclamation published, the *Maria* was about five weeks out of Norfolk. So five weeks after issuing his Proclamation, he would receive the instalment of resources needed to equip and animate not only his new army but Loyalists throughout Virginia as well. But this reinforcement would be effective only if he were still in control of his enclave in Princess Ann and Norfolk Counties when it arrived. Five weeks proved to be too long. Having despaired of receiving help from the British ministry and perceiving an assault by Colonel Woodford's burgeoning army was imminent, he would attack the entrenched 2nd Virginia Regiment at Great Bridge three weeks after his Proclamation was published and ten days before his shipment of arms arrived.[*]

༄

With the victory at Kemp's Landing in November, Governor Dunmore had tenuous control of a place of refuge in Princess Ann and Norfolk Counties. To secure his control, he took the initiative in his Proclamation to issue two directives he could enforce locally. He executed martial law and instituted a draft to fill the ranks of a personal army—the army to which he referred in his letter to Lord Dartmouth of December 6. Regarding the draft he mandated, "every person capable of bearing arms to resort to his majesty's standard." And he was explicit this draft include the slaves of rebels. To that end, he declared the slaves "appertaining to rebels" free. Regarding the size of his army, he explained to Lord Dartmouth he was recruiting two regiments, the Queen's Own Loyal Virginia Regiment and Lord Dunmore's Ethiopian Regiment.[7] The rank and file of this latter regiment were freed

---

[*] Lord Dartmouth promised Governor Dunmore 2000 stand of arms in a letter of July 5, 1775. According to Dunmore, the arms arrived on December 19—over five months after they were promised—when the 36-gun frigate *Liverpool* and store ship *Maria* anchored off Norfolk. In reporting the arrival of the arms, Lord Dunmore told Lord Germaine if they had arrived two months earlier—when they were expected— "… it would have made a wonderful change in the face of affairs in this country." "Governor Earl of Dunmore to Lord George Germaine, 30 March, 1776, *Dunmore*, Elizabeth River, Virginia," Davies, DAR, 12:101.

slaves. The regiments' officers and non-commissioned officers were white, in keeping with British policy[8] but–in such a case as this—also an expedient imposed by the need to train freed slaves as officers and there was no time for such training.

In addition to instigating martial law and a draft, Lord Dunmore took one more step to secure his enclave. He told General Howe, "I determined to take possession of the pass at the Great-Bridge, which secures us the greatest part of two counties, to supply us with provisions." To effect this determination, he "ordered a stockade to be erected there, which was done in a few days."[9] Captain Leslie noted in a report to General Howe he had been ordered to erect the fort on November 14, the day he and his contingent of the 14th Regiment arrived at Great Bridge in pursuit of the rebel militia.[10]

At this point, Governor Dunmore had achieved his goals of keeping the country in some awe of government and securing a place of refuge. Arguably, his initiatives were taking effect, but his situation was precarious. Captain Squire's flotilla lacked a reliable and secure means of re-provisioning. Regarding Captain Leslie's detachment of the 14th Regiment, the Governor told General Howe, "… we are contending, with only a very small part of a regiment, against the extensive colony of Virginia."[11] He conceded his fort could not withstand any thing heavier than musket shot. Of his new recruits he admitted, "… the greatest part of these hardly ever made use of the Gun."[12] He was in desperate need of arms and supplies. On November 30, he told General Howe, "We are in great want of small arms; and if two or three field pieces and their carriages could be spared, they would be of great service to us; also some cartridge paper, of which not a sheet is to be got in this country, and all our cartridges are expended."

☙

Dunmore's victory at Kemp's Landing, his Proclamation freeing and arming slaves and the willingness of considerable numbers* in Princess Anne and Norfolk Counties to abjure the

---

* Lord Dunmore estimated the number to be 3000. "Lord Dunmore to Lord Dartmouth, Ship *Dunmore* off Norfolk, Virginia 6th December 1775," NDAR 2:1311.

authority of all "Committees, Conventions, and Congresses," and solemnly promise "... to bear faith and true allegiance to his sacred Majesty George III," would rouse the ire of every member of the Virginia Convention. In a response to what they called these "species of despotism,"—in particular the Proclamation—the Convention was unanimous in declaring they were "... compelled, by a disagreeable, but absolute necessity, of repelling *force by force*, to maintain our just rights and privileges." Regarding those who might join the Governor in his new army the Convention added, "... we shall think ourselves justified, by the necessity we are under, in executing upon them the law of retaliation."[13]

And now they could retaliate. No longer dependent on the poorly coordinated county militias, Virginia's army of regulars was in the field. They were ready to retaliate not only for the perceived disloyalty of intimidated and deluded countrymen, but also for a string of embarrassing losses to a man they considered an arrogant despot. Publisher Alexander Purdie opined in his *Virginia Gazette*, "it is to be hoped his [Dunmore's] sphere of mischief will soon be circumscribed within narrow bounds, as Colonel Woodford, with about eight hundred as brave troops as the world can produce, are now on their march to Norfolk; and, should his lordship incline to give them battle, we have not the smallest doubt they will give a very satisfactory account of him."[14]

As noted in the previous chapter, Captain Fordyce may have taken time for the courteous socializing expected of a conscientious officer and friend, but it is clear from the letter he wrote Captain Urquhart on December 1—two weeks after Purdie's editorial warning—he knew a confrontation was likely if not imminent. Consistent with the skill and wisdom he had displayed in managing the Indian alarm in Florida, his assessment of the maneuvering taking place as the Patriots tightened their grip on Governor Dunmore evinces an appreciation for the true cause for alarm at Great Bridge. He pointed out,

> A corps of about seven hundred men has been sent from Williamsburg, in order to take possession of this place, which they are most exceedingly desirous of doing. ... They have been for some days within about ten miles of us, but their farther progress

has been hitherto stopped by a fort constructed by [Lieutenant John] Batut, at a bridge where they must pass. ... [Lieutenant Hill] Wallace commands the fort; he has twenty-five of our regiment, a few militia, and some Negroes.[15]

Captain Fordyce appreciated the value of the fort at this strategic location, i.e., athwart the main line of communication between North Carolina, the interior of Virginia and the Chesapeake Bay, but he also recognized the limits of this defensive position where some twenty-five men with single-shot muskets might face eight hundred attackers who would likely have artillery before attempting an assault. He told Urquhart, "Would to God we had a few more men, and I think we should give a very good account of these rascals; but we are at present a very handful."

Colonel Woodford was on the march to Great Bridge when the Battle of Kemp's Landing occurred. On November 25, ten days after the battle and almost twenty days after he left Williamsburg, he reached Suffolk, Virginia, some forty-five miles from Williamsburg and about thirty miles from Great Bridge.

He had been proceeding with caution, which was consistent with the approach recommended by the Virginia Convention. After he started his march, the Convention directed him to "risk the success of his arms as little as possible."[16] It seems Colonel Woodford was taking this approach without explicit direction. On November 26, while at Suffolk, he wrote Edmund Pendleton, President of the Convention, regarding the disposition of his troops. At the time, Lieutenant Colonel Charles Scott was seven miles from Great Bridge with an advance party. Evidently, Colonel Scott was eager to attack what he believed was a weak force guarding Great Bridge but Colonel Woodford told the Convention he "cautioned him against taking that step without the very best Intelligence."[17] Colonel Scott harassed the British detachment but he did not mount a concerted attack.

Woodford was at Great Bridge by December 2[18] and he soon determined he needed reinforcements. In a status report to Pendleton on December 4, he advised that at least part of the 1st Regiment should be "Immediately ordered" to join him. His reasons for this reinforcement reflected the caution with which he was performing his mission and an appreciation of the variability in the training and equipping of the soldiers of other colonies. Woodford told Pendleton he needed the Virginia troops since, although North Carolina troops were thought to be on the way, "it is very uncertain how these Carolina Troops may be arm'd & what sort of men & officers they are." He was also concerned the approaching "Winter Campaign" might last "longer than is agreeable" to the Carolina troops, which were not under his command "so far as to order them to remain."[19]

Arguably, Colonel Woodford's request for reinforcements was based more on maintaining a direct chain of command and relieving his troops of some of the privations of camp life than engaging Governor Dunmore and his British regulars. Regardless of the reason, the requested reinforcements were sent. On December 7, Pendleton replied to Woodford, informing him Major Francis Eppes of the 1st Virginia Regiment was on his way to Great Bridge. Eppes left Williamsburg on the 7th with three infantry companies, 500 pounds of powder and 1500 pounds of lead.[20]

In assessing the preliminary maneuvers of the two commanders at Great Bridge — Colonel Woodford and Governor Dunmore — one might conclude Governor Dunmore was animated, impatient and over-confident while Colonel Woodford was cautious, patient and under-confident.[21] Regardless of their temperament, both men appreciated the strategic issue at hand. Governor Dunmore explained to Lord Dartmouth that losing control of the pass at Great Bridge meant he and his community of Loyalists would be "… cut off from every supply of Provisions from this Colony."[22] When Woodford arrived at Great Bridge, he assured the Virginia Convention he had positioned his forces on the south side of the Elizabeth River to do just that, i.e., to "cutt [sic] off all communication with this Neighborhood & the Enemy."[23]

Time was on Colonel Woodford's side and he could afford to be patient and cautious. He was aware Colonel Robert Howe from North Carolina was within a few days march of Great Bridge with as many as 900 men. He was also informed the North Carolina troops were bringing cannon and ammunition. In his report from

Great Bridge of December 4, he told the Virginia Convention he thought the enemy fort might have been taken but not without the loss of "many of our men," since "their Situation is very advantageous, & no way to attack them, but by exposing most of the Troops to their Fire upon a large open Marsh." But he also told the Convention that, as he waited for the Carolina troops and their cannon, "we are now making the necessary preparations to raise Batterys [sic] for these Cannon upon the most advantageous Ground to play upon their Fort & send a large detachment at the same time to intercept their Retreat."[24]

The British troops in the fort would have been watching these developments with concern. Time was not on their side. They had to act before the rebel army doubled in size and acquired artillery. It is likely Woodford's construction of batteries in which to place cannon to be trained on their fort precipitated a momentous meeting of Governor Dunmore and his military staff.

There is no record of such a meeting but there is anecdotal evidence it occurred, and that Governor Dunmore did lay his plans for attacking Colonel Woodford's position at Great Bridge before his subordinates. Given the meeting occurred, the participants would have included Governor Dunmore; the senior army officer in the field, Captain Samuel Leslie of the 14th Regiment; the senior naval officer on station, Captain Matthew Squire of the *Otter* and other ranking army and navy officers including Captains Charles Fordyce, John Dalrymple and David Cooper.

The meeting could have been held the evening of December 8, possibly aboard one of the ships anchored at Norfolk. It would have been a meeting where sober and concerned military officers conferred with a determined Commander-in-Chief—Governor Dunmore. The officers present would have known Dunmore to be a firm believer in British military prowess, a critic of American military capability and a former army officer who probably was pleased with his recent performance against the Shawnee Indians and his military and political successes in October and November. It is likely he exuded confidence. Arguably he did have the skill and experience to rout a force he had characterized as a mob. The officers also may have been aware of the zeal he ascribed to the Loyalists in Princess Ann and Norfolk Counties and his determination—as reported to Lord Dartmouth—to "run all risques [sic] for their support."

The Governor would have provided an overview of the situation as he saw it. This overview could have been the same he provided to Lord Dartmouth after the battle, namely,

> Being informed that the Rebels had procured some Cannon from North Carolina, and that they were also to be reinforced from Williamsburg, and knowing that our little Fort [at Great Bridge] was not in a Condition to withstand any thing heavier than Musquet [sic] Shot, I thought it advisable to risque [sic] Something to save the Fort, as the loss of it was not only exposing the well disposed People of this part of the Country, to the resentment of the Rebels, but the moment they pass that Bridge, we must expect to be cut off from every supply of Provisions from this Colony.[25]

It is not likely any of Lord Dunmore's advisors disputed the need to save the fort nor the high probability that task would be more difficult with the passing of time. Of course, the question raised by such an overview was then, what was the "Something to save the fort" he was willing to risk? In answering this question, Governor Dunmore would have explained he intended to attack Colonel Woodford's entrenchments on the south side of the river to deny him any position from which he could emplace cannon. He then would have given his staff—as he did Lord Dartmouth—the details of the attack. Early Saturday morning, Captain Leslie, with that portion of the 14th Regiment not already at Great Bridge, as many as 150 men, would march to the fort to reinforce the 25-man garrison there and, "if on his Arrival there he found no Material change, ... order two Companies of Negroes to make a detour, and fall in behind the Rebels a little before break of Day in the morning, and just as Day began to break, to fall upon the rear of the Rebels." This was to be a diversion which he expected "would draw their attention and make them leave the breast work they had made near the Fort." As this occurred, Captain Leslie "was then with the Regulars, the Volunteers and some recruits to sally out of the Fort, and attack their breast work."[26]

Chapter 10: The Battle of Great Bridge

This was a simple plan consistent with military practice. Arguably, it was "text book"—essentially a verbatim application of the "Assault on a Considerable Out-Work" delineated in General Humphrey Bland's 1746 *Treatise of Military Discipline*.[27] This *Treatise* was a popular guideline for training in military science at the time—George Washington had recommended it to Colonel Woodford as "foremost" of the texts on exercise and maneuver.[28] It is likely Governor Dunmore was introduced to it when he was an officer in the 3rd Foot Guards. The flanking maneuver proposed—if effected—was bound to divide the enemies' attention and diminish their firepower at just the time it would be needed to repel a frontal assault. Given his adherence to Bland's *Treatise*, Governor Dunmore might very well have assured his assembled staff none other than General Bland himself planned the operation.

After presenting his outline of the proposed assault, the Governor might have entertained questions from his military advisors as to possible risks associated with the plan. Any one of the officers might have brought up the challenges and risks associated with frontal assaults—risks demonstrated so clearly in the recent attack at Bunker Hill. They would have noted that despite the relatively even correlation of forces in that battle, the defensive forces had a distinct advantage and losses to the attacking British force were staggering. They might have reminded the Governor that two of their own officers, Ensign Robert Hesketh, nephew of Parliamentarian Sir Thomas Hesketh, and Lieutenant John Bruere, son of George James Bruere, Governor of Bermuda, had been killed in that battle and Lieutenant William Brown, also of the 14th Regiment, had been wounded. The death of Lieutenant Bruere and wounding of Lieutenant Brown, including their affiliation with the 14th Regiment, had been reported locally.[29]

One of the officers present might have had the temerity to point out a particular reference to Bunker Hill recently made by a local Patriot and published in the *Virginia Gazette*. This Virginian had asserted,

> I do not, in the least, suspect the courage of my countrymen. I know their cool intrepidity, and will affirm that no troops in the

world are superiour [sic] to them in the use of their arms; I mean not in the anticks [sic] of a parade, but in the true use of fire-arms; for, as marksmen, they are unequalled. Whenever an engagement happens, I make no doubt the list of killed and wounded will equal that of Bunker's Hill.[30]

If such a report were presented, it is likely it would have been dismissed as bravado. To the extent Governor Dunmore wanted to emphasize this point, he might have taken the opportunity such melodrama afforded to remind his commanders he did not expect the Virginians to stand for more than one volley from the British regulars. In an after-action account of the Battle of Great Bridge by one of the officers of the 2nd Virginia Regiment, Dunmore was alleged to have instructed his troops the Virginians would shirk their duty in this way.[31]

At some point, the planners may have elicited the opinions of Captain Fordyce. He might have voiced his concern over the number of British regulars available for the proposed attack. He had made this point in his December 1 letter to fellow Captain James Urquhart, and there had been no additions to the British contingent since then. Captain Fordyce might have brought his experience in defending the bridgehead at the Battle of Brucher Mühl to the attention of the gathered staff. Referring to this battle, he could have made the points that, when supported with reserves, a determined defensive force in a well-placed redoubt might withstand a fifteen-hour cannonade and that Colonel Woodford had prepared just such a combination of fortification and reserves for his defense of Great Bridge.

The Governor and his staff probably addressed the risks associated with the attack in some detail, although it is likely there was considerable deference to the rank and determination of the Commander-in-Chief. As Captain Dalrymple noted in his report of the battle, "we hinted to him as far as Delicacy in our situation would permit, the Absurdity & extravagant Folly of so unnecessary an Attempt—it was in vain."

Regardless of whether or not there was a frank and open assessment of the risks, they were undeniable. There were, in fact, significant and numerous risks. There were high risks associated

Chapter 10: The Battle of Great Bridge   159

with geography, timing, communication, training and the unfavorable correlation of forces.

Risks associated with geography were high because the terrain limited access to the rebel fortifications. Figure 14 is a map of the village of Great Bridge and its environs based on a map said to be the work of Francis Rawdon, a British army officer who was active in America throughout the Revolutionary War, most notably in the Southern campaign of 1780-1781. The most prominent feature

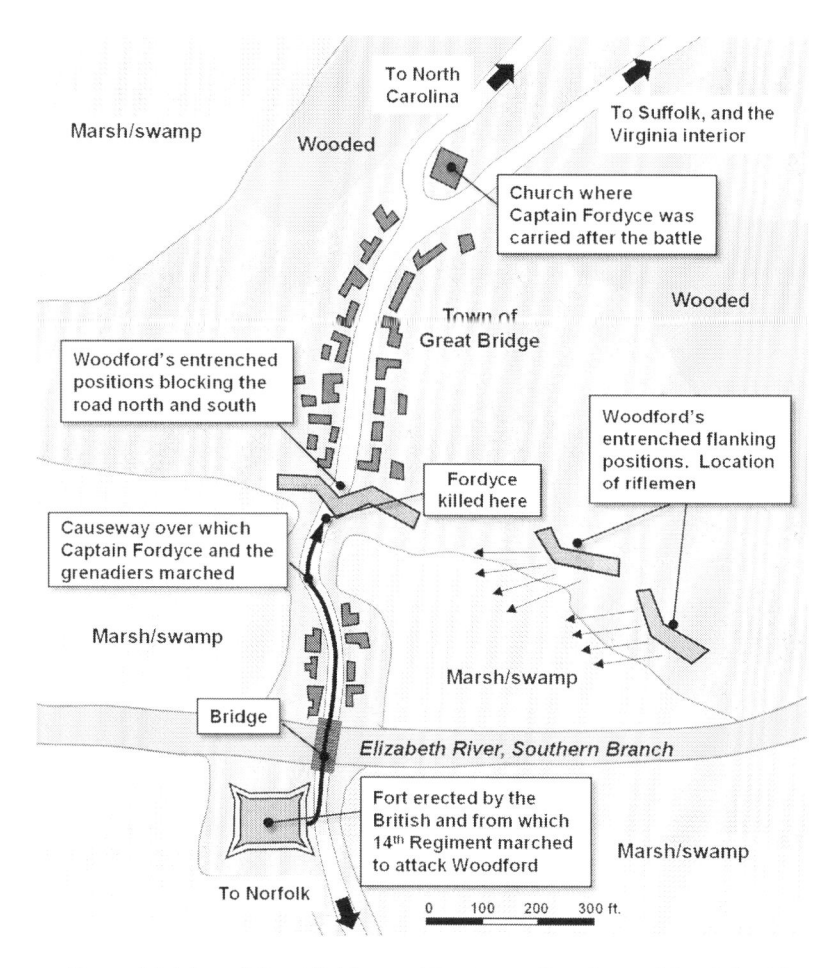

Figure 14. Map of Great Bridge and Environs. Based on a "sketch" said to be the work of Francis Rawdon, 1775. (Authorship of the map is uncertain. Lieutenant John Batut is another candidate.)

of the terrain depicted is the swamp and marsh surrounding the village and Woodford's entrenchments. The swamp precluded the possibility of finding any "detour" to reach the rear of the rebel position. Second in prominence is the width of the causeway between the British fort and the rebels. This causeway was built atop the narrow stretch of high ground running through the swamp, so the causeway itself was narrow. From Norfolk, the causeway was accessed by crossing a bridge over the Southern Branch of the Elizabeth River. This arrangement of bridge, causeway and swamp effectively funneled any force attacking the rebel position into a narrow column where defensive fire could be applied with ferocious intensity. Thus, the terrain features made the risks associated with both elements of Lord Dunmore's attack plan—a flanking maneuver combined with a frontal assault—quite high.

Timing was crucial to the effectiveness of Governor Dunmore's plan. Neither component of his force—the "Regulars, the Volunteers and some recruits" who would sally out of the fort nor the two companies of Negroes who would fall on the enemy's rear—had any chance of success unless the attack was coordinated. This coordination was difficult—risky—for a number of reasons. It was to be done in the dark, that is, at daybreak, the volunteers and Negros lacked training and the irregular, swampy terrain over which the flanking component had to march was bound to make it difficult to accurately time the maneuver.

The risks accruing from inaccurate timing and the attendant lack of coordination of the proposed attack could have been reduced with good communication. Communication on any battlefield is difficult but, on this occasion, it was deliberately restricted because the effectiveness of the attack depended on surprise. To achieve surprise, it would be executed with a minimum of signals. And here again, the need to maneuver in the dark increased the risks of a breakdown in communication, especially since the volunteers and new recruits would not have the visceral communication skills developed with rigorous training and combat experience. Communication would also be limited by a battle plan that put the enemy between the two attacking elements of

Lord Dunmore's force—one in front and the other in the rear of the enemy. This orientation on the battlefield would deny the British forces line-of-sight communication when the battle started.

The difficult terrain coupled with the requirement for exacting coordination, which in turn put exacting requirements on timing and communication, made training a crucial component of the plan. Thus, the risk of the operation was elevated because the men Governor Dunmore recruited for the critical flanking maneuver he planned— "two companies of Negroes" —were very recent additions to his force and they were singularly unaccustomed to weapons and combat. They were former slaves and unlike the farm boys obliged to serve in the Virginia militia and now trained as soldiers in Virginia's state army, the Negroes had not been introduced to firearms and hunting at an early age.[32] On the contrary, they had been denied access to arms deliberately in order to preclude the possibility of the often vaunted but unlikely slave insurrection. Yet despite the need the Negroes might have for more than usual training, they had less. Lord Dunmore was still recruiting Negroes in November.[33] The risk associated with limited training was compounded by the fact the operation planned was an offensive action—the Negroes were to "fall upon the rear of the rebels," that is, attack them. Such an action would require skills in weapons handling, marching, communicating and forming ranks that would have been mastered in training more advanced than the minimal basic training they had received.

Given the plan devised by Governor Dunmore was strictly offensive, the unfavorable correlation of forces posed the primary risk to success. Although superior equipment, training and leadership may act as "force multipliers" on the battlefield, such superiority is limited in a frontal assault against a well-fortified position. In terms of total forces available to the two commanders, the ratio of defenders (Woodford's force) to attackers (Dunmore's force) was about 790 (accounting for the sick and non-combatants) to 174 or about 4.5 to 1. Even if as many as 50 marines and sailors are added to Governor Dunmore's force, the ratio still favors the defenders 3.5 to 1. This is the inverse of the ratio prescribed for an assault in modern combat doctrine. According to modern guidelines, the attacker should outnumber the defender 3 to 1.[34] True, Colonel Woodford had only a portion of his force on the entrenched line at Great Bridge but it is also true the geography of the attack, i.e., the narrow causeway approaching the American position, limited the ability of the British attackers to employ all their force simultaneously.

The correlation of forces related to reinforcements gave the Americans an insurmountable advantage. Woodford could count on almost two regiments of reinforcements and Governor Dunmore had none.

༂

In the final analysis, it seems there were four conclusions Governor Dunmore and his staff drew about their situation in the first days of December that account for the occurrence of the Battle of Great Bridge on the particular day of Saturday, December 9. First, the British planners concluded they would soon be surrounded and "cut off." It was clear to Governor Dunmore and his advisors the Patriot force was growing in number and capability and they also were growing more belligerent. When the Governor fled Williamsburg in June, some moderates still hoped for reconciliation.[35] With the aggressive disarmament campaign in October, the humiliation of Kemp's Landing in November and the proclamation freeing the slaves and imposing an oath of allegiance, hope for reconciliation evaporated. After the engagement at Kemp's, Governor Dunmore told General Howe, he had been informed 1000 rebels "… were on their march to attack us here, or to cut off our provisions."[36] As noted previously, he reported to Lord Dartmouth "… the moment they pass that Bridge, we must expect to be cut off from every supply of Provisions from this Colony."

The fact he was surrounded was compounded by the fact he had been given little encouragement from the military high command or the ministry regarding reinforcements or supply from any other quarter. The naval and army units Governor Dunmore had received had all been sent before the Battle of Bunker Hill. After that, General Gage told the Governor, "I can neither assist you with Men, Money, Arms or Ammunition, for I have them not to Spare."[37] Earlier Lord Dartmouth had reminded Governor Dunmore he was not the only one in a desperate situation. He affirmed General Gage's needs and plans as paramount, averring, "… it is His Majesty's express Command that you do exert every Endeavour & employ every means in your power to aid & support him & Admiral Graves in all such Operations as they may think proper to undertake for carrying the King's Orders into full Execution."[38] A week after Lord Dartmouth promised Dunmore 2000 stand of arms he wrote the Governor to inform him Josiah Martin, Governor of North Carolina, had also requested arms. Regarding Martin's request Dartmouth instructed, "… it will be proper that your Lordship should from the supply now sent you, deliver to Governor Martin's Order, such a portion of them as he shall want, and your Lordship may be able to spare him."[39]

Second, as already noted, Governor Dunmore and some of the officers in his cadre of advisors concluded the King's regular army forces were far superior to any military capability the rebels could field. They underestimated the spirit and capability of the Patriot forces and overestimated of the capability of the government forces—regulars as well as their newly-formed volunteer units. This conclusion rendered the most compelling reason *not* to attack—the unfavorable correlation of forces—moot, or of less consequence than prudence would warrant.

Regarding the correlation of forces, it is likely Governor Dunmore was confident of his qualitative superiority but appreciated its limits. In his correspondence with Lord Dartmouth after the battle, he was explicit his decision to attack was influenced by intelligence of rebel reinforcements on the way from Williamsburg and North Carolina.[40] The intelligence was accurate. Three days after the battle Colonel Woodford reported to the Virginia Convention, "Major Eppes arrived here this evening with his party, and Colonel Howe with three hundred and forty of the Carolina regulars."[41] As noted previously, Major Eppes was Major Francis Eppes in command of three companies of the 1st Virginia Regiment. Under these circumstances, even if Governor Dunmore were confident of his qualitative advantage, he would have wanted to apply it before the rebels increased their quantitative advantage beyond the over four-to-one they already had in the field. Concluding reinforcements were no more than hours away was then the third factor inciting the attack on December 9.

Finally, there is evidence Colonel Woodford and his staff organized a deception that could have influenced the timing of Governor Dunmore's attack. In reports to the Virginia Convention after the battle, Woodford includes intelligence the Governor had been tricked into believing there were no more than 300 poorly-armed rebels manning the Patriot fortifications. Woodford notes this intelligence was supplied by his prisoner, Lieutenant Batut of the 14th Regiment, so it seems credible. Captains George Johnston and Richard Kidder Meade, both of the 2nd Virginia Regiment, also mentioned the ruse in their after-action reports as did one of Lord Dunmore's volunteers and the author of a "Letter from Northampton County" who reported on the battle.[42]

Colonel Woodford does not take credit for the deception. And although he notes the false information was supplied by a servant of Major Thomas Marshall, whose arranged "desertion" from Lieutenant Colonel Charles Scott's party was part of the plot, there is no record of either Marshall or Scott planning the deception. Planned or not, Lieutenant Batut reported it and he seemed to think it influenced his commander. If indeed Governor Dunmore had received and believed such intelligence, he could have concluded the ratio of defenders to attackers implicated—less than 2 to 1—was in his favor. He could have concluded such a ratio greatly increased his probability of success since, as already noted, he seemed to be convinced his attacking force was superior in every respect except numbers.

෴

Given the risks associated with Governor Dunmore's plan, its failure has been relegated to the battle lore of foregone conclusions. That is, there could have been only one outcome and it was the outcome which occurred. The British diversion—poorly planned and risky for all the reasons just noted—failed, enabling Colonel Woodford to concentrate his force—which was actually rather small at the point of contact—on the funneled frontal assault and defeat it without losing a man.

All the accounts of the battle seem to adopt this perspective regarding the failed assault to a greater or lesser extent. Synopses of many of the eyewitness and early reports of the battle are presented in the Appendix. There are inconsistencies in the various accounts of the battle that suggest some of the earliest reporting included second-hand details and the histories and memoirs written after the fact were affected accordingly. That said, the fundamentals of the battle were reported consistently.

It seems Governor Dunmore made the final decision to attack the evening of December 8 or in the early morning hours of December 9, the day of the battle. This decision was made at Norfolk and most of the regulars were at Norfolk with Captain Leslie at the time. Once the attack was ordered, this contingent, which would have included Captain Fordyce and his company of grenadiers, marched to the British fort at Great Bridge, ten miles distant, arriving about 4:00 AM.

According to the eyewitness and other contemporary reporters, the battle began at daybreak with the regulars of the 14th Regiment marching out of the British fort and across the bridge over the Southern Branch of the Elizabeth River. To prevent Patriot access to the fort, the wood planks comprising the bed of the bridge had been removed and these had to be replaced. Lieutenant Batut led an advance party. It was probably this group that relaid the planks on the bridge and encountered the rebel sentries, one of whom was identified in later accounts of the battle as William "Billy" Flora, a free Negro who reportedly distinguished himself by repeatedly firing on the advance party in this early stage of the engagement.[43] Mr. Flora would go on to serve in the Continental Army for three years.[44]

The attack on Woodford's entrenchment consisted of about 120 men, all regulars, commanded by Captains Fordyce and Dalrymple. Fordyce was in the van with the company of grenadiers. Since they were obliged to march over the narrow causeway through what had been the village of Great Bridge, the British soldiers marched in ranks said to be no more than six men abreast. Given there were 120 soldiers in the attack, such a restriction would mean there were about twenty ranks marching in a column at Colonel Woodford's entrenchments. Marching in close order—one pace apart, or about 36 inches—the ranks would have formed a column about sixty feet long. This would have been the maximum extent of the column. By some accounts, the number of soldiers in Fordyce's main attack numbered only 60. With this number of troops, the column would have been about thirty feet long. Captain Fordyce would have been leading from the head of the column. Although none of the accounts of the attack mention drums and fifes, these resources were available.

To begin the attack, a detachment of gunners from Captain Squire's *Otter* started firing two cannon at the entrenchments. These cannon were mounted near the British fort, about 100 yards from Woodford's position.

The attack was a surprise in that no more than sixty men of Woodford's 2nd Virginia Regiment were manning the barricade when the firing commenced. The battle was of short duration—no more than 45 minutes—but very intense. The circumstances of the attack put the British at a great disadvantage. Their diversionary attack never occurred. While approaching on the narrow causeway, the main Patriot force could fire directly at them. At the same time, another Patriot element enfiladed their ranks from entrenchments to the right and rear of their column.

Evidently the British column advanced with resolution, discipline and order and despite the insurmountable disadvantages, some of the force, including Captain Fordyce, made it to the entrenchments. At his death, the attack ended, and the broken column retreated back across the causeway and bridge to their fort. British casualties were high while only one man of Woodford's force was shot, resulting in a minor hand wound. It was the consensus of those reporting on the British attack at the time and in later histories that it was ill conceived and ill advised.

༄

The harshest critics were British officers directly involved in the attack. They often credited the Patriot force with considerably larger numbers than were actually brought to bear at the battle. A midshipman from the *Otter* who was at the battle asked the rhetorical question, "But how can it be supposed, that with 200 men we could force a strong intrenchment, defended by at least 2000? yet this was attempted, and we marched up to their works with the intrepedity of lions."[45] In the same vein but with some difference in the number of forces involved, a "Gentleman" aboard the ship *William* asked, "The Rebels were posted in great strength, 1100 in number; so what could our small party do, upwards of four to one against them, and strongly entrenched?"[46] But the criticisms of the British officers addressed more than the unfavorable correlation of forces. They were appalled with a plan of attack that did not account for any of the risks involved.

By far the most vehement denunciation of the plan was penned in a letter to one of Charles' relatives, Patrick McDouall-Crichton, the 6th Earl of Dumfries, a third cousin. The author of the letter was another relative (third cousin once removed) and comrade-in-arms, Captain John Dalrymple of the 14th Regiment. It seems Captain Dalrymple and Captain Fordyce were very close friends. He opens his letter to Lord Dumfries with the "melancholy" news of "having lost a Friend, an Acquaintance of yours, the most exemplary man I ever knew. —Poor Chas Fordyce—he died as he lived—his conduct as a Soldier was equal to his Courage. I had the most perfect friendship for him."

Regarding the situation at Great Bridge and the battle which unfolded, Captain Dalrymple explained to the Earl with unapologetic sarcasm,

> Our only hope was therefore in a little Wooden Fort, which we immediately erected, at a pass called the Great Bridge, twenty miles from Norfolk, the only inlet by land from the rest of the colony to those two Counties, & which we defended for many Days against all their Effort & Numbers, and might with some little Precautions have done so still; but as they could not force us, His Excellency (& certainly he excels all Men as a General) wisely proposed to us, to pass the Bridge & dislodge them from their Entrenchments; we hinted to him as far as Delicacy in our situation would permit, the Absurdity & extravagant Folly of so unnecessary an Attempt—it was in vain.

Dalrymple was obviously incensed at the loss of his friend, but it seems his loss did not seem to cloud his recollection of the battle, which he also provided his correspondent, noting,

> We passed the Bridge exposed to the Enemy, drove in their Out-Posts and advanced towards their Entrenchments, over a narrow Causeway which led from the Bridge through a Morass at the End of which they were securely posted. The approach to it was so narrow we were obliged to march up by files, & by a Curve in the Causeway & Breastworks on the opposite Side of the Morass on our Right, we were flank'd & our Rear almost equally exposed as our Front: in less than ten Minutes that we were exposed to the Enemy's Fire, upwards of Seventy of our little Detachment were killed & wounded.[47]

This account is dramatic but quite consistent with that of Mr. William Eddis, one of His Majesty's Customs Surveyors based in Annapolis, Maryland. Not a military officer and not in the battle, it is likely Mr. Eddis received his information on the battle second hand—he cites "Letters from Virginia"—but whatever the source, his account of the battle corroborates Dalrymple's. According to Mr. Eddis,

> Both parties fortified themselves within cannon shot of each other; and as a narrow causeway lay between them, which must necessarily be passed previous to an attack, they appeared to be mutually secured from any danger of surprise.
>
> Thus circumstanced, they continued inactive several days, till, at length, a design was formed of surprising the American troops in their intrenchments. Captain Fordyce, a very gallant officer, at the head of about sixty grenadiers, led the attack: they passed the causeway with the utmost intrepidity, and with fixed bayonets rushed on an enemy, who were properly prepared for their reception; for Captain Fordyce's party were not only exposed, naked, to a heavy fire in front, but were enfiladed from another part of the works. The brave leader, with several of his men, fell; the lieutenant, with the residue, all of whom were severely wounded, were taken prisoners.[48]

Mr. Eddis forbears calling the plan an "Absurdity & extravagant Folly," but his description is, in effect, an appeal for an answer to the question asked by the midshipman from the *Otter*, "But how can it be supposed, that with 200 men we could force a strong intrenchment?"

Another reporter, this one from Northampton County, Virginia, told his correspondent Lord Dunmore sent all his regulars,

> ...with orders to storm the Provincial entrenchments in the morning by day break; the regulars accordingly began a most furious attack upon the only part of the breast work which was accessible, but the works were so constructed, that when they attacked this point, they were flanked by part of the Provincial lines—the causeway over which they were obliged to march, admitted only a few men abreast, and those were cut off as fast as they approached.

This reporter, like Mr. Eddis, made no explicit criticism of the plan but he did include in his report, "It seems Capt. Leslie, who commands the regulars, did absolutely refuse to act any more on shore, 'till he could be better supported, as he had already sacrificed many of his men in so desperate a service."[49] In the same vein, Virginia's Committee of Safety sent the Virginia Congressional delegation a report of the battle that included unattributed intelligence Captain Leslie "declared no more of his troops should be sacrificed to whims."[50]

CHAPTER 11: TRIBUTES

Other than officers Captain Charles Fordyce, Lieutenant William Napier and Lieutenant Peter Henry Leslie, the British soldiers who gave their lives at Great Bridge—the ultimate sacrifice—are unknown. Lord Dunmore, in his account of the battle to Lord Dartmouth of December 13, 1775, summarized the casualties as: "three Officers killed and one Wounded, who was made a prisoner, 14 Privates were killed and 43 Wounded."[1] In his report to the Virginia Convention of December 10, 1775, Colonel Woodford notes, "We buried 12, besides the captain (him with all the military honours due to his rank) and have prisoners lieutenant [John] Batut, and 16 privates; all wounded."[2] Woodford also noted he had two wounded Negro prisoners, James Anderson, wounded "in the forearm, Bone shattered & flesh much torn," and Caesar, wounded "in the Thigh by a Ball, & 5 Shot, one lodged."[3] It is likely these men were from the Ethiopian Regiment.

Although the names of the fourteen privates killed are unknown, Colonel Woodford did identify the sixteen British prisoners in a December 10 letter to the Virginia Convention. The men and the wounds they received are listed in Table 9.

Five of the men listed in Table 9, Samuel Hale [Heal], Francis Jackson, William Stokes, John Stokes and William Unwin, had served in Captain Fordyce's grenadier company at least since the muster taken in Boston in 1769 and most likely before then. Four of the men, Richard Abbot, Francis Jackson, William Unwin and Peter Wyatt (possibly Mayett), were still prisoners of war a year later. In October 1776, they petitioned the Virginia Assembly for "necessary clothing," praying the House "in their wonted lenity and tenderness" would grant them "such supplies of necessary clothing as shall be judged reasonable."[4]

One man in the list, Robert Calder, held the rank of corporal. It is possible this is the soldier to whom Captain Dalrymple referred in his letter to Lord Dumfries when he observed,

The Rebels behaved with the greatest Humanity, ceasing to fire when we were retreating with the wounded, as also to fifteen that fell into their Hands; they have since informed us that eight of them are dead, but that they have still some Hopes of a Corporal who has seventeen balls through him.

Table 9. Enlisted Men of the 14th Regiment Wounded at Great Bridge, December 9, 1775.[5]

NAME	WOUNDS
Abbot, Richard	Both Thighs, one with Ball lodged & bone Shattered, the other passed thro', & no fracture
Allen, James	Shoulder & foot, no Ball lodged, no Fracture
Calder, Robert, Cpl.	Thigh, Ball lodged & Bone Shattered
Chalmers, William	Leg & Knee Ball lodged in the Leg, no Fracture
Chislet, Stephen	Thigh, passed thro' Bone Fractured
Drisson, Thomas	Leg & Knee, passed thro', Bone much Shattered
Hale, Samuel	Shoulder, Side, both Hands with fractures, no Balls lodged
Jackson, Francis	Thigh wth. two Balls Both passed thro' Bone shattered
Reeder, George	Breast & Arms, Ball lodged in his Breast, judged mortal
Stokes, John	Breast & Thigh, Balls passed thro' each
Stokes, William	Thigh, Ball passed thro' without Fracture
Tilley, George	Both Thighs, in 5 Places, one Ball lodged, no fracture
Unwin, William	Forearm, Ball passed thro', Bone shattered
Villis, Edward	Thigh, Arm and Belly, Ball lodged in Bowels, judged Mortal
Windsor, Samuel	Thigh, no Ball lodged, no Fracture
Wyatt, Peter	One Side of Breast, Ball passed thro'

In his letters to the Virginia Convention, Colonel Woodford notes "most of their dead and wounded, with two pieces of cannon, were carried off under cover of their guns from the fort."[6] Evidently the two slain lieutenants, William Napier and Peter Henry Leslie, were among those taken from the causeway back to the fort. Based on details in General Howe's announcement of

Lieutenant Napier's replacement in his General Orders of March 9, 1776, it seems he died of his wounds on December 11.[7]

William Napier first appears in the *Army Commission Book for 1763-1767* as a 2nd lieutenant in the 21st Regiment of Foot with a date-of-rank of October 18, 1763. That same year, on December 1, he is listed again, this time as an ensign in the 14th Regiment of Foot commanded by Major General Charles Jefferyes.[8] His first appearance in the 14th Regiment is as an ensign in the *Army List* of 1765. In that *List*, his army date-of-rank as a 2nd lieutenant is noted as October 18, 1763. It is likely William was between sixteen and eighteen years old when he was commissioned in 1763. If so, his birth year would have been between 1745 and 1747.

In the index of the 1765 *Army List*, William is listed as William Napier Jun. [junior] of the 14th Regiment, and Lieutenant Colonel William Napier of the 14th Regiment is listed as William Napier Ser [i.e., senior].[9] However, these index entries should not be considered proof these two Napiers are related as father and son.

The elder William Napier—Lieutenant Colonel William Napier—was commissioned a 1st lieutenant in John Huske's 23rd Regiment of Foot (Royal Welsh Fusiliers) on December 9, 1745.[10] He could have been old enough—perhaps 20 to 25—to be married and have a child at this time. Since 1745-1747 is the estimated birth year range of the younger Napier, these men could be father and son if Lieutenant Colonel Napier had married in 1745. However, the only marriage recorded for Lieutenant Colonel Napier is that of July 9, 1764 when he married Miss Jean Milliken.[11] By this time, the younger William Napier was already a 2nd lieutenant in the 21st Foot. If he were the son of Lieutenant Colonel Napier, it would have been by an earlier marriage.

William Napier (the younger) was an ensign in the 14th Regiment in 1765, so it is likely he sailed with the regiment to Nova Scotia in 1766. And again, based on the possibility he was commissioned as a teenager, he could have been a teenager on this first deployment. He was with the regiment when it deployed to Boston since he is listed as the ensign in Captain William Blackett's company in the April 24, 1769 muster taken there. He was promoted to lieutenant on September 16, 1771 while the regiment was still in Boston but at Castle William.[12] In the muster of May 15, 1772, taken just before the regiment left Boston for St. Vincent, he was listed as a lieutenant in Blackett's company.[13]

After the deployment to St. Vincent, Captain Blackett and his company were deployed to New Providence while the rest of the 14th was deployed to St. Augustine. Since William had been the lieutenant in Blackett's company in Boston and St. Vincent, it is reasonable to assume he was Blackett's lieutenant when the company deployed to New Providence. But it seems this was not the case. Captain Blackett's lieutenant at New Providence was Daniel Mattear, a fact established by Blackett's report of Lieutenant Mattear's death at New Providence on September 12, 1773.[14] Furthermore, two years later, in September 1775, when Blackett's contingent from New Providence arrived in Virginia, Lieutenant Napier was not with them. He arrived a month later, on October 20, with Captain Fordyce and the second detachment of the 14th Regiment from St. Augustine. These circumstances support the conclusion Lieutenant Napier was deployed to St. Augustine after the action in St. Vincent and he remained in St. Augustine until deployed to Virginia.

Lieutenant Napier was not a soldier of renown. Other than his meritorious service at Great Bridge, he seems to have served with diligence but without fanfare. He was made aware of the contentiousness and determination of the Yankee Patriots during his deployment to Boston. He and the rest of the 14th Regiment were indirectly involved in the Boston Massacre of March 5, 1770. On the evening of that engagement, the 14th had been called to arms and Lieutenant Napier found himself in the thick of the mob rushing to and from the scene of the shooting. He described the frenzy of that evening in a deposition he made for the trial of the soldiers of the 29th Regiment who had actually fired on the mob. He told the court, he "was much abused and threatened by the townspeople." He added he took decisive action, noting, "I drew my sword to defend myself." He also noted he defended his fellow officers when he "observed Ensign Hallwood lying on his back, and a man just going to strike him. I run up and made a cut at him with my sword, upon which they moved off."[15]

Whether or not Ensign (at the time) Napier used appropriate force on that occasion may be debated but given the alarming and threatening situation in which this young officer found himself, it seems his instincts and training as a soldier were sound. He evaluated the situation, maintained his post, defended himself, was alert to the threats to his comrades, defended them and was instrumental in ending the melee. It is likely he performed as this kind of soldier on December 9, 1775. This seems to be the opinion of Colonel Woodford who included him among "the brave fellows" who fell with Captain Fordyce, and who, like Fordyce, "behaved like heroes."[16]

ಲ

The other lieutenant killed at the Battle of Great Bridge was Peter Henry Leslie. Lieutenant Leslie was born in Dublin, Ireland on April 6, 1755. Given this birth date, he was twenty years old on December 9, 1775, so he was one of the youngest soldiers at the battle.* Peter's father was the Reverend Henry Leslie, L.L.D. of Ballybay, in the county of Monaghan. At the time of Peter's birth, Rev. Leslie was rector of Tandragee, in Armagh. Rev. Leslie was born October 23, 1719 and one of his younger brothers was Samuel Leslie, the senior captain in the 14th Regiment in Virginia. So Captain Leslie was Peter's paternal uncle. Peter's mother was Catherine Meredyth, daughter of the Very Reverend Charles Meredyth, dean of Meath. Peter was the oldest of three children. His younger brother was Charles Albert Leslie and his youngest sibling was his sister, Catherine Letitia Leslie.[17]

Peter purchased a commission as an ensign in the 14th Regiment on August 12, 1771.[18] At the time, his uncle, Samuel Leslie, was third in the succession of captains in the regiment. When he was commissioned most of the regiment was in Boston Harbor at Castle William. Given his birthdate, he would have been sixteen years old when he joined the 14th in 1771.

Peter is listed on the muster roll taken at Castle William on May 15, 1772 as the ensign in Captain Brabazon O'Hara's Company,

---

* At sixteen years old, Ensign James Lindsay was probably the youngest soldier on the field. More of his *curricula vitae* are presented in the Epilogue.

but the listing includes the note "by the King's leave." This means Peter was not with his company at this time, a point Captain O'Hara makes explicitly in another note where he lists the ensign as not present.[19] It so happens Peter's uncle, Captain Samuel Leslie, was also on the King's leave when this muster was taken. One explanation for the absence of both Captain Leslie and his nephew at this time is that they were back home in Ireland or England making last-minute preparations for the young Ensign Leslie—now just seventeen years old—to join his regiment in the actual theater of military operations in North America. This possibility, that both Captain Leslie and his nephew were in Britain at this time, is supported to some extent by the announcement of Captain Leslie's August 17, 1772 arrival in Boston on board a ship from England.[20] No mention is made of Ensign Leslie in this announcement but if the speculation that Captain Leslie was preparing his nephew for this first deployment is correct, then his escorting his nephew on the voyage to America could have been a part of those preparations.

The 14th Regiment sailed from Boston for St. Vincent on July 27, 1772 so if Ensign Leslie did not arrive with his uncle until August 17, 1772, he was not included in the initial cadre of the regiment deployed to St. Vincent.

The campaign in St. Vincent was rather short—Colonel Dalrymple concluded peace negations in February of 1773, about six months after the 14th arrived. Given this circumstance, it is possible Peter never did sail to join the 14th in St. Vincent if he missed the transports that departed July 27. Furthermore, the company commander to whom Ensign Leslie had been assigned, Captain Brabazon O'Hara, was one of the first casualties of the campaign against the Caribs. He died of a fever at St. Vincent on October 5, 1772.[21] O'Hara's death was reported in Boston on November 16,[22] so if Peter had not sailed to join the regiment by then, this news might have delayed his departure until he could join the regiment at their next duty station, St. Augustine.

On December 16, 1773—after the 14th had redeployed from St. Vincent to St. Augustine and New Providence, eighteen-year-old Peter was promoted to lieutenant in the 14th Regiment, taking the place of Lieutenant Henry Hallwood.[23] Hallwood died of disease in New Providence on September 22, 1773. In the May 15, 1772 muster at Castle William, Hallwood had been listed as the ensign in Lieutenant Colonel Dalrymple's company. He had been promoted to lieutenant on March 22, 1773 to take the place of Edward Gower of Major Jonathan Furlong's company. Gower died in St. Vincent as the result of an accident.[24]

Lieutenant Hallwood was assigned to Captain William Blackett's detachment of the 14th Regiment at New Providence when he died.[25] He was one of the two subalterns in the company. The other was Lieutenant Daniel Mattear. Since the normal compliment of subalterns in a company was two, and Captain Blackett had two, it is unlikely Peter was posted to New Providence with Captain Blackett's initial detachment. In fact, based on the way the various detachments of the 14th arrived in Virginia when called to that post in 1775, it seems Lieutenant Leslie was in St. Augustine while Blackett was in New Providence. Lieutenant Leslie was with the first detachment to arrive in Virginia, that commanded by his uncle and this detachment came directly from St. Augustine. Furthermore, a comparison of the officers listed in Captain Leslie's detachment—a captain and two lieutenants[26]— with the officers listed in a muster of the combined detachments after Captain Blackett arrived—two captains, two lieutenants and one ensign[27]—suggests the only officers in Blackett's detachment were Captain Blackett himself and an ensign. These lists provide a strong case Lieutenant Leslie was stationed in St. Augustine and never went to New Providence.

If Peter's introduction to overseas duty at a military station occurred in St. Augustine, it would have been an introduction similar to that experienced by the soldiers who landed in Halifax in 1766. That is, the locals were not hostile—they supported the British administration. The only threat would have been the Native Americans. And these natives were at peace with the British despite alarming accounts to the contrary of fighting in the frontier regions of neighboring Georgia.

At St. Augustine, it is probable Peter—like the rest of his regiment—would have been exasperated by the steady stream of news recounting what they must have considered insults and offenses committed by the Patriots, especially those in Boston and Virginia. These reports might have incited in him the kind of indignation voiced by the Governor of Virginia who was eager to "reduce the whole of his Southern part of His Majesty's Continent to a proper State of Submission"[28] when he arrived at that post in 1775.

In the muster roll of August 1, 1775, Major Furlong lists the number of officers in Virginia as two captains, two lieutenants and one ensign.[29] Most likely these officers were Captains Samuel Leslie and William Blackett, Lieutenants Peter Leslie and John Batut and Ensign Thomas Wools. Major Furlong's muster was made at St. Augustine and it was based on the orders for Leslie's and Blackett's troops to sail for Virginia. In the muster these troops are listed as "On Command." Captain Blackett was still *en route* to Virginia with his detachment on August 1 but since Major Furlong was in St. Augustine, he could not have known whether either Leslie or Blackett had actually landed in Virginia.

Peter saw action, possibly his first in the army, within weeks of his arrival in Virginia. On October 17, a detachment of soldiers, marines and seamen made a foray to Kemp's Landing in search of arms. The detachment included Peter, Captains Leslie and Cooper, Lieutenants Batut and Laurie, Ensigns Wools, Boyes, Ogle, and Lindsay, three Sergeants, and seventy rank and file of the 14th Regiment, twenty marines and ten or twelve seamen. They found and destroyed a cache of small arms and returned to their shipping the next day, "without interruption."[30] Governor Dunmore took part in this raid and two others performed a few days later. In his account of the actions to Lord Dartmouth, he noted, "upon all these occasions both Officers and Soldiers behaved with that order and Spirit that does them honor."[31]

On November 30, Governor Dunmore reported to General Howe he had taken "our little corps" and "hearing that a body, between 2 and 300, of our rebels were within about ten miles of us, we determined to beat up their quarters."[32] This was the Battle of Kemp's Landing, an action distinct from the earlier raids at that location. Since the little corps in question was the 14th Regiment, it is likely Peter participated in this engagement as well. So in the course of two months Lieutenant Leslie had been involved in several patrols and these included encounters where shots were fired and men were killed, wounded and taken prisoner.

Like his comrade-in-arms, Lieutenant Napier, Peter was not a soldier of renown. As noted previously, at twenty years old, he was one of the youngest and least experienced officers on the battlefield at Great Bridge. One might be tempted to believe he received some preferential treatment in his military assignments because he was the nephew of the commander of the detachment of the 14th Regiment in Virginia. One might also be tempted to surmise his status as the eldest son of a well-respected family could have imbued him with an unseemly sense of entitlement. But these influences, actual and speculated, which might have affected Lieutenant Leslie's behavior as a man and a soldier—might have caused him to stay behind in the stockade, might have caused him to panic and run, might have caused him to stop and find shelter—were proven inconsequential by his actual behavior on the causeway at Great Bridge on December 9. As already noted, Colonel Woodford told the Virginia Convention all the British soldiers "behaved like heroes" and Major Spotswood of Woodford's regiment echoed this sentiment in a letter to a friend in Williamsburg observing of the King's troops they behaved "like true-born Englishmen."[33]

☙

Recognition of the spirit and heroism of the British troops at the Battle of Great Bridge is common to almost every account of the battle. Captain John Dalrymple provides a clue as to why this is so in his account to the Earl of Dumfries. He observed of the rebels, "They were astonished at Men marching up with such Courage, or rather Madness, to certain Death."[34] And nowhere is this astonishment more pronounced than in the tributes to one particular individual in the King's service on this occasion, Captain Charles Fordyce. Without exception, glowing tributes to Captain Fordyce are included in every complete account of the battle.

The Battle of Great Bridge was of genuine strategic significance, a claim which will be defended in more detail in the next chapter. But it is easy to make the case that Captain Fordyce is the individual who made the battle significant; the individual who was the heart and soul of the fight. No doubt Captain Fordyce would insist on sharing this distinction with two groups of soldiers at the battle, namely the true-born Englishmen on the causeway with him and the sixty Virginians behind the earthworks under attack, few of whom had ever seen a regular British soldier and many of whom had never fired a musket in anger. But as an individual, Captain Fordyce is preeminent.

With fourteen years of active duty service, having fought in the large-scale battles in Germany and the guerrilla war in St. Vincent, having served as town major in Halifax and brigade major in Boston and having served as commander of the regiment in St. Augustine, there is little doubt Captain Fordyce was the most experienced soldier on the field at Great Bridge. It is likely Charles was well acquainted with most of the grenadier company he led across the causeway the morning of December 9. As noted earlier, five of the men wounded had served in Charles' company of the 14th Regiment for at least six years—since the muster roll was taken in Boston in 1769. Such continuity of service is not, in itself, a testament the rank and file admired or respected their commander. However, Captain Fordyce's efforts to resolve the disputes between the refractory citizens of Boston and his soldiers in their favor surely encouraged an appreciation of their commander. Already noted is the way both American and British officers respected Charles' military capabilities. So even before the definitive display of courage, determination and heroism at Great Bridge, Charles Fordyce had distinguished himself as a man and a soldier.

Given Charles was a man of consistently good character, the tributes paid after his death at Great Bridge do not come as a surprise nor is there any reservation or skepticism these tributes might have been made as a courtesy to a man who simply died a remarkable death due to a tragic tactical blunder. The tributes were sincere and accurate assessments of a man who, as Captain Dalrymple observed, "… died as he lived."

The validity of this observation—and the fact it was a compliment—was affirmed in the testimonies of other officers and civilians who engaged Captain Fordyce at this time. Just before he left St. Augustine, two of his comrades-in-arms wrote letters wherein his attributes as an officer and a gentleman were commended either explicitly or insinuated. On October 4, while Captain Fordyce and his detachment waited for the fair winds that would set them on their way from St. Augustine to Virginia, Lieutenant Alexander Ross, still at the garrison in St. Augustine, wrote a letter to Captain John Stanton who had been deployed to Halifax, Nova Scotia with a detachment of the 14th Regiment. The letter dealt with bills Captain Stanton was obliged to pay and, in particular, with what seems to have been a £20 debt Stanton owed Captain Fordyce, possibly for payments Fordyce made to new recruits on Stanton's behalf. Regarding that debt, Lieutenant Ross informed Captain Stanton, "I offered Captain Fordyce the twenty pounds you desired me to pay him, but he would not accept of it."[35] Based on Lieutenant Ross' brief statement it is not possible to tell whether or not this was a noble gesture on the part of Captain Fordyce, but it does suggest he was providing his friend some support and encouragement. From such a gesture—which was certainly generous—one may insinuate Captain Fordyce had a healthy perspective concerning duty, money and friends.

Frederick Mulcaster of the Royal Engineers was more explicit regarding Fordyce's virtues in a letter he wrote to General James Grant—former Governor of East Florida—and entrusted to Charles for delivery. Mulcaster wrote from St. Augustine on September 29, 1775 and provided this introduction of his emissary.

> This letter is given to the care of Captain Charles Fordyce, of the Fourteenth Regiment. He has been here about two years and a half; he goes now to Virginia with the detachment; his own Company of Grenadiers is part of it. He has for these two years past been one of a cabinet junto, consisting of the Padre [John Forbes[36]] and myself, where the state of the Province and its welfare has been duly considered. He of course is well acquainted

with the characters, and had he been here in your time, I am confident would have been a frequent guest in the Print room [probably a parlor or gallery for meeting and relaxing], and a no small sharer of the wicked bottle. When your friend General [Alexander] McKay [MacKay] was at Boston, he was his Brigade-Major. I have often mentioned to you the *propreté* [order, cleanliness] of this Regiment, for which it is not a little indebted to this gentleman. ... As he is the particular friend of the parson and myself, I forbear to say so much as I wish and he deserves; but I may venture to assert, that should you ever meet, you will find in him that uprightness, honour, and sincerity, which constitute the character of a worthy man, and one you will be much pleased with.[37]

Charles's character as an officer and a gentleman was also marked by a Scottish engineer who evidently met him in connection with the Battle of Kemp's Landing in November. The engineer was Thomas McKnight, brother of Reverend James McKnight, still living in Scotland. After the Battle of Great Bridge, Thomas wrote his brother with an account of the action and informed him, "Slain was a Charles Fordyce Captain of Grenadeers [sic] a Gentleman exceedingly regretted by all who knew him." Of his personal relationship with Charles he added, "I had a particular affection for him which commenced at the affair at Kemps."[38]

Mrs. Maxwell, who hosted Charles at her home in Norfolk, also developed an appreciation of his character as a soldier as well as a gentleman. In her *Memoir* she noted Governor Dunmore's plan was a foolhardy undertaking and remarked that, although Captain Fordyce "saw at once the folly and rashness of the order," he was "too brave a man and too good a soldier to flinch from any duty."[39]

The American commander at Great Bridge, Colonel William Woodford of the 2nd Virginia Regiment, paid tribute to the British soldiers in the report he sent to the Virginia Convention the day of the battle. In that report he noted, "… none marched up but his Majesty's soldiers, who behaved like Englishmen." The next day he wrote the Convention with more details. In this second report, he singled out Captain Fordyce for his "coolness and bravery." In another dispatch of a day later, Woodford told the Convention, "As the Captain was a gallant and brave officer, I promised to inter him with all the military honours [sic] due to his great merit."[40]

Another American officer, Captain George Johnston of the 2nd Virginia, was impressed with the way the "brave Captain Fordyce" rallied his men at "every hazard" and "brought them up to the very muzzles of our Guns."[41] Captain Richard Kidder Meade, also of the 2nd Virginia, was impressed with the same heroic leadership. In his description of the battle, he noted the British troops "fell back a little" when the Americans at the breastwork opened fire, "but soon rallied, by the vast bravery of Capt. Fordyce, who marched with many bullets through him, within twenty yards of the breastwork, before he fell."[42] An unidentified correspondent for the *Virginia Gazette* echoed Johnston and Meade in a report filed on December 14. According to that account, "the enemy had crossed the bridge … and attacked our guard in the breastwork. Our men returned the fire, and threw them into some confusion, but they were instantly rallied by a Captain Fordyce, and advanced along the causeway with great resolution, keeping up a constant and heavy fire as they approached."[43]

Governor Dunmore paid his tribute in a letter he wrote Secretary Dartmouth four days after the battle. In that letter he told Lord Dartmouth, "Captain Fordyce's bravery and good conduct (who fell with his hand on the breast work) would do honor to any Corps of any Country, His loss is most Sincerely lamented by all who knew him."[44]

One of the participants in the battle was a midshipman from the *Otter*. He was probably part of the naval detachment Captain Squire of the *Otter* sent to support the attack with two cannon from his ship. In a letter he wrote describing the battle he called Charles "the gallant Captain Fordyce," and praised all the men who "fell fighting for their King and Country" for their "unparalleled courage."[45]

Captain John Dalrymple, who fought alongside Charles at the battle, offered the most comprehensive of all the tributes to his friend, relation and comrade-in-arms. In his letter to Lord Dumfries he declared,

> A truer man, a finer fellow (in the right meaning of the words) or completer Officer never lived. His Majesty could not have lost a braver or more excellent Officer, nor one whose loss could be more severely felt by his Corps, & all who knew him; & whose Character as a Soldier & Gentlemen (in their estimation) was as perfect as the World can produce. He fell covered with 11 wounds.

The Battle of Great Bridge was reported in considerable detail in numerous newspapers published in Great Britain. The letters of Major Alexander Spotswood and Colonel Woodford, which provided the information upon which many other later accounts were based, were published in *The Edinburgh Advertiser*, *Derby Mercury*, *Norfolk Chronicle*, *Stamford Mercury*, *Hibernian Journal*, *Caledonian Mercury* and the 1776 edition of the *Scots Magazine*.[46] Besides these rather extensive accounts, summary accounts—usually based on one of Woodford's letters or Spotswood's letter—were published in at least nine other British newspapers.[47] All these accounts mention the death of Captain Fordyce and those that include Colonel Woodford's letter of December 10 repeat his assessment of Fordyce's coolness and bravery.

Such coverage of the extraordinary courage and poise of an army captain—especially coverage provided by the opposing commander and coverage of a failed attack—was rare. It must have elevated Charles in the esteem of his countrymen and, given his otherwise modest rank and renown, it must have prompted questions about his history and his family. In many such instances, these questions would have been answered in an obituary and at least two obituaries for Charles were published in British newspapers.

The obituaries are brief, but they honor the fallen warrior and provide answers to some of the questions regarding his history and family. The short notice in the paper published in his hometown, *The Edinburgh Advertiser*, addresses family. The two sentences of the tribute are,

Capt. Charles Fordyce, who is killed in Virginia by the provincials, was brother to Mr. Fordyce of Ayton, and nephew to the late General Sir John Whiteford. He was much esteemed as an officer and a man.[48]

This obituary seems to be rather perfunctory, especially since Charles' brother—mentioned in the obituary—was a notable in Edinburgh and news of the exploits of a family member would bolster reputations. As noted in the chapter "Charles Fordyce's Family," John Fordyce—the brother named as Mr. Fordyce of Ayton—was Receiver General of the Land Tax in Scotland. Captain Dalrymple, in his letter to Lord Dumfries announcing Charles' death, provides an item of anecdotal evidence which supports a hypothesis the brevity and dispassion of this announcement could be due to an estrangement between the brothers. In his letter, Dalrymple told Lord Dumfries he would take care to provide Charles' brother with a proper account of his effects but determined Mr. Fordyce did not deserve to benefit from Charles' estate. Whether or not Charles would have agreed with this determination is unknown, but the comment suggests a possible estrangement, and this could explain the perfunctory obituary.

A much more eloquent and edifying obituary addressing Charles' record in the army and his qualities as a soldier and a man was published in an English newspaper, the *Derby Mercury*. According to this obituary,

The Loss of Captain Fordyce, of the 14th Regiment of Infantry, (Captain of Grenadiers) who was killed by the Rebels in Virginia, is greatly lamented by a pretty numerous and affectionate Acquaintance, whose Feelings on the Occasion do much Honour to his Memory. This Gentleman had served three or four Campaigns in Germany last War, and since distinguished himself in the West-Indies, and in north-America. He was an excellent Example, in his Profession, of Steadiness, Activity, and unwearied Attention. He possessed a most engaging Disposition, was a firm Friend, and a pleasing, useful Companion. His Loss is great to his Corps in particular (by whom he was ever beloved) and, indeed, to the Service in general.[49]

The tribute makes no reference Charles' family, but it is quite personal and complementary. It includes sentiments similar to those Captain Dalrymple expressed in his letter to Lord Dumfries as well as details of Charles' military service that would be known to a fellow officer but probably not known outside the service. Given the similarities with Dalrymple's letter and the details of Charles' service, one might speculate Dalrymple composed the obituary. Regardless of who wrote it, Charles' service record coupled with the vignettes presented in this biography of his mentoring, his concern for his men, his support of fellow officers, his leadership, his devotion to duty—even his conscientious care of government property—give this obituary credence.

༄

In his assessment of the Battle of Great Bridge, Captain George Johnston reported that, after the battle, Charles was, "lying dead in our Church." It is likely "our church" was the church in the village of Great Bridge at the fork in the Great Road at the south end of town. Colonel Woodford notes in his account Charles was buried with military honors. It is reasonable to conclude he was buried in the cemetery at the same church where Captain Johnston saw his body. Such a conclusion is supported by a brief history of the church included in William Stewart's *History of Norfolk County, Virginia*. In that history, Mr. Stewart claims the church was the first Episcopal Church (Church of England) built in St. Brides Parish. He determined it was built in 1762* and it was located "at Great Bridge, on the Great Road just opposite the point where the New Mill Creek road joins this great highway to North Carolina." Regarding Captain Fordyce's funeral, he notes,

> It is said that the funeral rites of Captain Fordyce, the English officer, who was killed in the battle of Great Bridge, took place

---

*In Mr. Stewart's *History* there seems to be a printing error regarding the date the church was built—1662 has been changed here to the correct 1762. His estimate of the date the church was torn down—about 1845—is also at variance with the "official" record on the historical marker for the site. According to the marker, the church "survived until 1853."

in this church, and that Rev. John Hamilton Rowland, grandfather of Thomas B. Rowland of Norfolk, officiated.[50]

Rev. Rowland was a Loyalist minister assigned to St. Bride's Parish by Governor Dunmore on January 23, 1775.[51] Concerning the later fate of the church, Mr. Stewart adds, "The church went into disuse and was torn down about the year 1845."

Based on an entry in the *Orderly Book* of the 2nd Virginia Regiment for December 10, 1775, Colonel Woodford was true to his word regarding the military funeral for Captain Fordyce. On that day he ordered,

> The long Roll to Beat when the commanding Officer orders which will be in less than an Hour the whole to fall in upon their parade with their arms and wait for orders[.] all the Officers and men off Duty are to Attend and the party to be formed to attend the funeral of Capt Fordice [sic].[52]

The day before, Woodford had given orders for graves to be dug in the "Church yard," and for a "good joiner" to construct as good a coffin "as the place can afford" for Captain Fordyce.[53]

Charles was buried with "full military honors." The details of these honors are not provided but based on guidelines published in 1811, such a ceremony would involve the attendance of three companies of soldiers, including an escort detachment and a firing detachment. Six officers of the same rank—in this case, captain—would be the pall bearers. Other than the attendance of three companies of soldiers it seems the honors were paid in the way the corpse was moved to the grave site and interred. These honors were quite detailed. They are presented here—although it is likely there were differences in the ceremony performed in 1775 and those prescribed in 1811—as a tribute to Captain Fordyce.

> The Corpse is then brought out, accompanied by the *Pall Bearers*, and received by the troops with *presented* arms. It is then placed in the procession…. The escort *shoulder arms*; break into open column of platoons; *reverse arms*. Officers draw their swords; reverse swords, carrying them under the left arm; the point towards the rear; the left hand at the hilt to support it. The

Procession ... then moves; music playing a dead march, or funeral dirge; drums muffled.

When the procession arrives at the place of *interment*, the escort will file from the right and left *of* platoons to the front; forming two lines; *halt, face* inwards, and *rest on arms reversed*. Officers handle their swords with the right hand; place the point on the ground, at the right foot; rest the right hand lightly on the hilt; the eyes cast down ward.

Platoon Officers, with espontoons [polearm similar to a pike or halberd] reversed, and the point placed on the ground by the right foot, supported against the hollow of the shoulder; the right arm extended downward, nearly full length, and the hand around the espontoon; the back of the hand towards the rear; eyes fixed on the ground. The Corpse is carried through the avenue, between the lines of the troops; they continuing to rest on arms reversed, until the Corpse is let down into the grave. They then shoulder arms; wheel inwards to re-form platoons; and immediately form a line.

The Commandant, by signal, causes the troops to load, and fire three volleys over the grave, at an elevation of forty-five degrees. These orders should be communicated by *tap of the drum*. All orders should be given without noise or bustle; and by signal, if practicable. The party having completed their firings, they shoulder arms; wheel again into open column of platoons; right in front, and march in quick time.[54]

Thus was 34-year-old Captain Charles Fordyce of His Majesty's 14th Regiment of Foot laid to rest, 3500 miles from home, in a country church yard in enemy territory and with the admiration and respect of a roughhewn but worthy adversary. Although in enemy territory, his comrades—Lieutenant Batut and some of the other wounded prisoners—could have attended the service. As noted earlier, it is likely the clergyman conducting the funeral was Rev. John Hamilton Rowland of the Church of England. As part of the service, Reverend Rowland would have reminded all present the soul Almighty God was pleased to take unto himself that day was that of "our dear brother."[55]

Based on Colonel Woodford's December 10 letter to the Virginia Convention,[56] and the Orderly Book entry for December 10, it seems Charles was buried on that day. The location of his grave is unknown, but it is probably in the vicinity of the Great Bridge Battlefield and Waterways Historic Park in Chesapeake, Virginia. There is no record of his grave having been marked and there is no marked grave for Captain Fordyce now. The Great Bridge Battlefield and Waterways History Foundation is installing a monument at the Park to honor all the British soldiers who fought in the battle.

CHAPTER 12: SIGNIFICANCE OF THE BATTLE OF GREAT BRIDGE

The Battle of Great Bridge, Virginia was fought in the first months of the Revolutionary War on December 9, 1775. The most significant action prior to the battle at Great Bridge had been the Battle of Bunker Hill, fought almost six months earlier on June 17, 1775. The "battle" prior to that had been the engagements at Lexington and Concord, Massachusetts on April 19—the engagements that started the War.

This third battle of the Revolutionary War—the Battle of Great Bridge—was of modest size and duration. On the British side, there were some 120 regular soldiers, perhaps that many loyalist militia and a contingent of no more than 300 of Governor Dunmore's Ethiopian Regiment—the regiment he raised of former Negro slaves he freed by proclamation a few weeks prior to the battle. The highest ranking, regular British army officer in the field (in fact, in all Virginia) was a captain. On the American side, there was a force of some 400 soldiers of the 2nd Virginia Regiment, about as many in the Culpeper Minute Battalion and a small detachment—less than 200 soldiers—from North Carolina.[1] The battle lasted about 45 minutes.

By contrast, the battles of Lexington and Concord and Bunker Hill lasted hours. The engagements at Lexington and Concord, followed by the incessant American enfilade of the British column on their return march to Boston, involved 700 British regulars and some 3,000 Massachusetts' militia and minutemen. Bunker Hill was one of the largest battles of the Revolutionary war. In that battle, 2,400 militia defended Bunker Hill and Breed's Hill from the assaults of 3,000 British regulars.

༄

Inasmuch as the British were certain the most direct and effective way to end the rebellion in America was the subjugation of New England, the skirmishing in the South was considered a distraction and even worse, a drain on the resources General William Howe, the British Commander-in-Chief, wanted for the crucial Northern campaigns. Under these circumstances, the loss at Great Bridge may have been welcome news to General Howe in that it confirmed his position the Southern governors—at least to some extent—had encouraged and enabled the rebels in their successes by their own "irresponsible conduct" and supporting them was "inconsistent with the general plan of operations."[2]

But prior to the Battle of Great Bridge, Governor Dunmore had been quite successful in defeating and disarming the rebels in Virginia. His successes were recognized by some as worthy affirmations a southern strategy could reduce his Majesty's rebellious subjects to obedience just as effectively as the Northern strategy General Howe had determined to be "of so much consequence."[3]

That the Northern campaign was of so much consequence implied a campaign in the South—including, of course, Virginia—was of relatively little consequence. Such dissension over consequences in New England and consequences in Virginia and the South occurred because both the British authorities and the American rebels were expecting immediate results from whatever action they took. Accounting for the longer-term consequences of establishing military control in New England at the expense of relinquishing control in the South was unnecessary because it implied a wider breach between the motherland and her colonies than either side was prepared to acknowledge.

On the ground in Virginia, Captain Charles Fordyce of the British 14th Regiment determined the province was worth saving regardless of how the consequences might be measured. With his nine years of experience in the Americas, during which time he had seen no abatement in the colonists' rejection of British authority, it is likely he discerned the unfolding "war" would be protracted. Under these circumstances he opined, "What a pity it is that this Colony should have been so much neglected; a couple of thousand men would settle everything here in the course of this winter."[4] By having everything settled he must have meant having the rebel forces neutralized, the resources of Virginia at the disposal of the King and the Chesapeake available as a staging area for a Southern campaign.

Charles went no further in assessing the long-term consequences of subjugating Virginia than to observe "everything," that is, the unrest and rebellion in this valuable region, would be settled. On the other hand, Sir John Dalrymple, Charles' third cousin and one of the judges of the English Court of the Exchequer, was outraged at the ministry's neglect and abandonment of Virginia. He delineated his views of the catastrophic consequences of this neglect in a 1778 letter to Secretary of War Barrington. Dalrymple was convinced that by settling everything in Virginia "the subsequent repulse at Charlestown, abandonment of Boston, surrender at Saratoga, and unconsequential [sic] campaigns around New York and Philadelphia, might all have been prevented." Aware he might be ridiculed for this rather grandiose assessment he added, "... if these opinions be too sanguine, it is at least morally certain, that Chesapeake bay might, at this hour, have been in his Majesty's possession."[5]

Shortly after the loss at Great Bridge an unnamed correspondent on the Ship *William* off Norfolk drew the same conclusion. He reported, "Lord Dunmore has done every thing for the cause of King and country which man could do; and had a thousand troops arrived two months since, he would have had Virginia totally reduced to obedience by this time."[6] In the same vein, another correspondent observed, "Lord Dunmore has been shamefully neglected" and suggested—as did Sir John Dalrymple—Britain's strategic focus had been misdirected. There had been a rather half-hearted attempt at a Southern campaign aimed at South Carolina after Governor Dunmore's loss at Great Bridge, a campaign that included a British fleet commanded by Sir Peter Parker. Regarding this campaign and the attendant neglect of Governor Dunmore the correspondent noted, "a colony of great importance [was] lost to Britain (at least for one year); and a communication between the northern and southern provinces left open to the rebels." He concluded "had that unfortunate fleet of Sir Peter Parker got orders to join his Lordship, Virginia and Maryland might have been as effectually scoured [i.e., cleared of enemies] as Canada."[7]

૭

Although less dramatic than the loss of a staging area for a Southern campaign of war-changing consequence, it is conceivable, if not likely, the loss at Great Bridge prevented the demise of the American Navy at birth. While Governor Dunmore was tightening his grip on the sea lines of communication through the Chesapeake Bay in 1775, Congress was "taking into consideration the report of the Committee appointed to prepare a plan, for intercepting vessels coming out with stores and ammunition." As a result of these considerations, on October 13, 1775, Congress authorized the fitting out of "a swift sailing vessel" directed to "… cruize eastward, for intercepting such transports as may be laden with warlike stores and other supplies for our enemies."[8] This authorization marked the birth of the United States Navy. About six weeks later, on December 2, Congress narrowed the geographic purview of the new navy in direct response to reports of Governor Dunmore's activities. They directed the "Committee for fitting out armed vessels" to engage Captain William Stone of the *Hornet* "for the purpose of taking or destroying the cutters and armed vessels in Chesapeake Bay, under Lord Dunmore."[9]

In that same session of Congress, Colonel Benjamin Harrison was ordered to Maryland and directed to work with the delegates of that colony to procure "… two or three armed vessels to proceed immediately to cruize on, take or destroy as many of the armed vessels, cutters, and ships of war of the enemy as possible, that may be found in the bay of Chesapeake, or any of its dependencies, or coasts of Virginia and Maryland." The Congress also acknowledged "… partizans in the counties of Norfolk and Princess Ann, and some other parts of Virginia" were "under the influence of Lord Dunmore, to contravene the non-exportation agreement"—in particular, by exporting provisions and other produce to the West Indies. As a result, Congress resolved the armed vessels Harrison was to procure were "… to seize and detain … all such ships and vessels as they may find employed in such exportations." Along with the flotilla Harrison was to procure, Congress resolved Captain Abraham Whipple of Rhode Island should be dispatched with his armed sloop "to aid the marine business to the southward."[10]

In December 1775, Christopher Gadsden, one of South Carolina's delegates to the Continental Congress and famous as the designer of the coiled-rattlesnake "Don't-Tread-on-Me" flag, provided a "pleasing account of the actual sailing from that place of the first American fleet that ever swelled their sails on the Western Ocean" to the American press. He noted, "This fleet consists of five sail, fitted out from Philadelphia, which are to be joined at the Capes of Virginia by two ships more from Maryland and is commanded by Admiral [Esek] Hopkins." Regarding the mission of the fleet Gadsden observed, "Their destination is a secret, but generally supposed to be against the Ministerial Governours, those little petty tyrants that have lately spread fire and sword throughout these Southern Colonies."[11] Scottish-born First Lieutenant John Paul Jones was aboard the *Alfred*, Hopkins' flag ship, and in his *Journal* he explained, "The object of the first expedition was against Lord Dunmore in Virginia."[12] Hopkins received definitive orders to this effect on January 5, 1776.[13] Thus, containing Governor Dunmore was to be the first campaign of America's new Navy.*

It turned out the American Navy's campaign to contain Dunmore was fought indirectly. Despite his orders, Commodore Hopkins focused on the broader objective of "intercepting such transports as may be laden with warlike stores and other supplies for our enemies." When he took his fleet into action, he bypassed the Chesapeake to raid the British base at New Providence—until July 1775, garrisoned by Captain Blackett's detachment of the 14th Regiment. The reasons for the change of plans are unclear, although it is likely Commodore Hopkins was exercising the caution often commended as the better part of valor for his new navy.[14] It is less likely, but conceivable, a raid on Dunmore's fleet was considered unnecessary—at least from a military standpoint—after the loss

---

* This was, incidentally, the first time the "Union Flag, with thirteen stripes in the field" was displayed. Of this event Lieutenant Jones journaled, "On board of that ship [*Alfred*], before Philadelphia I hoisted the flag of America with my own hands, the first time it was ever displayed." Henry E. Waite, *Extracts Relating to the Origin of the American Navy*, Boston: Berwick and Smith, 1890, p. 29.

at Great Bridge. The threat posed by his fleet was diminished greatly after the battle. On December 13, Governor Dunmore reported to Lord Dartmouth, "All who were friends to Government took refuge on board of the Ships, with their whole families, and their most valuable Effects, some in the Men of War, some in their own Vessels, others have chartered such as were here, so that our Fleet is at present Numerous tho' not very powerfull."[15]

Whether or not Dunmore's dilapidated fleet would have been a match for America's new Navy is unknown. An American victory would have been a stunning political triumph. But disappointments over this missed opportunity were mollified to some extent when the raid on New Providence proved to be of substantial military worth. Hopkins brought away four hundred and fifty tons of cannon and other military stores along with numerous high-profile prisoners, including the Governor of the island.[16]

The victory at New Providence not only provided much-needed equipment for the Americans, it established the credibility of the new navy—a vitalizing, definitive accomplishment. The kind of accomplishment that convinced one naval historian the new Navy "… played a very important part in forcing the Mistress-of-the-Seas to yield American independence, because their ships demoralized British commerce and increased insurance rates, besides causing considerable actual loss and capturing valuable and needed war materials." This same historian concluded, "The prestige of American exploits at sea helped in inducing open and direct aid from France and Spain."[17]

These accomplishments would have been jeopardized had Governor Dunmore been reinforced. Such a possibility had been quite likely when General Henry Clinton arrived in the Chesapeake with a naval squadron in February 1776. At that time, he met with Governor Dunmore but was not inclined to provide reinforcements confessing, "I could not see the Use of his Lordship's remaining longer there, especially after the failure of his Attack on the Rebel Post at the Great Bridge."[18] Given this conclusion, no reinforcements were provided, Dunmore's "Navy" remained enervated and a British Southern campaign based in the Chesapeake entirely frustrated.[19]

Chapter 12: Significance of the Battle of Great Bridge 195

Both George Washington and his third in command, General Charles Lee,* were adamant control of Virginia at this time was vital to the American war effort. When intelligence of Governor Dunmore's plans to "reduce this colony to a proper sense of their duty"—articulated in his letters to General Howe[20]—reached the Continental Army high command, Washington told the President of Congress, "I do not mean to dictate, but I am Sure they will pardon me for giving them freely my opinion, which is, that the fate of America a good deal depends, on his [Dunmore] being obliged to evacuate Norfolk this Winter.[21] A few days later he told Virginia Congressional delegate Richard Henry Lee, Governor Dunmore would "become the most formidable enemy America has," if he were not "crushed" before spring.[22]

In his assessment of the significance of Dunmore's hold on Virginia, General Lee made it clear the British Northern and Southern campaigns were of equal consequence. In fact, he seemed to be certain—like Sir John Dalrymple—a Southern campaign was of more consequence than a Northern campaign at this time. He warned Richard Henry Lee, "You may depend upon it, that if the war is continued, Norfolk will be the Boston—that is the chief place of arms—to your enemies the next year; and it is a place which in their hands will be infinitely more dangerous."[23]

Congress was concerned over the threat Lord Dunmore posed even before Washington and Lee voiced their opinions. As previously noted, on December 2, 1775, they ordered Captain Stone of the *Hornet* to take or destroy Lord Dunmore's cutters and armed vessels. Two days later, on December 4, they resolved the Virginians should "resist to the utmost the arbitrary government intended to be established ... by their Governor Lord Dunmore."[24] Although no official record exists to support it, several British newspapers reported Congress was so outraged with Governor

---

* General Lee was a former Lieutenant Colonel in the British army and served for a time as a general in the Polish army. Historically he has been characterized as eccentric and his loyalty to the American cause has been questioned. That said, he was a combat veteran credited with a firm grasp of the vital elements of the unfolding war.

Dunmore's "Proceedings," they advertised him to be "a public incendiary, and offered a £500 reward for taking him dead or alive."[25]

~

By the 20th century, professional historians were making more dispassionate assessments of the British defeat at Great Bridge while still acknowledging the strategic significance of Virginia. In his 1958 assessment of the British activities in Virginia in 1775, historian W. Hugh Moomaw noted one of the keys to the successful British prosecution of the war lay in "… the retention of the highly important Chesapeake Bay region." He also noted, "… the British situation and American hostility prevented an early concentration in this strategic area" and concluded, "ultimately this proved disastrous."[26] Of course, one of the foremost instances of American hostility was their challenge to Lord Dunmore at Great Bridge.

Hamilton Eckenrode, first archivist at the Virginia State Library, assessed the consequences of the loss of Virginia in his *The Revolution in Virginia*, published in 1916. In this landmark study, Eckenrode linked this loss of Virginia to the loss at Great Bridge. In his assessment he speculates on the consequences of a victory at Great Bridge in promoting the success of British arms throughout the continent, and the modest resources such a victory would have required. He was aware "The first successes in a war, trifling as they usually are, have an effect altogether disproportionate to their importance," and of the Battle of Great Bridge he surmised,

> If at this time, as might well have chanced, a British regiment had arrived under the command of a competent officer, there is no telling the result. The willingness of so many under a little urging to take the oath of allegiance to the king is evidence that no great enthusiasm for the American cause animated the inhabitants along the lower Chesapeake. The coming of troops, entailing a prolonged and doubtful military struggle, might have changed indifference into royalist partisanship; and a Tory party would have arisen in Virginia as in other colonies. The energies of the Revolutionary government would have been largely expended on the internal contest at the very time when

the resources of the colony were most needed to maintain the American arms in the North. From this situation Virginia and the Confederation were saved by the speedy collapse of Dunmore's defense.[27]

Mr. Eckenrode's primus the American victory at Great Bridge saved Virginia and the Confederation from the shortages of men and materials that likely would have ensued with a British victory is certainly reasonable.[28] In his pleas for help after the Gunpowder Incident, Governor Dunmore assured General Howe he could, with victory in the Chesapeake, supply the "… army and navy with every necessary of life, and that in the greatest abundance." He added, without exaggeration, this was "… more than any other Colony on the Continent could do."[29]

Sir John Dalrymple, noted earlier as a strident critic of Britain's abandonment of Governor Dunmore and Virginia, was specific in his commendation of Dunmore's accomplishments—accomplishments affecting the war in terms of access to strategic resources. In his letter to Lord Barrington, he reminded the Secretary of the outstanding cost-effectiveness of Lord Dunmore's activities, observing, "With a fleet of three ships, and an army of one hundred and eight soldiers, he stopt [sic] the trade of that bay, from end to end of it for six months, he prevented five provinces from sending a single soldier to the continental army."[30] This was at a time when one of Virginia's delegates to the Second Continental Congress reported on the intelligence received in New York the British were planning to reinforce their army in that state in order to "cut off communication between the southern and eastern colonies." The delegate noted, in consequence of such a plan, the New Yorkers were "forming themselves, and beg assistance from the southward."[31]

Regarding the value of Virginia's contribution of manpower to the Continental Army, George Washington acknowledged the fact almost as soon as the Virginians arrived. At the time—September 1776—Washington was defending New York City after his all but fatal loss at Long Island. He credited the men of George Weedon's Virginia Brigade with his first victory against British regulars at The Battle of Harlem Heights on September 16, 1776.[32]

Of this victory Washington's *aide de camp*, Colonel Joseph Reed observed, "You can hardly conceive the change it has made in our army. The men have recovered their spirits and feel a confidence which before they had quite lost."[33] Weedon's Brigade included the 1st and 3rd Virginia Regiments which had arrived on Manhattan Island the day before the battle. Many of the men in these regiments had been involved in finally expelling Governor Dunmore from Virginia a few months earlier and it is quite likely they would have remained in Virginia had Dunmore continued to threaten the colony.

Just over three months later, when Washington attacked the Hessian outpost at Trenton on December 26, the Continental Army had been reinforced with three more Virginia regiments, the 4th, 5th, and 6th. These regiments, along with the 1st and 3rd, were among the approximately 2400 men who crossed the Delaware River with Washington for the assault on Trenton. The Virginia regiments were assigned to Stephen's and Stirling's Brigades in General Greene's Division—the Division that led the main attack. The five Virginia regiments accounted for almost half the Division's strength.[34] Again, it is likely these Virginians would have remained in Virginia had Governor Dunmore not been expelled.

It is also possible the energies of Virginians like Thomas Jefferson, who was writing the Declaration of Independence while Governor Dunmore was making his last stand at Portsmouth and Gwynn's Island in July of 1776, would have been diverted had Governor Dunmore remained in Virginia.

One may argue George Washington would have won at Harlem Heights and Trenton with regiments other than those from Virginia, even though the Virginias were some of the best trained and most experienced in his new army. One may also argue the Declaration of Independence could have been written by other able political thinkers at the disposal of Congress. These arguments elicit the concession from the humble historian, the humble general and the humble philosopher, that the salvation of Virginia and the Confederation was not dependent on the Patriot victory at Great Bridge. Having made these concessions, it is still reasonable to conclude the victory at Great Bridge did save George

Washington the inconvenience of finding two crack regiments of Continental soldiers at the Battle of Harlem Heights and another three when he attacked Trenton. The case for the victory saving Congress the inconvenience of finding a statesman other than Thomas Jefferson to write the Declaration of Independence is weaker although he did appreciate the "temporary holiday" Dunmore's expulsion afforded Virginia's executives.[35]

As is often the case in trying to assess the impact of a battle on a war or even a campaign, it may be difficult to link the victory or defeat to the secondary and tertiary impacts of victory or defeat with certainty because the links disperse. But the links between the American victory at Great Bridge and the redirection of two strategic resources that changed the course of the Revolutionary War are intact. First, there is a viable link between the victory over Governor Dunmore and way the fledging American Navy was able to make its auspicious and timely debut. It may be argued this link is somewhat convoluted, but only somewhat. The loss promoted a refugee crisis that compromised the fighting capability of Governor Dunmore's fleet and confused plans for the Southern campaign just as the new navy left port for the first time. These circumstances greatly enhanced the probability of success for the navy and the greater American cause.

Second, the victory at Great Bridge relieved the Virginians of the need to field almost all their army (the third largest in America) to secure one of the most populous and productive agricultural regions in the country.[36] Until Dunmore was defeated, the commanders of the Continental Army and Virginia's State Army made his containment a priority and applied their resources accordingly. After his defeat and the dissolution of the Southern campaign, the Virginians and their southern neighbors redirected their resources. The flow of agricultural and human resources was directed north, resources which furnished and sustained the American Continental Army on that front at this most critical juncture in the war.

EPILOGUE

After the loss at Great Bridge, Captain Leslie abandoned his fort and marched what was left of the 14th Regiment the ten miles back to Norfolk. Both Colonel Woodford and Governor Dunmore reported the casualties of the battle. In his report to the Virginia Convention of December 10, Colonel Woodford identified seventeen prisoners by name (one officer and sixteen privates, all wounded). He also reported he buried twelve besides Captain Fordyce for a total of thirteen killed. In a letter to the Convention of December 11, Woodford passed on intelligence he received from "people from the other side of the river" that 65 of the enemy crossed in boats and of Captain Fordyce's Grenadiers, eleven escaped. In the same letter, he included the claim of Mr. William Calvert that the enemy's losses were 102 killed and wounded.[1]

In his report to Lord Dartmouth of December 13, Governor Dunmore counted the casualties as, "… three Officers killed and one Wounded, who was made a prisoner, 14 Privates were killed and 43 Wounded."[2] Other than the one officer, Lieutenant Batut, Governor Dunmore made no mention of prisoners.

On January 11, 1776, Captain Leslie submitted a "Return of Strength of Detachment of 14th Regiment," and noted the casualties since the last return (December 1) as 23 killed, 6 prisoners and 20 wounded.[3] Based on the reports of Governor Dunmore and Captain Leslie, it seems the 14th Regiment suffered between 17 killed and 44* wounded (Dunmore) and 23 killed, 20 wounded and 6 made prisoner (Leslie). According to these two reports the total casualties were between 49 and 65. Given the strength of the 14th Regiment just prior to the battle was 174, the reported losses would mean the detachment was reduced by as much as 37% and the number of men available after the battle was between 109 and 125. If the intelligence available to Colonel Woodford was accurate,

---

* This number is also reported as 49, Davies, DAR Vol. 10, p. 291, note iv.

and the casualties amounted to 102, then the strength of the detachment was reduced by 58% to 72. In any event, losses were such the detachment no longer functioned as a viable military unit.[4]

Although Lord Dunmore had fortified Norfolk, he was not confident he could withstand an attack by the combined force now under the command of Colonel Robert Howe—some 1,275 men.[5] Colonel Howe was from North Carolina but senior in rank to Colonel Woodford. When he arrived at Great Bridge with his North Carolina Regiment a few days after the battle, Woodford relinquished his command, leaving Howe in charge of a brigade of three regiments. Under the circumstances, Governor Dunmore, along with his troop of regular soldiers, volunteers and Loyalist supporters, took refuge on a rather substantial fleet of ships anchored off Norfolk. Colonel Howe occupied Norfolk and a standoff between his brigade and Dunmore's sea-borne community ensued.

The standoff was punctuated with violence beginning with the British cannonading of Norfolk on January 1, 1776 followed a month later by the complete destruction of what was left of the town by direction of Virginia's Committee of Safety. At the same time, Governor Dunmore's forces were making forays into the countryside along the coast lines to obtain water and provisions. In mid-February, Lord Dunmore's modest amalgamation of regulars and volunteers made landings at Tucker's Mills, just below Portsmouth on the Elizabeth River—across the river from Norfolk. Here they were able to secure a supply of water and establish a base from which they could monitor the Patriot forces and Dunmore's armed forces could exercise and train.

In an intelligence report of March 31, 1776, Lieutenant Colonel Francis Eppes of the 1st Virginia Regiment estimated forty regulars of the 14th Regiment were among those exercising at Tucker's Mills. In this same report, Eppes commented on the "heavy firing" from the ships in the bay or at sea which he speculated was in response to repositioning elements of the fleet.[6] A week later Lieutenant Colonel Eppes reported on his efforts to "bring the enemy out of their entrenchments by a smart fire upon them." He said his force started firing at daybreak "which occasioned an almost constant discharge of artillery thro' the whole day."[7]

Governor Dunmore was outnumbered and effectively surrounded but he never seemed to be deterred by these circumstances. He fought and maneuvered with determination and resolve for months, which meant the men of the 14th Regiment were often under arms. On March 10, Captain Andrew Snape Hamond, one of the naval officers with the Governor's fleet, reported on a search-and-destroy mission he initiated to prevent the Patriots from unloading powder and arms thought to be aboard a French vessel off Currituck inlet on the Virginia-North Carolina border. The plan involved sending twenty men on a sloop to board the vessel. Evidently the mission was a success, but the sloop was stranded with a detachment of men from the 14th Regiment on a bar at the inlet. Hamond reported the stranded men "marched thro' the Enemy's Country, and came to the Ships at Norfolk, having saved their Arms and destroyed the Vessel."[8]

Later that month, Governor Dunmore reported to Lord Germain on the way he was using vessels taken from the Patriots. He noted the vessels were "employed constantly running up the Rivers, where they have orders to Seize, burn or destroy every thing that is Water Born." He added, "they often Land and take off what Provisions they can get, which keeps the Rebels in constant motion, and I generally send a few of the 14th Regiment with them."[9] In April, when Lieutenant Colonel Eppes was reporting on the developments at Tucker's Mills, Purdie's *Virginia Gazette* carried an article describing the fighting between Eppes' forces and those of Governor Dunmore in which two grenadiers of the 14th Regiment were killed.[10]

But by mid-May, the lack of access to resupply was taking its toll. At this time, Captain George Johnston of the 2nd Virginia Regiment noted, "I have had skirmishes with the enemy every day; they hazard their lives to procure wood & water."[11] On May 20, 1776, Dunmore's forces attempted a landing at Norfolk. This would result in their last significant fight on mainland Virginia. They were repulsed by Captain Johnston and a detachment of about fifty men from the 1st and 2nd Virginia Regiments.[12] On May 22, 1776, Colonel Woodford wrote Brigadier General Andrew Lewis from Kemp's Landing and informed him, "The vigilance of my guards has occasioned the enemy to abandon their lines at Portsmouth. This and some fire rafts I was preparing, has likewise occasioned the fleet to go off."[13]

Governor Dunmore sailed from Norfolk on May 23, 1776 and arrived at Gwynn's* Island, some 70 miles north on Virginia's Middle Peninsula, on May 28.[14] Gwynn's Island was not a stronghold, although it did it offer some of the resources he needed to sustain his cadre of British soldiers, volunteers and refugees. But the Governor knew the island was vulnerable. In a letter to Lord Germain he acknowledged "it lies too near the Main, which the Rebels occupy, all around us, as the Haven between it and the Main, in some places don't exceed two hundred Yards wide."[15]

About a month after Governor Dunmore arrived, the Patriots took advantage of the vulnerabilities he described. On July 9, Brigadier General Lewis, in command of Virginia's regiments on the mainland, opened fire on Dunmore's ships and his encampment on the island. Here again the men of the 14th Regiment were involved. Editors Dixon and Hunter of the *Virginia Gazette* reported "ten or more privates of the 14th regiment" were killed at Gwynn's Island.[16] When the fighting stopped on the day of the battle, Lord Dunmore abandoned the island and sailed for St. George's Island, Maryland, about sixty miles up the Chesapeake Bay at the mouth of the Potomac River.[17]

At this point, Governor Dunmore's quixotic campaign to "reduce the whole of his Southern part of His Majesty's Continent to a proper State of Submission" was all but over. Captain Hamond noted Lord Dunmore landed troops on St. George's Island to search for water but found none. The enfeebled fleet continued up the Potomac River with the "detachment of the 14th Regt & a part of the Queens" stopping occasionally to "harass & annoy the Enemy by landing at different places."[18] On July 23 they landed at

---

* Gwynn's is the accepted spelling today. In reports published in 1776, the spelling is often Gwin's or Gwyn's.

the "House of a Mr. Brent on the Virginia side" and engaged a large number of the "Enemy's Troops." In another letter to Lord Germain of July 31, Lord Dunmore reported, "We were no sooner landed, than the Rebels fled on all quarters from the House and Offices, all of which we burnt, and having done all the Mischief in our power, we reimbarked."[19]

But even this rather inept landing was not without consequences for the 14th Regiment. Governor Dunmore told Secretary Germain four or five of his men were wounded, including Lieutenant Hill Wallace. It is difficult to imagine the men of the 14th considered such harassing and annoying worth the risks, but they continued to serve with distinction. Regarding Lieutenant Wallace's performance the Governor noted, "… every praise is due to the Spirit of this Young* Gentleman."

Despite such spirit, it seems Governor Dunmore finally recognized the futility of further engagement. He closed his report of July 31 with questions of exasperation if not defeat, asking, "… where we are to go, or what we can do next to render Service to His Majesty I own I am puzzled to know, and as I find there is now not even a Chance of our receiving any assistance, I really am at a loss what to determine on, for next Month it will become very unsafe for the Ships to keep the Bay, and I do declare I know not where we can go with our present force to make a Harbour of any tollerable safety."[20]

Four days later the Governor submitted another report to Lord Germain and reiterated his exasperation. He also reiterated another theme dominant in his correspondence during the months of privation he and his troops endured in 1776—the theme of serving King and country. On August 4, he lamented, "I am left without even the hope of being able to render His Majesty the smallest Service, this I must say is truely discouraging, and leaves me in the utmost difficulty to determine what to do; my utmost desire is (when I do resolve) that I may do what may be most agreeable to His Majesty's wishes and the best for His Service."[21]

---

* Based on a memorial for Lieutenant Wallace in the Drumbeg Churchyard near Belfast, Ireland, he was born in 1754, so he was twenty two years old at this time.

Epilogue 205

The next day he quit the Potomac and sailed for New York. He arrived at Sandy Hook, New Jersey, on August 13.[22]

Dunmore remained in New York as the campaign for that city unfolded, a campaign that began with the Battle of Long Island on August 27. In a letter to Lord Germain of September 4, Lord Dunmore alludes to his having been at that battle. He told the Secretary, "I was with the Highlanders and Hessians the whole day, and it is with the utmost pleasure I can assure your Lordship that the ardour [sic] of both these corps on that day must have exceeded his Majesty's most sanguine wish."[23]

This battle was followed by the fighting on Manhattan Island in September. Here the regiments from Virginia made their debut as regulars in the Continental Army at the Battle of Harlem Heights on September 16.

A report of an "engagement" of September 15—the day before the battle at Harlem Heights—puts Governor Dunmore in the thick of the action on Manhattan. According to an article published in British newspapers, "Lord Dunmore was in the engagement on the 15th of September, and showed great spirit and intrepidity, having with his own hands torn down the American colours [sic] that were flying on the castle, and hoisted the British ensigns in their stead."[24] "The engagement on the 15th" was probably the successful British landing at Kips Bay, Manhattan Island, on that date, and it is conceivable Lord Dunmore—demonstrating again his insuperable devotion to the British cause—found a way to participate. This successful amphibious operation led to the occupation of New York City on the same day, and it is possible Lord Dunmore's demonstration of "great spirit" occurred there.

In other newspaper articles, Dunmore was reported as present at the Battle of White Plains on October 28—another British victory. Here again the Governor praised the British soldiers, reportedly declaring "… nothing ever equaled the ardor of the British battalions which attacked."[25]

As General Howe's New York Campaign came to a close and the prospect of survival for George Washington's Continental Army dimmed, Governor Dunmore finally left America, sailing from New York on November 10, 1776. He was accompanied by another evicted governor, William Campbell of South Carolina. They arrived in London on December 19, 1776[26] –just over a year after the loss at Great Bridge and one week before George Washington would cross the Delaware River with a Continental Army that included five Virginia regiments and defeat the Hessians at Trenton.

It seems Governor Dunmore's zeal for King and country never flagged. Shortly after he returned to England, he was sent to Paris by Lord Stormont, then Secretary of State for the Northern Department, in an effort to assuage the growing rancor between the French and English related to American affairs.[27]

A report that Lord Dunmore was "again looking towards his government in Virginia" was published in British newspapers in July of 1780.[28] In 1781, a few months before General Cornwallis was defeated at Yorktown, the King endorsed Governor Dunmore's plan to return to Virginia "… under the idea that he will be able to form several corps there of the Virginians, and to arm them in assisting towards the reduction of the rebellion in that part of America, which, his Lordship is inclined to think, may, ere long, be put an end to."[29] Dunmore sailed in October 1781[30] and arrived at Charleston, South Carolina—at the time, British controlled—on December 20. He was given a hero's welcome by the well disposed of that city. Reportedly, the not-so-well-disposed citizens of Virginia offered a $5,000 reward for his apprehension—dead or alive.[31] But Cornwallis' defeat at Yorktown—possibly on the same day Governor Dunmore sailed for Virginia—meant the mission to Virginia was moot.

Ever devoted to the King's service, upon hearing of the loss of Cornwallis' army, Lord Dunmore would make one last proposal to General Clinton to raise an army of ten thousand Blacks as "the most efficacious, expeditious, cheapest, and certain means of reducing this country to a proper sense of their duty."[32] His proposal was ignored and he made his way back to England, arriving in London in June, 1782.[33]

After the war, on May 1, 1787, Dunmore was appointed Governor of the Bahamas.[34] Evidently he served honorably and enjoyed the Bahamas but was recalled in 1797, possibly over an intrigue involving the clandestine marriage of his daughter, Augusta Murray, to the King's son, Prince Augustus Frederick, the Duke of Sussex.[35] The Duke was twenty years old at the time and Lady Augusta was thirty. The King disapproved the match. Governor Dunmore returned to England from the Bahamas on April 10, 1797. This rebuff seems to have ended his involvement in the court and politics. Among other retirement pursuits, it seems he passed some of his time with agricultural experiments.[36] He died at Ramsgate, Kent, England on February 25, 1809 at age 78 and was interred in St. Lawrence Church in Ramsgate on March 3.[37]

※

When Governor Dunmore sailed from Maryland for New York in August of 1776, some of the original detachments of the 14th that had joined him in Virginia sailed with him. This is clear from his reports and those of his subordinates as well as Patriot observers. Based on a report addressing measures General Howe took to secure his base at Staten Island as he began the campaign to take New York in August, some of the 14th may have sailed directly from Virginia to New York. According to the report, Lieutenant Colonel Dalrymple "and a detachment of the 14th Regiment from Virginia" were assigned the duty of protecting the British depot at Staten Island.[38] Of course these men could have taken the indirect route with Governor Dunmore and still been considered a detachment from Virginia.

The detachment of the 14th Regiment on Staten Island in August 1776 may have been most of the officers and men who survived the Battle of Great Bridge and the rather arduous passage from Virginia with Governor Dunmore. However, it seems some of the men in the 14th were assigned to other regiments a few weeks after the Battle of Great Bridge. This would explain why—in some reports—the strength of the detachment of the 14th remaining with Governor Dunmore during his escapades in the Chesapeake was said to be no more than forty. The reassignments could have occurred in February of 1776, when General Clinton visited Lord Dunmore on his way to South Carolina to salvage the on-again, off-again Southern campaign. This was while the Governor was still with his "fleet" off the coast of Norfolk.[39]

Two reports published in Britain at the time support this possibility. The assertion was made in one report, alleged to be from an officer in the 14th Regiment, the King's troops had been ordered to embark with General Clinton's forces "and they were to go upon a secret mission." The editors then speculated the secret mission was to South Carolina.[40] According to another report, "in the late skirmish there [i.e., Virginia], the [14th] regiment had only 75 rank and file escaped the slaughter of that day; and these are to be incorporated into other regiments on the Continent."[41] At least one instance of a reassignment to St. Augustine seems to have occurred. This was the case of Captain John Dalrymple, to be considered in more detail later in this Epilogue.

And it was not only the three undermanned companies of the 14th Regiment from Virginia that were scattered. It seems as many as six more—also undermanned—were detached from one end of North America to the other. Two "companies" were at Halifax, Nova Scotia with Captain John Stanton, enough rank and file to make two more were at Boston with Captain James Urquhart and two were at St. Augustine with Major Jonathan Furlong.[42] And it seems the distribution changed frequently. In a letter to General Gage of October 5, 1775, Major Furlong apprises his commanding officer of his need in St. Augustine for officers coopted by Governor Dunmore, but he also acknowledges the arrival of 23 recruits.[43] These were probably from the detachment at Boston. Such a wide, fluid distribution of the regiment rendered it ineffectual as a fighting force. In fact, the 14th was not even enumerated in the "State of the British Forces" published in July 1776. In explaining the omission of the regiment's status in the report, the publishers noted it was not included because it was "so very much disbursed."[44] The regiment returned to England piecemeal in 1777.[45]

ॐ

Charles Fordyce served with thirteen other officers of the 14th Regiment at Great Bridge. These included three captains, six lieutenants (including the adjutant, Lieutenant Cornelius Smelt) and four ensigns. Some of the officers had served with Charles throughout his army career. Others had known him only for the few months they were together in Virginia in 1775. Of the thirteen officers, brief sketches of the backgrounds of Lieutenants William Napier and Peter Henry Leslie were presented in Chapter 11, "Tributes." Sketches of the backgrounds and post battle histories of the other eleven officers are presented here. The officers are:

>Captain Samuel Leslie
>Captain David Cooper
>Captain John Dalrymple
>Lieutenant John Batut
>Lieutenant Hill Wallace
>Lieutenant Andrew Laurie
>Lieutenant Cornelius Smelt
>Ensign Thomas Appleford Wools
>Ensign James Boyes
>Ensign Charles Ogle
>Ensign James Lindsay.

Samuel Leslie was born October 7, 1728 in Hillsborough, Northern Ireland. His parents were Reverend Peter Leslie, rector of Ahoghill in the county of Antrim, and Jane Dopping. Samuel had two older brothers, Henry and James, and a younger brother, Edmond. He had at least two sisters, Margaret and Jane. His great-great grandfather, Henry Leslie, was from Scotland. He moved to Ireland in 1614, so Samuel's family had been in Ireland for over one-hundred years when he was born.[46]

Evidently Samuel made the decision to pursue a military career while still a teenager. He was commissioned a 2nd Lieutenant in Huske's Regiment on June 2, 1748.[47] Born in October of 1728, he would have been nineteen years old when commissioned. He seems to have progressed through the ranks at a modest pace. Six years after he was commissioned, he was still listed as a 2nd lieutenant, at this time in the 23rd Regiment of Foot (Royal Welsh Fusiliers). He was promoted to first lieutenant in the 23rd Regiment on July 5, 1755, having served in the regiment for eight years. His next promotion was quicker and seems to have been related to the formation of a new regiment—the 68th—in 1758. He was assigned to the new regiment and promoted to captain lieutenant on May 20, 1758. He remained in the 68th at this rank for the next four years. In 1762 he was assigned to the 14th Regiment of Foot as a captain, with a date-of-rank of February 8, 1762.[48] He remained a captain in the 14th for the next fifteen years—including the entire time the regiment was in North America. Since Charles Fordyce also joined the 14th in 1762, he and Captain Leslie were comrades-in-arms for thirteen years. At 47 years old in 1775, Captain Leslie would have been one of the oldest soldiers at Great Bridge.

Captain Leslie may have continued to serve with Governor Dunmore after the battle then returned to England in 1777. He was promoted to major on September 6, 1777.[49] He seems to have held this rank as a "supernumerary," that is he was an "extra" with the rank of "brevet major."[50] There was only one officer in the regiment assigned duty as the regimental major and that was Major Johnathan Furlong. When Furlong retired in 1778 he was replaced by Captain John Stanton—an officer inferior in rank to Samuel although he had served in the 14th Regiment longer than Samuel. Major Leslie remained on the rolls of the 14th until 1779, when he retired at the age of 51. If his commission as a second lieutenant in the 23rd Regiment on June 2, 1748, marked the beginning of his service, he had served king and country for 31 years when he retired. He was never married. In 1764, he had inherited property in the county of his birth, County Antrim, from his Uncle, Edmund Leslie Corry.[51] He may have spent his retirement years there.

༄

David Cooper was commissioned a lieutenant in the 50th Regiment of Foot on May 1, 1762. On June 1, 1763, he received his commission as a lieutenant in the 14th Regiment. At this time, Charles Fordyce had been in the regiment for one year, so he and David Cooper served together for twelve years. On the muster roll at Boston in 1769, Cooper is listed as the lieutenant in Captain Fordyce's company of grenadiers. Lieutenant Cooper was promoted to adjutant of the 14th Regiment on July 24, 1772. On March 25, 1774, he was promoted to Captain.[52]

As has been speculated for Captain Leslie, Captain Cooper may have continued to serve with Governor Dunmore after the Battle of Great Bridge then returned to England with the officers of the 14th in 1777. On March 19, 1783, he was commissioned a major.[53] This was a year after the 14th was deployed to Jamaica in the closing months of the American Revolutionary War.[54] He died in Jamaica, possibly of disease, while serving with the 14th in December 1786. The following obituary for Major Cooper was published in London.

> On Friday last [December 15] died Major David Cooper, commanding officer of his Majesty's 14th, or Bedfordshire regiment of foot; an officer whose conduct engaged the esteem, affection and respect of all who had the happiness to be under his command. His remains, attended by his Honor the Lieutenant Governor, and the field officers of the different regiments were buried with the military honors due to his rank.[55]

John Dalrymple was born July 4, 1746 in Old Luce, Wigtownshire, Scotland. He was commissioned an ensign in the 14th Regiment on March 27, 1765, a few months before his nineteenth birthday. He served with Charles Fordyce for ten years. He was promoted to lieutenant on January 6, 1772. On February 27, 1775—a few months before he arrived in Virginia—he bought out James Gifford to become captain in the 14th.[56]

Based on reports published in British newspapers some months after the Battle of Great Bridge, it is likely Captain Dalrymple joined General Clinton on his voyage to South Carolina in February 1776. According to the reports, General Clinton sent Captain Dalrymple to St. Augustine, "to secure that place, in case the rebels should attack it."[57] He probably returned to England with the officers of the 14th Regiment in 1777.

On April 15, 1779, he married Susan (or Susannah) Hay, only daughter of Sir Thomas Hay of Park. Later that year, on June 12, Francis Elliot took Captain Dalrymple's place in the 14th Regiment.[58] Evidently Captain Dalrymple left the military at this time and made his home in Wigtown, Scotland. Sometime after his marriage he changed his name to Dalrymple-Hay. It seems he was active in the local government and the militia units formed in response to the Militia Act of 1797. In June of 1797, he was made Major-Commandant of the Wigton [Wigtown] Volunteers. He was created 1st Baronet Dalrymple-Hay in 1798. In 1802 he was promoted to Colonel of the Kirkcudbright and Wigtown Regiment of North British Militia. In 1807, he was made Deputy Lieutenant of the county of Wigtown.[59] Captain Dalrymple (later Colonel) and his wife Susan were the parents of seven children.[60] He died in Edinburgh on May 5, 1812.[61] The Dalrymple-Hay baronetcy is still active. As noted earlier in the book, Captain Dalrymple was Charles Fordyce's third cousin, once removed.

∽

John Batut was commissioned an ensign in the 33rd Regiment of Foot on November 4, 1758. He was promoted to lieutenant in the 33rd on March 17, 1761.[62] The 33rd Regiment was posted to Germany during the Seven Years War, fighting in the battles of Cloister Camp, October 16, 1760, Villinghausen July 16, 1761, and Wilhelmsthal, June 24, 1762. Although in a different regiment than Charles Fordyce at this time—Charles was in the 88th—it is conceivable Lieutenant Batut met Charles in Germany since they were involved in the same campaigns.

With the end of the Seven Years War in 1763, Lieutenant Batut was put on half pay* in the 33rd Regiment. He remained in that status through 1770 when he was commissioned lieutenant in the 14th Regiment on December 25.[63] As noted, Lieutenant Batut could have met Charles Fordyce during some of the campaigns in Germany during the Seven Years War. In any event, they were fellow officers in the 14th Regiment from 1770 to 1775—five years.

Lieutenant Batut was promoted to captain lieutenant in the 14th Regiment on October 15, 1775,[64] but was still denominated a lieutenant at the Battle of Great Bridge in December 1775. On December 10, 1775, he was promoted to captain, taking the place of Captain Fordyce.[65]

---

* Retired officers or those in inactive status received half their normal pay.

Lieutenant Batut was wounded—shot through the leg—and captured at the Battle of Great Bridge but it is possible he was returned to active duty in a prisoner exchange soon after the battle. Governor Dunmore initiated such an exchange in a letter to Colonel Howe of December 25.[66] If returned to active duty, he may have continued to serve with Governor Dunmore through the summer of 1776. However, by one account, he was paroled[67] and would have been ineligible for active duty. In either case, he probably returned to England in 1777 with the rest of the officers in the 14th.

On the *Army Lists* of 1777 to 1783, he is identified as a captain in the 14th Regiment. He could have been part of a Marine force that included the 14th sent to the relief of Gibraltar in 1781. The 14th was also part a force deployed to Jamaica in 1782. It is not clear Captain Batut was with the regiment in Jamaica since he was again placed on half pay in 1783, and William Burnett took his place as captain January 24, 1784.[68] He died in Colyton, County Devon, England January 2, 1788.[69]

༄

Andrew Laurie (sometimes Lawrie) was commissioned an ensign in the 14th Regiment on June 24, 1767. In the muster rolls of 1769 and 1772, he is listed in the company commanded by Captain Alexander Murray. Although in different companies, he and Charles Fordyce served together in the 14th for eight years. Laurie was promoted to lieutenant on December 22, 1772.[70]

Just before the Battle of Great Bridge, Laurie was promoted to captain in the 2nd Battalion of the 71st Regiment in America. This regiment, like the 78th, was also known Fraser's Highlanders. Although his promotion occurred on November 30, 1775, it is not clear when he joined the 71st. Evidently, he was still serving in the 14th Regiment in 1776 since he purchased the adjutancy of the 14th from Cornelius Smelt on January 13, 1776.[71] Given this link to the 14th after the Battle of Great Bridge, Lieutenant Laurie may have continued to serve with Governor Dunmore then joined his new regiment, the 71st, when the governor quit the Chesapeake Bay and sailed to New York in August 1776.

The 71st Regiment was very active during the Revolutionary War, joining General Howe on Staten Island as he began the New York Campaign in 1776.[72] Laurie could have arrived at Staten Island with the detachment of the 14th Regiment in August 1776 and joined the 71st at that time. If so, he could have been with the 71st at the Battle of Long Island and the engagements at Fort Washington and Fort Lee later in that campaign. In 1777 the 71st fought at Brandywine, Pennsylvania, and a detachment fought with General Burgoyne in his operations along the Hudson River. The 71st was especially active in General Clinton's second Southern campaign (the first had been the fractured and ineffective effort of 1775-1776), fighting at Savannah, Georgia in 1778 and 1779, Charleston, South Carolina in 1780, Camden, South Carolina ("Gates' Defeat") in 1780, the Battle of Cowpens, South Carolina in February 1781 and the Battle of Guilford Court House, North Carolina in March 1781. The regiment was besieged at Yorktown, Virginia in September 1781 and surrendered with General Cornwallis. On July 16, 1782, William Narin took Captain Laurie's place in the 71st Regiment.[73] Based on this replacement and an annotation "dd" in the *Army List* of 1782, it is possible Captain Laurie died of disease in the Carolinas in 1781 or 1782.[74]

※

Cornelius Smelt was born August 1748 to William Smelt, Receiver General of Casual Revenue of Barbados and his wife Dorothy Caley. He was commissioned an ensign in the 14th Regiment on June 12, 1765, when he was sixteen years old. Ensign Smelt would have been with the 14th Regiment when they were deployed to Halifax in 1766. In the Monthly Return for the regiment at Boston in 1769, he is listed in Captain Gifford's Company. Cornelius was promoted to Lieutenant on February 22, 1772. On the *Monthly Return* for the regiment of April 24, 1772, three months before they sailed for St. Vincent, Lieutenant Smelt is listed as on the King's leave. Lieutenant Smelt is still listed on the King's leave on the *Return* at Fort Tyrell, St Vincent, of September 18, 1772 and based on the number of lieutenants listed in the *Returns* for the regiment at St. Vincent in 1773, it seems Lieutenant Smelt did not join the regiment on the island.[75] He was promoted to adjutant of the 14th Regiment, June 18, 1775 and was with Captain Leslie's detachment in Virginia in October 1775. At the time of the Battle of Great Bridge, he was twenty seven years old and he had served with Captain Fordyce for ten years.[76]

Lieutenant Smelt purchased a captaincy in the 35th Regiment on June 13, 1776, so it is possible he did not remain with the detachment of the 14th Regiment that stayed with Governor Dunmore after the Battle of Great Bridge. The 35th Regiment was active in the Americas throughout the Revolutionary War. They were present on Long Island during the battle there in August 1776. In September 1776 they were part of the amphibious assault at Kip's Bay and the occupation of New York City which followed. They were at the Battle of White Plains in October 1776. The regiment wintered in New Jersey in 1777. Evidently they were posted to New York with General Clinton in 1778. In November of 1778, the 35th was assigned to the West Indies and remained in that theater for the duration of the war.[77]

On October 6, 1785, Captain Smelt married Mary Trant Otley. He was appointed Deputy Governor of Southsea Castle on July 17, 1787. On June 15, 1805, he was appointed Lieutenant Governor of the Isle of Man, a position he held for the next twenty-seven years. After the death of his first wife, Mary, Cornelius married Ann Hale, daughter of General Sir John Hale. He died at age 84 on November 28, 1832 while serving on the Isle of Man.[78]

༄

Hill Wallace, also known as St. John Wallace, was born in 1754. He joined the army as an ensign on March 20, 1771, when he was seventeen years old. Ensign Wallace's initial service in the 14th was in Captain Edmond Mason's company at Boston in 1771, so he served with Charles Fordyce for four years. He was promoted to lieutenant in the 14th Regiment on December 15, 1773, about seven months after the regiment arrived in St. Augustine from the campaign in St. Vincent. He arrived in Virginia with Captain Fordyce on October 20, 1775. After the Battle of Great Bridge, he continued to serve with Governor Dunmore. As noted previously, he was wounded in an action against the rebels in Maryland on July 23, 1776. He probably returned to England with the officers of the regiment in 1777.

Wallace had been promoted to captain lieutenant on October 24, 1776 and was promoted to captain May 11, 1781.[79] He married Miss Ellen Legg in Belfast, Northern Ireland, on January 2, 1784 and it seems he inherited a sizeable fortune—some £5,000—at the same time.[80] On December 18, 1784, Captain Alexander MacBean of the "late 71st Regiment" took his place in the 14th Regiment[81] and it seems Wallace was put on half pay in the disbanded 71st at that time. He remained on the half-pay list for the rest of his life.[82] He died on April 29, 1794 at the age of 40.[83]

୪

Thomas Appleford Wools (also spelled Woolls) joined the 14th Regiment as an ensign on June 18, 1773. His first service in the regiment would have been at St. Augustine that same year. Charles Fordyce arrived at St. Augustine with the 14th after the campaign in St, Vincent in 1773 and remained there until deployed to Virginia. So at the time of the Battle of Great Bridge he and Ensign Wools had served together for about two years. Wools was promoted to lieutenant in November 22, 1775,[84] but in Captain Leslie's return of the strength of his detachment on December 1, 1775, he is still listed as an ensign. Ensign Wools may have arrived at Norfolk with Captain Blackett but it is also possible he was the ensign "on his way over land" reported in Dixon and Hunter's *Virginia Gazette* of August 5, 1775.

On January 4, 1779, while stationed at Chatham Barracks in Kent, England, Lieutenant Wools submitted a "Memorial to King George" wherein he petitioned the King to allow him to resign from the service "on account of his own private affairs." [85] As was common for this type of memorial, Lieutenant Wools asked not only to resign his commission but, in his case, to sell his lieutenancy at the regulated price—£550 in 1776.[86] In the memorial he also noted he had served five years and seven months in the regiment and that he "was with a detachment of his regiment against the Rebels in Virginia." He added he "acted" as adjutant during the "Campaign of 1776." This campaign could have been with Governor Dunmore in Virginia after the Battle of Great Bridge, or with General Clinton in the "campaign" in North and South Carolina, which also occurred in 1776. His official commission as adjutant is dated December 6, 1776, when he took the place of Andrew Laurie.[87] The fact he acted as adjutant in 1776 is consistent with the fact Lieutenant Laurie had accepted a captaincy in the 71st Regiment in November 1775, and was probably with that regiment in 1776.

Lieutenant Wool's memorial was forwarded to General Jeffery Amherst, Commander-in-Chief of the British Army, by his former commander, William Dalrymple. In forwarding the memorial, Colonel Dalrymple noted Lieutenant Wools had "discharged his duty with fidelity and ability."[88] Evidently his petition was granted since Lieutenant John Brownrigg took his place as adjutant on June 7, 1779[89] and it seems he left the service at this time.

It is possible Lieutenant Wools was the son of Thomas Appleford Wools, vicar of Fareham, Hants. This conclusion is based on the unusual name—Thomas Appleford Wools—and speculating Thomas' was about 20 years old when he entered the service. If he were the son of this Thomas Appleford Wools, he would have been born July 12, 1750, in Fareham and his mother's name would have been Elizabeth.[90] Given this birthdate, he would have been twenty-two years old when he joined the 14th Regiment on June 18, 1773. Again, if this connection to the Thomas and Elizabeth Wools family is correct, Thomas matriculated at Pembroke College, Oxford November 12, 1767,[91] almost six years before enlisting in the 14th. After resigning his commission in 1779, he would have returned to Fareham and died at nearby Kitknocks, Hampshire, August 6, 1796, at age 46.[92]

In addition to his military service in the 14th Regiment, it is possible Lieutenant Wools was instrumental in raising a troop of "Gentleman Yeomanry Cavalry" in Hampshire in 1795 for "internal defense," and that he served in the troop as captain.[93]

༄

James Boyes (often spelled Boys) joined the 14th Regiment as an ensign on December 16, 1773. This was the same day Peter

Henry Leslie joined.[94] As noted earlier, Peter Leslie was sixteen when he was commissioned and it is possible Ensign Boyes was about the same age. Based on the possibility he was a sixteen to nineteen-year-old teenager when commissioned, he would have been born between 1754 and 1757.

Like fellow ensigns James Lindsay and Charles Ogle, he was probably among the thirteen officers and 74 privates of the 14th Regiment who sailed from Dover to Boston on March 28, 1775, and was one of three ensigns arriving at Gosport from Boston on August 12. Given the date of his commission—December 16, 1773—the action in Virginia in 1775 was probably the first he had seen in the army. Under these circumstances, it is likely Ensign Boyes only served with Charles Fordyce for the few months they were together in Virginia.

On October 15, 1775, shortly after he arrived in Virginia, Ensign Boyes was promoted to lieutenant. He took the place of John Batut who had been promoted from lieutenant to captain lieutenant at the same time.[95] It is possible Lieutenant Boyes continued to serve with Governor Dunmore after the Battle of Great Bridge and through the summer of 1776. If he did serve through 1776, he would have returned to England with the remnants of the 14th Regiment in 1777. On October 5, 1779, he was promoted to captain and transferred to the 87th Regiment. This was one day before fellow lieutenant, Charles Ogle, was promoted and transferred to the same regiment.[96]

The 87th Regiment left Plymouth England for the West Indies in January 1780.[97] On that station, the 87th served as a Marine unit that was part of a British naval force sent to check the French fleet in the West Indies. The British fleet saw action near Martinique and detachments of the 87th were deployed to the islands of Martinique and St. Lucia. The confrontation between the British and French in the West Indies ended with the end of the American Revolution in 1782. The 87th returned to England in October of that year.[98] That Captain Boyes served in the West Indies at this time is borne out by an award of £24 7s he received in February 1787 for "losses he sustained by the hurricane in the West Indies, in the year 1780."[99]

Epilogue

On May 20, 1783, the 87th was disbanded, and Captain Boyes was put on half pay.[100] In August 1795, he was promoted from half-pay status in the 87th Regiment to be the major of "A Regiment of Foot" commanded by Lieutenant Colonel John Podmore. A notice that "Major __ Boys from Lieutenant Colonel Podmore's Regiment" was to be Major of the 53rd Regiment, commanded by Lieutenant Colonel Stafford Lightburne, was published by the War Office on September 12, 1795.[101] It seems his posting to the 53rd was for a short time since the *Army Lists* of 1795, 1796 and 1797 do not include a Major Boys or Boyes in the 53rd Regiment. James was still listed on half pay in the *Army List* of 1796, with the rank of Major and no regimental affiliation.[102] In the 1797 *Army List* he is included as a Major in the "late" 131st Regiment of Foot with a date-of-rank of March 1, 1794.[103] The 131st Regiment was formed in response of France's declaration of war against England in 1793 and the emerging threat of a French invasion of England at that time. This listing in the 131st is consistent with the notice of a promotion in *The London Gazette* of January 6, 1798. According to *The Gazette*, "James Boys, of the late 131st Foot," was promoted to lieutenant colonel January 1, 1798.[104] It is not clear the regiment was ever activated, nevertheless, Lieutenant Colonel Boyes continued in the army at half pay until his death in 1808.[105] At some point he married Mrs. Jane Owen, who is designated his "Dear wife, Mrs. Boys, late Mrs. Jane Owen" in his will of 1797.[106] The probate date of the will was January 26, 1808.

༄

Charles Ogle purchased the commission of ensign in the 14th Regiment on March 25, 1774.[107] He was commissioned just a few days before fellow ensign James Lindsay. As with other ensigns in the 14th, it is reasonable to conclude Ensign Ogle was a teenager—probably between the ages of sixteen and nineteen—when commissioned. If so, he could have been born between 1755 and 1758. As has been speculated for fellow ensign James Boyes, he was probably among the thirteen officers and 74 privates of the 14th Regiment who sailed from Dover to Boston on March 28, 1775 and was one of three ensigns arriving at Gosport from Boston on

August 12. Having just arrived in America and commissioned the year before, the fighting in Virginia would have been his first in the army. As was the case with Ensign Boyes, Ensign Ogle would only serve with Charles Fordyce for the few months they were together in Virginia.

On December 10, 1775, the day after the Battle of Great Bridge, Ensign Ogle was promoted to lieutenant, taking the place of Peter Henry Leslie, who died in the battle.[108] As has been speculated for Lieutenant Boyes, it is possible Lieutenant Ogle served with Governor Dunmore through the summer of 1776 and returned to England with the officers of the 14th Regiment in 1777. On October 6, 1779, he was promoted to Captain and transferred to the 87th Regiment.[109] Fellow lieutenant, James Boyes, had been promoted and transferred to the 87th the day before.

Serving as a Marine with the 87th Regiment, he was with a naval force sent against the French in the West Indies in 1780. He was wounded in an engagement between the British and French fleets on April 17, 1780 near Martinique.[110] Evidently Captain Ogle was aboard the *Montague* when he was wounded because an officer on that ship reported his wounds to be "desperate," noting he "… lost an arm, wounded in the other, and in many parts of his body, head and legs."[111] Ogle retired from the 87th Regiment in 1783, no doubt due to disability resulting from the injuries sustained at Martinique. On July 26, 1786, he was awarded an annual allowance of £100 "in consideration of his having been severely wounded and disabled in the service." He was receiving the allowance as late as 1817.[112]

જ

James Lindsay, also known as James Stair Lindsay, was the fourth son of James Lindsay, 5th Earl of Balcarres and his wife, Anne Dalrymple. He was born in Kilconquhar, Fife, Scotland on December 16, 1758.[113] James was commissioned an ensign in the 14th Regiment on April 27, 1774 when he was fifteen years old.[114] He was probably one of the thirteen officers and 74 privates of the 14th Regiment who left Dover on March 28, 1775 bound for Boston,[115] and was one of three ensigns arriving at Gosport from

Boston on August 12, 1775. The action he saw in Virginia would have been his introduction to combat. Given this timing, it is likely he only served with Charles Fordyce for the few months they were together in Virginia.

Born December 16, Ensign Lindsay was sixteen years old on the day of the Battle of Great Bridge—December 9. He was promoted to lieutenant on December 11, 1775—five days before his seventeenth birthday—taking the place of William Napier, who died December 10 of wounds sustained in the battle.[116] After the battle, it is possible Lindsay continued to serve with Governor Dunmore through the summer of 1776, then returned to England with the officers of the 14th in 1777.

On December 25, 1777, at age 19, he was promoted to captain in the 1st Battalion of the 73rd Regiment of Foot, serving with his brothers, Colin and John.[117] The 73rd was deployed to India in 1779 to support the East India Company in what came to be known as the Carnatic War. James was wounded in a battle with the French Mahrattas at Cuddalore, India on June 13, 1783, "by a grape-shot which entered below his left knee." He died in a French hospital on June 22 of "mortification" of the wound and was buried that day.[118] He was 24 years old and never married.[119] He and Captain Fordyce were related as third cousins. Their common ancestor was their 2nd Great-Grandfather, James Dalrymple, 1st Viscount Stair.

APPENDIX

ANNOTATED LIST OF ACCOUNTS OF THE BATTLE OF GREAT BRIDGE

APPENDIX

As noted in the text, numerous accounts of the Battle of Great Bridge were published shortly after the battle. Twenty-two of those accounts are abstracted in this Appendix. This collection is not comprehensive, but it contains the origins—the earliest publication—of most of the remarkable claims made about the battle.

Although there are inconsistencies in the accounts, they are actually quite consistent regarding the key elements of the engagement. The inconsistencies seem to occur when reporters want to emphasize a particularly exciting or dramatic aspect of the battle. For example, Captain Fordyce is said to have been shot "numerous" times in most of the accounts. But for some of the reporters this kind of estimate did not convey the fortitude and resolve they wanted to ascribe to a man who was such a presence on the battlefield that day. In her memoir, Mrs. Maxwell, Captain Fordyce's sometime hostess while he was in Norfolk, claimed he was shot no less than 17 or 18 times. Captain John Dalrymple, Fordyce's comrade-in-arms and fast friend, claimed he died "covered with 11 wounds." Caleb Mason of the North Carolina detachment at the battle claimed Fordyce was shot seven times and another American veteran, William White of Colonel Edward Stevens' minuteman battalion, deposed he was shot ten times.

In what seems to be another instance of dramatic flair, Mrs. Maxwell noted the first wound Captain Fordyce received was a bullet to the knee "but he tied a handkerchief round it, and marched on cheering his men." In a compilation of the accounts of officers from Colonel Woodford's camp published in the *Virginia Gazette*, Captain Fordyce was said to have waved his hat over his head and told his men the day was their own. At the same time, veteran Caleb Mason observed Captain Fordyce "on the bridge at the head of his men with his sword in one hand and a torch in the other to burn our breastworks."

Some reports of the battle include the exciting account of a deception planned and executed by the American forces. The deception involved the dissemination of a false report of the Patriot strength at Great Bridge. It was a plan of some sophistication that included the arranged "desertion" of a servant of Major Marshall's with false intelligence Colonel Woodford had only 300 poorly armed shirtmen* at his entrenchments on the road through the village. The deception added excitement to the battle by highlighting the cleverness of the Patriots and the gullibility of the villainous Lord Dunmore. In some reports, this excitement was amplified by representing the deception as pivotal to the Patriot victory. But there are questions regarding the feint. For example, given its alleged importance, why was the American commander, Colonel Woodford, ignorant of it? He reported learning of the ploy from his prisoner, Lieutenant Batut, after the battle (accounts 2, 3 and 4). Questions also arise because many accounts, including one of the most comprehensive, that of the "Officers who have just arrived in town from Colonel Woodford's camp" (account 16), do not mention the deception. Neither does John Marshall, Major Marshall's son, in the account of the battle he included in his *Life of George Washington*.[1] Additional questions arise because, other than Lieutenant Batut, only one British participant reports the deception. And this report, the "Extract of a letter from Elizabeth River, Norfolk, Virginia dated Jan. 3, 1776" (account 11), is of dubious credibility since it was written by a Loyalist volunteer—someone unlikely to have had first-hand knowledge of intelligence informing the British plan. In the other reports by the British participants, the Patriot strength was always overestimated.

In addition to this kind of drama, the accounts also include information that is remarkable but unique to a single report. For example, the claim in the "Extract of a letter from Northampton County, in Virginia" (account 12), that Captain Fordyce was "an old acquaintance" of Colonel Woodford's is quite intriguing, but

---

* As noted in a footnote in Chapter 9, the "uniform" of most of the soldiers in Virginia's army at this time was the "hunting shirt," an open-front garment of osnaburg with distinctive fringes at the seams. The soldiers wearing these shirts were called shirtmen.

absent from any other report. So too is Mrs. Maxwell's unique claim (account 17) Captain Fordyce was married. She certainly infers as much when she notes, "It was said that he [Captain Fordyce] gave his watch to his friend, with a message for his wife."

None of these inconsistencies or peculiarities will be resolved or explained in this Appendix. As noted earlier, this list is provided in an attempt to establish the origin of the various "particulars" of the battle which were highlighted in contemporary accounts as well as later histories. For each of the twenty-two accounts, a synopsis is presented that is a list of the key elements of the battle as provided in the particular account.

The collection is divided into four parts, Colonel Woodford's Letters, Letters from Participants in the Battle, Contemporary Reports and Accounts Included in Revolutionary War Pension Applications.

Colonel Woodford Letters

It seems Colonel Woodford wrote four letters directly related to the battle. These letters contain much of the often-quoted information about the incident. One was dated December 9, two December 10 and another December 11. All four letters are transcribed in: Dice Robins Anderson, editor, *Richmond College Historical Papers*, Volume 1 (1915), pp. 115, 116, 119 and 120. Some are included in *Naval Documents of the American Revolution* (NDAR) 3:28, 39 and 40, *American Archives* 4:224, 228, 233 and newspapers, in particular various editions of the *Virginia Gazette*. In addition to American newspapers, these letters were published in numerous newspapers in Great Britain. Since all of Colonel Woodford's letters may be cited as "Colonel Woodford to the President of the Convention," they are distinguished here by quoting the first line of the letter. The letters are:

1. "William Woodford on the Virginia Service to the President of the Convention at Williamsburg, December 9, 1775." *American Archives* 4:224. Also in: *Virginia Gazette*, Pinkney, December 13, 1775, p. 2, *Virginia Gazette*, Dixon and Hunter, December 16, 1775, p. 3.

In the newspaper accounts, this letter is not attributed to Colonel Woodford.

>This letter begins, "The enemy were reinforced about 3 o'clock this morning with (as they tell me) every soldier of the 14th regiment at Norfolk ...." The letter includes the following particulars of the battle:

A. British reinforcements arrived at their fort at about 3:00 AM the morning of December 9.
B. At this point the British force included every soldier of the 14th Regiment at Norfolk, amounting to 200.
C. Captain Leslie had overall command of the British force.
D. The attack commenced in the morning after reveille beating.
E. The British had to lay planks on the bridge to cross it.
F. The British attack was "to force our breast-work."
G. After the battle, the British prisoners told their captors Dunmore's entire force amounted to 500, which included "volunteers and blacks."
H. The British employed two pieces of cannon.
I. Only "his Majesty's soldiers" marched against the entrenchments.

2. "Extract of a letter from Col. William Woodford to the Hon. Edmund Pendleton, Esq; President of the General Convention, Great Bridge, December 10, 1775." Also in: *American Archives*, 4:233, *Virginia Gazette*, Pinkney, December 13, 1775, p. 2, *Virginia Gazette*, Dixon and Hunter, December 16, 1775, p. 3.

>This letter begins, "I must apologize for the hurry in which I wrote you yesterday ...." These are the particulars:

A. A prisoner, Lieutenant [John] Batut, sent a message to Captain Leslie informing him of the humane treatment of the prisoners.
B. Captain Leslie returned the compliment and thanked Colonel Woodford "for his kind treatment of the prisoners."
C. Captain Fordyce led the grenadiers of the 14th Regiment; most of the soldiers were grenadiers of that regiment.
D. Colonel Woodford noted Captain Fordyce was a gallant and brave officer and promised to inter him with all the military honors due to his great merit.

Appendix: Annotated List of Accounts of the Battle of Great Bridge 227

    E. Lieutenant Batut informed Woodford that a servant of Major Marshall "deserted" and told Lord Dunmore that not more than 300 shirtmen were at Great Bridge.
    F. Woodford surmised, "That imprudent man caught at the bait, and dispatched Capt. Leslie with all the regulars, who arrived at the fort about 4 in the morning."

3. "Extract of a letter from Col. William Woodford to the Hon. Edmund Pendleton, Esq; President of the General Convention, Great Bridge, December 10, 1775." Also in: *American Archives*, 4:228, *Virginia Gazette*, Purdie, December 15, 1775, p. 2.

    This letter begins, "A servant belonging to major Marshal, who deserted the other night from col. Scott's party …." Particulars include:
    A. A servant belonging to major Marshal, said to have deserted from Colonel Scott's party, duped Lord Dunmore.
    B. British prisoner Batut told Colonel Woodford the servant told them not more than 300 shirtmen were at hand and Lord Dunmore believed him.
    C. Captain Leslie with all the regulars (about 200) arrived at the bridge about 3:00 AM and were joined by about 300 black and white slaves.
    D. They laid planks upon the bridge, and crossed just after reveille beat.
    E. Lieutenant Batut commanded the advance party.
    F. Captain Fordyce of the grenadiers led the van with his company.
    G. Fordyce "for coolness and bravery, deserved a better fate."
    H. The brave fellows who fell with him behaved like heroes.
    I. They "marched up to our breastwork with fixed bayonets."
    J. The blacks and volunteers in the rear, with Captain Leslie, did not advance any farther than the bridge.
    K. Woodford's forces buried 12, besides Captain Fordyce who was buried "with all the military honours due to his rank."
    L. British prisoners included Lieutenant Batut and 16 privates, all wounded.
    M. In this letter, Woodford makes the famous assessment, "This was a second Bunker's Hill affair, in miniature; with

this difference, that we kept our post, and had only one man wounded in the hand."

4. "William Woodford to the Honble President of the Convention at Williamsburg, Great Bridge, December 11, 1775." Evidently this letter and the previous letter were the basis for an account published as "From a Correspondent, December 13," in *Virginia Gazette*, Pinkney, December 13, 1775, pp. 2, 3.

> This letter begins, "Several people from the other side the River have come in to me this morning, & informs they saw Smallwood at the Ferry …." Particulars include:
> A. Smallwood counted the British dead and wounded at a ferry at the river.
> B. He noted 65 men crossed the river at the ferry in the boats.
> C. He was informed eleven of Fordyce's grenadiers escaped.
> D. Mr. Max Calvert of Norfolk said the Enemy's whole loss was 102 Killed and wounded, among them several officers.
> E. Mr. Calvert claimed he was present "when his Lordship rec[eive]d the news of the defeat, at which he Raved like the madman he is, & swore to Hang the Boy that gave the Information this Day."

Letters from Participants in the Battle

5. "Major Spotswood of Col. Woodford's Regiment to a Friend in this City, Great Bridge, December 9, 1775." *Virginia Gazette*, Purdie, December 15, 1775, p. 2, *American Archives* 4:224.

> A. He heard Adjutant [Christopher] Blackburn call out, "Boys! stand to your arms!"
> B. He and Colonel Woodford "immediately got equipped, and ran out; the Colonel pressed down to the breastwork in our front."
> C. A very heavy fire ensued at the breastwork.
> D. There were no more than sixty men at the breastwork.
> E. The firing continued for about half an hour.
> F. The King's troops gave way after sustaining considerable loss.
> G. They behaved like "true-born Englishmen."

Appendix: Annotated List of Accounts of the Battle of Great Bridge 229

    H. "They mounted up to our intrenchments with fixed bayonets; our young troops received them with firmness, and behaved as well as it was possible for soldiers to do."
    I. Captain Leslie commanded the fort on the other side of the bridge.
    J. Captain Fordyce of the grenadiers led the van with his company.
    K. Lieutenant Batut commanded the advance party.
    L. Fordyce was killed within a few yards of the breastwork, with twelve privates.
    M. Lieutenant Batut and sixteen soldiers were taken prisoners, all wounded.
    N. Several others were carried into the fort under cover of their cannon.
    O. The amount of blood on the bridge suggested they must have lost one-half of their detachment.
    P. The only American casualty was a soldier slightly wounded in the hand.
    Q. Colonel Woodford had Captain Fordyce buried with the military honors due to his rank.

6. "Report of Captain [George] Johnston to Major Leven Powell, G Bridge Dec 9, 1775," *Leven Powell Papers 1774 – 1810*, Special Collections Research Center, Earl Gregg Swem Library, College of William and Mary, "Folder 3, Item 3: 9 Dec. 1775. George Johnston, Great Bridge, Va. to Leven Powell, Loudoun County, Va."

    A. The enemy attacked at about half an hour before sun rise.
    B. The attacking force was comprised of about 150 Regulars of the 14th Regiment, volunteers "without number" and three field pieces.
    C. "They marched boldly up to our Breast work."
    D. The breast work was about 200 yards from their fort.
    E. The attackers were exposed all the way to the "fullest fire of about thirty Men stationed always to defend that place."
    F. They began to retreat when they got within 50 yards of the breast work.
    G. "Captain Fordyce at every hazard rallied and brought them up to the very muzzles of our Guns."
    H. By this time, about sixty men were at the breastwork.

I. For about twenty minutes there was a "warm fire."
J. British casualties: One Captain and ten men killed, twenty wounded, four or five mortally.
K. Captain Fordyce's body was placed in "our Church."
L. Lieutenant Batut told Captain Leslie he and the other prisoners had met with kind treatment.
M. The officer who carried the flag of truce, Ensign Holmes, was on the bridge. He said the dragging of the dead over made a bloody path.
N. Thanks for the victory was due in part to "a little villain, who deserted from us a few nights ago." He informed Lord Dunmore Woodford had no more than three hundred men. With this intelligence, Lord Dunmore determined to attack with fixed bayonets.
O. The fight lasted about 45 minutes.
P. No more than 100 men of Woodford's force were engaged.

7. "'JD' [Captain John Dalrymple, 14th Regiment] to the Earl of Dumfries, Virginia, January 14, 1776," National Archives, UK PRO CO 5/40 folio 124.

   A. Captain Fordyce's "relations" named in the letter are his "brother" [John Fordyce], "Sir J. [John] Whitefoord," [a first cousin] and "Sir A. [Adam] Ferguson" [a second cousin].
   B. Dalrymple tells Lord Dumfries, "This is the second and last time they will mourn his death." [A false report of Captain Fordyce's death at St. Vincent in 1773 had been published in numerous British newspapers.]
   C. Fordyce fell "covered with 11 wounds" on the morning of December 9.
   D. Attack was "absurd, ridiculous and unnecessary."
   E. "Our little Detachmt, consisting of 121 rank & file, were ordered by the Governor to [attack] a strong Body of the rebels, consisting of upwards of 1000 ... securely intrenched."
   F. Dalrymple reasons that, after the battle of Kemps Landing, "The News of this reaching Williamsburg ... two Regiments were ... immediately sent down to oppose us."
   G. During the battle, the British force passed the bridge exposed to the Enemy.

Appendix: Annotated List of Accounts of the Battle of Great Bridge 231

    H. They "drove in their Out-Posts and advanced towards their Entrenchments, over a narrow Causeway which led from the Bridge through a Morass at the End of which they were securely posted."
    I. The approach was so narrow the attacking force had to march up by files.
    J. By a "Curve in the Causeway & Breastworks on the opposite Side of the Morass on our Right, we were flank'd & our Rear almost equally exposed as our Front."
    K. In less than ten Minutes, upwards of seventy of the "little Detachment" were killed or wounded.
    L. Captain Fordyce fell within four yards of the breastwork and stockade.
    M. Some of the grenadiers fell against it.
    N. The stockade was seven feet high with loop holes through which to fire.
    O. In Dalrymple's "Division," which was next to Fordyce's, five out of twenty two escaped.
    P. Lieutenants Napier, Leslie and Batut fell. Batut a prisoner.
    Q. "They were astonished at Men marching up with such Courage, or rather Madness, to certain Death."
    R. The rebels had one casualty, a man with a slight wound in the hand.

8. "Letter of Richard Kidder Meade, Norfolk, Town Camp, Dec. 18th, 1775," in: Theodorick Bland, *The Bland Papers*, Petersburg, Virginia: 1840, pp. 38, 39 and *The Southern Magazine and Monthly Review*, Vol. 1, Issues 1-2, Petersburg, Virginia: 1841, pp. 75, 76.

    A. A servant lad deserted from an officer of the minutemen and went to the enemy. He told them Woodford's force did not exceed 300 men. He deserted "without cause."
    B. Governor Dunmore, "pleased with this account, and sure of success, mustered his whole force."
    C. The British force was marched in the night to the fort with orders to force the breastworks early next morning, or die in the attempt.
    D. Lord Dunmore taught his troops to believe the provincials would not stand more than one fire.

- E. It was also reported the British were told no quarter would be given if the rebels conquered.
- F. The firing began before the men were out of their tents.
- G. The British advance was along a causeway, six abreast.
- H. A small guard at the American breastwork began the fire.
- I. This guard was soon reinforced.
- J. The enemy "fell back a little, but soon rallied, by the vast bravery of Capt. Fordyce."
- K. Fordyce "marched with many bullets through him, within twenty yards of the breastwork, before he fell."
- L. Colonel Stevens flanked them with a handful of riflemen.
- M. They "fought, bled, and died, like Englishmen and were treated as such."
- N. Many of the attackers were shot ten and twelve times. Their limbs were broken in two or three places, their "brains turning out."
- O. British casualties: about 100 killed and wounded.
- P. American casualties: one man wounded in the finger.
- Q. Many Negroes were sent off to the islands. Reports say the governor intends to send the rest, except those which may be useful as pilots or in similar jobs.

9. "Letter of Richard K. Meade to his Brother, Norfolk, Town Camp, December 19, 1775," in: John R. Thompson, ed., "Two Letters of Richard Kidder Meade," *The Southern Literary Messenger*, Volume 24 (New Series Volume 3) January to July 1857, Richmond: McFarlane, Fergusson & Co., 1857, pp. 23-25.

- A. A few days after Meade arrived at Great Bridge the British fort was reinforced by all the regulars.
- B. This occurred as a result of false information provided to Governor Dunmore by a deserter. The deserter informed the British Woodford's force did not exceed 250.
- C. The officer of the British reinforcement arrived the night before the attack with orders to "carry our Breast Work or Die in the Attempt."
- D. The British force crossed the bridge at about day break "with shouts of joy and advanced on the causeway toward [the] breast work."

Appendix: Annotated List of Accounts of the Battle of Great Bridge 233

- E. The breastwork was guarded by only a "Lieutenant's Guard" commanded by Ned [sic, Edward] Travis.
- F. Lieutenant Travis, "with some small assistance gave such a reception as the 14th Reg's had not been us'd to."
- G. Captain Leslie was first in command of the enemy.
- H. Captain Fordyce led the advance party "with a Bravery not to be equal'd."
- I. Many of the attackers fell and were wounded before they got within 150 yards.
- J. The numbers at the breast work were few and the enemy "got near the Breast Work" before the guard was increased.
- K. Fordyce, "with many bullets through him," got within fifteen yards of the breast work before he died.
- L. As the British retreated, many of them were cut off by a small flanking party commanded by Colonel Stevens.
- M. Enemy casualties: nearly 70 Grenadiers were killed and wounded, possibly 100, and a few Negroes.
- N. Volunteers came out of the fort but were driven back at the first fire.
- O. The British "fought Bled and Died like Englishmen, and … were treated with the utmost humanity."
- P. Many men were shot ten and twelve times. Almost every bone in those so wounded was broken.
- Q. Captain Fordyce, Lieutenant Nippier [sic] and Lieutenant Leslie were killed. Wounded (prisoner): Lieutenant Batut.
- R. One of the defenders slightly wounded in the finger.
- S. Reportedly many Negroes were sent to the West Indies and the rest would follow.
- T. The 14th Regiment had been "in many engagements and never worsted before."
- U. "Our men shot well."

10. "Extract of a Letter from a Midshipman on Board H.M. Sloop *Otter*, December 9, 1775" NDAR 3:29, *American Archives*, 4:540 and British newspapers: *Lloyd's Evening Post and British Chronicle*, March 4 to March 6, 1776, *The Scots Magazine*, Volume 38, p. 92, *Leeds Intelligencer*, 12 March 1776, p. 1, *Bath Chronicle and Weekly Gazette*, 7 March 1776, p. 3.

A. British forces: the British regulars, about sixty townsmen from Norfolk and a detachment of Sailors from the ships.
B. The combined force set out from Norfolk to attack "the Rebels at the great bridge."
C. The Rebels had been lodged there some time and had erected a breastwork on their side of the river opposite the British fort.
D. The British force arrived at the fort at 3:30 AM.
E. They refreshed themselves and prepared to attack the Rebels in their entrenchments.
F. Captain Squires sent his gunners and men to manage two pieces of cannon.
G. The cannon were put in the front, and ordered to begin the attack.
H. Rhetorical question: "How can it be supposed, that with 200 men we could force a strong intrenchment, defended by at least 2000?"
I. The British "marched up to their works with the intrepedity of lions."
J. Their fire was so heavy the British retreat was necessary to prevent everyone from being "cut off."
K. The Americans had built a strong breastwork across the causeway.
L. The width of the causeway limited the advance of the British troops to ranks of six men a-breast.
M. The causeway was almost surrounded by a large swamp.
N. Two small breastworks were built at the back of the swamp. From these the Rebels could direct flanking fire on those attacking the entrenchments.
O. Under these disadvantages it was impossible to succeed.
P. The British attackers "were so enraged, that all the intreaties, and scarcely the threats of their Officers, could prevail on them to retreat."
Q. British casualties: sixty killed, wounded, and taken prisoners. Among the slain were "the gallant Captain Fordyce, of the Grenadiers of the 14th Brigade, Lieutenants Napier and Leslie." Lieutenant Batut was wounded and taken prisoner.
R. The attack reflected the "greatest honour on the men for their unparalleled courage."

S. The British force left for the return trip to Norfolk at about 7:00 PM. They arrived at midnight and boarded the ships prepared to receive them.

11. "Extract of a letter from Elizabeth River, Norfolk, Virginia dated Jan. 3, 1776, to a Merchant in Liverpool," *Caledonian Mercury*, 16 March 1776, p. 1.

   A. We were led "into a very disagreeable error, by a prisoner we took from them, who informed us there were only 200 of them, which proved 1700."
   B. They "had created a breast work across a narrow passage on the other side the road, which we were obliged to pass along to attack them."
   C. "We marched out of a fort built on purpose to stop the rebels from marching into Norfolk county."
   D. British force: "about 180 regulars, 100 negroes [sic], and 60 volunteers."
   E. We "marched up to the breast works, and mounted them."
   F. "Only about four could march abreast."
   G. "About sixty-seven grenadiers [were] killed, wounded, and missing, before any other of the troops could march up to their assistance."
   H. Five of our commanding officers were killed on the spot.
   I. I was marched, with other volunteers, three times up to the bridge.
   J. The bullets flew there as thick as hail stones about us.

Contemporary Reports

12. "Extract of a letter from Northampton County, in Virginia," *The Remembrancer, or Impartial Repository of Public Events*, 1776, Vol. 2, Part 1, p. 225.

   A. Colonel Woodford, with the troops under his command, had been at Great-bridge "some time."
   B. Great Bridge was the only pass by which Woodford could march to Norfolk.
   C. Supposedly Woodford was waiting for artillery "to batter a fort which Lord Dunmore had erected" at Great Bridge.

D. Part of Woodford's force had entrenched within gun shot of the fort. They prevented the enemy from strengthening their fort, which it seems was not "cannon proof."
E. Lord Dunmore was informed by a deserter that the detachment near the fort consisted of about three hundred men, badly provided with ammunition. It is supposed this deserter was sent to Dunmore on purpose.
F. Governor Dunmore sent all his regulars to the fort the night of December 8 and early morning of December 9.
G. They had orders to "storm the Provincial entrenchments in the morning by day break."
H. The regulars "began a most furious attack upon the only part of the breast work which was accessible."
I. The works were so constructed that when they attacked this point they were flanked by part of the Provincial lines.
J. The causeway over which the attackers had to march was only wide enough to allow the attackers to advance "a few men abreast."
K. The attackers were cut off as fast as they approached.
L. In a few minutes, the attackers "were obliged to sound a retreat."
M. British casualties: Sixty-two men killed wounded and taken prisoner. The prisoners were all wounded. Evidently some of those taken had died by the time the report was made. Ten were still alive including "Captain" Batut.
N. Captain Fordyce, who headed the grenadiers, and a young "Captain" Leslie were killed.
O. The Provincials did not lose a man.
P. After the action, Colonel Woodford sent a flag to the fort proposing that all firing should cease until the dead were buried.
Q. Woodford desired to inter Captain Fordyce "who was a brave officer, and an old acquaintance" with military honors.
R. In the night the enemy evacuated the fort.
S. Evidently, Captain Leslie, in command of the regulars, absolutely refused to act any more on shore, until he could be better supported. He took this position because "he had already sacrificed many of his men in so desperate a service."

Appendix: Annotated List of Accounts of the Battle of Great Bridge 237

    T. The Norfolk volunteers and Governor Dunmore's black battalions refused to act without the assistance of the regulars.
    U. Governor Dunmore carried off his cannon, abandoned the entrenchments at Norfolk, and took shelter on board the ships.

13. "Extract of a Letter from a Gentleman dated Ship *William* off Norfolk, Virginia, December 25, 1775," NDAR 3:242. Also: *Scots Magazine*, Vol. 38, p. 91.

    A. Lord Dunmore received intelligence about a month earlier that a large body of the rebel army was on the march to destroy Norfolk.
    B. The rebel army took this action because the inhabitants of Norfolk had professed their loyalty to the government.
    C. In order to stop the rebels, Lord Dunmore sent a party of the 14th Regiment to a "narrow pass through which the rebels were to march." He erected a fort at the pass about eighteen miles from Norfolk.
    D. The fort was garrisoned with twenty-five men and a few volunteers from Norfolk.
    E. The rebels approached the fort and made several unsuccessful attacks.
    F. On December 8, Lord Dunmore received intelligence a party of the rebels had "crossed" and planned to attack the British fort "on both sides."
    G. Governor Dunmore judged it necessary to attack the main body.
    H. The attack occurred early on the morning of December 9.
    I. British forces: About 130 men in a detachment of the 14th Regiment under Captain Leslie, a party of marines, and some volunteers from Norfolk and Princess Anne [County]. Total force: about 250.
    J. "This small detachment made a furious attack upon the rebels intrenchments" but "after every effort which British soldiers could do, were obliged to retreat."
    K. British casualties: "The brave Capt. Fordyce, two lieutenants, and about fifteen privates killed." Forty wounded, fifteen of whom were captured including a lieutenant.

- L. The rebels were posted in great strength, 1100 in number.
- M. Rhetorical question: "So what could our small party do, upwards of four to one against them, and strongly intrenched?"
- N. "Lord Dunmore has done every thing for the cause of his King and country which man could do; and had a thousand troops arrived two months since, he would have had Virginia totally reduced to obedience by this time."

14. "Lord Dunmore to Lord Dartmouth, December 13, 1775, on board the Ship *Dunmore* off Norfolk," NDAR 3:140, 141. This letter is, in effect, Governor Dunmore's official after-action report. In it, he explains his rational for the attack, his plan of action and the reason the attack failed. This letter may have been intercepted by the Americans. This possibility is based on the fact much of its content (with some derisive editorializing) was published in an article headlined "A Remarkable Instance of Lord Dunmore's Humanity" in the *Virginia Gazette*, Pinkney, December 30, 1775, p. 4. Also in: *American Archives*, 4:292, 293. Most of this synopsis is left in the Governor's own words.

- A. He "thought it advisable to risque Something to save the Fort" after he was "informed that the Rebels had procured some Cannon from North Carolina, and that they were also to be reinforced from Williamsburg, and knowing that our little Fort was not in a Condition to withstand any thing heavier than Musquet Shot."
- B. The fort was across a critical line of communication and he knew "the loss of it was not only exposing the well disposed People of this part of the Country, to the resentment of the Rebels," but "the moment they pass that Bridge," he would "be cut off from every supply of Provisions from this Colony."
- C. Captain Samuel Leslie, commander of the detachment of the 14th Regiment, marched from Norfolk on Friday December 8, after dark, to reinforce the garrison at the fort.
- D. He had orders from Governor Dunmore "to order two Companies of Negroes to make a detour, and fall in behind the Rebels a little before break of Day in the morning, and

Appendix: Annotated List of Accounts of the Battle of Great Bridge 239

just as Day began to break, to fall upon the rear of the Rebels."

E. Governor Dunmore expected this would draw the rebels' attention, and make them leave the breastwork they had constructed near the fort. Leslie was then "with the Regulars, the Volunteers and some recruits to sally out of the Fort, and attack their breast work."

F. This plan was to be activated only if Captain Leslie found no "Material Change" on his arrival.

G. Leslie arrived at the fort in the night unperceived by the Rebels but "the Negroes by some mistake were sent out of the Fort to guard a pass, where it was thought the Rebels might attempt to pass, and where in fact some of them had Crossed a Night or two before."

H. It seems Governor Dunmore considered this a material change. He tells Lord Dartmouth, "Captain Leslie not finding the Negroes there, imprudently Sallied out of the Fort at break of Day."

I. Furthermore, Governor Dunmore tells the Secretary he supposed the Rebels "got intelligence of his design" and "were prepared to receive him from behind their Trenches, and kept a very heavy fire upon" the British force.

J. Despite the heavy fire, the advance Guard forced their way up to the breastwork.

K. Captain Fordyce fell with his hand on the breastwork.

L. British casualties: Three officers killed, one officer wounded and captured. 14 Privates killed and 43 wounded.

M. "Captain Fordyce's bravery and good conduct ... would do honor to any Corps of any Country, His loss is most Sincerely lamented by all who knew him."

N. "Lieutenants Napier and Leslie who were the other two Officers that fell, were both very deserving young Men and are really a loss to their Corps."

O. "The greatest praise is due to both Officers and Soldiers of the 14th for the undaunted Spirit they shewed on this occasion."

P. Captain [Samuel] Leslie was "much depressed by the loss of Lieutenant Leslie [Peter Henry Leslie], his Nephew."

15. Letter of William Eddis, Annapolis, January 16, 1776," in: William Eddis, *Letters from America, Historical and Descriptive: Comprising Occurrences from 1769, to 1777*, London: Printed for the author, and sold by C. Dilly in the Poultry, 1792, pp. 250 – 254.

　　A. On November 7, Governor Dunmore issued a Proclamation from the ship *William* lying off Norfolk, declaring martial law and requiring "all persons capable of bearing arms, to repair to his majesty's standard, or to be considered as traitors." The Proclamation included the provision "all indented servants, negroes, or others appertaining to persons in opposition to government, who were able and willing to bear arms, and who joined his majesty's forces, to be free."
　　B. Emancipating the Negroes excited a "universal ferment." It is likely the measure greatly strengthened "the general confederacy."
　　C. The proclamation had immediate effect in the "opulent town of Norfolk, where many of the inhabitants were well affected to government."
　　D. The governor "was speedily joined by hundreds of all complexions. He doubtless formed an idea, that the disposition to loyalty, which he discovered in that neighbourhood, would have been sufficiently general for enabling him to raise a force competent to re-establish, what he deemed a proper degree of subordination."
　　E. "This delusive expectation was interrupted by information, that a party of provincials, under the command of Colonel Woodford, were on their march to oppose his measures."
　　F. To obstruct their progress, and to support those who were well-affected, Lord Dunmore immediately took possession of a post at Great Bridge, some miles distant from Norfolk.
　　G. Great Bridge is a pass, of great consequence, and the only practicable way of approaching Norfolk.
　　H. The British and rebels fortified themselves within cannon shot of each other.
　　I. Since the only way they could approach each other was over a narrow causeway that lay between them, they appeared to be mutually secured from any danger of surprise.

Appendix: Annotated List of Accounts of the Battle of Great Bridge 241

- J. "Thus circumstanced, they continued inactive several days."
- K. At length, a design was formed of surprising the American troops in their entrenchments.
- L. "Captain Fordyce, a very gallant officer, at the head of about sixty grenadiers, led the attack."
- M. The attackers "passed the causeway with the utmost intrepidity, and with fixed bayonets rushed on an enemy, who were properly prepared for their reception."
- N. "Captain Fordyce's party were not only exposed, naked, to a heavy fire in front, but were enfiladed from another part of the works."
- O. "The brave leader, with several of his men, fell; the lieutenant, with the residue, all of whom were severely wounded, were taken prisoners."
- P. The fire of the artillery from the British fort, enabled the forces under the command of the governor, to retreat from the post without pursuit.
- Q. "All hopes in this quarter were terminated by the defeat."

16. Account from "Officers who have just arrived in town from Colonel Woodford's camp," *Virginia Gazette*, Pinkney, December 20, 1775, p. 2, *American Archives* 4:228 and NDAR 3:187. This seems to be the most comprehensive account of the battle. The officers providing input probably included Colonel Woodford and Major Spotswood. Given the details presented, officers who never published an account of their own could have provided input. The compiler of this account begins with a description of the scene of the action. He or she also notes the heroic action of the sentinels blunting the first advance of the British. This mention of the sentinels is key to understanding the actions ascribed to William "Billy" Flora. This synopsis is quoted from the published account with minor revisions designed to improve readability.

- A. The great bridge is built over the southern branch of the Elizabeth River, twelve miles above Norfolk. The land on each side is marshy to a considerable distance from the river, except at the two extremities of the bridge, where there are two pieces of firm land, which may not improperly be called islands, being surrounded entirely by water and marsh, and joined to the main land by causeways.

B. On the little piece of firm ground on the farther, or Norfolk side, Lord Dunmore erected his fort. It was situated such that his cannon commanded the causeway on his own side and the bridge between him and the rebels, with the marshes around him.

C. The island on the south side of the river contained six or seven houses, some of which were burnt down by the enemy, after the arrival of the rebel troops; in the others, adjoining the causeway on each side, Colonel Woodford stationed a guard every night. These were withdrawn before day that they might not be exposed to the fire of the enemy's fort in recrossing the causeway to our camp, this causeway being also commanded by their cannon.

D. Causeway on our side [the rebel side] was in length about one hundred and sixty yards. Breastwork was constructed at the south end of the causeway. From the breastwork ran a street, gradually ascending, about four hundred yards, to a church, where our main body were encamped.

E. On Saturday, December 9, after reveille beating, two or three great guns and some musketry were discharged from the enemy's fort, which, as it was not an unusual thing, was but little regarded by Colonel Woodford.

F. Soon afterwards he heard a call to the soldiers to stand to their arms; upon which, with all expedition, he made the proper dispositions to receive the enemy.

G. In the meantime, the enemy had crossed the bridge, fired the remaining houses upon the island, and some large piles of shingles, and attacked our guard in the breastwork.

H. Our men returned the fire, and threw them into confusion.

I. They were instantly rallied by a Captain Fordyce, and advanced along the causeway with great resolution, keeping up a constant and heavy fire as they approached.

J. Two field-pieces, which had been brought across the bridge and planted on the edge of the island, facing the left of our breastwork, played briskly at the same time upon us.

K. Lieutenant [Edward] Travis, who commanded in the breastwork, ordered his men to reserve their fire till the

Appendix: Annotated List of Accounts of the Battle of Great Bridge 243

    enemy came within the distance of fifty yards, and then they gave it to them with terrible execution.

L. The brave Fordyce exerted himself to keep up their spirits, reminded them of their ancient glory, and, waving his hat over his head, told them the day was their own.

M. He fell within fifteen steps of the breastwork. His wounds were many, and his death would have been that of a hero had he met it in a better cause.

N. The progress of the enemy was now at an end; they retreated over the causeway with precipitation, and were dreadfully galled in their rear.

O. Hitherto, on our side, only the guard, consisting of twenty-five, and some others, upon the whole amounting to not more than ninety, had been engaged.

P. Only the regulars of the Fourteenth Regiment, in number one hundred and twenty, had advanced upon the causeway; and about two hundred and thirty Tories and Negroes had, after crossing the bridge, continued upon the island.

Q. The regulars, after retreating along the causeway, were again rallied by Captain Leslie, and the two field-pieces continued to play upon our men.

R. At this time, Colonel Woodford was advancing down the street to the breastwork with the main body, and against him was now directed the whole fire of the enemy. Never were cannon better served; but yet, in the face of them and the musketry, which kept up a continual blaze, our men marched on with the utmost intrepidity.

S. Colonel Stevens, of the Culpepper battalion, was sent round to the left to flank the enemy, which was done with such activity and spirit that a rout immediately ensued.

T. The enemy fled into their fort, leaving behind them the two field-pieces, which they spiked with nails.

U. Many were killed and wounded in the flight, but Colonel Woodford very prudently restrained his troops from urging their pursuit too far.

V. From the beginning of the attack till the repulse from the breastwork, might be about fourteen or fifteen minutes; till the total defeat upwards of half an hour.

W. It is said that some of the enemy preferred death to captivity, from a fear of being scalped, which Lord Dunmore inhumanly told them would be their fate should they be taken alive. [See more on this claim in *Virginia Gazette*, Pinkney, December 23, 1775, p. 2.]
X. British casualties: Thirty-one, killed and wounded, fell into our hands, and the number borne off was much greater.
Y. Through the whole of the engagement, every officer and soldier behaved with the greatest courage and calmness.
Z. The conduct of our sentinels: Before they quitted their stations they fired at least three rounds as the enemy were crossing the bridge, and one of them, who was posted behind some shingles, kept his ground till he had fired eight times, and, after receiving a whole platoon, made his escape over the causeway into our breastwork.
AA. The scene was closed with as much humanity as it had been conducted with bravery. ... every one's attention was directed to the succor of the unhappy sufferers.
BB. Only American casualty: slight wound to a soldier's hand.
CC. The field-pieces raked the whole length of the street, throwing double-headed shot as far as the church, and afterwards, as our troops approached, cannonaded them heavily with grape-shot.

17. Account of Mrs. Maxwell, from: William Maxwell, "My Mother," in Edward W. James, ed., *Lower Norfolk County Virginia Antiquary*, Number 2, Part 3, Baltimore: The Friedenwald Co., 1897, p. 137. This was published after the fact but it does contain information referenced in various accounts of the battle. The account is referenced as "Copy of Memoir of Mrs. Helen Read (in the State Library, Richmond, Va.), entitled 'My Mother,' written from his mother's lips, by the late William Maxwell," in: *Lower Norfolk County Virginia Antiquary*, Number 1, Part 1, 1895, p. 60. Mrs. Maxwell (Mrs. Read at the time) died in 1833 so this material was recorded sometime before 1833.

A. Lord Dunmore, elated by his easy victory over the Norfolk and Pungo [northern part of Princess Ann County] militia, determined to attack our troops at the Great Bridge.

Appendix: Annotated List of Accounts of the Battle of Great Bridge 245

    B. Colonel Woodford's force was comprised of about a thousand men.
    C. They were strongly posted behind a breastwork which they had thrown up at the further end of the long causeway which led into the village.
    D. The attack was, indeed, a foolhardy undertaking but Governor Dunmore thought his grenadiers were invincible.
    E. He ordered Capt. Fordyce to lead the attack. "Capt. F. saw at once the folly and rashness of the order, but was too brave a man and too good a soldier to flinch from any duty."
    F. It was said that he gave his watch to his friend, with a message for his wife, for he knew, as he said, that he was going to his death.
    G. It was reported, too, that Col. Woodford, to deceive the British, had sent a Negro boy into their camp, who told them that our men were out of ammunition, had no powder, and had been obliged to melt up their shoe buckles for shot.
    H. This story, perhaps, duped Lord Dunmore and made him more confident of success.
    I. The gallant Fordyce led his men in the assault in the morning.
    J. Our people opened a deadly fire upon them with their rifles and shot them down like sheep.
    K. Fordyce himself was killed among the first, having received no less than 17 or 18 balls in different parts of his body.
    L. The first was in his knee, but he tied a handkerchief round it, and marched on cheering his men.
    M. There was a song made upon it: Come my brave boys, the day is our own.
    N. There were a number killed and many wounded, whom they brought back to Norfolk in wagons and carts.

18. "Extract of a letter from Thomas Ludwell Lee to Richard Henry Lee, Williamsburg, Decr. 9, 1775," NDAR 3:26. This account was written before the battle. It is included because it seems to be the account from which the denomination of Governor Dunmore's fort as a "hog pen" originates.

A. Account based on intelligence received at Headquarters from the camp at the [great] bridge.
B. The Virginia Army had been arrested for some time in its march to Norfolk by a redoubt, or stockade, or hog pen, as they call it here, by way of derision.
C. My apprehension is that we shall be amused at this outpost, until Dunmore gets the lines at Norfolk finished; where he is now entrenching, & mounting cannon, some hundreds of Negro's being employ'd in the work.
D. There is a strong expectation, based on intercepted intelligence, of a reinforcement arriving every hour from St. Augustine.

Information from Revolutionary War Pension Applications

19. Caleb Mason, S1917, Hertford County, North Carolina, Robert Howe's Regiment, transcribed and annotated by Pat Mason Harris and C. Leon Harris at revwarapps.org.

A. We remained a short time at Edenton, North Carolina. We were marched to Virginia and fought at Great Bridge.
B. Captain Fordise [sic: Charles Fordyce] of the British Grenadiers was killed.
C. When we got to the great bridge we made breastworks and entrenched ourselves behind them.
D. Fordise was in a Fort in an open Savanna.
E. Fordyce had orders from Governor Dunmore to drive us from the breastworks just at the break of day.
F. Capt Fordise appeared on the bridge at the head of his men with his sword in one hand and a torch in the other to burn our breastworks.
G. He called to his men to follow him that the day was theirs.
H. Just as he spoke those words he was shot down, seven balls having passed through his body.

20. William White, S1735, Colonel Stephen's [sic, Stevens'] Regiment of Minutemen in Fauquier County, Virginia, transcribed by Will Graves at revwarapps.org.

Appendix: Annotated List of Accounts of the Battle of Great Bridge

> "Fordyce marched out of the fort to storm our breastworks, and we killed, wounded and took prisoner his whole company except one Ensign who made his escape. Capt. Fordyce was shot through the body with ten balls."

21. Joseph Bridges, W4646 (wife Frances), Caroline County Virginia, 2nd Virginia Regiment, transcribed by Will Graves at revwarapps.org.

> "… he was marched with the Regiment down to Williamsburg and from thence to the great bridge and was at the Battle fought there the British commander Captain Fordice [sic, Capt. Charles Fordyce] fell within 30 feet of the American breastwork."

22. Samuel Templeman, S6204, Westmorland County, Virginia Militia, Transcribed by Will Graves at revwarapps.org.

   A. American troops at Great Bridge: a Company from North Carolina commanded by Captain William Goodman, the company commanded by Captain Grimes, in which I was Lieutenant [and] a detachment of minute men commanded by Major Ruffin from the lower part of Virginia.
   B. This force was employed in fortifying the American position until December 7, at which time the 2nd Virginia Regiment commanded by Colonel Woodford and a Battalion of minute men from Culpeper and Fauquier Counties, commanded by Major [Thomas] Marshall (father of the Chief Justice), arrived.
   C. Two days after the arrival of this force the battle of the great bridge occurred.
   D. Fordyce fell within a few yards of our Breast-work.
   E. Result: The entire rout of the British force, with a considerable loss on their side in killed, wounded & prisoners.

NOTES

Abbreviations and Acronyms

American Archives: Force, Peter, ed. *American Archives, Fourth Series, A Documentary History of the English Colonies in North America*. Vols. 1-4. Washington: M. St. Clair Clarke and Peter Force, 1839-1843.

DAR: Davies, K. G., ed. *Documents of the American Revolution 1770-1783, Colonial Office Series*, Shannon: Irish University Press, 1972.

NDAR: Clark, William Bell, ed. *Naval Documents of the American Revolution (NDAR)*. Vols. 1-7. Washington: GPO, 1964-1968.

Notes: Introduction

[1] In a note in his history of British colonial policy, George Beer observed, "In the controversial literature of 1764 and 1765, a large number of colonial writers asserted that the colonies had contributed their full proportion during the war." George Louis Beer, *British Colonial Policy, 1754-1765*, New York: Macmillan Company, 1907, p. 270. In the note, Beer cites Thatcher, Otis, Hopkins and Franklin.

[2] George Louis Beer, *op cit*, p. 14.

[3] Thomas Carter, *Historical Record of the Forty-Fourth, Or the East Essex Regiment of Foot*, London: W. O. Mitchell, 1864, p. 9.

[4] Braddock is said to have told Benjamin Franklin, "The savages may be formidable to your raw American militia; upon the king's regulars and disciplined troops it is impossible they should make any impression." George Bancroft, *A History of the United States*, Vol. 4, Boston: Little, Brown, 1852, p. 184.

[5] George Washington's report of the battle "George Washington to Robert Dinwiddie, Fort Cumberland, Md., 18 July 1755," Worthington Chauncey Ford, editor, *The Writings of George Washington*, Vol. 1, New York: G. P. Putnam, p. 173.

[6] Arthur Granville Bradley, *The Fight with France for North America*, Westminster: A. Constable and Co., Ltd., 1900. p. 104.

[7] Ron Chernow, *Washington, a Life*, New York: Penguin Books, 2010, p. 53.

[8] *Ibid*, p. 58-60.

[9] "Extract of a Letter from Will's Creek dated July 10, 1755," *Derby Mercury*, 22 August 1755, p. 4. *Caledonian Mercury*, 2 September 1755, p. 4. See also: N. Darnell Davis, "British Newspaper Accounts of Braddock's Defeat," *The Pennsylvania*

Magazine of History and Biography, Vol. 23 (1899), Philadelphia: Historical Society of Pennsylvania, 1899, pp. 310-328.

[10] Edmund Burke, "Mr. Burke's Speech on Moving His Resolutions for a Conciliation with the Colonies, March 22, 1775," *The Works of Edmund Burke*, Vol. 1, New York: Harper and Brothers, 1847, p. 228.

[11] Governor Dunmore observed this predilection first hand and reported on it in a letter to Lord Dartmouth, informing the Secretary, "I have learnt from experience that the established authority of any government in America, and the policy at home are both insufficient to restrain the Americans, and they do and will remove as their avidity and restlessness incite them." He added such characteristics were "impressed upon their earliest infancy." "Dunmore to Dartmouth, December 24, 1774," Public Record Office, CO 5/1353, Library of Congress Transcripts. Letter in Isaac S. Harrell, "Some Neglected Phases of the Revolution in Virginia," *The William and Mary Quarterly*, Vol. 5, No. 3 (Jul., 1925), pp. 161, 162.

[12] John Fortescue, editor, *The Correspondence of King George the Third*, Vol. 3, London: MacMillan and Co., 1928, pp. 318-320. Huntington Library.

[13] "Philip Stephens, Lieutenant Evans, 28 October 1766," National Maritime Museum: The Caird Library, Manuscripts Section - Admiralty, Navy, Royal Marines, and Coastguard, Reference: ADM 354/179/36.

[14] Use of the navy for "administrative purposes." Beer, *op cit*, p. 287.

[15] Alden Bradford, *History of Massachusetts from 1764, to July, 1775 When General Washington Took Command of the American Army*, Boston: Richardson and Lord, 1822, p. 168.

[16] Whether or not it was a massacre was a question raised in one of the earliest accounts of the event published in London, *A Fair Account of the Late Unhappy Disturbance at Boston: In New England*, London: B. White, 1770. An earlier account by the "Freeholders and other Inhabitants of the Town of Boston," made the massacre interpretation part of the title, namely, *A Short Narrative of the Horrid Massacre in Boston: Perpetrated in the Evening of the Fifth Day of March 1770*, Boston, printed, by order of the town, by Messrs. Edes and Gill; and reprinted for W. Bingley, London, 1770.

[17] "Letter from the Earl of Hillsborough to the Lords of the Admiralty, Whitehall, April 16, 1772," William Cobbett, ed. *Cobbett's Parliamentary History of England*, Vol. 17 (1771-1774), London: T. C. Hansard, 1803, p. 631.

[18] *The London Gazette*, 3 April 1773, Issue 11341, p. 1.

[19] Losses in manpower and equipment were replaced incrementally using weeks-old status reports. Supplies and reinforcements made their way to the deployed units over irregular and vulnerable lines of communication. And while awaiting replacements, the regiments continued to exercise, patrol and fight. It is an overstatement to say they were considered expendable but it seems the regiments were often overextended. Such a conclusion is supported by the report of the regiment's arrival back in England in 1778. According to the *Stamford Mercury*, "The 14th regiment of foot (if a corps of Officers only without men may

be called a regiment) is to receive the levies to be raised in the County of Norfolk. The above regiment went abroad in the year 1766, and did not return till ten years after to England; they had not 40 men besides invalids." *Stamford Mercury,* 12 February 1778, p. 1.
[20] "Hugh Wallace to General Haldimand, October 22, 1771," *Haldimand Papers,* H-1431, image 351.
[21] *Virginia Gazette,* Purdie and Dixon, Oct. 21, 1773, p. 2.
[22] "Articles of Association," *Journals of the Continental Congress, 1774-1789,* Thursday, October 20, 1774. *Virginia Gazette,* Purdie and Dixon, Nov. 03, 1774, p. 1.
[23] "Lord Dunmore to General Howe, November 30, 1775," Hezekiah Niles, *Principles and Acts of the Revolution in America,* Baltimore: W.O. Niles, 1822, pp. 138, 139.

Notes: Chapter 1: Charles Fordyce's Family

[1] Birth record of Charles Fordyce. Scotland's People, National Records of Scotland. 01/10/1741 Fordyce Charles (Church registers Old Parish Records 685/1 230 119) p. 119 of 548. Thursday, 1st October 1741 To Mr. Thomas Fordyce of Ayton & Ms Elizabeth Whiteford his spouse asn [a son named] Charles N [nephew] Sir John Whiteford of that ilk Mr. Allan Whiteford Receiver General of the Land Tax John Stevenson Doctor of Medicine Mr. Alexander Grant Merchant in Ed[r] [sic, Edinburgh?]. Born the same day & Baptized by the Rev. Mr. George Fordyce Minister of the Gospel at Corstorphine. Transcription by Roy Randolph 07 October 2016. Marriage of Thomas Fordyce and Elizabeth Whitefoord, "sister to Sir John W. of Blairquhan, baronet," on 20 July 1729 in: Scottish Record Society, *The Register of Marriages for the Parish of Edinburgh, 1595-,* Vol. 35, edited by Rev. Henry Paton, Edinburgh: James Skinner and Company, 1908, p. 191.
[2] Cathcarts listed in: James Balfour Paul, *The Scots Peerage: Founded on Wood's Edition of Sir Robert Douglas's Peerage of Scotland,* Vol. 2, Edinburgh: Davis Douglas, 1905, pp. 518–520. Whitefoords in: George Edward Cokayne, ed, *The Complete Baronetage,* Vol. IV, Exeter: William Pollard, 1904, pp. 400–401.
[3] Charles Rogers, *The Book of Robert Burns: Genealogical and Historical Memoirs of the Poet, His Associates and Those Celebrated in His Writings,* Vol. 2, Edinburgh: Grampian Club, 1890, p. 322.
[4] Sir Walter Scott, *The Waverley Novels: With the Author's Last Corrections and Additions,* Vol. 1, Philadelphia: Carey and Hart, 1846, Introduction.
[5] Appreciation of Whitefoord by his contemporaries documented in: Charles Rogers, *The Book of Robert Burns, op cit,* pp. 317, 318.
[6] W. A. S. (William Albert Samuel) Hewins, editor, *The Whitefoord Papers: Being the Correspondence and other Manuscripts of Colonel Charles Whitefoord and Caleb Whitefoord, from 1739 to 1810,* Oxford: Clarendon Press, 1898, p. xxii.
[7] "Warrants &c. for Regulating the Army," *A List of the General and Field-Officers as they Rank in the Army,* [Army List] 1753, image 55.

[8] David Croal Thomson, "The National Gallery of Scotland: The French School," *The Art Journal*, 1904, London: Virtue & Co., 1904, p. 311.

[9] Alexander Dingwall Fordyce, *Family Record of the Name of Dingwall Fordyce in Aberdeenshire*, Toronto: C. Blackett Robinson, 1885, p. xlv.

[10] There may have been a sixth child, James, born in 1745, for whom there is no birth record. In a letter of March 1745, Thomas reports: "I wish it [childbirth] were over with my wife ... who is not at all well, I never saw her soe unweldy, she's hardly able to walk, and not able to goe in either coach or chaise." ("Thomas Fordyce to George Innes, Ayton, March 19, 1745," National Archives of Scotland, Papers of George Innes, GD 113/3/220.) Evidently, this child died in infancy. Another letter from Thomas of June 1746, contains the news, "James, writer's son, is dead." (Abstract at: "Thomas Fordyce to George Innes, Ayton, June 17, 1746," National Archives of Scotland, Papers of George Innes, GD 113/3/243, item 1.)

[11] National Archives of Scotland, Court of Session: Unextracted processes, 1st arrangement, Adams-Dalrymple office, Earl of Home and others v Fordyce of Ayton and others, CS228/H/2/31, item 4.

[12] "Thomas Fordyce to George Innes, Ayton, April 26, 1742," National Archives of Scotland, Papers of George Innes, GD 113/3/167.

[13] "Thomas Fordyce to George Innes, Ayton, November 17, 1746," National Archives of Scotland, Papers of George Innes, GD 113/3/248.

[14] *Family Record of the Name of Dingwall Fordyce in Aberdeenshire*, op cit, p. xlix.

[15] Erroneous reports of Charles' death in St. Vincent in: *Bath Chronicle and Weekly Gazette*, March 4, 1773, p. 3, *Kentish Gazette*, March 6, 1773, pp. 3, 4, *Shrewsbury Chronicle*, March 6, 1773, p. 3, *The Ipswich Journal*, March 6, 1773, pp. 1, 2, *Oxford Journal*, March 6, 1773, p. 1, *Hampshire Chronicle*, March 4, 1773, p. 1, *The Scots Magazine*, Vol. 35, 1773, p. 53, *Weekly Magazine, or, Edinburgh Amusement*, Vol. 19-20 (Jan.-Apr. 1773), p. 351.

[16] "Scotland, Births and Baptisms, 1564-1950," Database, FamilySearch citing Edinburgh Parish, Edinburgh, Midlothian, Scotland, references 2:17NWBGW and 2:17NVP9M of FHL (Family History Library) microfilm 1,066,668 and references 2:17NSMPH, 2:17NQS9L and 2:17NRR5Q of FHL microfilm 1,066,667.

[17] *Derby Mercury*, May 30, 1746, p. 4. See also, Joseph Randall, *An Account of the Academy at Heath, Near Wakefield, Yorkshire*, London: 1750.

[18] "Thomas Fordyce to George Innes, Ayton, May 27, 1751," National Archives of Scotland, Papers of George Innes, GD 113/3/345.

[19] *The History of Parliament: the House of Commons*, 1790-1820, ed. R. Thorne, 1986.

[20] *The Scots Magazine*, Vol. 29, (1767), pp. 55, 557.

[21] Francis Hindes Groome, editor, *Ordnance Gazetteer of Scotland*, Edinburgh: T. C. and E. C. Jack, 1901, p. 476.

[22] "Monthly Return for His Majesty's 14th Regiment of Foot, Salisbury, 1 March, 1766," National Archives, Monthly Returns, 14th Foot 1759-1805, WO 17/115, image 46.

Notes: Chapter 2: Deployed to Germany

[1] Secretary at War UK, *Army Commission Book, 1761-1762*, WO 25/28, pp. 7, 39, 49.

[2] Secretary at War, *A List of the General and Field-Officers as They Rank in the Army, of the Officers of the Several Regiments of Horse, Dragoons, and Foot on the British and Irish Establishments*, to November 1761. London: J. Millan, 1761, pp. 67, 154 and image 143. UK National Archives, WO 65/10.

[3] Secretary at War, *A List of the General and Field-Officers as They Rank in the Army, of the Officers of the Several Regiments of Horse, Dragoons, and Foot on the British and Irish Establishments*, Complete for 1761. London: J. Millan, 1761, p. 150. UK National Archives, WO 65/9.

[4] *Army Commission Book, 1761-1762*, WO 25/28, *op cit*, p. 47.

[5] Secretary at War, *A List of the General and Field-Officers as They Rank in the Army, of the Officers of the Several Regiments of Horse, Dragoons, and Foot on the British and Irish Establishments*, for 1763. London: J. Millan, 1763, p. 154. UK National Archives, WO 65/12.

[6] Secretary at War, *A List of the General and Field-Officers as They Rank in the Army, of the Officers of the Several Regiments of Horse, Dragoons, and Foot on the British and Irish Establishments*, to November 1763. London: J. Millan, 1763, p. 67. UK National Archives, WO 65/13.

[7] *The London Gazette*, 18 January 1757, Issue 9654, p. 1.

[8] *The London Gazette*, 21 August 1759, Issue 9924, p. 2. *Caledonian Mercury*, 29 August 1759, p. 2, *Caledonian Mercury*, 17 September 1759, p. 3, *Aberdeen Press and Journal*, 30 October 1759, p. 3, *The London Gazette*, 19 January 1760, Issue 9967, p. 1, *Derby Mercury*, 18 January 1760, p. 4, *Oxford Journal*, 26 January 1760, p. 2, *Caledonian Mercury*, 26 January 1760, p. 1, *Manchester Mercury*, 29 January 1760, p. 1, *Leeds Intelligencer*, 29 January 1760, p. 1, *Dublin Courier*, 01 February 1760, p. 1.

[9] *Caledonian Mercury*, 30 January 1760, p. 3.

[10] *Aberdeen Press and Journal*, 05 February 1760, p. 3. Also see: *Caledonian Mercury*, 30 January 1760, p. 3, *Oxford Journal*, 09 February 1760, p. 2.

[11] Murray Keith's promotion: *The London Gazette*, 21 August 1759, Issue 9924, p. 2. Campbell's promotion: *Army List Complete for 1761*, WO 65/9, *op cit*, pp. 154, 155.

[12] *Caledonian Mercury*, 13 April 1761, p. 3, *Derby Mercury*, 24 April 1761, p. 1, "John Clevland [sic] [to Admiralty]," National Maritime Museum: The Caird Library, Manuscripts Sections, ADM 354/166/344, 1761 May 18, *Derby Mercury*, 10 July 1761, p. 3.

[13] "Copy Orders, Pr. Ferdinand of Brunswick, Delivered the Day after the Battle of July 16," *The Scots Magazine*, v.23, 1761, p. 376.

[14] "An Officer Who Served in the British Forces," *The Operations of the Allied Army, Under the Command of His Serene Highness, Prince Ferdinand*, London: T. Jefferys, 1764, p. 232.

[15] *Caledonian Mercury*, 14 October 1761, p. 2.

[16] Secretary at War, *A List of the General and Field-Officers as They Rank in the Army, of the Officers of the Several Regiments of Horse, Dragoons, and Foot on the British and Irish Establishments*, November 1761, WO 65/11, pp. 153, 154.
[17] *Oxford Journal*, 24 October 1761, p. 1.
[18] *The London Gazette*, 17 November 1761, Issue 10158, pp. 8, 9.
[19] "British Camp at Worwolde, Nov. 8," *The London Gazette*, 17 November 1761, Issue 10158, p. 9. "…our Corps consisted of the British Grenadiers, and Highlanders."
[20] "A Letter from an Officer in the Artillery, dated from the Camp at Williamsthall, June 25," *Derby Mercury*, 02 July 1762, p. 1.
[21] *The London Gazette*, 17 July 1762, Issue 10227, pp. 1, 2, *Manchester Mercury*, 27 July 1762, p. 1, *The Operations of the Allied Army, op cit*, p. 255.
[22] *The London Gazette*, 23 November 1762, Issue 10264, p. 1.
[23] *Manchester Mercury*, 30 November 1762, p. 4.
[24] "Hague, October 1," *The London Gazette*, 2 October 1762, Issue 10249, p. 6. Killed and wounded are listed.
[25] *Leeds Intelligencer*, 19 October 1762, p. 2, *The Edinburgh Magazine*, Vol. 6, October 1762, p. 516.
[26] *Bath Chronicle and Weekly Gazette*, 18 November 1762, p. 4.
[27] *Oxford Journal*, 05 February 1763, p. 1, *Derby Mercury*, 18 March 1763, p. 1. *Leeds Intelligencer*, 12 April 1763, p. 3. *Aberdeen Press and Journal*, 02 May 1763, p. 3, *Caledonian Mercury*, 02 May 1763, p.2, *Manchester Mercury*, 10 May 1763, p. 2. *Manchester Mercury*, 24 May 1763, p. 2. *Aberdeen Press and Journal*, 30 May 1763, p. 4, *Manchester Mercury*, 31 May 1763, p. 2.
[28] *Newcastle Courant*, 15 August 1761, p. 1.
[29] *Manchester Mercury*, 16 November 1762, p. 2.
[30] *Bath Chronicle and Weekly Gazette*, 24 February 1763, p. 4.
[31] Secretary at War UK, *Army Commission Book, 1762-1767*, WO 25/30, p. 67. *Army List for 1763*, WO-65/12, *op cit*, p. 67, image 81.

Notes: Chapter 3: Deployed to Nova Scotia

[1] William Cobbett, editor, *Cobbett's Parliamentary History of England*, Vol. 16, (1765-1771), London: T. C. Hansard, 1813, p. 83.
[2] The possibility of "Stamp Duties" was first made known in America when Lord Halifax sent a circular letter to the governors informing them "it may be proper to charge certain stamp duties." ("Circular Letter from the Earl of Halifax, St. James's 11 August 1764," Frederick Ricord and William Nelson, editors, *Documents Relating to the Colonial History of the State of New Jersey*, Vol. 9, Newark: Daily Advertiser, 1885, p. 448.) A report of the disaffection in Virginia was published in the *Oxford Journal*, 23 February 1765, p. 1 and reports of continued disaffection there followed throughout the year, see: *Newcastle Chronicle*, August 17,

1765, p. 1. The reaction in Rhode Island was published in the *Aberdeen Press and Journal*, October 21, 1765, p. 3, the reaction in Philadelphia in the *Derby Mercury*, November 22, 1765, p. 2 and a report from Boston of the "utmost violence of their Diabolical Phrenzy," in the *Derby Mercury*, October 25, 1765, p. 1.

[3] John Romeyn Brodhead *Documents Relative to the Colonial History of the State of New York*, Vol. 7, Albany: Weed, Parsons and Company, 1856, p. 759.

[4] "Lieutenant-Governor Colden to General Gage. Spring Hill Sept 2d 1765," *Documents Relative to the Colonial History of the State of New York*, Vol. 7, *op cit*, p. 758.

[5] William Cobbett, editor, *Cobbett's Parliamentary History of England*, Vol. 16, *op cit*, pp. 84, 87. HathiTrust, transcribed by Roy Randolph.

[6] George Louis Beer, *British Colonial Policy, 1754-1765*, New York: Macmillan Company, 1907, p. 266.

[7] Map of troop deployments in 1763, John W. Shy, *Toward Lexington: The Role of the British Army in the Coming of the American Revolution*, Princeton, N.J.: Princeton University Press, 1965, p. 112 ff.

[8] Lord North to King George, February 4, 1774, Letter 204. W. Bodham Donne, editor, *The Correspondence of King George the Third with Lord North from 1768 to 1783*, Vol. 1, London: J. Murray, 1867, p. 164.

[9] Danby Pickering, *The Statutes at Large: From Magna Charta to the End of the Eleventh Parliament of Great Britain*, Vol. 27, Cambridge: John Archdeacon, 1767, p. 19.

[10] Beer noted how, under the circumstances, "impossible it was to enforce the law without resorting to exceptional measures." George Louis Beer, *British Colonial Policy, 1754-1765*, New York: Macmillan Company, 1907, p. 291.

[11] *The Boston Gazette and Country Journal*, 3 March 1766, p. 3.

[12] "To the Lords of the Admiralty, October 15, 1765," Joseph Redington, editor, *Calendar of Home Office Papers of the Reign of George III*, Vol. 1, London: Longman & Company and Trübner & Company, 1878, p. 608.

[13] *Leeds Intelligencer*, 20 May 1766, p. 1. King George III's "Foreign Garrisons and Reliefs" in John Fortescue, ed., *The Correspondence of King George the Third*, Vol. 3, London: MacMillan and Co., 1928, p. 319, 320. Huntington Library. General Gage requests troops for garrisons on the western frontiers of North America: *Caledonian Mercury*, 07 April 1766, p. 2.

[14] The duration of deployments in this era was variable and uncertain. As the regiment prepared to leave England for Nova Scotia in 1766, the *Newcastle Courant* reported "the 14th Regiment … is to embark next week for America, and to remain there for three years." *Newcastle Courant*, May 31, 1766, p. 1.

[15] James Balfour Paul, *The Scots Peerage: Founded on Wood's Edition of Sir Robert Douglas's Peerage of Scotland*, Vol. 8, Edinburgh: Davis Douglas, 1911, pp. 147-151.

[16] Lieutenant Colonel Dalrymple's birthdate, January 5, 1736 and parents, George Dalrymple and Euphame Myreton from: "Scotland, Births and Baptisms, 1564-1950," FamilySearch database, reference 2:17NSMRW; FHL microfilm 1,066,667.

[17] Charles' great grandmother, Elizabeth Dalrymple, was the sister of John Dalrymple, 1st Earl of Stair. James Balfour Paul, *The Scots Peerage: Founded on Wood's*

Edition of Sir Robert Douglas's Peerage of Scotland, Vol. 8, *op cit*, p. 147. Parents of Charles' mother, Elizabeth Whitefoord, identified as Adam Baronet Whitefoord and Margaret Cathcart in: "Scotland, Births and Baptisms, 1564-1950," FamilySearch database, reference 2:15HDG2D; FHL microfilm 1,041,471. Relationship between Margaret Cathcart and the 1st Earl of Stair in: "The Family of Whitefoord," George W. Marshall, editor, *The Genealogist*, Vol. 4, London: George Bell & Sons, 1880, p. 141, 142.

[18] "The 14th Regiment of Foot, commanded by Major General Jefferys, is to be reviewed by his Majesty in Hyde-Park on the 8th of next Month." *Derby Mercury*, 27 April 1764, pp. 2, 3. London, May 8. "Yesterday his Majesty, attended by his Brothers the Princes William Henry, and Frederick, the Marquis of Granby, the French Ambassador, and several other Persons of Distinction, reviewed Gen. Jefferies Regiment of Foot in Hyde Park; the Soldiers were hearty looking well-proportioned Men, and went through their Exercise with inimitable Dexterity, and imitated a Bush Fight against the Indians, to the great Delight of the numerous Spectators; his Majesty was pleased to express the Highest Approbation." *Derby Mercury*, 04 May 1764 p. 4.

[19] Reviewed at Hyde Park in: *Oxford Journal*, Saturday 07 June 1766, p. 3.

[20] Great Britain, Public Record Office, Joseph Redington, editor, *Calendar of Home Office Papers of the Reign of George* III, Vol. 2 (1766-1769), London: H.M.S.O., 1879, p. 40.

[21] Notice of news from London dated July 1, 1766, "We hear from Portsmouth, that for three successive days Kepple's Regiment has been marching from their cantonment round this Country to Portsmouth and Gosport, in order to embark for North America, to relieve some Troops that are coming home from thence." *The Boston Gazette and Country Journal*, 8 September 1766, p. 2. Notices in English newspapers: *Manchester Mercury*, 17 June 1766, p. 4, *Dublin Courier*, 30 June 1766, p. 1 and *Newcastle Chronicle*, 05 July 1766, p. 2. In this last reference "London [Tuesday] July 1, 1766. Friday morning the transports, with Keppel's regiment on board for North America, got under sail at Spithead, with a fine wind down the Channel." Also, *Newcastle Courant*, 05 July 1766, p. 1. Just before they left, notice that Lieutenant Colonel William Dalrymple would command the regiment in America was published in the *Caledonian Mercury*, 28 June 1766, p. 2.

[22] "Letter from J. J. W. Des Barres, to General Haldimand, Halifax, August 28, 1766," in French, Sessional Papers, First Session of the Sixth Parliament, 1887, Vol. 20, Issue 11 p. 488, *Haldimand Papers*, H-1438, image 1130. Arrival of 14th published in *Dublin Courier*, November 14, 1766, p. 1 and *Newcastle Chronical*, November 15, 1766, p. 2. Boston was apprised of the arrival with the news, "We hear that Admiral Durnell in His Majesty's Ship Launceston, and a Number of Transports with Troops arrived a Fortnight ago at Halifax. That Admiral Durrell died there two Days after." *The Boston Gazette and Country Journal*, 15 September 1766, p. 3.

[23] Historian Murdoch observed, "Besides, the personal welfare and comfort of so many of our people depended on the expenditure of public money which flowed freely hither in naval and military channels, and otherwise, that no serious opposition to any measures of the crown could be reasonably looked for in this quarter." Beamish Murdoch, *A History of Nova-Scotia, or Acadie, op cit*, pp. 448, 449. In a letter of September 7, 1767, Governor Campbell told Lord Selbourne the possibility one of the two regiments in the province might "soon be embarked for the continent" was "a matter of much concern," since "what little commerce there is here … almost wholly depends on the specie introduced by the navy and army." "Campbell to Shelburne, Halifax, September 7, 1767," Canadian Archives, Nova Scotia and Cape Breton, Original Correspondence (CO 217) C-9130, image 528.

[24] When the General Assembly of Nova Scotia received the "Circular Letter" from the Assembly of Massachusetts Bay in 1768, Lieutenant Governor Franklin reported to Lord Shelburne, "… it was not allowed to be read or answered which fully answers his Majesty's pleasure of treating it with the contempt it deserves, and there would have been no difficulty in procuring a vote of their disapprobation in strong terms if it had been thought necessary." He told Lord Shelburne he could assure the King, "… the people of this province have the highest reverence and respect for all acts of the British legislature." "Michael Franklin to Shelburne, Halifax, July 10, 1768," Canadian Archives, Nova Scotia and Cape Breton, Original Correspondence (CO 217), C-9130, image 1093. See also "Michael Franklin to Shelburne, Halifax, March 29, 1768," image 880. In a letter of September 9, 1768, Franklin tells Hillsborough, "I know of no obstruction the officers of the Customs have hitherto ever met with in this colony nor is there the least appearance of their being deterred in future from exerting themselves in their respective offices," image 1208. As usual, it seems there were exceptions to the view the Stamp Duties were not challenged in Nova Scotia. In a report datelined New York, December 19, 1765, one Captain Malony from Nova Scotia claimed, "the people at Halifax are very uneasy under the influence of the Stamp-law: And the distributor of stamps there, one Heinselwood, is so detested by the inhabitants, on account of the office he holds, that he never dares to appear abroad. And certainly he can have but little peace at home, being obliged to transact all his business under the protection of a file of musqueteers, and to be continually guarded by them." *Leeds Intelligencer*, February 11, 1766 p. 3.

[25] *Derby Mercury*, January 17, 1766 p. 2.

[26] On July 9, 1768, General Gage informed Lieutenant Governor Franklin he had ordered Lieutenant Colonel Dalrymple to withdraw his troops from Forts Cumberland, Annapolis Royal, Frederick, Amherst and the Town of Louisbourg. "Michael Franklin to Hillsborough, Halifax, July 20, 1768," Canadian Archives, Nova Scotia and Cape Breton, Original Correspondence (CO 217), C-9130, images 1109-1110.

[27] Census records in: Canadian Archives, Nova Scotia and Cape Breton, Original Correspondence (CO 217), C-9130, August 24, 1766, images 14-16, December 31, 1766, image 270, December 16, 1767, image 673 (primary source for the data presented) and "A General Return of the several Townships in the Province of Nova Scotia the first day of January 1767," Commissioner of Public Records Nova Scotia Archives RG 1 vol. 443 no. 1. Demographics of Halifax and Nova Scotia at this time are addressed in detail in: Arthur Eaton, "Chapters in the History of Halifax, Nova Scotia," *Americana Illustrated*, Vol. 11 (1916), New York: The National Americana Society, 1916. For specifics regarding the numbers presented in the text see pp. 143, 144, 149, 171-175.

[28] Beamish Murdoch, *A History of Nova-Scotia, or Acadie*, Vol. 2, Halifax: James Barnes, 1866, p. 463.

[29] "To Barrington, New York, October 20, 1767," Clarence Edwin Carter, *Correspondence of Thomas Gage with the Secretaries of State, and with the War Office and the Treasury 1763-1775*, Vol. 2, New Haven: Yale University Press, 1933, p. 441.

[30] William C. Lowe, "The Parliamentary Career of Lord Dunmore, 1761-1774," *The Virginia Magazine of History and Biography*, Vol. 96, No. 1 (Jan., 1988), pp. 13, 14.

[31] *Ibid*, p. 15.

[32] William Cobbett, ed., *Cobbett's Parliamentary History of England*, Vol. 16, *op cit*, p. 181. *Journals of the House of Lords*. Vol. 31 (1765-1767), *op cit*, pp. 305.

[33] "The Parliamentary Career of Lord Dunmore, 1761-1774," *op cit*, p. 15.

[34] *Ibid*, p. 14.

[35] Captain, 3rd Foot Guards, *Commission Book*, WO 25/21, 1744-1746, p. 113.

[36] "The Parliamentary Career of Lord Dunmore," *op cit*, pp. 8-10.

[37] "Thomas Fordyce to George Innes, Ayton, March 26, 1750," National Archives of Scotland, Papers of George Innes, GD 113/3/317.

[38] Governor Bernard told Lord Hillsborough "if the troops from Halifax were to come of a sudden, there would be no avoiding an insurrection." "Governor Bernard to the Earl of Hillsborough, Boston, September 16, 1768," Sir Francis Bernard, Thomas Gage, Samuel Hood (Viscount), *Letters to the Ministry from Governor Bernard, General Gage, and Commodore Hood*, Boston: Edes and Gill, 1769, p. 70.

[39] "American Board of Customs to the Lords Commissioners of the Treasury, Boston 28th March 1768," *The Papers of Francis Bernard*, Vol. 4: 1768, *Publications of the Colonial Society of Massachusetts*, Vol. 86, p. 369 and "Letter from the Honourable Commissioners of his Majesty's Customs to Governor Bernard," on board his Majesty's ship Romney, 12th June 1768, *Letters to the Ministry from Governor Bernard, General Gage, and Commodore Hood*, *op cit*, p. 128.

[40] Governor Bernard reported his precarious situation, including threats of violence, to Secretary Hillsborough in numerous letters in 1768. The Secretary could only construe these reports as pleas for help. See: *Letters to the Ministry from Governor Bernard, General Gage, and Commodore Hood*, *op cit*, pp. 10-67. The commissioners made their explicit pleas for protection in letters of June 11, 13, 15, 16 and July 11, *ibid*, pp. 114-121, 127, 133, 137, 142.

Notes: Chapter 4: Unrest in Boston

[1] Danby Pickering, *The Statutes at Large: From Magna Charta to the End of the Eleventh Parliament of Great Britain*, Vol. 27, Cambridge: John Archdeacon, 1767, p. 505.
[2] *The Boston Gazette and Country Journal*, 9 November 1767, p. 3.
[3] *The Boston Gazette and Country Journal*, 2 November 1767, p. 1 and Adam Anderson, *An Historical and Chronological Deduction of the Origin of Commerce, From The Earliest Accounts*, Vol. 4, London: J. Walter, 1789, p. 106.
[4] *The Boston Gazette and Country Journal*, 31 July 1769, p. 1. (599).
[5] *The Boston Evening Post*, 14 August 1769, p. 2.
[6] *Journals of the House of Representatives of Massachusetts*, Vol. 44 1767-1768, Massachusetts Historical Society, Portland, Main: Anthoensen Press, 1975 (originally published in Boston by Green and Russell, 1767), pp. 236-239.
[7] *The Boston Gazette and Country Journal*, 4 July 1768, p. 1.
[8] *The Boston Gazette and Country Journal*, 28 March 1768, p. 3.
[9] Plans for the celebration in Boston announced in *Boston Gazette and Country Journal*, 7 April 1766, p. 2. Accounts of celebrations in London published in *Bath Chronicle and Weekly Gazette*, 20 March 1766, p. 4, *Derby Mercury*, 21 March 1766, p. 4, *Newcastle Courant*, 22 March 1766, p. 2.
[10] Samuel Gardner Drake, *The History and Antiquities of Boston: The Capital of Massachusetts*, Boston: Luther Stevens, 1856, p. 769. Captain John Montresor observed this same kind of nurturing of a spirit of disaffection among the citizens of New York at this time. In his *Journal* entry for April 4, 1766, he recorded the public burning at the "Coffee house" of "Stamps" and "play bills" said to have been found in the street "all to prevent their Spirits to flag." Gideon D. Scull, editor, "The Montresor Journals," *Collections of the New York Historical Society for 1881*, New York, 1882, p. 358.
[11] John Rowe, *Letters and Diary of John Rowe: Boston Merchant, 1759-1762, 1764-1779*, edited by Anne Rowe Cunningham, Boston: W. B. Clarke Company, 1903, pp. 156, 157.
[12] *The Boston Gazette and Country Journal*, 21 March 1768. General Gage agreed. In a letter to Lord Hillsborough of October 31, 1768, he noted, "… according to the best Information I have been able to procure, the Disturbance in March was trifling." "General Gage to Hillsborough, Boston, October 31st 1768." Clarence Edwin Carter, *Correspondence of Thomas Gage with the Secretaries of State, and with the War Office and the Treasury 1763-1775*, Vol. 1, New Haven: Yale University Press, 1933, p. 204.
[13] "Governor Bernard to the Earl of Shelburne, Boston March 19, 1768," Sir Francis Bernard, Thomas Gage, Samuel Hood (Viscount), *Letters to the Ministry from Governor Bernard, General Gage, and Commodore Hood*, Boston: Edes and Gill, 1769, pp. 16, 17.
[14] *Ibid*, p. 20.

[15] Alden Bradford , editor, *Speeches of the Governors of Massachusetts, from 1765 to 1775; and the Answers of the House of Representatives, to the Same*, Boston: Russell and Gardner, 1818, pp. 109, 112.

[16] Danby Pickering, *The Statutes at Large: From Magna Charta to the End of the Eleventh Parliament of Great Britain*, Cambridge: Joseph Bentham, 1764, v.26, p. 309. William MacDonald, editor, *Select Charters and Other Documents Illustrative of American History*, Vol. 1, New York: Macmillan Company, 1904, p. 309. Re-published in *The Boston Evening Post*, 10 October 1768, p. 4.

[17] *Journals of the House of Representatives of Massachusetts*, Vol. 44, *op cit*, p. 56.

[18] William F. Wells, *The Life and Public Services of Samuel Adams, Being a Narrative of His Acts and Opinions, and of His Agency in Producing and Forwarding the American Revolution*, Vol. 1, Boston: Little, Brown, and Company, 1865, pp. 141, 142.

[19] Reported in *The Boston Gazette and Country Journal*, 13 October 1766, p. 1.

[20] *Letters to the Ministry from Governor Bernard, General Gage, and Commodore Hood*, *op cit*, p. 23. The Malcom incident along with other such incidents that gave the smugglers reason to "triumph in their success" delineated in "Commissioners of the Customs to the Lords of the Treasury," Boston February 12, 1768, *Proceedings of the Massachusetts Historical Society*, Third Series, Vol. 55 (Oct., 1921 - Jun., 1922), p. 264.

[21] *The Boston Gazette and Country Journal*, 27 October 1766, p. 3.

[22] *Letters to the Ministry from Governor Bernard, General Gage, and Commodore Hood*, *op cit*, pp. 22-25.

[23] "American Board of Customs to the Lords Commissioners of the Treasury, Boston 28th March 1768," *The Papers of Francis Bernard*, Vol. 4: 1768, *Publications of the Colonial Society of Massachusetts*, Vol. 86, p. 369.

[24] *The Boston Gazette and Country Journal*, 4 July 1768, p. 1. Also: *The American Gazette, a Collection of All the Authentic Addresses, Memorials Petitions, and Other Papers, Which Have Been Published from the Date of the Circular Letters, (sent from the House of Assembly of Massachusetts-Bay, in February 1768), to the Present Time*, London: G. Kearsly, 1770, p. 2.

[25] Alden Bradford, *History of Massachusetts from 1764, to July, 1775 When General Washington Took Command of the American Army*, Boston: Richardson and Lord, 1822, p. 168. On June 11, Hillsborough told Governor Bernard "His Majesty has thought fit, upon the most mature Consideration of what has been represented by yourself, and by the Commrs of the Customs established at Boston, to direct the Commander in Chief of His Majesty's Forces in America to station One Regiment at least in the Town of Boston." Letter "From the Earl of Hillsborough, Whitehall 11th June 1768," *The Papers of Francis Bernard, op cit*. 373.

[26] "Hillsborough to General Gage, Whitehall, June 8th 1768." Clarence Edwin Carter, *Correspondence of Thomas Gage with the Secretaries of State, and with the War Office and the Treasury 1763-1775*, Vol. 2, New Haven: Yale University Press, 1933, pp. 69, 191.

[27] "General Gage to Lieutenant Colonel William Dalrymple, New York, June 25th 1768," *The Papers of Francis Bernard, op cit*, pp. 271, 397. "General Gage to Hillsborough, New York, June 28th 1768." Clarence Edwin Carter, *Correspondence of Thomas Gage with the Secretaries of State, and with the War Office and the Treasury 1763-1775*, Vol. 1, New Haven: Yale University Press, 1933, p. 182. On July 9, 1768, Gage informed the Lieutenant Governor of Nova Scotia, Michael Franklin, he had ordered Lieutenant Colonel Dalrymple to withdraw his troops from Forts Cumberland, Annapolis Royal, Frederick, Amherst and the Town of Louisbourg. "Michael Franklin to Hillsborough, Halifax, July 20, 1768," Canadian Archives, Nova Scotia and Cape Breton, Original Correspondence (CO 217), C-9130, images 1109-1110.

[28] "Letter from the Commissioners of the Customs at Boston to Commodore Hood [with copies to General Gage and Lieutenant Colonel Dalrymple] Boston, June 15th, 1768," *Letters to the Ministry from Governor Bernard, General Gage, and Commodore Hood, op cit*, pp. 137, 138.

[29] "Letter from Colonel Dalrymple, to the honourable the Commissioners of the Customs at Boston, dated Halifax, June 23d, 1768," *Letters to the Ministry from Governor Bernard, General Gage, and Commodore Hood, op cit*, pp. 145, 146.

[30] "General Gage to Hillsborough, New York, September 7th 1768." *Correspondence of Thomas Gage*, Vol. 2, *op cit*, p. 191.

Notes: Chapter 5: Deployed to Boston

[1] *The Boston Gazette, and Country Journal*, 3 October 1768, p. 2 and *Derby Mercury*, 11 November 1768, p. 2. Bostonians were given informal notice of the deployment of troops from Nova Scotia to Boston about a month before they arrived. *The Boston Evening Post*, 29 August 1768, p. 3. A more formal notice of the troops being ordered to Boston was published just a few days before they arrived. *The Boston Gazette, and Country Journal*, 26 September 1768, p. 3.

[2] The following "Extract of a Letter from Halifax" provides anecdotal support for this observation: "This Place [Halifax] is very dull since the Troops and the Navy have left us. I hope we shall soon have others in their Room, and make us alive again." *The Boston Gazette and Country Journal*, 14 November 1768, p. 1.

[3] The Commissioner's oath was published in *The Boston Evening Post*, 26 September 1768, p. 1. Governor Bernard's oath of 1761 in: Albert Matthews, editor, *Publications of the Colonial Society of Massachusetts*, Vol. 2, Cambridge: University Press, John Wilson and Son, 1913, p. 157.

[4] *The Boston Gazette and Country Journal*, 19 September 1768, pp. 1, 2.

[5] *The Boston Evening Post*, 3 October 1768, p. 3.

[6] Norman, John. *Plan of the town of Boston, with the attack on Bunkers-Hill, in the peninsula of Charlestown, the 17th of June, 1775*. Map. 1781. Norman B. Leventhal Map & Education Center, Boston Public Library. No known copyright restrictions. No known restrictions on use.

[7] Muster Roll for 14th Regiment at Boston, April 24, 1769, WO 12/3117.

[8] Sibbald David Scott, *The British Army: Its Origin, Progress, and Equipment*, Vol. 3, London: Cassell, Petter, Galpin, 1880, pp. 337, 338 and Edward E. Curtis, *The Organization of the British Army in the American Revolution*, New Haven: Yale University Press, 1926, p. 4.

[9] *The Boston Gazette and Country Journal*, 5 December 1768, p. 3. Headquarters, 20 November 1768, Boston, "Richard Maitland, Deputy Adjutant General, Headquarters, Boston, November 20, 1768," *Haldimand Papers*, H-1431 image 1258.

[10] *The Boston Evening Post*, 1 May 1769, p. 3.

[11] *The Boston Evening Post*, 21 August 1769, p. 3. Charles addressed as "Major" Fordyce in correspondence between Governor Hutchinson and Lieutenant Colonel Dalrymple dated September 9, 1770. Peter Orlando Hutchinson, *The Diary and Letters of His Excellency Thomas Hutchinson: Captain-General and Governor-in-Chief of His Late Majesty's Province of Massachusetts Bay in North America*, London: Sampson Low, Makston, Seaele & Rivington, 1883, p. 28.

[12] Humphrey Bland, *A Treatise of Military Discipline*, sixth edition, London: John and Paul Knapton, 1746, pp., 210-212 and Richard Kane, *A System of Camp Discipline, Military Honours, Garrison Duty, and Other Regulations for the Land Forces*, London: J. Milan, 1757, pp. 1, 7, 26, 73.

[13] *The Boston Evening Post*, 29 May 1769, p. 3, 5 June 1769, p. 1, *The Boston Gazette and Country Journal*, 5 June 1769, p. 4, 12 June 1769, p. 4, 19 June 1769, p. 4, 26 June 1769, p. 4 and *The Massachusetts Gazette*, 8 June 1769, p. 2.

[14] John Rowe, *Letters and Diary of John Rowe: Boston Merchant, 1759-1762, 1764-1779*, edited by Anne Rowe Cunningham, Boston: W. B. Clarke Company, 1903, p. 184.

[15] Ann Hulton, *Letters of a Loyalist Lady: Being the Letters of Ann Hulton, Sister of Henry Hulton, Commissioner of Customs at Boston, 1767-1776*, E Rhys Jones (Editor), Cambridge: Harvard University Press, 1927, p. 19.

[16] Margaret E. May, "Brookline in the Revolution," *Brookline Historical Publication Society*, Brookline: Riverdale Press, 1897, p. 18 and R. G. F. Candage, "The Gridley House, Brookline and Jeremy Gridley," *Brookline Historical Publication Society*, Boston: Rockwell and Churchill, 1903, pp. 4, 5.

[17] *The Boston Gazette and Country Journal*, 6 October 1766, p. 2, *The Boston Evening-Post*, 9 January 1769, p. 3.

[18] "Journal of the Times," January 26, 1769, *The Boston Evening Post*, 20 March 1769, p. 1 (435) and "Journal of the Times," February 16, 1769, *The Boston Evening Post*, 10 April 1769, p. 1. (459)

[19] "Memoir of Alfred Moore," Charles Kitchell Gardner, editor, *The Literary and Scientific Repository, and Critical Review*, Vol. 1, New York: Wiley and Halstead, 1820, p. 25.

[20] Samuel A'Court Ashe, *Biographical History of North Carolina from Colonial Times to the* Present, Vol. 2, Greensboro, N.C.: Charles L. Van Noppen, 1905, p. 303. For a more measured assessment of the battle at Moores Creek see Hugh F. Rankin,

"The Moores Creek Bridge Campaign, 1776," *North Carolina Historical Review*, Vol. 30 Issue 1, Jan 1953, pp. 23-60.

[21] William Heath, *Memoirs of Major General Heath*, New York: William Abbatt, 1901, p. 27.

[22] John Rowe, *Letters and Diary*, op cit, p. 188.

[23] John Frost, *The American Generals*, Columbus Ohio: William and Thomas Miller, 1855, p. 416.

[24] George Trevelyan, *The American Revolution*, Vol. 1, London: Longmans, Green, and Co., 1921, pp. 86-88. On October 10, 1768, a "Gentleman from New York" observed, "It gives pain to the Inhabitants of Boston, as well as this city, that the Ministry should send his Majesty's troops upon so ungrateful an errand, that they cannot receive that respect which would otherwise be shewn them for their heroism and intrepidity against the enemies of our common country, (Great-Britain, Ireland, and the colonies) during the late war, which has always been paid them on former occasions." *The Boston Gazette and Country Journal*, 31 October 1768, p 1.

[25] Charles Fordyce deposition, Massachusetts Historical Society, Frederick Lewis Gay transcripts, 1632-1786., Ms. N-2012 (Tall), State Papers, Vol. 12. Pages 40-97, (UK National Archives CO 5/88). The Patriot view of the affair may be ascertained in affidavits dated 25 July 1769 in *The Boston Evening Post*, 2 October 1769, p. 1.

[26] *A Fair Account of the Late Unhappy Disturbance at Boston: In New England*, London: B. White, 1770, p. 22. Another account by the "Freeholders and other Inhabitants of the Town of Boston," also credits the leaders of both parties with preventing additional violence and bloodshed. *A Short Narrative of the Horrid Massacre in Boston: Perpetrated in the Evening of the Fifth Day of March 1770*, Boston, printed, by order of the town, by Messrs. Edes and Gill; and re-printed for W. Bingley, London, 1770, p. 31.

[27] See: G. D. Scull, ed., "The Montresor Journals," *Collections of the New York Historical Society for the Year 1881*, New York: New York Historical Society, 1882, pp. 400, 401, 407, 410.

[28] Peter Orlando Hutchinson, *Diary*, op cit, pp. 27, 28.

[29] *Journals of the House of Representatives of Massachusetts*, Vol. 47 1770-1771, Massachusetts Historical Society, Portland, Main: Anthoensen Press, 1978, pp. 173, 174.

[30] *The Boston Gazette and Country Journal*, 5 November 1770, p. 2.

[31] *The Boston Gazette and Country Journal*, 5 February 1770, p. 4.

[32] *The Massachusetts Gazette: and the Boston Weekly News-Letter*, 1 March 1770, p. 2.

[33] *The Boston Gazette and Country Journal*, 15 October 1770, p. 1 and 29 October 1770, p. 3.

[34] *The Boston Gazette and Country Journal*, 5 November 1770, p. 2. Also: *The Boston Gazette and Country Journal*, 11 February 1771, p. 3. Botetourt had been appointed Governor of Virginia just two years earlier, in August, 1768, just as the 14th

departed Halifax for Boston, *The Boston Gazette and Country Journal*, 19 September 1768, p. 5.

[35] Lord Hillsborough notified Dunmore of his nomination as Governor of Virginia in a letter of December 11, 1770. "Earl of Hillsborough to the Earl of Dunmore, Whitehall December 11, 1770," John Romeyn Brodhead *Documents Relative to the Colonial History of the State of New York*, Vol. 8, Albany: Weed, Parsons and Company, 1857, p. 260.

[36] *The Boston Evening Post*, 24 December 1770, p. 2. Assembly acknowledges their interest in renewing commerce with the mother country, *The Boston Evening Post*, 31 December 1770, p 3.

[37] *The Boston Evening Post*, 2 February 1771, p. 3. Dunmore's salary dictated in: "Earl of Hillsborough to the Earl of Dunmore," *Documents Relative to the Colonial History of the State of New York*, Vol. 8, *op cit*, p. 223. In a later criticism of this practice, the citizens of Boston would argue it was a "violent breach" of the Royal Charter of the province. *The Boston Gazette and Country Journal*, 8 March 1773, p. 3.

[38] *The Boston Gazette and Country Journal*, 11 February 1771, p. 1. Same point made in an editorial in *The Boston Gazette and Country Journal*, 11 March 1771, p. 2. The Assembly would offer Governor Tryon a salary too, which he declined. *The Boston Gazette and Country Journal*, 9 March 1772, p. 3.

[39] *Manchester Mercury*, 04 September 1770, p. 4.

[40] *Caledonian Mercury*, 11 January 1772, p. 2.

Notes: Chapter 6: Deployed to St. Vincent

[1] Description of plans to distribute land on St. Vincent in: *Caledonian Mercury*, 01 May 1765, p. 1.

[2] "Copy of a letter from an officer of the fourth regiment of foot, dated St. Vincent, Jan. 25, 1764," *Aberdeen Press and Journal*, 28 May 1764, p. 4.

[3] *The London Gazette*, 31 March 1764, Issue 10405, p. 1.

[4] "Barbados, January 19, 1765, By the Kings' Authority," *The Scots Magazine*, Vol. 27 (1765), pp. 291, 294.

[5] Date set for land sale: *Caledonian Mercury*, 01 May 1765, p. 1. Sale advertised in *The Halifax Gazette*, Jan 30, 1766, p. 3. Details of lands included in the sale: *Aberdeen Press and Journal*, 02 December 1765, p. 2. Also: *The Public Advertiser* November 22, 1765, p. 3.

[6] Parliament published much of the documentation relating to the war with the Caribbs in "Debate in Commons on the Expedition Against the Caribbs," and "Papers Relating to the Expedition against the Caribbs," in *The Parliamentary History of England,* Vol. 17, London: T.C. Hansard, 1813, pp. 567-639. Instructions to wait: "Memorial of William Young, esq. first Commissioner for the Sale of Lands in the Ceded Islands, to the Lords of the Treasury, 11 April 1767," p. 575. Instructions provided: "Instructions from the Lords of the Treasury to the

Commissioners for the Sale of Lands in the Ceded Islands," p. 584. Sale authorized: "Letter from the Earl of Shelburne to Governor Melville, 18 January 1768," p. 587.

[7] "Letter from Lieutenant Governor Fitzmaurice to the Earl of Hillsborough, dated St. Vincent, June 10, 1769," *Parliamentary History, op cit*, pp. 599, 600.

[8] "Letter from William Young, esq., First Commissioner for the Sale of Lands, to Harry Alexander, esq., President of the Island of St. Vincent, St. Vincent, May 1, 1769," *Parliamentary History op cit*, p. 588.

[9] Sir William Young, *Account of the Black Charaibs in the Island of St Vincent's*, London: Frank Cass and Company, 1795, p. 44.

[10] "Extract from a Report of the Commissioners for the Sale of Lands in the Ceded Islands, to the Lords Commissioners for Trade and Plantations, July 26, 1769," *Parliamentary History op cit*, p. 624.

[11] "Letter from the Earl of Hillsborough to Lieutenant Governor Fitzmaurice, Whitehall, 4 August, 1769," *Parliamentary History op cit*, p. 597.

[12] "Gage to Hillsborough, New York, October 7, 1769," Clarence Edwin Carter, *Correspondence of Thomas Gage with the Secretaries of State, and with the War Office and the Treasury 1763-1775*, Vol. 1, New Haven: Yale University Press, 1933, p. 238.

[13] "Letter from Lieutenant General Fitzmaurice to the Earl of Hillsborough, Grenada, February 12, 1770," *Parliamentary History op cit*, p. 621.

[14] "Representation of the Board of Trade to the King, March 29, 1770," *Parliamentary History op cit*, p. 625.

[15] "Letter of the Commissioners for the Sale of Lands in the Ceded Islands, to the Lords of the Treasury, Dominica, October 16, 1771," *Parliamentary History op cit*, p. 607.

[16] "Letter from the Earl of Hillsborough to the Lords of the Admiralty, Whitehall, April 16, 1772," *Parliamentary History op cit*, p. 631.

[17] "Letter from the Earl of Hillsborough to Lieutenant General Gage, Whitehall, April 18, 1772," *Parliamentary History, op cit*, pp. 635, 636.

[18] "J. Pownall to Lieut. General Gage, Whitehall, Oct. 7, 1772," CO 5/90.

[19] "To Barrington, New York June 29th 1772," Clarence Edwin Carter, *Correspondence of Thomas Gage with the Secretaries of State, and with the War Office and the Treasury 1763-1775*, Vol. 2, New Haven: Yale University Press, 1933, pp. 607, 608.

[20] In a letter to Lord Hillsborough of July 1, 1772, General Gage observed, "I have thought that I could not be ... too careful in concealing the Destination of the Regiments ordered from this Country till they are sailed; for this place is much frequented by French Merchants from the French Islands and are so many Spies upon our Motions." "General Gage to Lord Hillsborough, New York, July 1, 1772," *Correspondence of General Gage*, Vol. 1, *op cit*, p. 237.

[21] *Boston Gazette and Country Journal*, 3 August 1772, p. 2.

[22] *Boston Gazette and Country Journal*, 27 July 1772, p. 2.

[23] "Governor William L. Leyborne to the Earl of Hillsborough, St. Vincent, September 12, 1772," *Manuscripts of the Earl of Dartmouth, Vol. 2, American Papers,*

Historical Manuscripts Commission, Vol. 14, Appendix, Part 10, London: Eyre and Spottiswoode, 1895, p. 531.

[24] "Dalrymple to Barrington, St. Vincent, Oct. 3, 1772," War Office (UK), In-Letters, c. West Indies, Campaign against Charibs on St. Vincent, (Documents from the National Archives, 1772-1773), WO 1/57, item 55. General Gage notified Lord Barrington he had received a report the 14th Regiment arrived at St. Vincent on September 3. "To Barrington, November 5th 1772," *Correspondence of Thomas Gage*, Vol. 2, *op cit*, pp. 624, 625.

[25] "William Leyborne to Secretary Barrington, St. Vincent, 9 Oct. 1772," WO 1/57, *op cit*, item 82.

[26] WO 1/57, *op cit*, item 16.

[27] *Ibid*.

[28] Muster Roll for 14th Regiment at Castle William, May 15, 1772, WO 12/3117.

[29] *Derby Mercury*, 18 May 1764, p. 2

[30] Byres, John, J Bayly, and S Hooper. *Plan of the island of St. Vincent laid down by actual survey under the direction of the Honorable the Commissioners for the Sale of Lands in the Ceded Islands*. London, S. Hooper, 1776. Map. Retrieved from the Library of Congress, <https://www.loc.gov/item/74691678/>.

[31] *The Ipswich Journal*, 20 February 1773, p. 2.

[32] *The Boston Evening-Post*, 16 November 1772, p. 2.

[33] *Berrow's Worcester Journal*, 31 December 1772, Issue Number: 4099.

[34] *Derby Mercury*, 25 December 1772, p. 2, *Edinburgh Advertiser*, Dec 22, 1772, p. 3.

[35] "Return of the Casualties of the Several Regiments in St. Vincents, February 20, 1773," War Office (UK), In-Letters, c. West Indies, Campaign against Charibs on St. Vincent, (Documents from the National Archives, 1772-1773), WO 1/57, item 28.

[36] *The Parliamentary History of England*, Vol. 17, p. 722 and *Bath Chronicle and Weekly Gazette*, 18 February 1773, p. 1.

[37] *Hampshire Chronicle*, 05 April 1773, p. 2.

[38] *The Halifax Gazette*, March 9, 1773, p. 3, *The Pennsylvania Packet*, March 1, 1773, p. 3.

[39] *Caledonian Mercury*, 27 March 1773, p. 2. *Weekly Magazine, or, Edinburgh Amusement*, Vol. 20 (April 1773), p. 27.

[40] *Stamford Mercury*, 28 January 1773, p 3.

[41] "Colonel Dalrymple to Lord Barrington, St. Vincent, Dec 26, 1772," John Fortescue, ed., *The Correspondence of King George the Third*, Vol. 2, London: MacMillan and Co., 1928, p. 424.

[42] "Adam Wood to Lord [Dartmouth], April 5, 1773," *Manuscripts of the Earl of Dartmouth, Vol. 2, American Papers, op cit*, p. 535.

[43] According to historian Charles Shephard, the rather quick resolution of the conflict was due in large part to a political assessment that exposed the mercenary motives for the campaign. Shephard notes, "… an enquiry was set on foot by the opponents of Lord North's Administration, respecting the justice, and

propriety of the motives, which gave rise to this expedition, and after a tedious investigation, it was finally resolved, that the measure was founded in injustice, and reflected dishonour on the National Character, a violation of the natural rights of mankind, and totally subversive of that liberty it gloried to defend. This conclusion was productive of immediate orders to suspend hostilities against the Caribs, and to negotiate a Treaty with them on reasonable terms. In obedience to these instructions, General Dalrymple made overtures of peace, which were joyfully embraced by the enemy. Charles Shephard, *An Historical Account of the Island of Saint Vincent*, London: W. Nicol, 1831, pp. 29-36.

[44] "Major General William Dalrymple to Lord Dartmouth, St. Vincent, February 22, 1773," *Manuscripts of the Earl of Dartmouth, Vol. 2, American Papers, op cit*, p. 534.

[45] *The London Gazette*, 3 April 1773, Issue 11341, p. 1.

[46] *Bath Chronicle and Weekly Gazette*, March 4, 1773, p. 3. Same report published in: *Shrewsbury Chronicle*, March 6, 1773, p. 3, *The Ipswich Journal*, March 6, 1773, p. 2, *Oxford Journal*, March 6, 1773, p. 1, *Kentish Gazette*, March 6, 1773, p. 3, *Hampshire Chronicle*, March 8, 1773, p. 1.

[47] Several officers reported as killed in a "Letter from St. Vincent's, dated Jan 18 [1773]." *Northampton Mercury*, 29 March 1773, p. 1.

[48] *Caledonian Mercury*, December 7, 1772, p. 1. In a later assessment the reporter claimed the war was illegal, oppressive, cruel and perfidious and it was conducted "to gratify the avarice and injustice of a few rapacious planters," *Hampshire Chronicle*, March 1, 1773, p. 1. For a summary of the arguments against the Carib War see "The Languages of Empire and the Carib War in St. Vincent" in the Prologue of Jack P. Greene, *Evaluating Empire and Confronting Colonialism in Eighteenth-Century Britain*, New York: Cambridge University Press, 2013, pp. 1-19.

[49] "Debate on the Papers Relating to the Expedition against the Caribbs," William Cobbett, ed. *Cobbett's Parliamentary History of England*, Vol. 17 (1771-1774), London: T. C. Hansard, 1803, p. 741.

[50] Furlong's arrival in St. Augustine in command of the 14th Regiment reported in: "Maurice Carr to Haldimand, April 28 1773, St. Augustine," Haldimand Papers, H-1439, image 396. Dalrymple's arrival in London and his conferences with the King reported in numerous newspapers including, *Kentish Gazette*, 17 April 1773, p. 2, *Derby Mercury*, 23 April 1773, p. 1, *Caledonian Mercury*, 21 April 1773, p. 2.

Notes: Chapter 7: Deployed to St. Augustine, Florida

[1] "Letter from the Earl of Hillsborough to Lieutenant General Gage, Whitehall, April 18, 1772," *Parliamentary History of England*, Volume 17, pp. 635, 636. "To Barrington, New York, June 29th 1772," Clarence Edwin Carter, *Correspondence of Thomas Gage with the Secretaries of State, and with the War Office and the Treasury 1763-1775*, Vol. 2, New Haven: Yale University Press, 1933, p. 608. (Also in: War Office (UK), In-Letters, WO 1/57, item 1.)

[2] "To Dartmouth, New York, May 5, 1773," Clarence Edwin Carter, *Correspondence of Thomas Gage with the Secretaries of State, and with the War Office and the Treasury 1763-1775*, Vol. 1, New Haven: Yale University Press, 1933, p. 351.

[3] Charles Loch Mowat, *East Florida as a British Province, 1763-1784*, Berkeley: University of California Press, 1943, p. 8.

[4] William Stork, John Bartram, *A Description of East-Florida, with a Journal Kept by John Bartram*, Third Edition, London: W. Nicoll, 1769, p. 7. Charles L. Mowat, describes the town as "The whole town site was not much more than ¾ mile long and ¼ mile broad. The number of houses standing before 1775 was disputed: Dr. Stork mentioned 900 but admitted that several were constructed of wood and palmetto leaves and were in a state of decay; Romans put the number at only 300." "St. Augustine under the British Flag, 1763-1775," *The Florida Historical Quarterly*, Vol. 20, No. 2 (Oct., 1941), p. 134.

[5] Helen Eloise Boor Tingley, "Florida under the English Flag, 1763-1783," *The Journal of American History*, Vol. 11, 1917, p. 75.

[6] Map based on: Samuel Dunn, Jonathan Carver, and Robert Sayer and John Bennett. *A New Map of the United States of North America with the British Dominions on that Continent &c*. London, Printed for R. Sayer & J. Bennett, Map & sea chartsellers, 1783. Map. Retrieved from the Library of Congress, <https://www.loc.gov/item/74693119/>.

[7] Mowat, *East Florida as a British Province, op cit*, pp. 26, 27.

[8] "Edward Maxwell to General Haldimand, St. Augustine, May 25, 1770," *Haldimand Papers*, H-1439 Image 159, p. 117.

[9] Mowat, *East Florida as a British Province, op cit*, pp. 30, 31.

[10] Mowat, *East Florida as a British Province, op cit*, p. 17.

[11] "Edward Maxwell to General Haldimand, St. Augustine, April 5, 1771," *Haldimand Papers*, H-1439, images 239, 240 pp 194, 195.

[12] "Maurice Carr to Haldimand, April 28 1773, St. Augustine," *Haldimand Papers*, H-1439, image 396, p. 41.

[13] "Maurice Carr to Haldimand, June 13, 1773, St. Augustine," *Haldimand Papers*, H-1439, image 437, p. 82.

[14] *Bath Chronicle and Weekly Gazette*, 9 February 1769, p. 1.

[15] "William Blackett to Haldimand, New Providence, October 1 1773," *Haldimand Papers*, H-1439, image 636.

[16] "Jonathan Furlong to Haldimand, St. Augustine, October 17 1773," *Haldimand Papers*, H-1439, image 685, p. 310.

[17] "Haldimand to Carr, New York, July 28, 1773," *Haldimand Papers*, H-1432, image 968.

[18] "Carr to Haldimand, St. Augustine, 26 September 1773," *Haldimand Papers*, H-1439, image 623, p. 248.

[19] "Fordyce to Haldimand, St. Augustine, December 17, 1773," *Haldimand Papers*, H-1439, image 749. Report of the death of Ensign Scrimshire at St. Augustine in East Florida in: *Leeds Intelligencer*, 22 March 1774, p. 3.

[20] "State of His Majesty's Forces in the Province of East Florida," *Haldimand Papers*, H-1431, images 15, 18.
[21] "Memorandum by the King," Fortescue, John, ed. *The Correspondence of King George the Third*, Vol. 3, London: MacMillan and Co., 1928, p. 325 and "Lord Dartmouth to General Gage, Whitehall, Aug 2, 1775," *Gage Correspondence* 2:204.
[22] "Fordyce to Haldimand, St. Augustine, January 9 1774," *Haldimand Papers*, H-1439, image 791, p. 15.
[23] "Fordyce to Haldimand, St. Augustine, February 6 1774," *Haldimand Papers*, H-1439, image 810, p. 33.
[24] "Fordyce to Haldimand, St. Augustine, February 15, 1774," *Haldimand Papers*, H-1439, image 822, p. 45.
[25] "Fordyce to Haldimand, St. Augustine, February 17, 1774," *Haldimand Papers*, H-1439, image 836, 837, pp. 59, 60.
[26] "Haldimand to Fordyce, New York, March 14, 1774," *Haldimand Papers*, H-1432, images 1174, 1175, p. 228.
[27] "Fordyce to Haldimand, St. Augustine, March 13, 1774," *Haldimand Papers*, H-1439, image 851, p. 74.
[28] K. G. Davies, editor, *Documents of the American Revolution 1770-1783*, Colonial Office Series, Vol. 7, Shannon: Irish University Press, 1972, p. 56. (Huntington Library)
[29] *The Boston Gazette and Country Journal*, 4 January 1773, p. 1. *The Boston Gazette and Country Journal*, 21 June 1773, p. 3.
[30] First report, *The Boston Gazette and Country Journal*, 22 June 1772, p. 3 (v4 101). Dartmouth letter to the Governor of Rhode Island, *The Boston Gazette and Country Journal*, 4 January 1773, p. 1. *The Boston Gazette and Country Journal*, 21 June 1773, p. 3.
[31] *The Boston Gazette and Country Journal*, 20 December 1773, p. 3. *Virginia Gazette*, Purdie and Dixon, Jan. 06, 1774, p. 3. More details in Jan. 13, 1774, p. 2.
[32] *Virginia Gazette*, Purdie and Dixon, Jan. 20, 1774, p. 2.
[33] Indian uprising reported in *Virginia Gazette*, Purdie and Dixon, March 10, 1774, p. 2, with dateline February 2, 1774. Details of the rather sordid affair in *Virginia Gazette*, Purdie and Dixon, March 24, 1774, p. 1. Detailed account of the resolution of the affair, datelined Charleston, March 4, 1774, in: *Virginia Gazette*, Purdie and Dixon, April 07, 1774, p. 2.
[34] *Virginia Gazette*, Purdie and Dixon, May 26, 1774, p. 2.
[35] *Virginia Gazette*, Purdie and Dixon, July 21, 1774 (postscript), p. 1.
[36] *Virginia Gazette*, Purdie and Dixon, Aug. 25, 1774, p. 1.
[37] *Virginia Gazette*, Purdie and Dixon, Sept. 15, 1774, p. 3
[38] "Meeting of the Freeholders of Boston, January 2, 1775," *The Boston Gazette and Country Journal*, 2 January 1775, p. 2, *Virginia Gazette*, Dixon and Hunter, February 04, 1775, p. 1.

[39] Articles of Association, *The Boston Gazette and Country Journal*, 7 November 1774, p. 1. Dartmouth's powder import/export prohibition, *The Boston Gazette and Country Journal*, 12 December 1774, p. 4.
[40] "Dunmore to Gage, Williamsburg 1st May 1775," NDAR 1:258.

Notes: Chapter 8: Lord Dunmore and the "Spirit of Faction"

[1] "Lord Dunmore to Lord Dartmouth, on board the Ship *Dunmore* off Norfolk, December 13, 1775," NDAR 3:140, 141.
[2] John Pendleton Kennedy, editor, *Journals of the House of Burgesses of Virginia, 1773-1776*, Richmond: 1905, p. 93.
[3] Commissioned ensign, 30 May 1749, *Commission Book*, 1746-1750, WO 25/22, p. 258. Promoted to Lieutenant and Captain, 5 November 1755, *Commission Book*, 1750-1755, WO 25/23 p, 276. Secretary at War, *A List of the General and Field-Officers as They Rank in the Army, of the Officers of the Several Regiments of Horse, Dragoons, and Foot on the British and Irish Establishments, September 1758*. London: J. Millan, 1758, pp. 44, 45. UK National Archives, WO 65/6.
[4] Richard Cannon, editor, *Historical Records of the British Army: The Third Regiment of Foot, or The Buffs*, London. William Clowes and Sons, 1836, p. 181.
[5] William C. Low and the *Dictionary of Virginia Biography*. "John Murray, fourth earl of Dunmore (ca. 1730–1809)." *Encyclopedia Virginia*. Virginia Foundation for the Humanities, 21 Nov. 2016. Web. 2 Nov. 2018.
[6] *Dictionary of National Biography*, Volumes 1-20, 22, p. 1247.
[7] *The Virginia Magazine of History and Biography*, Vol. 10, p. 80, and *Edinburgh Advertiser*, 1775 March 17, p. 2.
[8] *Virginia Gazette*, Pinkney, Dec. 15, 1774, p. 3 and *Virginia Gazette*, Purdie and Dixon, Dec. 22, 1774, p. 2. The Mayor, Recorder, Aldermen and Common Council of Williamsburg as well as the President and Professors of the College of William and Mary offered similar expressions of approbation in *Virginia Gazette*, Purdie and Dixon, Dec. 08, 1774 (supplement), p. 1. Representatives from the frontier county of Fincastle were rather effusive in their praise. *Virginia Gazette*, Dixon and Hunter, April 08, 1775, p. 3.
[9] King George was a strong proponent of the campaign. Historian George Trevelyan called it the "pet scheme" of the King and William Cullen Bryant claimed "The expedition to the southern colonies was the King's favorite project." George Trevelyan, *The American Revolution*, Vol. 1, London: Longmans, Green, and Co., 1921, p. 364. William Cullen Bryant, Sydney Howard Gay and Noah Brooks, *Scribner's Popular History of the United States*, Vol. 3, New York: Charles Scribner's Sons, 1898, p. 463. Despite the King's favor, the campaign was always second to the campaign in New England in the first years of the war. Eric Robson has written the definitive account of the "Southern Campaign," in "The Expedition to the Southern Colonies, 1775-1776," *English Historical Review*, Vol. 66 (1951),

535-560. See also: "The British Leave Colonial Virginia," W. Hugh Moomaw, *The Virginia Magazine of History and Biography*, Vol. 66, No. 2 (Apr., 1958), p. 151.

[10] "Lord Dunmore to Vice Admiral Graves, June 17, 1775," NDAR 1:710.

[11] One of Connolly's cohorts, Dr. John Smyth, explained the significance of the plan in a history he wrote after the War. Dr. Smyth noted the plan was to move on "Pittsburg, which we were to seize on and establish as head-quarters, until the disaffected interest was entirely crushed, and the whole strength of the country collected and formed into regular disciplined regiments. "After leaving a sufficient garrison at Pittsburg, we were to advance across the Allegany Mountains with our whole force upon the back of Virginia; and after establishing a strong post at Fort Cumberland, it was proposed to fall down the river Potomac, and seize on Alexandria, where the Earl of Dunmore was to meet us with the fleet, and all the force of the lower part of the province. Alexandria was to be strongly fortified, as a place of arms, and the communication between the southern and northern parts of the continent thereby cut off." John Ferdinand Smyth, *A Tour in the United States of America*, Vol. 2, London: G. Robinson, 1784, pp. 246, 247.

[12] Connolly provided this summary of the significance of the operation: "It was evident, on consulting with Lord Dunmore, and informing him of the plan I had concerted, and the confederacy I had formed, that when his Lordship was reinforced with supplies from Britain, a co-operative body of troops from Canada, and the western frontiers of Virginia, with Indian auxiliaries, would be ready to act at the time that Sir William Howe would draw their principal attention to the northward. This would not only be productive of the restitution of the royal authority of this colony, but have a general tendency to promote the success of his Majesty's arms, and the like happy effects universally." John Connolly, "A Narrative of the Transactions, Imprisonment, and Sufferings of John Connolly, an American Loyalist and Lieut.-Col. in His Majesty's Service," *The Pennsylvania Magazine of History and Biography*, Vol 12, Philadelphia: The Historical Society of Pennsylvania, 1888, p. 407.

[13] "Gage to Dartmouth," Boston September 20, 1775, Clarence Edwin Carter, *Correspondence of Thomas Gage with the Secretaries of State, and with the War Office and the Treasury 1763-1775*, Vol. 1, New Haven: Yale University Press, 1933, p. 415. Probably received in November. General Gage was not the only one who saw merit in the plan. After Connolly was captured, George Washington told Congress, "I am much pleased…that Connolly and his associates are taken; it has been a very fortunate discovery." General Washington to the President of Congress, Cambridge, December 14, 1775.

[14] *Virginia Gazette*, Purdie, Dec. 15, 1775, p. 2.

[15] "Major John Pitcairn, R. M., to Lord Sandwich Boston, 4th March 1775," NDAR 1:126.

[16] "Captain Matthew Squire, R.N., to Vice Admiral Samuel Graves, *Otter* Sloop off Norfolk. 2d Decr 1775," NDAR 2:1240.

[17] "Captain Samuel Leslie to Major General William Howe, Gosport Virginia, 1st Novr 1775," NDAR 2:844.
[18] "Beesly Joel to Joseph Wright, *Otter* Sloop Octr 1775, Norfolk Virginia," Dice Robins Anderson, editor, *Richmond College Historical Papers*, Vol. 1 (1915), p. 97.
[19] The Resolve quoted was the fifth of five introduced by Patrick Henry on May 29, 1765, but it was not included in the final four Resolves passed by the House of Burgesses on May 30. This fifth Resolve was, however, published in the newspapers of the time and, no doubt, would have been known to Lord Dunmore and the other members of the House of Lords. John Pendleton Kennedy, editor, *Journals of the House of Burgesses of Virginia, 1761-1765*, Richmond: 1908, pp. lxv, lxvii, 360.
[20] The Burgesses published their Resolution in support of Boston on May 24, 1774. *Journals of the House of Burgesses of Virginia 1773 - 1776, op cit*, p. 124. Lord Dunmore dissolved the Burgesses on May 26 *ibid*, p. 132.
[21] Lord Dunmore explained his concern to Lord Dartmouth in a letter of May 29, 1774. Letter published in *Virginia Gazette*, Pinkney, June 08, 1775, p. 1.
[22] Governor Dunmore named the discord he witnessed in 1774 a "spirit of faction" in a "Proclamation" issued on May 3, 1775, in response to the uproar over his confiscation of the gunpowder in Williamsburg on April 20, 1775. *Virginia Gazette*, Dixon and Hunter, May 6, 1775, p. 2.
[23] Dinwiddie told the Earl of Halifax the Burgesses were, "making Encroachments on the Prerogative of the Crown" and feared it would be difficult to bring them to order. "Governor Dinwiddie to the Earl of Halifax, March 12, 1754," *Collections of the Virginia Historical Society*, New Series, Vol. 3, Richmond: 1883, p. 100.
[24] *Journals of the House of Burgesses of Virginia, 1761-1765, op cit*, p. 364 and "Governor Fauquier to the Lords of Trade, Williamsburg, June 5, 1765," Jared Sparks, editor, *The Library of American Biography*, Vol. 1, Boston: C. C. Little and J. Brown, 1844, pp. 391, 392.
[25] John Pendleton Kennedy, editor, *Journals of the House of Burgesses of Virginia, 1766-1769*, Richmond: 1906, p. 214.
[26] *Ibid*, p. 218.
[27] Lord Dunmore explained his concern to Lord Dartmouth in a letter of May 29, 1774. Letter published in *Virginia Gazette*, Pinkney, June 08, 1775, p. 1.
[28] "Murray Esq., commonly known as Lord Fincastle, to be a Lieutenant in the said Regt. And to take your rank as Captain of Foot." 5 November 1755. *Commission Book*, WO 25/23, 1750-1755, p. 276.
[29] William C. Lowe, "The Parliamentary Career of Lord Dunmore, 1761-1774," *The Virginia Magazine of History and Biography*, Vol. 96, No. 1 (Jan., 1988), p. 5.
[30] See for example the list of letters, assembly records, memorials, petitions and council minutes presented to the House of Lords during the February and March session of 1766. *Journals of the House of Lords*, Vol. 31, 1765-1767, pp. 263, 267, 268, 271, 279, 282, ff. Also, *Cobbetts Parliamentary History of England*, Vol. 16, pp. 112-137.

[31] The Resolves affected attitudes about sovereignty and authority throughout the colonies. Francis Bernard, Governor of Massachusetts, wrote Lord Halifax of rioting in Boston as a result of the passage of the Stamp Act in 1765, and in the letter he noted, "I thought that this People would have submitted to the Stamp Act ... But the publishing the Virginia Resolves proved an Alarm bell to the disaffected." "Governor Bernard to Lord Halifax, August 15, 1765," quoted in: Edmund Sears Morgan, editor, *Prologue to Revolution: Sources and Documents on the Stamp Act Crisis, 1764-1766*, Chapel Hill: The University of North Carolina Press, 1959, p. 106. Letter to Secretary Conway entered into the Parliamentary Record, "The resolves of the assembly of Virginia ... gave the signal for a general out-cry over the continent." *Cobbetts Parliamentary History of England*, Vol. 16, p. 123. In a letter to Lord Hillsborough of December 4, 1769, Cadwallader Colden, Lieutenant Governor of New York, expressed his concern parts of the Assembly's proceedings "Have not so good an appearance as I wish, particularly their concurring with and adopting the Resolves of the Virginia Assembly." "The Colden Letter Books, Vol. 2, 1765 – 1775, *Collections of the New York Historical Society for the Year 1877*, New York: 1878, p. 194

[32] "Governor Fauquier to Lord Halifax, Williamsburg, Virginia June 14, 1765." *Cobbett's Parliamentary History of England*, London: T. C. Hansard, 1813, p. 1254.

[33] "Governor Fauquier to the Lords of Trade, Williamsburg, Virginia, June 5, 1765," Alexander Everett, "Life of Patrick Henry," in Jared Sparks, editor, *Lives of Robert Cavelier de La Salle and Patrick Henry*, Boston: Little, Brown, 1848, pp. 391-394.

[34] "Lieutenant Governor Fauquier to the Board of Trade, Williamsburg, Virginia, December 17, 1766." "Letters of Governor Francis Fauquier," *The William and Mary Quarterly*, Vol. 21, No. 3 (Jan., 1913), p. 170.

[35] "Extract of a Letter from the Earl of Dunmore to the Earl of Dartmouth, dated Williamsburg, December 24, 1774. Received Feb. 11, 1775," *The Parliamentary Register: or, History of the Proceedings and Debates of the House of Commons, 14th Parliament*, Vol. 1, p. 187.

[36] "Lord Dunmore to Lord Dartmouth (No 32) the Ship William by Norfolk, Virginia 5th October 1775," NDAR 2:316, 317. Dunmore was not alone. Regarding the on-again-off-again Southern Expedition, Lord Germain reminded Lord Dunmore, "this Expedition has been formed (in great Measure at least) upon the Assurances given, with equal Confidence, from each of the Southern Provinces, that the bare Appearance of a Military Force would encourage the Friends of Government to shew themselves." "Lord Germain to Lord Dunmore, Whitehall, Dec 23rd 1775." NDAR 3:445.

[37] Dunmore to Dartmouth, May 29, 1774. Published in *Virginia Gazette*, Pinkney, June 08, 1775, p. 1.

[38] Thomas Jefferson, *The Writings of Thomas Jefferson: Being His Autobiography, Correspondence, Reports, Messages, Addresses, and Other Writings, Official and Private*, Vol. 6, edited by Henry Augustine Washington, Washington: Taylor & Maury,

1854, p. 366. Five hundred guineas in Robert R. Howison, *A History of Virginia: from Its Discovery and Settlement by Europeans to the Present Time*, Philadelphia: Carey & Hart, 1846-1848, p. 51.

[39] "Lord Dartmouth to Lord Dunmore, (No. 21) Whitehall 5th July 1775," NDAR 1:1311-1313.

[40] "Lord Dartmouth to Lord Dunmore, (No. 22) Whitehall, 12th July 1775," NDAR 1:1324, 1325.

[41] "The Parliamentary Career of Lord Dunmore, 1761-1774," *op cit*, pp. 21-24.

[42] *Ibid*, pp. 24, 25, 26.

[43] The details of Governor Dunmore's reluctance to leave New York and his initial encounters with Virginia's ruling elites is recorded in detail in George Morrow, *A Cock and Bull for Kitty: Lord Dunmore and the Affair that Ruined the British Cause in Virginia*, Williamsburg: Telford Publications, 2011, pp. 16-22. Regarding Dunmore's governorship in general see also, Percy Scott Flippin, *The Royal Government in Virginia, 1624-1775*, New York: Columbia University, 1919, pp. 142 ff.

[44] In a letter to the Earl of Dartmouth in 1773, Dunmore provided this explanation for his lenient interpretation of instructions related to the printing of paper money: "I thought it not advisable to let them feel the weight of govern't to severely, by adhering rigidly to the exact letter of the Instructions, at a time when I saw, that it must have greatly distressed their trade." "Lord Dunmore to Lord Dartmouth, Williamsburg, March 31, 1773," *Journals of the House of Burgesses of Virginia 1773 - 1776, op cit*, p. x.

[45] William Lecky, *The American Revolution, 1763-1783*, New York and London: D. Appleton and Company, 1898, p. 346.

[46] Vote against repeal of the Stamp Act: *Virginia Gazette*, Purdie and Dixon, May 19, 1768, p. 1. Move to read *Boston Gazette* in House of Lords: *Virginia Gazette*, Rind, March 24, 1768, p. 3. Other unfavorable reports: *Virginia Gazette*, Purdie and Dixon, April 27, 1769, p. 3, *Virginia Gazette*, Purdie and Dixon, May 25, 1769, p. 2.

[47] William Lee to Richard Henry Lee, London, March 17, 1774, in *Virginia Gazette*, Purdie and Dixon, May 19, 1774, p. 4.

[48] *Virginia Gazette*, Purdie, April 14, 1775 (supplement), p. 2.

[49] *Virginia Gazette*, Purdie and Dixon, March 28, 1771, p. 2. Disaffection with this act was documented in *Virginia Gazette*, Purdie and Dixon, Feb. 22, 1770, p. 2.

[50] *Virginia Gazette*, Purdie and Dixon, March 07, 1771, p. 3 and *Virginia Gazette*, Rind, March 07, 1771, p. 3.

[51] *Virginia Gazette*, Purdie and Dixon, Sept. 26, 1771, pp. 2, 3.

[52] When Governor Botetourt arrived editors Purdie and Dixon reported "… all ranks of people vied with each other in testifying their gratitude and joy that a Nobleman of such distinguished merit and abilities is appointed to preside over, and live among, them." *Virginia Gazette*, Purdie and Dixon, Oct. 27, 1768, p. 3.

[53] In a letter of May 8, 1771, the Lieutenant Governor of New York, Cadwallader Colden, told Arthur Maris, "It is said he [Lord Dunmore] does not intend going

soon to the Gov' of Virginia, as he hopes to obtain leave to remain here [i.e., New York]" "The Colden Letter Books, Vol. 2, 1765 - 1775 or The Colden Papers," *Collections of the New York Historical Society for the Year 1877*, New York: 1878, pp. 323, 324.

[54] Both responses are in: *Virginia Gazette*, Purdie and Dixon, Oct. 3, 1771, pp. 2, 3.

[55] *Journals of the House of Burgesses of Virginia 1773 - 1776, op cit*, p. xxxiii. The Proclamation was published in *Virginia Gazette*, Rind, Sept. 26, 1771, p. 2.

[56] *Journals of the House of Burgesses of Virginia 1773 - 1776, op cit*, p. 124.

[57] *Ibid*, pp. 124, 132.

[58] (Prince William) *Virginia Gazette*, Rind, June 09, 1774 (supplement), p. 2 (Westmoreland, Prince George) *Virginia Gazette*, Rind, June 30, 1774, p. 2; (Richmond) *Virginia Gazette*, Purdie and Dixon, July 07, 1774, p. 2; (Spotsylvania) *Virginia Gazette*, Purdie and Dixon, July 07, 1774, p. 3; (Norfolk) *Virginia Gazette*, Purdie and Dixon, July 14, 1774, p. 3; (James City, Culpeper and Norfolk) *Virginia Gazette*, Rind, July 14, 1774, p. 3; (York, New Kent, Dinwiddie, Chesterfield) *Virginia Gazette*, Purdie and Dixon, July 21, 1774 (postscript), p. 1; (Essex, Middlesex, Surry) *Virginia Gazette*, Purdie and Dixon, July 21, 1774 (postscript), p. 2; (Hanover, Caroline) *Virginia Gazette*, Purdie and Dixon: July 28, 1774 (supplement), p. 1; (Henrico, Nansemond) *Virginia Gazette*, Purdie and Dixon: July 28, 1774 (supplement), p. 2; (Isle of Wight, Stafford, Gloucester, Caroline) *Virginia Gazette*, Rind, July 28, 1774, p. 2; (Elizabeth City, Henrico) *Virginia Gazette*, Rind, July 28, 1774, p. 3; (Albemarle, Princess Ann, Buckingham, Fauquier, Dunmore) *Virginia Gazette*, Rind, Aug. 04, 1774, p. 1; (Fairfax) *Virginia Gazette*, Rind, Aug. 04, 1774, p. 2: (Accomack), Peter Force, *American Archives*, 4: 639, 640. See also, Arthur Meier Schlesinger, *The Colonial Merchants and the American Revolution*, 1763-1776, Vol. 78, New York: Columbia University, 1918, p. 365.

[59] *Virginia Gazette*, Rind, June 09, 1774 (supplement), p. 2.

[60] Kate Mason Rowland, *The Life of George Mason, 1725-1792*, Vol. 1, New York: G. P. Putnam's Sons, 1892, footnote, pp. 181, 182.

[61] *Virginia Gazette*, Pinkney, June 08, 1775, p. 1.

[62] "Letter from the Earl of Dunmore to the Earl of Dartmouth, Williamsburg, December 24, 1774," William Cobbett, editor, *Cobbett's Parliamentary History of England*, Vol. 18, London: T. C. Hansard, 1813, p. 315. *Virginia Gazette*, Pinkney, April 28, 1775, p. 3. The House of Burgesses referred to this letter in an address to Governor Dunmore after he had fled Williamsburg in June of 1775. *The Journals of the House of Burgesses of Virginia 1773 - 1776, op cit*, pp. 254-255.

[63] *The Journals of the House of Burgesses of Virginia 1773 - 1776, op cit*, pp. xvii-xviii. "Lord Dunmore to Lord Dartmouth, Williamsburg 1st May 1775," NDAR 1:259.

[64] "Spirit of faction" named in "Proclamation" of May 3, 1775, published in *Virginia Gazette*, Dixon and Hunter, May 6, 1775, p. 2. "Pretending to contend for Liberty" quote from "Lord Dunmore to Lord Dartmouth, Williamsburg 1st May 1775," *op cit*.

Notes: Chapter 9: Deployed to Virginia

[1] "Lord Dunmore to Lord Dartmouth, Williamsburg, 1st May 1775," NDAR 1:259 – 261.

[2] NDAR 1:257, 258. Also referenced in: Great Britain, Public Record Office, Richard Arthur Roberts, editor, *Calendar of Home Office Papers of the Reign of George III*, Vol. 4 (1773-1775), London: H.M.S.O., 1899, p. 360.

[3] "Dunmore to Gage, Williamsburg 1st May 1775," NDAR 1:258.

[4] *Otter* ordered to Virginia: NDAR 1:297, 311, 785, also reported as 20 guns, p. 428.

[5] "Graves to Dunmore, May 20, 1775," NDAR 1:372. *Otter* sails for Virginia: NDAR 1:510, 518. *Otter* arrives Yorktown: NDAR 1:643. Purdie notes arrival of *Otter*: *Virginia Gazette*, Purdie, June 09, 1775 (supplement), p. 2.

[6] "Lord Dunmore to Vice Admiral Samuel Graves, *Fowey*, York River, June 17, 1775," NDAR 1:710.

[7] Dunmore in Portsmouth: *Virginia Gazette*, Dixon and Hunter, July 15, 1775, *Virginia Gazette*, Purdie, July 28, 1775.

[8] *Virginia Gazette*, Purdie, July 14, 1775 (supplement), p. 1. Arrival of the 24 gun *Mercury* at Yorktown, Captain John McCartney.

[9] "Lord Dunmore to Lord Dartmouth, *Fowey* in York River 25th June 1775," NDAR 1:754 – 757. Some of the outrage (not-so-righteous indignation) in response to this second incident involving the magazine in Williamsburg did support a conclusion the citizens might want revenge. The report of the incident in Purdie's *Gazette* ended with the warning, "had any person lost his life, the perpetrator or perpetrators, of this diabolical invention, might have been justly branded with opprobrious title of MURDERERS. *Virginia Gazette*, Purdie, June 09, 1775 (supplement) p. 2. Editor Pinkney linked the incident to a plot by Dunmore to blow up the city of Williamsburg. *Virginia Gazette*, Pinkney, June 08, 1775, p. 3. See also: *Virginia Gazette*, Dixon and Hunter, June 10, 1775, p. 2 and John Pendleton Kennedy, editor, *Journals of the House of Burgesses of Virginia, 1773-1776*, Richmond: 1905, p. 260.

[10] "Lord Dunmore to Lord Dartmouth, P.S. [to letter of June 25] 27th of June 1775," NDAR 1:764.

[11] William Eddis, Surveyor of Customs in Maryland, claimed Governor Dunmore's Proclamation freeing the slaves "had some immediate effect in the opulent town of Norfolk, where many of the inhabitants were well affected to government." "Letter of William Eddis, January 16, 1776." William Eddis, *Letters from America, Historical and Descriptive: Comprising Occurrences from 1769, to 1777*, London: Printed for the author, and sold by C. Dilly in the Poultry, 1792, p. 251. One observer of the turmoil in Virginia at this time told Admiral Graves' Secretary, George Giffarina, he thought one reason Colonel Woodford had been ordered to march to Great Bridge was "to punish the Norfolk people for declaring

for Government." "W. Griffin to George Giffarina, Secretary to Admiral Graves." *Kingfisher*, Jamestown, Virginia, November 14, 1775, *American Archives* 4:343. The observations of another observer, to the same effect, were published in England. In a letter dated December 25, this observer told his correspondent Lord Dunmore took action when he learned "of a large body of the rebel army being on their march to destroy Norfolk, because its inhabitants had professed their loyalty to government." Ship *William*, off Norfolk, December 25, *The Scots Magazine*, February 1776, Vol. 38, p. 91.

[12] Maps evaluated in developing this figure include, Collet, John, J Bayly, and S Hooper. *A compleat map of North-Carolina from an actual survey*. London: S. Hooper, 1770. Map. Retrieved from the Library of Congress, https://www.loc.gov/item/83693769/, Faden, William. *A Plan of the entrance of Chesapeak Bay, with James and York rivers; wherein are shewn the respective positions in the beginning of October 1.⁰ of the British Army commanded by Lord Cornwallis at Gloucester and York in Virginia; 2.⁰ of the American and French forces under General Washington; 3.⁰ and of the French Fleet under Count de Grasse*. London, Wm. Faden, 1781. Map. Retrieved from the Library of Congress, https://www.loc.gov/item/74692131/, Worret, Ch, and Thomas Jefferson Cram. *S.E. portion of Virginia and N.E. portion of N'th Carolina*. [186, 1861] Map. Retrieved from the Library of Congress, https://www.loc.gov/item/2003630424/and *Part of the Province of Virginia*. [?, 1791] Map. Retrieved from the Library of Congress, https://www.loc.gov/item/74693199/.

[13] "Captain George Montagu, R.N., to Vice Admiral Samuel Graves, *Fowey* at York 17th June 1775, NDAR 1:711. "Journal of His Majesty's Sloop *Otter*, Matthew Squire, Commanding, June 28, 1775," NDAR 1:772.

[14] *Virginia Gazette*, Dixon and Hunter, Aug. 05, 1775, p. 3. *Virginia Gazette*, Purdie, Aug. 04, 1775 (postscript), p. 1. Holt, The *Virginia Gazette or the Norfolk Intelligencer*, Aug. 2, 1775, p. 2, col. 3 and Aug. 16, p. 3. (google.com/newspapers).

[15] K. G. Davies, editor, *Documents of the American Revolution 1770-1783*, Colonial Office Series, Vol. 10, Shannon: Irish University Press, 1976, p. 53.

[16] "Captain Samuel Leslie to General Thomas Gage, August 20, 1775," NDAR 1:1192.

[17] *Virginia Gazette*, Dixon and Hunter, August 12, 1775, p. 3. *Virginia Gazette*, Purdie, August 11, 1775 (postscript), p. 2 and August 25, p. 7, NDAR 1:1162.

[18] Ms. Hunter notes the arrival of Captain John Dalrymple and Lieutenant Andrew Laurie in "Katherine Leslie Hunter, Gosport, Virginia, to Miss Logan, Nov. 5, 1775," Robert L. Scribner and Brent Tarter, editors, *Revolutionary Virginia, The Road to Independence*, Vol. 4, Charlottesville: The University Press of Virginia, 1979, p. 323.

[19] "Jonathan Furlong to General Gage, St. Augustine, October 5, 1775," *American Archives* 4:319.

[20] *Ibid*.

[21] *Virginia Gazette*, Purdie, Sept. 15, 1775 (supplement), p. 2.

[22] "Monthly Return of His Majesty's Forces in the Province of East Florida, St. Augustine, August 1, 1775," *American Archives*, 4:321, 322.
[23] "Monthly Return of His Majesty's Forces in the Province of East Florida, St. Augustine, September 1, 1775," *American Archives*, 4: 323, 324.
[24] "Monthly Return of a Detachment of His Majesty's Fourteenth Regiment of Infantry, Gosport Virginia, October 1, 1775," *American Archives* 4:349.
[25] "Captain Samuel Leslie to General Thomas Gage, August 20, 1775," NDAR 1:1192, "Captain Samuel Leslie to General Howe, Gosport, Virginia, November 1, 1775," *American Archives*, 3:1716.
[26] "An Ordinance for Raising and Embodying a Sufficient Force for the Defense and Protection of This Colony," *The Proceedings of the Convention of Delegates for the Counties and Corporations in the Colony of Virginia: 17th of July, 1775*, p. 29, transcribed by Roy Randolph. The text of the entire Ordinance was published in the *Virginia Gazette*, Purdie, August 25, 1775, pp. 1-5.
[27] *Ibid*, p. 45, transcribed by Roy Randolph.
[28] *The Proceedings of the Convention of Delegates for the Counties and Corporations in the Colony of Virginia: Held at Richmond Town, in the County of Henrico, on the 20th of March, 1775*, Richmond: Ritchie, Trueheart & Du-Val, printers, 1816, pp. 5, 6. HathiTrust, transcribed by Roy Randolph.
[29] Despite the urgent need for troops, there was still some pageantry involved in the training. Purdie provides this report of a display of martial competence by Woodford's volunteer company: "Last Thursday the volunteer company of Caroline, commanded by William Woodford, esq; went through the manual exercise, with a great variety of new and useful evolutions, at the Fowling Green in that county, before upwards of 1500 spectators, who were exceedingly pleased with the dexterity and alertness of the men, they performing only by the beat of the drum, and did credit to the abilities of Mr. Thomas Davis, adjutant, late of Fairfax county, who instructed them." *Virginia Gazette*, Purdie, August 11, 1775 (postscript), p. 2.
[30] *Virginia Gazette*, Dixon and Hunter, August 26, 1775, p. 3, transcribed by Roy Randolph. Purdie reported these additional facts: "Williamsburg August 25. From Norfolk we learn, that lord Dunmore seized last Tuesday a fine new ship lately launched, frigate built, and pierced for 22 guns, belonging to Eilbeck, Ross, & co. of that place...for the king's service! He has likewise seized a brig belonging to Mr. Daniel Barraud, merchant in Norfolk for the same pious intent, no doubt!" *Virginia Gazette, Purdie*, August 25, 1775, p. 7.
[31] "Lord Dunmore to Lord Dartmouth, Ship William off Norfolk October 22d 1775," NDAR 2:574, 575. Also: *The London Gazette*, 12 December 1775, Issue 11622, p. 8.
[32] "Captain Samuel Leslie to General Howe, Gosport, Virginia, November 1, 1775," *American Archives* 3:1716.
[33] "Distribution of His Majesty's Forces in North America, July 19, 1775," 1 drummer and 95 rank and file at Castle William, *Gage Correspondence* 2:690. This is a

large detachment but it seems to lack the officers necessary to be considered a company (or companies).
[34] Date of embarkation noted in: "C. Shirreff to General Robertson, St. Augustine, October 2, 1775," *American Archives*, 4:334. "Captain Fordice [Fordyce] to Captain Urquhart, Norfolk, December 1, 1775," *American Archives*, 4:350.
[35] "Captain Samuel Leslie to General Howe, Gosport, Virginia, November 1, 1775," *op cit*. Captain Matthew Squire of the *Otter* recorded the arrival of the *Betsey* Sloop & *Unicorn* Snow with part of the 14th Regiment from St. Augustine on October 19 in his ship's Journal. "Journal of H.M. Sloop *Otter*, Captain Matthew Squire October 1775 Elizabeth River [Virginia] Thursday 19," PRO, Admiralty 5 1/663. *Unicorn* seized by Lord Dunmore to transport 14t Regiment, *Virginia Gazette or the Norfolk Intelligencer*, Aug 30, 1775, p. 3.
[36] Captain Blackett's funeral and burial at Portsmouth were recorded in Purdie's *Virginia Gazette*. According to the report, "Last Sunday [October 15] a captain of the regiment with lord Dunmore was buried at Portsmouth, his funeral being attended by his lordship, the gentlemen of the navy, and 91 men rank and file, besides officers, which it seems composed the whole corps under lord Dunmore's command at that time. Four of the soldiers were so feeble, occasioned by sickness, that they could not carry their arms." *Virginia Gazette*, Purdie, October 20, 1775 (supplement), p. 2. Transcribed by Roy Randolph.
[37] "Monthly Return of a Detachment of His Majesty's Fourteenth Regiment of Infantry, Gosport, Virginia, November 1, 1775," *American Archives*, 4:350.
[38] Captain Leslie said he was supported with twenty marines and twelve seamen in his raid of October 17. "Letter from Captain Leslie to General Howe," *American Archives*, 3:1716.
[39] "Letter to Patrick Henry from the Virginia Committee of Safety [manuscript], October 21, 1775," Boston Public Library American Revolutionary War Manuscripts Collection. <https://archive.org/details/lettertopatrickh00pend>
[40] *Virginia Gazette*, Purdie, October 20, 1775, (Supplement), p. 2.
[41] Robert L. Scribner and Brent Tarter, *Revolutionary Virginia, the Road to Independence*, Vol. 4, Charlottesville: University Press of Virginia, 1979, pp. 269, 270. On October 25, the 2nd Regiment and the Culpeper Minute Battalion were ordered to "hold themselves in Readiness to march," as soon as they "could be provided with Necessarys." Brent Tarter, "The Orderly Book of the Second Virginia Regiment: September 27, 1775-April 15, 1776," *The Virginia Magazine of History and Biography*, Vol. 85, No. 2 (Apr., 1977), pp. 172, 173.
[42] John Burk, Skelton Jones and Louis Hue Girardin, *The History of Virginia: From Its First Settlement to the Present Day*, Vol. 4, Petersburg, Virginia: M. W. Dunnavant, 1816, Appendix p. ii. Also see: Robert L. Scribner and Brent Tarter, *Revolutionary Virginia, the Road to Independence*, Vol. 4, Charlottesville: University Press of Virginia, 1979, pp. 270, 271.

[43] "The Orderly Book of the Second Virginia Regiment: September 27, 1775-April 15, 1776," *The Virginia Magazine of History and Biography* Vol. 85, No. 2 (Apr, 1977), pp. 157, 180.

[44] "Lord Dunmore to Lord Dartmouth, on Board the Ship *Dunmore* off Norfolk Virginia 6th December 1775," NDAR 2:1309 ff.

[45] "Lord Dunmore to Lord Dartmouth, 6th December 1775," *op cit*. In this account Governor Dunmore estimated the number of militia to be between three and four hundred. This estimate is consistent with that reported by John Brown in a letter to his brother, William Brown, of London in *Virginia Historical Society, The Virginia Magazine of History and Biography*, Vol. 14, Number 3, January 1907, Richmond: Wm. Ellis Jones, 1907, pp. 255, 256. In this same edition of *The Virginia Magazine of History*, pp. 247-250, William Calderhead and Robert Shedden also provide accounts of the battle and they too estimated the rebel force as between three and four hundred. In an earlier account, Governor Dunmore estimated the rebel force at two to three hundred. "Lord Dunmore to Major General William Howe on Board the Ship *William* off Norfolk, November 30, 1775," NDAR 2:1210. According to the report in one edition of the *Virginia Gazette*, "The Governor himself was in the action, with all his forces, far superior in number to ours." *Virginia Gazette*, Dixon and Hunter, November 18, 1775, p. 3.

[46] "Colonel William Woodford, On the Virginia Service, to The Honble The President of the Convention at Wms:burg, with Enclosures," Great Bridge, December 10, 1775, in Robert Scribner and Brent Tarter, editors, *Revolutionary Virginia, the Road to Independence*, Vol. 5, Charlottesville: University Press of Virginia, 1978, pp. 102, 103. Used by permission.

[47] Account of John Brown in a letter to his brother, William Brown, of London in *Virginia Historical Society, The Virginia Magazine of History and Biography*, Vol. 14, *op cit*, p. 256, transcribed by Roy Randolph.

[48] Note 72, "The Orderly Book of the Second Virginia Regiment," *op cit*, p. 180.

[49] "W. P. W. Curll [William Curle], Portsmouth, Novemr 16th, 1775," Dice Robins Anderson, editor, *Richmond College Historical Papers*, Vol. 1, No. 1 (1915), p 100.

[50] "Lord Dunmore to Lord Dartmouth, on Board the Ship *Dunmore* off Norfolk Virginia 6th December 1775," NDAR 2:1309 ff.

[51] Proclamation published in Pinkney, November 23, 1775, p. 2, Purdie, November 24, 1775, p. 2 and Dixon and Hunter, November 25, 1775, p. 3.

[52] William Maxwell, "My Mother," in Edward W. James, ed., *Lower Norfolk County Virginia Antiquary*, Number 2, Part 3, Baltimore: The Friedenwald Co., 1897, pp. 32, 61, 137.

[53] Ships' Remark Books, "HMS Launceston: assigned 'Captain John Gell, Commander', 'James Maxwell' and '[?] Maude'; 6 May 1766 to 5 May 1767; England, SE Coast, English Channel to United States, E Coast and Nova Scotia," National Archives UK, Records of the Admiralty, Naval Forces, Royal Marines, Coastguard, and Related Bodies, ADM 346/17/5.

[54] *The Boston Evening Post*, 3 October 1768, p. 3.

55 *Virginia Gazette*, Purdie and Dixon, Dec. 01, 1768, p. 3.
56 William Crozier, editor, *Virginia County Records*, Vol. 6, Hasbrouck Heights, New Jersey: The Genealogical Association, 1909, p. 250. Republished, Baltimore: Genealogical Publishing Co., 1971.
57 *Virginia Gazette*, Rind, Aug. 11, 1768, p. 2
58 William Maxwell, "My Mother," *op cit*, p. 27.
59 Proclamation signed November 7, 1775. Published in *Virginia Gazette*, Pinkney, Nov. 23, 1775, p. 2. Oath published in *Virginia Gazette*, Dixon and Hunter, Dec. 2, 1775, p. 3.
60 "Katherine Leslie Hunter, Gosport, Virginia, to Miss Logan, Glasgow, Scotland, Nov. 5, 1775," *Revolutionary Virginia*, Vol. 4, *op cit*, p. 324.

Notes: Chapter 10: The Battle of Great Bridge

[1] "Lord Dunmore to Lord Dartmouth, *Fowey* in York River 25th June 1775," NDAR 1:754, 757.
[2] "Lord Dunmore to Vice Admiral Graves, Williamsburg 1st May 1775," NDAR 1:257, 258. "Lord Dunmore to Lord Dartmouth, the Ship *William* in Elizabeth River Virginia 24th September 1775," NDAR 2:195, 196.
[3] On May 1st, 1775, Dunmore told Lord Dartmouth he was awaiting "His Majesty's orders to regulate my future conduct." On May 15th, he told Lord Dartmouth he hoped he, i.e., Lord Dartmouth, would "See the Necessity of Sending me Instructions upon the occasion, and of putting me in a Situation of Safety." "Lord Dunmore to Lord Dartmouth, Williamsburg 1st May 1775, NDAR, 1:259-261. "Lord Dunmore to Lord Dartmouth [Extract], Williamsburg 15th May 1775, NDAR 1:341, 342.
[4] "Extract of a Letter from Lord Dunmore to General Howe, November 30, 1775," Hezekiah Niles, *Principles and Acts of the Revolution in America*, Baltimore: William Ogden Files, 1822, p. 139.
[5] "Lord Dunmore to Lord Dartmouth, on Board the Ship *Dunmore* off Norfolk Virginia 6th December 1775," NDAR 2:1309 ff.
[6] "Philip Stephens to Vice Admiral Samuel Graves, 6th September 1775," NDAR 2:705.
[7] "Lord Dunmore to Lord Dartmouth, on Board the Ship *Dunmore* off Norfolk Virginia 6th December 1775," NDAR 2:1309 ff. Also called "Black Fusiliers" *Virginia Gazette*, Purdie, April 26, 1776 supplement, p. 2 or "Dunmore's Royal Regiment of Black Fusiliers," *Virginia Gazette*, Purdie, March 22, 1776, p. 3.
[8] Such would be American policy as well. See *Journals of the Continental Congress*, March 29, 1779, p. 387.
[9] "Lord Dunmore to General Howe, November 30, 1775," Hezekiah Niles, *op cit*.
[10] "Captain Samuel Leslie to Major General William Howe, Norfolk 26th November." NDAR 2:1148.

[11] "Lord Dunmore to General Howe, November 30, 1775," Hezekiah Niles, *op cit*. Two days later Governor Dunmore wrote General Howe pleading for troops to augment his regulars. He told the General, "Pray spare us some troops, if you can possibly do it consistent with your orders; even the recruits of the Fourteenth Regiment would be of service to us." "Lord Dunmore to General Howe," on board the *Dunmore*, off Norfolk, Virginia, December 2, 1775," *American Archives* 4:357.

[12] "Lord Dunmore to Lord Dartmouth, 6th December 1775," *op cit*.

[13] Virginia House of Delegates, *Proceedings of the Convention of Delegates for the Counties and Corporations in the Colony of Virginia, December 1775*, Richmond: Ritchie, Trueheart & Du-Val, 1816, pp. 63, 64.

[14] Taken from an account of the skirmish at Kemp's Landing in *Virginia Gazette*, Purdie, November 17, 1775, p. 3. A less opinionated account of this skirmish was published in *Virginia Gazette*, Dixon and Hunter, November 18, 1775, p. 3.

[15] "Captain Fordice [Fordyce] to Captain Urquhart, Norfolk, December 1, 1775," *op cit*.

[16] Virginia House of Delegates, *Proceedings of the Convention of Delegates for the Counties and Corporations in the Colony of Virginia, December 1775*, op cit, p. 59.

[17] "Colonel Woodford to Edmund Pendleton, Camp at Suffolk 26th Novr. 1775," Dice Robins Anderson, editor, *Richmond College Historical Papers*, Vol. 1 (1915), p 104.

[18] "The Orderly Book of the Second Virginia Regiment: September 27,1775-April 15, 1776," *op cit*, p. 181.

[19] "Colonel Woodford to Edmund Pendleton, Great Bridge 4th Decmr. 1775," *Richmond College Historical Papers*, *op cit*, p 109.

[20] "Edmund Pendleton to Colonel William Woodford, Wmsburg, December 7th 1775," Robert L. and Brent Tarter, *Revolutionary Virginia, the Road to Independence*. Vol. 5. Charlottesville: University Press of Virginia, 1978, p. 76.

[21] Assessing Colonel Woodford as "under confident" is certainly subject to dispute. That said, it is remarkable that Woodford wrote General George Washington after his appointment as commander of the 2nd Virginia Regiment asking for advice on how to do his new job and admitting his lack of experience. This is consistent with the caution ascribed to Woodford and it also demonstrates a valuable characteristic in a commander, humility. Washington did advise Colonel Woodford and he assured him, "I do not mean to flatter, when I assure you, that I highly approve of your appointment. The inexperience you complain of is a common case, and only to be remedied by practice and close attention. The best general advice I can give, and which I am sure you stand in no need of, is to be strict in your discipline." Washington went on to give Colonel Woodford a rather extensive lesson in the art of commanding. "George Washington to Colonel William Woodford, Cambridge, November 10, 1775," John Clement Fitzpatrick, editor, *The Writings of George Washington from the Original Manuscripts*, Vol. 4, Washington: GPO, 1931, p. 80.

[22] "Lord Dunmore to Lord Dartmouth, on board the Ship *Dunmore* off Norfolk, December 13, 1775," NDAR 3:140, 141.
[23] "Colonel Woodford to Edmund Pendleton, Camp at Suffolk 26th Novr. 1775," *op cit*.
[24] "Colonel Woodford to Edmund Pendleton, Great Bridge 4th Decmr. 1775," *op cit*.
[25] "Lord Dunmore to Lord Dartmouth, Ship *Dunmore* off Norfolk, 13th of December," *op cit*. Also, "Earl of Dunmore to the Earl of Dartmouth, 6 and 13 December 1775, *Dunmore* off Norfolk," K. G. Davies, editor, *Documents of the American Revolution 1770-1783, Colonial Office Series*, Vol. 12, Shannon: Irish University Press, p. 60. This was the same point Governor Dunmore had made to Lord Dartmouth in a letter of September 24. In that letter he told the Secretary, "I wait with great impatience for a full Answer to my former letters which I trust in God will relieve me from the very disagreeable Situation I now find myself in, Surrounded with Enemies, and Seeing them every day grow more formidable, both as to Numbers and discipline, without a Single instruction how to Act." "Lord Dunmore to Lord Dartmouth, Ship *William* in Elizabeth River Virginia 24th September 1775," NDAR 2:195, 196.
[26] "Lord Dunmore to Lord Dartmouth, Ship *Dunmore* off Norfolk, 13th of December," *op cit*.
[27] "Assault on a considerable Out-work" in Humphrey Bland, *A Treatise of Military Discipline*, sixth edition, London: John and Paul Knapton, 1746, pp. 277-280. Although "text book," Governor Dunmore did not have the complement of forces Bland posited as necessary for such an attack.
[28] "George Washington to Colonel William Woodford, Cambridge, November 10, 1775," *op cit*.
[29] *Virginia Gazette*, Purdie, July 22, 1775 (supplement), p. 2.
[30] *Virginia Gazette*, Purdie: Oct. 27, 1775, p. 2.
[31] "Letter of Richard Kidder Meade, Norfolk, Town Camp, Dec. 18, 1775," *The Southern Magazine and Monthly Review*, Vol. 1:no. 1-2 (1841), p. 76.
[32] Governor Dunmore freely admitted to the ignorance of his recruits—Negro and white. After the Battle of Kemp's Landing he told Lord Dartmouth most of the men who had taken the oath of loyalty "hardly ever made use of the Gun." Nevertheless, he reported he hoped that "a Short time (if they are willing) will make them as good if not better than those who are come down to oppose them." "Lord Dunmore to Lord Dartmouth, December 6, 1775," NDAR 2:1311.
[33] *American Archives*, 3:1714.
[34] See for example, *The Infantry Battalion*, Field Manual 3-21.20 (FM 7-20) Washington: Headquarters, Department of the Army, 2006, pp. 8-25, 26. In his *Treatise of Military Discipline*, p. 277, General Bland notes the number of troops making the attack depends on the "Strength of the Place to be attacked and the Number of Men who can be brought to Defend it."

[35] This claim "moderates" hoped for reconciliation is based on the exchange of addresses between the House of Burgesses and the Governor reported in the *Journals of the Hose of Burgesses* throughout June 1775. In an address of June 8, the Governor told the Burgesses, "I am perfectly disposed to contribute all in my power, if opportunity be given me to restore that harmony, the interruption of which is likely to cost so dear, to the repose, as well as to the comfort of every individual." The House responded, "it is with much pleasure we receive your Lordship's assurance of your disposition to establish that harmony so essential to the repose and comfort of every individual …. We therefore earnestly entreat your Lordship that you will be pleased to return, with your Lady and family, to the Palace; which we are persuaded will give the greatest satisfaction, and be the most likely means of quieting the minds of the People." In the session of June 15, the House agreed on a resolution assuring the Governor, "in the warmth of our hearts of the sincerest disposition on our part to have the utmost harmony and most perfect tranquility restored." These exchanges continued through the last session of the House of Burgesses, June 24, 1775. It may be argued the addresses of both parties were disingenuous, but they were addressing each other. *Journals of the House of Burgesses of Virginia 1773 - 1776*, edited by John Pendleton Kennedy, Richmond: Virginia State Library, 1905, pp. 206-207, 214-215, 219-221, 241, 248, 282.

[36] "Lord Dunmore to General Howe, November 30, 1775," Hezekiah Niles, *op cit*.

[37] "General Thomas Gage to Lord Dunmore, Boston 10th September 1775," NDAR 2:72, 73.

[38] "Lord Dartmouth to Lord Dunmore, Whitehall 5th July 1775," NDAR 1:1311-1313.

[39] "Lord Dartmouth to Lord Dunmore, Whitehall 5th July 1775," NDAR 1:1312 and Same to Same, Whitehall, 12th July 1775, NDAR 1:1324.

[40] "Lord Dunmore to Lord Dartmouth, December 13, 1775, on board the Ship *Dunmore* off Norfolk," NDAR 3:140, 141.

[41] *Virginia Gazette*, Purdie, December 15, 1775, p. 3

[42] Woodford (two letters): "Extract of a letter from Col. William Woodford to the Hon. Edmund Pendleton, Esq; President of the General Convention, Great Bridge, December 10, 1775." *Virginia Gazette*, Purdie, December 15, 1775, p. 2 and *Virginia Gazette*, Dixon and Hunter, December 16, 1775, p. 3. Johnston: "Report of Captain [George] Johnston to Major Leven Powell, G Bridge Dec 9, 1775," Leven Powell Papers 1774 – 1810, Special Collections Research Center, Earl Gregg Swem Library, College of William and Mary, "Folder 3, Item 3: 9 Dec. 1775. George Johnston, Great Bridge, Va. to Leven Powell, Loudoun County, Va." Meade (two letters): "Letter of Richard Kidder Meade, Norfolk, Town Camp, Dec. 18th, 1775," in: Theodorick Bland, *The Bland Papers*, Petersburg, Virginia: 1840, pp. 38, 39. "Letter of Richard K. Meade to his Brother, Norfolk, Town Camp, December 19, 1775," in: John R. Thompson, ed., "Two Letters of Richard

Kidder Meade," *The Southern Literary Messenger*, Vol. 24 (New Series Vol. 3) January to July 1857, Richmond: McFarlane, Fergusson & Co., 1857, pp. 23-25. Report from one of Dunmore's volunteers: "Extract of a Letter from Elizabeth River, Norfolk, Virginia dated Jan. 3, 1776, to a Merchant in Liverpool," *Caledonian Mercury*, 16 March 1776, p. 1. Northampton County letter: "Extract of a letter from Northampton County, in Virginia," *The Remembrancer, or Impartial Repository of Public Events*, 1776, Vol. 2, Part 1, p. 225.

[43] In his *Gazette* of December 20, 1775, editor Pinkney included a comprehensive account of the Battle of Great Bridge. Pinkney provided no attribution for the account but this report provides the first documented record of the performance of the "sentinels." According to Pinkney's report, "The conduct of our sentinels I cannot pass over in silence. Before they quitted their stations they fired at least three rounds as the enemy were crossing the bridge, and one of them, who was posted behind some shingles, kept his ground till he had fired eight times, and, after receiving a whole platoon, made his escape over the causeway into our breastwork." *Virginia Gazette*, Pinkney: Dec. 20, 1775, p. 2. Based on an account of the battle by one of the soldiers present, Thomas Nash (later Captain Nash), documented in 1846 and published in 1853, it is likely Billy Flora was the sentinel in question. Mr. James Jarvis, who recorded Captain Nash's account, notes, "Captain Nash informed me that at this famous battle, Billy Flora, a colored man, was the last sentinel that came into the breast work, and that he did not leave his post until he had fired several times. Billy had to cross a plank to get to the breast work, and had fairly passed over it when he was seen to turn back, and deliberately take up the plank after him, amidst a shower of musket balls. He was probably the very sentinel who is mentioned in the account as having fired 'eight times.'" "The Battle of Great Bridge," William Maxwell, editor, *The Virginia Historical Register, and Literary Companion*, Vol. 6 (January 1853), Richmond: McFarland & Fergusson, 1853, p. 5.

[44] William Flora enlisted in one of the Virginia Regiments, probably the 15th, for three years on November 22, 1776. Later he served in the 11th Regiment. The 11th was consolidated with the 5th in 1779. The last muster roll on which his name appears is that for Captain Carrington's Company in the consolidated regiment (5th and 11th) for October 1779. The regiment was in Woodford's Brigade. U.S. Revolutionary War Rolls 1775-1783, Virginia, 5th and 11th Reg (Consolidated), 1779 (Folders 156-164), image 542. Virginia 11th Regiment, 1776-1778 (Folder 282) image 205 ff. Rolls of 15th Regiment: Virginia 15th Reg, 1777-1778 (Folder 328-337).

[45] "Letter from a Midshipman on Board H.M. Sloop *Otter*," NDAR 3:29.

[46] "Extract of a Letter from a Gentleman, Dated Ship *William*, off Norfolk, Virginia, Dec. 25, 1775." NDAR 3:242.

[47] "JD" [Captain John Dalrymple, 14th Regiment] to the Earl of Dumfries, Virginia, January 14, 1776," National Archives, UK PRO CO 5/40 folio 124.

[48] William Eddis, *Letters from America, Historical and Descriptive: Comprising Occurrences from 1769, to 1777*, London: Printed for the author, and sold by C. Dilly in the Poultry, 1792, pp. 250–254.
[49] "Extract of a letter from Northampton County, in Virginia," *The New England Chronicle: or, the Essex Gazette*, 11 January 1776, p. 2., also, *The Remembrancer, or Impartial Repository of Public Events, 1776*, Vol. 2, Part 1, p. 225.
[50] *Pennsylvania Packet*, Philadelphia, January 1, 1776. Quoted in NDAR 3:132.

Notes: Chapter 11: Tributes

[1] "Lord Dunmore to Lord Dartmouth, December 13, 1775," NDAR 3:140, 141.
[2] *Virginia Gazette*, Purdie, Dec. 15, 1775, p. 2.
[3] "William Woodford to the Virginia Convention, Great Bridge, December 10, 1775," Dice Robins Anderson, editor, *Richmond College Historical Papers, op cit*, pp. 118.
[4] *Journal of the House of Delegates of Virginia, 1776*, Richmond: Samuel Shepherd, 1828, p. 13.
[5] "William Woodford to the Virginia Convention, Great Bridge, December 10, 1775," *Richmond College Historical Papers, op cit*, pp. 117, 118.
[6] "Extract of a letter from Col. William Woodford to the Hon. Edmund Pendleton, Esq; President of the General Convention, Great Bridge, December 10, 1775," *Virginia Gazette*, Purdie: Dec. 15, 1775, p. 2.
[7] "General Orders by Major General the Honourable William Howe, Head Quarters, Halifax, 9th April, 1776," *Collections of the New York Historical Society for the Year 1883*, New York: 1884, pp. 333, 334.
[8] Secretary at War UK, *Army Commission Book, 1763-1767*, WO 25/30, pp. 62, 163.
[9] Secretary at War, *A List of the General and Field-Officers as They Rank in the Army, of the Officers of the Several Regiments of Horse, Dragoons, and Foot on the British and Irish Establishments*, March 1765 WO 65/15, p. 157.
[10] Secretary at War UK, *Army Commission Book, 1744-1746*, WO 25/21, p. 199.
[11] "9 [July, 1764] - At Glasgow, Col. William Napier, of Culcroich, to Miss Jeanie Millikin, daughter to James Millikin of Millikin, Esq.," *The Scots Magazine*. v.26 (1764), p. 350.
[12] "William Napier Gent, to be Lieutenant in Our 14th Regt of Foot commanded by Major Genl William Keppel, 16 Sept [?] 1771," Secretary at War UK, *Army Commission Book, 1767-1772*, WO 25/31, p. 257. Listed as January 22, 1772 in *The London Gazette*, Number 11217, from Saturday January 25, to Tuesday January 28, 1772, p. 1.
[13] Muster Roll for 14th Regiment at Castle William, May 15, 1772, WO 12/3117.
[14] "William Blackett to Haldimand, New Providence, October 1 1773," *Haldimand Papers*, H-1439, image 636.

[15] Deposition of Ensign William Napier, 14th Regiment of Foot, before James Murray, J. P., March 13, 1770, *A Fair Account of the Late Unhappy Disturbance at Boston*, London: B. White, 1770, p. 45.

[16] William Woodford to Edmund Pendleton, 10 December 1775, *Virginia Gazette*, Purdie, Dec. 15, 1775, p. 2.

[17] Colonel Leslie, K. H., of Balquhain, *Historical Records of the Family of Leslie from 1067 to 1868-9: Collected from Public Records and Authentic Private Sources*, Vol. 2, Edinburgh: Edmonston and Douglas, 1869, pp. 152–156.

[18] Secretary at War UK, *Army Commission Book, 1767-1772*, WO 25/31, op cit, p. 256, image 260, *The London Gazette*, 20 August 1771, Issue 11172, p. 1. Secretary at War, *A List of the General and Field-Officers as They Rank in the Army, of the Officers of the Several Regiments of Horse, Dragoons, and Foot on the British and Irish Establishments,* for 1772. London: J. Millan, 1772, p. 58. UK National Archives, WO 65/22.

[19] Muster Roll for the 14th Regiment at Castle William, May 15, 1772, WO 12/3117.

[20] *The Boston Gazette and Country Journal*, 17 August 1772, p. 3. Based on an announcement in the *Kentish Gazette* of July 28, 1772, it is possible the Captain Symmes' ship was the *Mary Ann* out of London. *Kentish Gazette*, 31 July 1773, p. 4.

[21] In a report published December 31, 1772, Captain O'Hara's death is given as October 5. *Berrow's Worcester Journal*, 31 December 1772, Issue Number: 4099, so he died about a month after the 14th arrived in St. Vincent. In another report, O'Hara's death is listed as October 9. *Salisbury and Winchester Journal*, 28 December 1772, p. 2.

[22] *The Boston Evening Post*, 16 November 1772, p. 2.

[23] Secretary at War UK, *Army Commission Book, 1772-1776*, WO 25/32, p. 105, image 109. *The London Gazette*, 18 December 1773, Issue 11415, p. 1.

[24] *The London Gazette*, 20 March 1773, Issue 11337, p. 1. "As Lieutenant Gore [Gower] of the fourteenth Regiment was carelessly leaning on his Fusee it accidently went off, and killed him on the spot." *Virginia Gazette*, Purdie, March 25, 1773, p. 2.

[25] "Blackett to Haldimand, New Providence, October 1st 1773," *Haldimand Papers*, H-1439 Image 636.

[26] "Captain Samuel Leslie to General Thomas Gage, August 20, 1775," NDAR 1:1192.

[27] "Monthly Return of His Majesty's Forces in the Province of East-Florida, St. Augustine, August 1, 1775," *American Archives*, 4:321.

[28] "Lord Dunmore to Lord Dartmouth, the Ship *William* by Norfolk, Virginia 5th October 1775," NDAR 2:316, 317.

[29] "Monthly Return of His Majesty's Forces in the Province of East-Florida, St. Augustine, August 1, 1775," *op cit*.

[30] "Letter from Captain Leslie to General Howe," *American Archives*, 3: 1716. Lord Dunmore reported these actions to the Secretary of State and his account was published in *The London Gazette*, 12 December 1775, Issue 11622, p. 8.

[31] "Lord Dunmore to Lord Dartmouth, Ship *William* off Norfolk, October 22d 1775," NDAR 2:574, 575. Also: *The London Gazette*, 12 December 1775, Issue 11622, p. 8.
[32] J. Almon, editor, *The Remembrancer*, part 2, 1776, p. 24.
[33] *Virginia Gazette*, Purdie, Dec. 15, 1775, p. 2.
[34] "JD" [Captain John Dalrymple, 14th Regiment] to the Earl of Dumfries, *op cit.*
[35] "Alexander Ross to Captain Stanton, St. Augustine, October 4, 1775," *American Archives*, 4:335.
[36] Identified as Rev. John Forbes, Chaplain of the 14th Regiment, in Charles L. Mowat, "St. Augustine under the British Flag, 1763-1775," *The Florida Historical Quarterly*, Vol. 20, No. 2 (Oct., 1941), p. 140.
[37] "Frederick George Mulcaster to General Grant, St. Augustine, September 29, 1775," *American Archives*, 3:838. Charles Loch Mowat, *East Florida as a British Province, 1763-1784*, Berkeley: University of California Press, 1943, p. 44. Mulcaster is identified as the Godson of George II in *The Atlantic Pilot*, 1772, Gainesville: University of Florida, 1974, p. xxiv.
[38] "Thomas Macknight to Rev. Doctor Macknight, December 26, 1775," NDAR 3:260-261.
[39] William Maxwell, "My Mother," in Edward W. James, ed., *Lower Norfolk County Virginia Antiquary*, Number 2, Part 3, Baltimore: The Friedenwald Co., 1897, p. 137.
[40] "Colonel William Woodford to Edmund Pendleton, Great Bridge, near Norfolk, December 9, 1775," NDAR 3:28. "Letters from Colonel Woodford to Edmund Pendleton, Great Bridge, December 10, 1775," *Virginia Gazette*, Purdie, Dec. 15, 1775, p. 2, and on the same page, "Woodford to Pendleton, Great Bridge, December 11, 1775,"
[41] Leven Powell Papers 1774–1810, Special Collections Research Center, Earl Gregg Swem Library, College of William and Mary, Folder 3, Item 3: "9 Dec. 1775. George Johnston, Great Bridge, Va. to Leven Powell, Loudoun County, Va."
[42] "Letter of Richard Kidder Meade, December 18, 1775," Theodorick Bland, *The Bland Papers*, Vol. 1, Petersburg, Virginia: Edmund and Julian Ruffin, 1840, pp. 38, 39. Also: *The Southern Magazine and Monthly Review*, Vol. 1, Issues 1-2, Petersburg, Virginia: 1841, pp. 75, 76.
[43] *Virginia Gazette*, Pinkney, Dec. 20, 1775, p. 2.
[44] "Lord Dunmore to Lord Dartmouth, December 13, 1775," *op cit.*
[45] *Bath Chronicle and Weekly Gazette*, 07 March 1776, p. 3 and *The Scots Magazine*, Vol. 38, p. 92, *American Archives* 4:452.
[46] *Edinburgh Advertiser*, February 13, 1776, p. 3, *Derby Mercury*, 09 February 1776, p. 4, *Norfolk Chronicle*, 17 February 1776, *Stamford Mercury*, 15 February 1776, pp. 2, 3, *Hibernian Journal; or, Chronicle of Liberty*, 16 February 1776, p. 1, *Caledonian Mercury*, 14 February 1776, p. 2, *The Scots Magazine*, 1776 – Vol. 38, pp. 90-92.
[47] *Hampshire Chronicle*, 12 February 1776, p. 3 (Woodford 9 December letter). *Chester Chronicle*, 12 February 1776, p. 3 (Woodford 9 December letter). *Shrewsbury*

Chronicle, 17 February 1776, p. 1 (Spotswood). *Leeds Intelligencer*, 20 February 1776, p. 2 (Woodford 11 December letter). *Bath Chronicle and Weekly Gazette*, 15 February 1776, p.2 (Spotswood letter). *Caledonian Mercury*, 09 March 1776, p. 2 (Midshipman letter). *Saunders' News-Letter*, 19 February 1776, p. 1 (Woodford 11 December letter). *Manchester Mercury*, 20 February 1776, p. 1 (Woodford 11 December letter). *Kentish Gazette*, 14 February 1776 p. 3 (Woodford 9 December letter).

[48] *The Edinburgh Advertiser*, from Tuesday, February 13 to Friday, February 16, 1776, Vol. 25, No. 1266, p. 5.

[49] *Derby Mercury*, 01 March 1776, p. 2.

[50] William H. Stewart, *History of Norfolk County, Virginia: and Representative Citizens, 1637-1900*, Chicago: Biographical Publishing Company, 1902, pp. 189, 218.

[51] "The Founding of the Church of England in Shelburne," *Collections of the New Brunswick Historical Society*, Number 8, St. John, N.B.: Barns and Company, 1909, p. 291.

[52] "The Orderly Book of the Second Virginia Regiment: September 27, 1775-April 15, 1776, 'Camp at Great Bridge December the 10th 1775,'" *The Virginia Magazine of History and Biography* Vol. 85, No. 3 (July 1977), p. 305. Used by permission.

[53] *Ibid*, "Camp at Great Bridge December the 9th 1775."

[54] Isaac Maltby, *The Elements of War*, Boston: Thomas B. Wait, 1811, pp. 205-208.

[55] "The Burial of the Dead," *The Book of Common Prayer* (1662), Cambridge: John Baskerville, 1662.

[56] "William Woodford to Edmund Pendleton, Great Bridge, December 10, 1775," *Virginia Gazette*, Dixon and Hunter, December 16, 1775, p. 3.

Notes: Chapter 12: Significance of the Battle of Great Bridge

[1] On December 10, the day after the battle, Colonel Woodford of the 2nd Virginia Regiment and commander of the forces at Great Bridge, provided the president of the Virginia Convention with the "General Return of the Forces," an enclosure to "Colonel William Woodford, On the Virginia Service, to The Honble The President of the Convention at Wms:burg, with Enclosures," Great Bridge, December 10, 1775, in Robert Scribner and Brent Tarter, editors, *Revolutionary Virginia, the Road to Independence*, Vol. 5, Charlottesville: University Press of Virginia, 1978, pp. 102, 103. This information is summarized in Table 8.

[2] "Major General Howe to the Earl of Dartmouth, Boston, January 16, 1776," *The Parliamentary Register: or, History of the Proceedings and Debates of the House of Commons*, Vol. 11 (1779), Fifth Session of the 14th Parliament, London: J. Almon, 1779, p. 292. Howe was not alone is his assignment of culpability to the governors in aggravating the discontent in the colonies. William Drayton, Chief Justice in East Florida during the Revolution, observed, "In the South, many crimes of Omission & Commission in the general Conduct of the American Governors have marked the Annals of their History, & led the way to this ever-to-be-lamented

Catastrophe." Charles Loch Mowat, *East Florida as a British Province, 1763-1784*, Berkeley: University of California Press, 1943, pp. 86, 87.

[3] *The Edinburgh Advertiser*, Vol. XXV, No. 1254, 2-5 January 1776, p. 4 and *Caledonian Mercury*, January 6, 1776, at: The Colonial Records Project, North Carolina Office of Archives & History, Department of Cultural Resources, Raleigh, NC 27699-4622. Successful raids reported: *The London Gazette*, 12 December 1775, Issue 11622, p. 8.

[4] "Captain Fordice [Fordyce] to Captain Urquhart, December 1, 1775, Norfolk," *American Archives*, 4:350.

[5] "Letters from Sir John Dalrymple, Bart, One of the Barons of the Exchequer in Scotland, to the Right Honourable Lord Viscount Barrington, Late Secretary of War, on His Lordships Official Conduct," Letter I, *The Gentleman's and London Magazine: or Monthly Chronologer*, for January 1779, p. 223.

[6] *The Scots Magazine*, 1776, Vol. 38, p. 92. ALSO: Tuesday 12 March 1776, *Leeds Intelligencer*, West Yorkshire, England, p. 2.

[7] *The Scots Magazine*, Vol. 38 (1776), pp. 432, 433.

[8] *Journals of the Continental Congress*, October 13, 1775.

[9] *Journals of the Continental Congress*, December 2, 1775. Edward Field, *Esek Hopkins, Commander in chief of the Continental Navy during the American Revolution, 1775 – 1778*, Providence: Preston & Rounds, 1898, pp. 91, 92.

[10] *Journals of the Continental Congress*, December 2, 1775.

[11] *Virginia Gazette*, Dixon and Hunter, March 02, 1776, p. 2. In this *Gazette* the author of the article is identified as "A Gentleman from Philadelphia." Attribution to Gadsden is in NDAR 3:1189.

[12] John Paul Jones, *Life and Correspondence of J. Paul Jones*, New York: A. Chandler, 1830, p. 35.

[13] "Naval Committee to Esek Hopkins, Commander-in-Chief of the Fleet of the United Colonies, Philadelphia, January 5, 1776." Esek Hopkins, *The Letter Book of Esek Hopkins, Commander-in-Chief of the United States Navy, 1775-1777*, Providence: Rhode Island Historical Society, 1932, pp. 15, 16. The timing of Commodore Hopkins orders is not clear. According to one credible source, he received detailed orders on April 23, 1776, "Marine Committee of the Continental Congress to Commodore Esek Hopkins, Philada [23d] April 1776," NDAR 4:1217.

[14] Robert Morris, Vice-President of the Marine Committee in Congress, did not think it advisable for Hopkins to attack Dunmore. On January 10, 1776, he told General Charles Lee, "we had some Success against Dunmore but he is now reenforced with Naval Strength & we dare not look at him by Sea no more than he dare set his foot on Shoar [sic, shore]. "Robert Morris to Major General Charles Lee, January 10, 1776," NDAR 3:719. George Washington alluded to British naval assignments for Dunmore's protection in a letter to Richard Henry Lee of December 26, 1775. He told Lee, "I fear the destination of the naval armament at Philadelphia is too well known to answer the design." He added he was told "… two men-of-war, going into the harbor of New York, supposed to be those

for the relief of the *Asia*, were ordered and accordingly sailed immediately out, as is imagined for Virginia." "George Washington to Richard Henry Lee, Cambridge, 26 December, 1775," NDAR 3:253. On April 8, after his successful raid on New Providence, Commodore Hopkins reported to Congress some of the reasons he made that island his target. He explained he was concerned over sickness (small pox) among his crews and weather noting, "I did not think we were in a Condition to keep on a cold Coast." Esek Hopkins, *Letter Book op cit*, p. 47. It is also quite likely the prospect of obtaining much-needed gun powder was the reason Hopkins sailed for New Providence. *Journals of the Continental Congress*, November 29, 1775 and Edward Field, *Esek Hopkins, Commander-in-chief of the Continental Navy, op cit*, p. 104.

[15] "Lord Dunmore to Lord Dartmouth, on board the ship *Dunmore* off Norfolk, December 13, 1775," NDAR 3:142. "List of Ships in Lord Dunmore's Fleet, July 10, 1776," *American Archives*, 1:152.

[16] Samuel Prescott Hildreth, *Biographical and Historical Memoirs of the Early Pioneer Settlers of Ohio*, Cincinnati: H. W. Derby & Co., 1852, p. 130. *Virginia Gazette*, Dixon and Hunter, March 30, 1776, p. 3. *Virginia Gazette*, Dixon and Hunter, May 18, 1776, p. 1.

[17] Frank Colby and George Sandeman, editors, *Nelson's Encyclopedia*, Vol. VIII, New York and London: Thomas Nelson, 1907, p. 423A.

[18] NDAR 4:102. Consider also Clinton's remark, "I don't think it worth while to meddle with them," in *The New-England Chronicle: or, the Essex Gazette*, 28 March 1776, p. 2.

[19] Hopkins' report of the campaign to New Providence was published widely, e.g., *The New England Chronicle*, 25 April 1776, p. 1, *Virginia Gazette*, Dixon and Hunter, March 30, 1776, p. 3, May 04, 1776, p. 3. Alverda Beck noted in her "Introduction" to Hopkins' *Letter Book*, "The people were enthusiastic over the capture of the supplies, and they were very proud of the American Fleet." However, even though the debut of the American Navy was auspicious, the Navy—as such—was not employed in the Revolutionary War. The exploits of individual commanders were significant but Beck notes, "From this time [Hopkins' New Providence Campaign], the history of the American Navy during the Revolution consists of the exploits of individual ships, or of two or three ships together, acting rather as privateers than as an American fleet. Never again did the whole fleet get to sea together." Esek Hopkins, *Letter Book, op cit*, pp. 20, 23. Since the fleet was not a celebrated element of America's military *per se*, its birth was not particularly relevant so–by association—neither was the way Governor Dunmore's loss at Great Bridge contributed to that birth. This kind of historical slight of an otherwise decisive event—the birth of the US Navy—helps explain why the Battle of Great Bridge itself is too often slighted.

[20] Probably Dunmore's letters to General Howe of November 30 and December 2, 1775. "Lord Dunmore to General Howe, on board the ship *William*, off Norfolk

in Virginia, November 30, 1775," *American Archives*, 3:1713. "Lord Dunmore to General Howe, on board the *Dunmore*, off Norfolk, Virginia, December 2, 1775," *American Archives*, 4:357. Published in *Virginia Gazette*, Purdie, January 26, 1776, p. 1.

[21] "George Washington to John Hancock, Cambridge, December 18, 1775." See also: "George Washington to Joseph Reed, Cambridge, December 15, 1775."

[22] "General Washington to Richard Henry Lee, December 26, 1775."

[23] "From Gen. Charles Lee to R. H. Lee, Dec'r ye 18th, 1775," Charles Lee, *Lee Papers*, Vol. 1, New York: New York Historical Society, 1872, pp. 232, 233.

[24] *Journals of the Continental Congress*, December 4, 1775. See also debates of October 6, 1775 in the *Journals* of that date (pp. 482, 483).

[25] *Stamford Mercury*, 19 September 1776, p. 2, *Derby Mercury*, 13 September 1776, p. 1, *Shrewsbury Chronicle*, 14 September 1776, p. 3, *Oxford Journal*, 14 September 1776, p. 2, *et al.*

[26] "The British Leave Colonial Virginia," W. Hugh Moomaw, *The Virginia Magazine of History and Biography*, Vol. 66, No. 2 (Apr., 1958), p. 160.

[27] H. J. Eckenrode, *The Revolution in Virginia*, Boston: Houghton Mifflin Company, 1916, pp. 69, 72. Transcribed by Roy Randolph.

[28] George Washington, in New England and in desperate need of the kind of troops opposing Lord Dunmore in Virginia, was so concerned over the possibility of Dunmore establishing a British post in the Chesapeake he told his *aide de camp*, Colonel Joseph Reed, "Dunmore should be instantly crushed, if it takes the force of the whole colony to do it." "George Washington to Joseph Reed, Cambridge, December 15, 1775," John Clement Fitzpatrick, editor, *The Writings of George Washington from the Original Manuscripts*, Vol. 4, Washington: GPO, 1931, p. 167.

[29] "Lord Dunmore to General Howe, on board the *Dunmore*, off Norfolk, Virginia, December 2, 1775," *American Archives* 4:357 and NDAR 2:1239.

[30] "Sir John Dalrymple, Bart, to Lord Viscount Barrington," *op cit*, p. 222.

[31] *Virginia Gazette*, Purdie, May 05, 1775 (supplement) p. 2.

[32] George Washington, General Orders, September 17, 1776. George Washington, *George Washington Papers, Series 3, Varick Transcripts, 1775-1785, Subseries 3G, General Orders, 1775-1783, Letterbook 1: July 3, 1775 - Sept. 30, 1776*, Library of Congress.

[33] William Bradford Reed, *Life and Correspondence of Joseph Reed*, Vol. 1, Philadelphia: Lindsay and Blakiston, 1847, pp. 237, 238. General Howe's account of this engagement was published in *The Remembrancer or Impartial Repository of Public Events for the Year 1776*, Part 3, p. 116. In his account it is the Americans who retreat.

[34] William Stryker, *The Battles of Trenton and Princeton*, Boston and New York: Houghton and Mifflin and Company, 1898, pp. 351-353.

[35] Jefferson acknowledged "Dunmore's flight from Gwyn's island" gave Virginia's leaders a "temporary holiday" in a letter to Lieutenant Governor John

Page. "Thomas Jefferson to John Page, Philadelphia, July 20, 1776." Paul Leicester Ford, editor, *The Writings of Thomas Jefferson*, Vol. 2, New York and London: G. Putnam's Sons, 1893, p. 70. He was also aware of the way Governor Dunmore had stalled Virginia's trade. "Thomas Jefferson to the President of Congress, Williamsburg, June 19, 1779," *Ibid*, p. 242.

[36] When Congress established quotas for the supply of foodstuffs to the Continental Army in 1780, the Southern colonies, Maryland, Virginia, North Carolina and South Carolina, were called on to supply almost half of the beef, close to 40% of the rum and salt, 60% of the forage and 100% of the tobacco and rice. No colony surpassed Virginia in terms of the variety of food stuffs supplied. *Journals of the Continental Congress*, February 25, 1780. Over the course of the war, Virginia's contribution of 26,678 soldiers to the Continental Army placed it third in the list of colonies. Its contribution was surpassed by Massachusetts with 67,907 and Connecticut with 31,939. Francis B. Heitman, *Historical Register of Officers of the Continental Army During the War of the Revolution, April, 1775, to December, 1783, New, Revised, and Enlarged Edition*, Washington DC: Rare Book Shop Publishing Company, 1914, p. 691.

Notes: Epilogue

[1] "Colonel William Woodford, on the Virginia Service, to the Honble. The President of the Convention at Williamsburg Per Mr. Page, Great Bridge, 11th Decr. 1775," Robert Scribner and Brent Tarter, editors, *Revolutionary Virginia, the Road to Independence*, Vol. 5, Charlottesville: University Press of Virginia, 1978, Vol. 5, pp. 108, 109 and *Virginia Gazette*, Pinkney, December 13, 1775, pp. 2, 3.

[2] "Lord Dunmore to Lord Dartmouth, on board the Ship Dunmore off Norfolk, December 13, 1775," NDAR 3: 140, 141.

[3] *Documents of the American Revolution* 1770-1783, Colonial Office Series, ed. K. G. Davies, Vol. 10, Shannon: Irish University Press, 1976, p. 219, note xiv.

[4] The disparity between in estimates of the strength of the 14th after the Battle of Great Bridge continued throughout the time they remained in the Chesapeake. William Barry was questioned about Dunmore's force in June of 1776 and he deposed, "… on the twenty-fourth of May the fleet went to Gwin's island, being eighty-two sail, most of which were prizes; and on the twenty-sixth landed on the island one hundred men of the fourteenth regiment." ("Deposition of William Barry [Newcastle] June 11, 1776," NDAR 5:485.) In his *Virginia Gazette* of June 14, 1776, editor Purdie published intelligence supplied by the masters of two vessels recently arrived to the effect "Dunmore's whole army is now reduced to 40 regular soldiers." (*Virginia Gazette*, Purdie, June 14, 1776.) On June 22, 1776, Mr. E. Johnson of Maryland reported British deserters claimed Lord Dunmore's force included "about 40 men of the 14 Regiment." ("E. Johnson to Lieutenant Colonel Alexander Somerville," NDAR 5:685.) In a letter of July 25, 1776, a gentleman aboard the ship *Dunmore* in Chesapeake Bay notes Governor

Dunmore's force included "eighty of the 14th regiment." (*Shrewsbury Chronicle*, 21 September 1776, p. 3.)

[5] *American Archives* 4:294

[6] "From Lt. Col. Frank Eppes, Kemps, March 31, 1776," Charles Lee, *The Lee Papers*, Vol. 1, New York: New York Historical Society, 1872, pp. 365-367.

[7] *Ibid*, pp. 384-386.

[8] "Journal of Captain Andrew Snape Hamond, 10th of March [1776]," NDAR 4:303, 401.

[9] "Lord Dunmore to Lord Germain, Ship *Dunmore* in Elizabeth River Virginia, 30th March 1776," NDAR 4:585.

[10] *Virginia Gazette*, Purdie, April 26, 1776 supplement, p. 2.

[11] Leven Powell Papers 1774 – 1810, Special Collections Research Center, Earl Gregg Swem Library, College of William and Mary, "Box 2, Folder 3, Item 4: 22 May 1776. George Johnston, Kemp's Landing, Princess Anne County, Va., to Major Leven Powell."

[12] "Extract of a letter from capt. George Johnston, dated, May 20, 1776," *Virginia Gazette*, Purdie, May 24, 1776, p. 2.

[13] *Virginia Gazette*, Dixon and Hunter, May 25, 1776, p. 3. See also, *Virginia Gazette*, Purdie, May 24, 1776, p. 3.

[14] "Captain Andrew Snape Hamond, R.N., to Governor Robert Eden, *Roebuck* at Gwins Island, Virginia the 30th May 1776," NDAR 5:311. Also, "Lord Dunmore to Lord George Germain, Ship *Dunmore* in Gwins Island Harbour, Virginia, 26th June 1776," NDAR 5:756.

[15] "Lord Dunmore to Lord George Germain, Ship *Dunmore* in Gwins Island Harbour, Virginia, 26th June 1776," NDAR 5:756.

[16] *Virginia Gazette*, Dixon and Hunter July 27, 1776. NDAR 5:1250.

[17] *American Archives*, Series 5, 1:150-153. NDAR 5:1030, 1066.

[18] "Narrative of Captain Andrew Snape Hamond, H.M.S. *Roebuck*, July 15 to August 13, 1776, NDAR 6:172.

[19] "Lord Dunmore to Lord George Germain, Ship Dunmore in Potowmack River Virginia 31st July 1776," NDAR 5:1313. Incident reported with considerable detail by an eyewitness in: *Shrewsbury Chronicle*, 21 September 1776, p. 3.

[20] "Lord Dunmore to Lord George Germain, 31st July 1776,"*op cit*.

[21] "Lord Dunmore to Lord George Germain, Ship *Dunmore* in Potomac River, Virginia, 4th of August, [1776]," NDAR 6:51.

[22] "Narrative of Captain Andrew Snape Hamond, H.M.S. *Roebuck*, July 15 to August 13, 1776," NDAR 6:174.

[23] "Letter from Lord Dunmore to Lord George Germaine, Ship *Dunmore* off New York, September 4, 1776," *American Archives*, 2:158.

[24] *Kentish Gazette*, 20 November 1776, p. 4. *Norfolk Chronicle*, 23 November 1776, p. 2. *Northampton Mercury*, 25 November 1776, p. 1.

[25] *Stamford Mercury*, 26 December 1776, p. 1. *Bath Chronicle and Weekly Gazette*, 26 December 1776, p. 1.

[26] "Extract of a Letter from Portsmouth, December 18," *Derby Mercury*, 20 December 1776, p. 2, *Hampshire Chronicle*, 23 December 1776, p. 3.
[27] *Kentish Gazette*, 23 August 1777, p. 3.
[28] *Salisbury and Winchester Journal*, 24 July 1780, p. 2, *Stamford Mercury*, 27 July 1780, p. 1.
[29] King's endorsement: *Reading Mercury*, 23 April 1781, p. 1. Quote: *Caledonian Mercury*, 21 April 1781, p. 2.
[30] *Bath Chronicle and Weekly Gazette*, 11 October 1781, p. 2.
[31] *Stamford Mercury*, 07 March 1782, p. 2, *Northampton Mercury*, 10 June 1782, p. 3.
[32] "Earl of Dunmore to Sir Henry Clinton, Charles Town [Charleston], Feb. 2, 1782," *Proceedings of the Massachusetts Historical Society*, Vol. 6 (1862-63), pp. 228, 229.
[33] Move to New York: *Caledonian Mercury*, 08 June 1782, p. 2. Return to England: *Reading Mercury*, 17 June 1782, p. 3.
[34] *The London Gazette*, 28 April 1787, Issue 12851, p. 205.
[35] The disagreeable marriage and Governor Dunmore's "earnest solicitations" to stay in the Bahamas reported in: *Cambridge Intelligencer*, 22 October 1796, p. 2. The marriage and associated legal wrangling were news for some time. See, for example, *Oxford Journal*, 27 April 1793, p. 1, *Cambridge Intelligencer*, 22 October 1796, p. 2, *Exeter Flying Post*, 20 August 1801, p. 1, *Oxford Journal*, 13 May 1809, p. 4.
[36] *Lancaster Gazette*, 01 January 1803, p. 4.
[37] Return to England: *Caledonian Mercury*, 15 April 1797, p. 3. Death: *The Scots Magazine*, 1809, p. 239. Interred at St. Lawrence: *Kentish Weekly Post or Canterbury Journal*, 07 March 1809, p. 4.
[38] "Letter from General Howe to Lord George Germain, Camp at Newton, Long Island, September 3, 1776," *The Universal Magazine of Knowledge and Pleasure*, Vol. 59, 1776, p. 211.
[39] Deserter from the 14th reports troops on their way to Cape Fear. "Edmund Pendleton to Thomas Jefferson, Political Speculation; Naval Intelligence, May 24, 1776." Thomas Jefferson Papers at the Library of Congress.
[40] *Caledonian Mercury*, 06 April 1776, p. 2.
[41] *Kentish Gazette*, 06 March 1776, p. 4. Possibility of serving with General Clinton reported in *Caledonian Mercury*, 06 April 1776, p. 2.
[42] Stanton in Nova Scotia: *The Manuscripts of the Earl of Dartmouth*, Vol. 1, pp. 386, 388. Stanton's detachment: Two companies of the 14th at Halifax, April 4, 1776, *General Sir William Howe's Orderly Book: At Charlestown, Boston and Halifax*, p. 243, also in "General Thomas Gage to Lord Dartmouth, Boston September 20th 1775," *Gage Correspondence*, 1:416. Urquhart's detachment: Urquhart, NDAR, 2:844. "Distribution of His Majesty's Forces in North America, July 19, 1775," 1 drummer and 95 rank and file at Castle William, *Gage Correspondence* 2:690. "General Thomas Gage to Lord Dunmore, Boston 10th September 1775," NDAR 2:72. Urquhart to be captain of an "additional company" in *Howe's Orderly Book*, p. 149.

"Leslie to Howe, Gosport, 1 November 1775," NDAR 2:844-845. Furlong's detachment: Furlong with 98 men, *American Archives* 4:327. See also: "Corps in America, February 1776," *The Gentleman's Magazine*, Vol. 46, p. 91.

[43] "Jonathan Furlong to General Gage, St. Augustine, October 5, 1775," *American Archives* 4:319.

[44] *Caledonian Mercury*, 19 July 1776, p. 2.

[45] Admiral Howe arranged an escort for the transports carrying the officers and recruiting parties of the 6th and 14th Regiments to England on February 13, 1777. "Vice Admiral Lord Richard Howe to Philip Stephens, Eagle, off New York, February the 13th 1777," NDAR 7:1192. See also: *Stamford Mercury*, 12 February 1778, p. 1. *Norfolk Chronicle*, 14 February 1778, p. 2.

[46] Somerset Richard Lowry-Corry Earl of Belmore, *The History of the Corry Family of Castlecoole*, London: Longmans, Green & Company, 1891, pp. 223, 224. John Burke, *A Genealogical and Heraldic History of the Commoners of Great Britain and Ireland*, Vol 4, London: Henry Colburn, 1838, pp. 87, 88.

[47] *Commission Book*, 1746-1750, WO 25/22, p. 209, 214.

[48] *The London Gazette*, 9 March 1762, Issue 10190, p. 2.

[49] *The London Gazette*, 2 September 1777, Issue 11802, p.1.

[50] He is identified as a "Brevet Major" in announcement of his replacement in the 14th Regiment of 1780. *The London Gazette*, 8 January 1780, Issue 12056, p. 2.

[51] *The History of the Corry Family of Castlecoole, op cit*, pp. 99–101.

[52] Promotion to adjutant: *Commission Book*, 1772-1776, WO 25/32, p. 9. Promotion to captain: *Commission Book*, 1772-1776, WO 25/32, p. 122.

[53] Commission in the 50th: *Commission Book*, 1761-1762, WO 25/28, p. 108. Commissioned lieutenant: *Commission Book*, 1762-1767, WO 25/30, p. 42. Commissioned adjutant: *The London Gazette*, 29 August 1772, Issue 11279, p. 1. Dates for the commission to major vary widely for Cooper. In the *Army List* of 1784, WO 65/34, p. 76, the date of his promotion is listed as March 19, 1783. The date of the promotion is listed as March 12, 1783 in *The London Gazette*, 12 April 1783, Issue 12431, p. 5. In the *Commission Book*, 1782-1786 WO 25/38, p. 152, the date is two years later, 6 April 1785. This latter date is also the date listed in the *Army List* for 1786, WO 65/36, p. 76.

[54] *Bath Chronicle and Weekly Gazette*, 10 January 1782, p. 1. Arrived in Jamaica 11 April 1782: *Newcastle Chronicle*, 06 July 1782, p. 1

[55] *The Public Advertiser*, (from London) December 22, 1786, p. 3.

[56] Commissioned ensign: *Commission Book*, WO 25/30, 1762-1767, p. 144. Promoted to lieutenant: *Commission Book*, WO 25/31, 1767-1772, p. 276 and *The London Gazette*, 29 February 1772, Issue 11227, p. 1. Promoted to captain: *Commission Book*, WO 25/32, 1772-1776, p. 175 and *The London Gazette*, 25 March 1775, Issue 11547, p. 1.

[57] *Caledonian Mercury*, 13 July 1776, p. 3 and *The London Evening Post*, July 16, 1776, p. 4(?).

[58] Marriage published in: *Caledonian Mercury*, 03 April 1779, p. 3. Francis Elliot takes Dalrymple's place: *The London Gazette*, 8 June 1779, Issue 11986, p. 3.

[59] *The London Gazette*, 20 June 1797, Issue 14021, p. 592. *The London Gazette*, 18 December 1802, Issue 15542, p. 1346. *The London Gazette*, 22 September 1807, Issue 16070, p. 1262.

[60] *Debrett's Baronetage of England*, 5th Edition, Vol. 2, London: C. and J. Rivington, et al, 1824, p. 956.

[61] *Cumberland Pacquet, and Ware's Whitehaven Advertiser*, 19 May 1812, p. 3.

[62] *General Evening Post (London)*, November 7-9, 1758, p. 1, https://books.google.com/books?id=DHxMAAAAcAAJ. *Army List* 1759, WO 65/7, p. 80. *Commission Book*, 1760-1761, WO 25/27, p. 55.

[63] Lieutenant in 14th Regiment: *Commission Book*, 1767-1772, WO 25/31, p. 196. Half pay in 33rd Regiment: 1765 March WO 65/15, p. 152. *Army List* 1770, WO 65/20, p. 189. *The Scots Magazine*, Vol. 32, 1770, p. 686.

[64] *Commission Book*, 1776-1778, WO 25/33, p. 41, *Army List* 1777, WO 65/27, p. 68.

[65] *Commission Book*, 1776-1778, WO 25/33, p. 41. Promotion date of July 9, 1776 in *The London Gazette*, 6 July 1776, Issue 11681, p. 1. This record is at odds with the *Commission Book* record and it is confusing in that the promotion of Lieutenant John Batut to Captain Lieutenant *vice* William Brown is reported for the same date.

[66] *Virginia Gazette*, Dixon and Hunter, January 06, 1776, p. 3.

[67] *Virginia Gazette*, Purdie, January 05, 1776 (supplement), p. 2.

[68] *The London Gazette*, 20 January 1784, Issue 12512, p. 2.

[69] *The Gentleman's Magazine*, Vol. 58, p. 1027. George Philip R. Pulman, *The Book of the Axe*, London: Longman, Brown, Green and Longmans, 1854, p. 438.

[70] Commissioned ensign: *Commission Book*, 1762-1767, WO 25/30, p. 277. Promoted to lieutenant: *Commission Book*, 1772-1776, WO 25/32, p. 77 and *The London Gazette*, 12 January 1773, Issue 11318, p. 1.

[71] Promoted to captain, 71st Regiment, November 30, 1775: *Commission Book*, WO 25/33, 1776-1778, p. 28. Gazetted to captain, 71st Regiment, May 14, 1776: *The London Gazette*, 11 May 1776, Issue 11665, p. 2. Adjutant in place of Cornelius Smelt, January 13, 1776: *Commission Book*, 1776-1776, WO 25/32, p. 96. Gazetted adjutant in place of Cornelius Smelt, July 9, 1776: *The London Gazette*, 6 July 1776, Issue 11681, p. 1.

[72] For a detailed account of the actions of the 71st Regiment in the War see: J. P. MacLean, *An Historical Account of the Settlements of Scotch Highlanders in America*, Cleveland: Helman-Taylor Company, 1900, Chapter XIII.

[73] *The London Gazette*, 13 July 1782, Issue 12313, p. 4.

[74] *Army List*, 1782, WO 65/32, p. 146. In this same *Army List*, Lieutenant Magnus Murchieson (Murchison) of the 71st is also noted as "dd." Lieutenant Murchison died 23 January 1782 in Charleswood, Richland County, South Carolina, and is buried in Saint Philips Episcopal Church Cemetery, Charleston, South Carolina. Murchison was wounded in 1779 at the Battle of Stono Ferry, South Carolina. *The Scots Magazine*, Vol. 41 (1779), p. 552.

[75] *Monthly Return* for the 14th Regiment at Castle William, April 24, 1772, WO 12/3117, item 11. *Monthly Return* at Fort Tyrell, WO 1/57, item 16.

[76] Born August 1748 to William Smelt, Receiver General of Casual Revenue, Barbados and Dorothy Caley, History of Parliament online, http://www.historyofparliamentonline.org/volume/1715-1754/member/smelt-william-1690-1755. Ensign, 14th Regiment, 12 June 1765, *Commission Book* 1762-1767, WO 25/30, p. 155. Lieutenant, 14th Regiment, February 21, 1772, *Commission Book* 1767-1772, WO 25/31, p. 282. *The London Gazette* 29 February 1772, no. 11227. p. 1. Adjutant, 14th Regiment, June 18, 1775, *Commission Book* 1772-1776, WO 25/32, p. 212. September 12, 1775 in *The London Gazette*, 9 September 1775, Issue 11595, p. 1.

[77] Captain, 35th Regiment, June 13, 1776, by purchase, *Commission Book* 1776-1778, WO 25/33, p. 97. Richard Trimen, *An Historical Memoir of the 35th Royal Sussex Regiment of Foot*, Southampton: Southampton Times Newspaper and Printing and Publishing Company, 1873, pp. 48-61.

[78] Married to Mary Trant Otley, 06 Oct 1785: "England Marriages, 1538–1973," database, *FamilySearch*. Appointed Deputy Governor of South Sea Castle: *The London Gazette*, 14 July 1787, Issue 12903, p. 1 (333). Appointed Lieutenant Governor Isle of Man: *The London Gazette*, 11 June 1805, Issue 15815, p. 773. Death: Carlisle Patriot, 01 December 1802, p. 3.

[79] His date-of-rank in the 14th Regiment is actually a few days later than his army date-of-rank. He is listed as St. John Wallace, 51st Regiment, date-of-rank March 20, 1771, in *Commission Book*, 1767-1772, WO 25/31, p. 219 and Hill Wallace of the 14th Regiment with a date-of-rank of April 9, 1771 in the same *Commission Book*, p. 229. Named St. John Wallace in *The London Gazette*, May 11, 1771, Issue 11143, p. 1. Promoted to lieutenant: *Commission Book*, 1772-1776, WO 25/32, p. 105 and *The London Gazette*, 18 December 1773, Issue 11415, p. 1. Promoted to captain lieutenant, October 24, 1776: *Commission Book*, 1776-1778, WO 25/33, p. 159. Gazetted to captain lieutenant, June 10, 1777: *The London Gazette*, 7 June 1777, Issue 11777, p. 1. Promoted to captain: *Commission Book*, 1779-1781, WO 25/35, p. 278 and *The London Gazette*, 29 May 1781, Issue 12192, p. 2.

[80] Marriage published in: *Hibernian Journal; or, Chronicle of Liberty*, 09 January 1784, p. 3. *Saunders's News-Letter*, 12 January 1784, p. 1. In a letter dated January 3, 1784 Martha McTier of Belfast tells her brother, "Hill Wallace I believe was married last night, and gets £5,000 fortune – her brother has given them a chaise and behaves very well." "Martha McTier to William Drennan, January 3, 1784," *The Drennan-McTier Letters: 1776-1793*, William Drennan, Martha Drennan McTier, Maria Luddy, Irish Manuscripts Commission, Women's History Project in association with the Irish Manuscripts Commission, 1998, p. 149.

[81] *The London Gazette*, 14 December 1784, Issue 12604, p. 1.

[82] *Army List* 1784, WO 65/34, p. 76. *Army List* 1786, WO 65/36, p. 327. *Army List* 1787, WO 65/37, p. 322. *Army List*, 1794, WO 65/44, p. 335.

[83] *Journal for the Association for the Preservation of Memorials of the Dead in Ireland*, Vol. 9, 1913, Dublin: Ponsby and Gibbs, University Press, 1913, p. 37.

84 Commissioned ensign: *Commission Book*, 1772-1776, WO 25/32, p. 71. Promoted to Lieutenant: *Commission Book*, 1772-1776, WO 25/32, p. 283. Gazetted to lieutenant: *The London Gazette*, 6 July 1776, Issue 11681, p. 1.

85 "Memorial of Thomas Appleford Woolls to George III, Jan. 4, 1779," Library of Congress, British Manuscripts Project, Microfilm 041, reel PRO 338/1, (Vol. 1), Washington, DC, p. 71.

86 Edward Ely Curtis, *The organization of the British Army in the American Revolution*, Vol. 19, New Haven: Yale University Press, 1926, p. 160.

87 Promoted to adjutant: *Commission Book*, 1776-1778, WO 25/33, p. 124.

88 "William Dalrymple to Jeffery Amherst, January 25, 1779, London England," Library of Congress, British Manuscripts Project, Microfilm 041, reel PRO 338/1, (Vol. 1), *op cit*, pp. 386, 387.

89 *Commission Book*, 1778-1780, WO 25/34, p. 212, *The London Gazette*, 22 June 1779, Issue 11990, p. 3. Brownrigg had been promoted to lieutenant in the 14th on June 6, 1778, taking the place of James Lindsay. WO 25/34, p. 8 and *The London Gazette*, 20 June 1778, Issue 11885, p. 2.

90 "England Births and Christenings, 1538-1975," database, FamilySearch https://familysearch.org/ark:/61903/1:1:N5F3-F6J, index based upon data collected by the Genealogical Society of Utah, Salt Lake City; FHL microfilm 918,892.

91 Joseph Foster, *Alumni Qronieness: Members of the University of Oxford, 1715-1886*, Vol. IV, Oxford: Parker and Co., p. 1608.

92 *Kentish Gazette*, 09 August 1796, p. 3. *Hampshire Chronicle*, 06 August 1796, p. 4.

93 *Hampshire Chronicle*, 15 June 1795, p. 1.

94 *Commission Book*, 1772-1776, WO 25/32, p. 105.

95 Promoted to lieutenant, October 15, 1775: *Commission Book*, 1776-1778, WO 25/33, p. 41. Gazetted: *The London Gazette*, 6 July 1776, Issue 11681, p. 1. In the Army List of 1779, Boyes date-of-rank is listed as November 24, 1775. *Army List*, 1779, WO 65/29, p. 78.

96 *Commission Book*, 1778-1780, WO 25/34, p. 260, *The London Gazette*, 16 October 1779, Issue 12023, p. 2 and *The Scots Magazine*, Vol. 41, 1779, p. 575.

97 *Bath Chronicle and Weekly Gazette*, 27 January 1780, p. 3.

98 *Kentish Gazette*, 26 October 1782, p. 4.

99 *Journals of the House of Commons*, Vol. 43, p. 399.

100 *Army List*, 1784, WO 65/34, p. 302

101 Listed as Captain James Boys of the 87th Regiment on half-pay in: *Army List* 1795, WO 65/45, p. 377. Promotion to major March 1, 1794 in: *Commission Book*, 1794-1795, WO 25/44, p. 389. Major in Podmore's Regiment of Foot, 28 August 1794, *ibid*, p. 152. Major in the 53rd Foot, 1 September 1795, *ibid*, p. 230. Major in the late 131st Regiment, 5 October 1795, *Army List*, 1798, WO 65/48, p. 327. Also: *The London Gazette*, 4 August 1795, Issue 13802, p. 813. *The London Gazette*, 8 September 1795, Issue 13812, p. 930.

102 *Army List*, 1796, WO 65/46, p. 32.

[103] *Army List*, 1797, WO 65/47, p. 28.

[104] *The London Gazette*, 6 January 1798, Issue 14080, p. 23. 1 January 1798 in *Commission Book*, 1795-1798, WO 25/47, p. 320.

[105] Charles James, *A Collection of the Charges, Opinions, and Sentences of General Courts Martial, as Published by Authority; from the Year 1795 to the Present Time*, London: T. Egerton, 1820, p. 146.

[106] The National Archives; Kew, England; Prerogative Court of Canterbury and Related Probate Jurisdictions, "Will of James Boys, Major of Marylebone, Middlesex," 26 January 1808, PROB 11/1472/230.

[107] *Commission Book*, 1772-1776, WO 25/32, p. 122. Date of commission April 6 in *The London Gazette*, 5 April 1774, Issue 11446, p. 1.

[108] *Commission Book*, 1776-1778, WO 25/33, p. 41. Promotion date of July 9, 1776 in *The London Gazette*, 6 July 1776, Issue 11681, p. 1.

[109] *Commission Book*, 1778-1780, WO 25/34, p. 260, *The London Gazette*, 16 October 1779, Issue 12023, p. 2. *The Scots Magazine*, Vol. 41, 1779, p. 575.

[110] *Derby Mercury*, 26 May 1780, p. 1. *Oxford Journal*, 27 May 1780, p. 3.

[111] *Bath Chronicle and Weekly Gazette*, 08 June 1780, p. 1.

[112] *Royal Military Panorama, or, Officers' Companion*, Vol. 3, 1814, p. 431. *Estimate and Accounts: Army; Navy; Civil List; Pensions; &C.*, 28 January – 12 July, 1817, Vol. 13, p. 59.

[113] James Balfour Paul, *The Scots Peerage: Founded on Wood's Edition of Sir Robert Douglas's Peerage of Scotland*, Vol. 1, Edinburgh: David Douglas, 1904, p. 525.

[114] *Commission Book*, 1772-1776, WO 25/32, p. 128 and *The London Gazette*, 14 May 1774, Issue 11457, p. 1.

[115] *Saunders's News-Letter*, 07 April 1775, p. 1. "Philip Stephens to the Board of the Admiralty, February 28, 1775," UK National Archives, ADM 354/189/357.

[116] *Commission Book*, 1776-1778, WO 25/33, p. 41. Promotion date reported as July 9, 1776 in *The London Gazette*, 6 July 1776, Issue 11681, p. 1.

[117] *Commission Book*, 1776-1778, WO 25/33, p. 311. *Army List*, 1779, WO 65/29, p. 138.

[118] Alexander Lindsay, *Lives of the Lindsays: or, A Memoir of the Houses of Crawford and Balcarres*, Vol. 2, London: John Murray, 1858, pp. 347-349. Vol. 3, p. 235 ff. includes part of a journal kept by Captain Lindsay.

[119] James Balfour Paul, *The Scots Peerage*, Vol. 1, 1904, *op cit*, p. 525.

Notes: Appendix

[1] John Marshall, *The Life of George Washington*, Vol. 1, Philadelphia: James Crissy, 1836, p. 69.

SELECT BIBLIOGRAPHY

Alvord, Clarence W. "Virginia and the West, an Interpretation." *The Mississippi Valley Historical Review*. Vol. 3 (June 1916): 26, 27.

An Officer Who Served in the British Forces. *The Operations of the Allied Army, Under the Command of His Serene Highness, Prince Ferdinand, 1757-1762*. London: T. Jefferys, 1764.

Anderson, Adam. *An Historical and Chronological Deduction of the Origin of Commerce, From the Earliest Accounts*. London: J. Walter, 1789.

Ashe, Samuel A'Court. *Biographical History of North Carolina from Colonial Times to the Present*. Vol. 2. Greensboro, N.C.: Charles L. Van Noppen, 1905.

Bancroft, George. *A History of the United States*. Vol. 4. Boston: Little Brown, 1852.

—. *A History of the United States*. Vol. 7. Boston: Little Brown, 1858.

Beer, George Louis. *British Colonial Policy, 1754-1765*. New York: Macmillan Company, 1907.

Bernard, Francis, Thomas Gage and Samuel Hood. *Letters to the Ministry from Governor Bernard, General Gage, and Commodore Hood*. Boston: Edes and Gill, 1769.

Bland, Humphrey. *A Treatise of Military Discipline*, sixth edition. London: John and Paul Knapton, 1746.

Bradford, Alden. *History of Massachusetts from 1764, to July, 1775 When General Washington Took Command of the American Army*. Boston: Richardson and Lord, 1822.

—. *Speeches of the Governors of Massachusetts, from 1765 to 1775; and the Answers of the House of Representatives, to the Same*. Ed. Alden Bradford. Boston: Russell and Gardner, 1818.

Bradley, Arthur Granville. *The Fight with France for North America*. Westminster: A. Constable and Co., Ltd., 1900.

Brodhead, John Romeyn. *Documents Relative to the Colonial History of the State of New York*. Vol. 7. Albany: Weed, Parsons and Company, 1856.

—. *Documents Relative to the Colonial History of the State of New York*. Vol. 8. Albany: Weed, Parsons and Company, 1857.

Burk, John, Skelton Jones and Louis Hue Girardin. *The History of Virginia: From Its First Settlement to the Present Day.* Vol. 4. Petersburg, Virginia: M. W. Dunnavant, 1816.

Cannon, Richard, ed. *Historical Records of the British Army: The Third Regiment of Foot, or The Buffs.* London: William Clowes and Sons, 1836.

—. *Historical record of the Fourteenth, or the Buckinghamshire Regiment of Foot: containing an account of the formation of the regiment in 1685, and of its subsequent services to 1845.* Ed. Richard Cannon. London: Parker, Funivall and Parker, 1845.

Carter, Clarence Edwin. *Correspondence of Thomas Gage with the Secretaries of State, and with the War Office and the Treasury 1763 - 1775.* Vols. 1 and 2. New Haven: Yale University Press, 1933.

Carter, Thomas. *Historical Record of the Forty-Fourth, Or the East Essex Regiment of Foot.* London: W. O. Mitchell, 1864.

Channing and Coolidge, *The Barrington-Bernard Correspondence, 1717-1793.* Cambridge: Harvard University, 1912.

Chernow, Ron. *Washington, a Life.* New York: Penguin Books, 2010.

Clark, William Bell, ed. *Naval Documents of the American Revolution (NDAR).* Vol. 1. Washington: GPO, 1964.

—. *Naval Documents of the American Revolution (NDAR).* Ed. William Bell Clark. Vol. 2. Washington: GPO, 1966.

—. *Naval Documents of the American Revolution (NDAR).* Ed. William Bell Clark. Vol. 3. Washington: GPO, 1968.

Cobbett, William, ed. *Cobbett's Parliamentary History of England.* Vol. 16. London: T.C. Hansard, 1813.

—. *Cobbett's Parliamentary History of England.* Ed. William Cobbett. Vol. 17. London: T. C. Hansard, 1803.

—. *Cobbett's Parliamentary History of England.* Ed. William Cobbett. Vol. 18. London: T.C. Hansard, 1813.

Cokayne, George Edward, ed. *The Complete Baronetage.* Vol. 4. Exeter: William Pollard, 1904.

Commissary General of Musters Office. General Muster Books and Pay Lists, 14th Foot 1st Battalion, April 24 1769. 1769 (UK National Archives WO 12/3117).

—. General Muster Books and Pay Lists, 14th Foot 1st Battalion, May 15 1772. 1772 (UK National Archives WO 12/3117).

Connor, Robert D. W. *History of North Carolina*. New York: The Lewis Publishing Company, 1919.

Curtis, Edward E. *The Organization of the British Army in the American Revolution*. New Haven: Yale University Press, 1926.

Dalrymple, John. "'JD' [Captain John Dalrymple, 14th Regiment] to the Earl of Dumfries, Virginia, January 14, 1776." 1776. National Archives, UK PRO CO 5/40 folio 124.

Davies, K. G., ed. *Documents of the American Revolution 1770-1783, Colonial Office Series*. Vol. 7. Shannon: Irish University Press, 1972.

—. *Documents of the American Revolution 1770-1783, Colonial Office Series*. Ed. K. G. Davies. Vol. 10. Shannon: Irish University Press, 1976.

—. *Documents of the American Revolution 1770-1783, Colonial Office Series*. Ed. K. G. Davies. Vol. 12. Shannon: Irish University Press.

Donne, W. Bodham, ed. *The Correspondence of King George the Third with Lord North from 1768 to 1783*. Vol. 1. London: J. Murray, 1867. 2 vols.

Drake, Samuel Gardner. *The History and Antiquities of Boston: The Capital of Massachusetts*. Boston: Luther Stevens, 1856.

Edes and Gill. *A Short Narrative of the Horrid Massacre in Boston: Perpetrated in the Evening of the Fifth Day of March 1770*. Boston: Edes and Gill; reprinted for W. Bingley, London, 1770.

Family History Library. Scotland, Births and Baptisms, 1564-1950. Database, FamilySearch citing Edinburgh Parish, Edinburgh, Midlothian, Scotland, and Straiton, Ayrshire, Scotland.

Fitzpatrick, John Clement, ed. *The Writings of George Washington from the Original Manuscripts*. Vol. 4. Washington: GPO, 1931.

Force, Peter, ed. *American Archives, Fourth Series, A Documentary History of the English Colonies in North America*. Vols. 1-4. Washington: M. St. Clair Clarke and Peter Force, 1839-1843.

Ford, Paul Leicester, ed. *The Writings of Thomas Jefferson*. Vol. 2. New York and London: G. Putnam's Sons, 1893

Ford, Worthington Chauncey, ed. *The Writings of George Washington*. Vol. 1. New York: G. P. Putnam, 1889.

Fordyce, Alexander Dingwall. *Family Record of the Name of Dingwall Fordyce in Aberdeenshire*. Toronto: C. Blackett Robinson, 1885.

Fortescue, John, ed. *The Correspondence of King George the Third*. Vol. 3. London: MacMillan and Co., 1928.

Frost, John. *The American Generals*. Columbus Ohio: William and Thomas Miller, 1855.

Greene, Jack P. *Evaluating Empire and Confronting Colonialism in Eighteenth-Century Britain*. New York: Cambridge University Press, 2013.

Groome, Francis Hindes, ed. *Ordnance Gazetteer of Scotland*. Edinburgh: T. C. and E. C. Jack, 1901.

Haldimand, Frederick. *Haldimand Papers*. British Library, Public Archives of Canada, MG 21.

Heath, William. *Memoirs of Major General Heath*. New York: William Abbatt, 1901.

Heitman, Francis B. *Historical Register of Officers of the Continental Army During the War of the Revolution, April, 1775, to December, 1783, New, Revised, and Enlarged Edition*. Washington D.C.: Rare Book Shop Publishing Company, 1914.

Historical Manuscripts Commission. *Manuscripts of the Earl of Dartmouth*. Vol. 2, *American Papers*. Vol. 14, Appendix, Part 10. London: Eyre and Spottiswoode, 1895.

House of Commons. *Journals of the House of Commons, 1774-76*. Vol. 35. 1803.

—. *The Parliamentary Register: or, History of the Proceedings and Debates of the House of Commons, First Session of the 14th Parliament*. Vol. 1. London: J. Almon, 1775.

—. *The Parliamentary Register: or, History of the Proceedings and Debates of the House of Commons, Fifth Session of the 14th Parliament*. Vol. 11. London: J. Almon, 1779.

Hulton, Ann. *Letters of a Loyalist Lady: Being the Letters of Ann Hulton, Sister of Henry Hulton, Commissioner of Customs at Boston, 1767-1776*. Ed. E. Rhys Jones. Cambridge: Harvard University Press, 1927.

Hutchinson, Peter Orlando. *The Diary and Letters of His Excellency Thomas Hutchinson: Captain-General and Governor-in-Chief of His Late Majesty's Province of Massachusetts Bay in North America*. London: Sampson Low, Makston, Seaele & Rivington, 1883.

Johnston, George. "George Johnston, Great Bridge, Va. to Leven Powell, Loudoun County, Va. 9 Dec. 1775." *Leven Powell Papers 1774–1810. 1775*. Special Collections Research Center, Earl Gregg Swem Library, College of William and Mary, Folder 3, Item 3.

Jones, Charles Colcock. *The History of Georgia: Revolutionary Epoch. Vol. 2*. Boston: Houghton, Mifflin and Company, 1883.

Journals of the House of Lords. Vols. 31 (1765-1767). London: H.M.S.O., 1767.

Kane, Richard. *A System of Camp Discipline, Military Honours, Garrison Duty, and Other Regulations for the Land Forces*. London: J. Milan, 1757.

Kennedy, John Pendleton, ed. *Journals of the House of Burgesses of Virginia, 1761-1765*. Richmond, 1908.

—. *Journals of the House of Burgesses of Virginia, 1766-1769*. Ed. John Pendleton Kennedy. Richmond, 1906.

—. *Journals of the House of Burgesses of Virginia, 1770-1772*. Ed. John Pendleton Kennedy. Richmond, 1906.

—. *Journals of the House of Burgesses of Virginia, 1773-1776*. Ed. John Pendleton Kennedy. Richmond: E. Waddey, 1905.

Lecky, William Edward Hartpole. *The American Revolution, 1763-1783: Being the Chapters and Passages Relating to America from the Author's History of England in the Eighteenth Century*. New York and London: D. Appleton and Company, 1898.

Lee, Richard H. *Memoir of the Life of Richard Henry Lee, and His Correspondence with the Most Distinguished Men in America and Europe, Illustrative of Their Characters, and of the Events of the American Revolution*. Vol. 1. Philadelphia: William Brown, 1825.

Lewis, Virgil Anson. *History of the Battle of Point Pleasant*. Charleston, West Virginia: The Tribune Printing Company, 1909.

Lowe, William C., "The Parliamentary Career of Lord Dunmore, 1761-1774," *The Virginia Magazine of History and Biography*. Vol. 96, No. 1 (Jan., 1988).

MacDonald, William, ed. *Select Charters and Other Documents Illustrative of American History*. Vol. 1. New York: Macmillan Company, 1904.

Maltby, Isaac. *The Elements of War*. Boston: Thomas B. Wait, 1811.

Massachusetts Historical Society. "Frederick Lewis Gay transcripts, 1632-1786., Ms. N-2012 (Tall), State Papers. Vol. 12. Pages 40-97." (UK National Archives CO 5/88).

—. *Journals of the House of Representatives of Massachusetts 1767-1768*. Vol. 44. Boston: Anthoensen Press, 1975 (originally published in Boston by Green and Russell, 1767), 1975.

—. *Journals of the House of Representatives of Massachusetts, 1770-1771*. Vol. 47. Portland, Main: (Republished) Anthoensen Press, 1978.

Matthews, Albert, ed. *Publications of the Colonial Society of Massachusetts*. Vol. 2. Cambridge: University Press, John Wilson and Son, 1913.

Maxwell, William, "My Mother." Edward W. James, ed. *Lower Norfolk County Virginia Antiquary (1897)*: Number 2, Part 3, 32, 61, 137.

"Memoir of Alfred Moore." *The Literary and Scientific Repository, and Critical Review* 1 (1820): 25.

Montresor, John. "The Montresor Journals." *Collections of the New York Historical Society for the Year 1881 (1882)*: 400, 401, 407, 410.

Moomaw, W. Hugh. "The British Leave Colonial Virginia." *The Virginia Magazine of History and Biography*. Vol. 66 (April 1958): 147-160.

Morgan, Edmund Sears, ed. *Prologue to Revolution: Sources and Documents on the Stamp Act Crisis, 1764-1766*. Chapel Hill: The University of North Carolina Press, 1959.

Mowat, Charles Loch. *East Florida as a British Province, 1763-1784*. Berkeley: University of California Press, 1943.

Murdoch, Beamish. *A History of Nova-Scotia, or Acadie*. Vol. 2. Halifax: James Barnes, 1866.

National Records of Scotland, Scotland's People. "Birth Record for Charles Fordyce 01/10/1741." Church registers Old Parish Records (1741): 685/1 230 119, p. 119 of 548.

Niles, Hezekiah, ed. *Principles and Acts of the Revolution in America*. Baltimore: W.O. Niles, 1822.

Paul, James Balfour. *The Scots Peerage: Founded on Wood's Edition of Sir Robert Douglas's Peerage of Scotland*. Vol. 2. Edinburgh: Davis Douglas, 1905.

—. *The Scots Peerage: Founded on Wood's Edition of Sir Robert Douglas's Peerage of Scotland*. Vol. 8. Edinburgh: Davis Douglas, 1911.

Pickering, Danby. *The Statutes at Large: From Magna Charta to the End of the Eleventh Parliament of Great Britain*. Vol. 26. Cambridge: Joseph Bentham, 1764.

—. *The Statutes at Large: From Magna Charta to the End of the Eleventh Parliament of Great Britain*. Vol. 27. Cambridge: John Archdeacon, 1767.

Prince, Carl and Mollie Keller. *The U.S. Customs Service: A Bicentennial History*. Washington: U.S. Customs Service, 1989.

Redington, Joseph, ed. *Calendar of Home Office Papers of the Reign of George III*. Vols. 2 (1766-1769). London: H.M.S.O., 1879.

—. *Calendar of Home Office Papers of the Reign of George III*. Ed. Joseph Redington. Vol. 1. London: Longman & Company and Trübner & Company, 1878.

Ricord, Frederick and William Nelson, *Documents Relating to the Colonial History of the State of New Jersey*. Vol. 9. Newark: Daily Advertiser, 1885.

—. *Documents Relating to the Colonial History of the State of New Jersey*. Ed. Frederick Ricord and William Nelson. Vol. 10. Newark: Daily Advertiser, 1886.

Roberts, Richard Arthur, ed. *Calendar of Home Office Papers of the Reign of George III*. London: H.M.S.O., 1899.

Robson, Eric. "The Expedition to the Southern Colonies, 1775-1776." *English Historical Review*. Vol. 66 (1951): 535-560.

Romans, Bernard. *A Concise Natural History of East and West Florida*. New York: R. Aitken, 1776.

Rowe, John. *Letters and Diary of John Rowe: Boston Merchant, 1759-1762, 1764-1779*. Ed. Anne Rowe Cunningham. Boston: W. B. Clarke Company, 1903.

Rowland, Kate Mason. *The Life of George Mason, 1725-1792*. Vol. 1. New York: G. P. Putnam's Sons, 1892.

Saunders, William L., ed. *Colonial Records of North Carolina*. Vol. 9. Raleigh: Josephus Daniels, 1890.

—. *Colonial Records of North Carolina*. Ed. William L. Saunders. Vol. 10. Raleigh: Josephus Daniels, 1890.

Schlesinger, Arthur Meier. *The Colonial Merchants and the American Revolution, 1763-1776*. Vol. 78. New York: Columbia University, 1918.

Scott, Sibbald David. *The British Army: Its Origin, Progress, and Equipment*. Vol. 3. London: Cassell, Petter, Galpin, 1880.

Scribner, Robert L. and Brent Tarter, *Revolutionary Virginia, the Road to Independence*. Vol. 5. Charlottesville: University Press of Virginia, 1978.

—. *Revolutionary Virginia, the Road to Independence*. Ed. Robert L. Scribner and Brent Tarter. Vol. 4. Charlottesville: The University Press of Virginia, 1979.

Secretary at War, UK. *A List of the General and Field-Officers as They Rank in the Army, of the Officers of the Several Regiments of Horse, Dragoons, and Foot on the British and Irish Establishments, Complete for 1761*. London: J. Millan, 1761 (UK National Archives WO 65/9).

—. *A List of the General and Field-Officers as They Rank in the Army, of the Officers of the Several Regiments of Horse, Dragoons, and Foot on the British and Irish Establishments, for 1763*. London: J. Millan, 1763 (UK National Archives WO 65/12).

—. *A List of the General and Field-Officers as They Rank in the Army, of the Officers of the Several Regiments of Horse, Dragoons, and Foot on the British and Irish Establishments, for 1772*. London: J. Milan, 1772 (UK National Archives, WO 65/22).

—. *A List of the General and Field-Officers as They Rank in the Army, of the Officers of the Several Regiments of Horse, Dragoons, and Foot on the British and Irish Establishments, March 1765*. London: J. Milan, 1765 (UK National Archives, WO 65/15).

—. *A List of the General and Field-Officers as They Rank in the Army, of the Officers of the Several Regiments of Horse, Dragoons, and Foot on the British and Irish Establishments, November 1761*. London: J. Milan, 1761 (UK National Archives, WO 65/11).

—. *A List of the General and Field-Officers as They Rank in the Army, of the Officers of the Several Regiments of Horse, Dragoons, and Foot on the British and Irish Establishments, to November 1761*. London: J. Millan, 1761 (UK National Archives, WO 65/10).

—. *A List of the General and Field-Officers as They Rank in the Army, of the Officers of the Several Regiments of Horse, Dragoons, and Foot on the British and Irish Establishments, to November 1763*. London: J. Millan, 1763 (UK National Archives WO 65/13).

—. *Army Commission Book for 1763-1767*. 1763 WO 25/30.
—. *Army Commission Book for 1767-1772*. 1767 WO 25/31.
—. *Army Commission Book, 1744-1746*. 1744 WO 25/21.
—. *Army Commission Book, 1761-1762*. 1761 WO 25/28.
—. *Army Commission Book, 1772-1776*. 1772 WO 25/32.
Selby, John E. *The Revolution in Virginia, 1775-1783*. Colonial Williamsburg, 2007.
Shephard, Charles. *An Historical Account of the Island of Saint Vincent*. London: W. Nicol, 1831.
Shy, John W. Toward Lexington: *The Role of the British Army in the Coming of the American Revolution*. Princeton, N.J.: Princeton University Press, 1965.
Smith, William James, ed. *The Grenville Papers: Being the Correspondence of Richard Grenville Earl Temple, K.G., and the Right Hon: George Grenville, Their Friends and Contemporaries*. Vol. 4. London: John Murray, 1853.
Smyth, John Ferdinand. *A Tour in the United States of America*. Vol. 2. London: G. Robinson, 1784.
Sparks, Jared. *The Writings of George Washington*. Vol. 3. Boston: Russell, Odiorne and Metcalf, 1834.
"St. Augustine under the British Flag, 1763-1775." *The Florida Historical Quarterly* (Oct., 1941) 20.2 (1941): 134.
Stewart, William H. *History of Norfolk County, Virginia: and Representative Citizens, 1637-1900*. Chicago: Biographical Publishing Company, 1902.
Stork, William and John Bartram. *A Description of East-Florida, with a Journal Kept by John Bartram, Third Edition*. London: W. Nicoll, 1769.
The American Gazette, a Collection of All the Authentic Addresses, Memorials Petitions, and Other Papers. London: G. Kearsly, 1770.
"The Methodist Earl of Dartmouth." *Methodist Review*. Vol. 86 (1904): 957-962.
The Papers of Francis Bernard. Vol. 4: 1768, *Publications of the Colonial Society of Massachusetts*. Vol. 86. https://www.colonialsociety.org/node/2810
Thwaites, Reuben Gold. *Documentary History of Dunmore's War*, Madison: Wisconsin Historical Society, 1905.

Tingley, Helen Eloise Boor. "Florida under the English Flag, 1763-1783." *The Journal of American History*. Vol. 11 (1917): 75.

Trevelyan, George. *The American Revolution*. Vol. 1. London: Longmans, Green, and Co., 1921.

US Congress. "Articles of Association." *Journals of the Continental Congress, 1774-1789* (1774).

Virginia House of Delegates. *Proceedings of the Convention of Delegates for the Counties and Corporations in the Colony of Virginia, December 1775*, Richmond: Ritchie, Trueheart & Du-Val, 1816.

—. *Journal of the House of Delegates of Virginia, 1776*. Richmond: Samuel Shepherd, 1828.

War Office (UK). In-Letters, c. West Indies, Campaign against Charibs on St Vincent, 1772-1773. 1772-1773 (UK National Archives WO 1/57).

Washington, George. *George Washington Papers*, Series 3, Varick Transcripts, 1775-1785, Subseries 3G, General Orders, 1775-1783, Letterbook 1: July 3, 1775 - Sept. 30, 1776. Washington: Library of Congress, 1776.

Wells, William F. *The Life and Public Services of Samuel Adams, Being a Narrative of His Acts and Opinions, and of His Agency in Producing and Forwarding the American Revolution*. Vol. 1. Boston: Little, Brown, and Company, 1865.

White (publisher). *A Fair Account of the Late Unhappy Disturbance at Boston: In New England*. London: B. White, 1770.

"The Letters of Col. William Woodford, Col. Robert Howe and Gen. Charles Lee to Edmund Pendleton." *Richmond College Historical Papers* 1 (1915).

Wolkins, George Gregerson. "The Seizure of Hancock's Sloop 'Liberty'." *Proceedings of the Massachusetts Historical Society*. Vol. 55 (1922): 239-284.

Young, William. *Account of the Black Charaibs in the Island of St Vincent's*. London: Frank Cass and Company, 1795.

INDEX

1st Foot Guards, 64
1st Virginia Regiment, v, 135, 141, 154, 163, 198, 201
2nd North Carolina Regiment, v
2nd Virginia Regiment, v, vi, 1, 21, 135, 141, 158, 166, 182, 186, 189, 202, 203, 247
3rd Foot Guards, 46, 108, 115, 157
3rd Virginia Regiment, 198
4th Virginia Regiment, 198
5th Virginia Regiment, 198
6th Virginia Regiment, 198
14th (Bedfordshire) Regiment, iv
14th (Buckinghamshire) Regiment, iv
14th Regiment, vii, xii, 16, 18, 22, 25, 41, 43, 48, 71, 73, 75, 76, 80, 84, 88, 98, 101, 104, 106, 146, 147, 155, 172, 174, 175, 187, 208, 210, 211, 212, 213, 214, 215, 216, 217, 218, 219, 220, 221
    Arrives Halifax, 42
    Arrives St. Augustine, 90, 96
    Arrives St. Vincent, 81, 96, 265
    Arrives Virginia, 132, 133, 134, 138
    Boston, 10, 74, 173
    Bunker Hill, 157
    Departs Boston, 96, 175
    Departs England, 41
    Departs St. Augustine, 138
    Departs St. Vincent, 90
    Deployed to America, 41
    French and Indian War, 4, 5, 6
    Gibralter, 5, 213
    Great Bridge, wounded, 171, 200, 227, 228, 229, 230, 231, 232, 233, 234, 236, 237, 239, 241, 243, 245, 247

Grenadiers, vii, viii, 1, 62, 70, 83, 97, 138, 142, 145, 148, 165, 168, 179, 180, 184, 200, 202, 210, 226, 227, 228, 229, 231, 233, 234, 236, 241, 245, 246
Gwynn's Island, 203
Halifax, 8, 180
Jamaica, 211, 213
Kemp's Landing, 142, 145, 177
Muster at Boston, 63
Muster at Castle William, 83
Muster at St. Augustine, 99, 103, 134
Muster at St. Vincent, 81
Muster at Virginia, 136, 140, 200
New Providence, 13, 96, 176
Recruits, 52, 97, 208, 218, 219, 220
Reviewed by King George III, 41
St. Augustine, 12, 89, 94, 95, 97, 104
St. George's Island, 203
St. Vincent, 11, 21, 81, 86
Staten Island, 207, 214
Virginia, 14, 111, 128, 135, 139, 177, 201
15th Regiment, iv
19th Regiment, iv
21st Regiment, 94, 172
23rd Regiment, 172, 209, 210
25th Regiment, ii, xii
29th Regiment, 10, 12, 54, 57, 59, 67, 71, 73, 74, 96, 97, 98, 173
31st Regiment, 80, 87, 88, 90
33rd Regiment, iv, 212
35th Regiment, 215, 297
44th Regiment, 5
48th Regiment, 5

Index

50th Regiment, 210
51st Regiment, 297
59th Regiment, 59, 60, 67
64th Regiment, 55, 64, 67
65th Regiment, 55, 64
68th Regiment, 88, 210
70th Regiment, 86, 88
71st Regiment, 213, 214, 216, 217
73rd Regiment, 221
76th Regiment, iv
78th Regiment, Fraser's Highlanders, 28, 213
87th Regiment, Keith's Highlanders, 28, 30, 34, 218, 220
88th Regiment, Campbell's Highlanders, 2, 6, 26, 28, 29, 30, 34, 40
131st Regiment, 219
Abbot, Richard, Private, 170, 171
Adams, John, 50
Adams, Samuel, 50, 52
Alexander, Harry, 79
Alexander, William, Lord Stirling, General, 198
Allen, James, Private, 171
Almond, William, Private, 63, 83
American Ship
  Alfred, 193
  Hornet, 192, 195
  Liberty, 55
Amherst, Jeffery, General, 217
Ancient and Honorable Artillery Company of Massachusetts, 68
Anderson, James, Negro prisoner, 170
Articles of Association, 13, 106, 126
Ashworth, Amy, xii
Asymmetric warfare, 86, 87
Augustus Frederick, Prince, Duke of Sussex, 207
Ballantine, James, Private, 63

Barrington, William, Secretary at War, 41, 80, 81, 87, 90, 102, 191, 197
Bartram, John, 90
Batut, John, Lieutenant, 82, 98, 99, 134, 136, 140, 153, 159, 164, 165, 170, 177, 187, 200, 209, 212, 213, 218, 224, 226, 227, 229, 230, 231, 233, 234, 236
Bedford. *See* Russell, John
Beer, George Louis, 3, 38
Berkeley, Norborne, 4th Baron Botetourt, 74, 75, 113, 122
Bernard, Francis, Governor, 47, 48, 51, 52, 53, 55, 57, 60, 65, 69, 272
Blackburn, Christopher, Adjutant, 2nd Virginia, 228
Blackett, William, Captain, 40, 82, 97, 98, 132, 133, 134, 136, 137, 139, 173, 176, 177, 216
Bland, Humphrey, General, 157
Bollen, Edward, Corporal, 83
Boston Massacre, 10, 70, 71, 73, 74, 173
Boston Port Act, 13, 104, 113, 114, 118, 124
Boston Tea Party, 13, 104
Botetourt. *See* Berkeley, Norborne
Botton, Edward, Private, 63
Boyes, James, Ensign, 133, 136, 140, 177, 209, 217, 219
Braddock, Edward, General, 5, 6
Braddock's Defeat, 5, 6
Brandywine, 214
Breed's Hill, 189
Bridges, Joseph, 247
Brison, James, Private, 83
British Ship
  Betsey, 132
  Dunmore, 150
  Fowey, 128, 130, 132
  Gaspee, 11, 103, 104

Launceston, 146, 147, 255, 279
Liverpool, 150
Maria, 149, 150
Mercury, 130, 140, 149
Montague, 220
Otter, 111, 129, 132, 137, 140, 149, 155, 166, 169, 182, 233
William, 132, 137, 140, 149
Brown, John, 60
Brown, John, Loyalist, 144, 145
Brown, William, 144
Brown, William, Lieutenant, 82, 88, 99, 157
Brownrigg, John, Lieutenant, 217
Brucher Mühl, 32, 33
Bruere, George James, Captain, 34, 40
Bruere, George James, Governor, 157
Bruere, John, Lieutenant, 157
Bunker Hill, 111, 129, 157, 158, 162, 189
Burgoyne, John, General, 214
Burnett, Peter, Ensign, 82, 99
Burns, Robert, 16
Caesar, Negro prisoner, 170
Calder, Robert, Corporal, 171
Caley, Dorothy, 214
Calvert, Helen, Mrs. James Maxwell, 145, 146, 147, 181, 223, 225, 244
Calvert, Max, 228
Camatic War, 221
Cameron, John, Private, 63
Campbell, John, 4th Earl of Loudoun, 18, 46
Campbell, John, Lieutenant Colonel, 2, 26, 28, 29, 33
Campbell, Lieutenant, 30
Campbell, Ronald, Lieutenant, 30
Campbell, William, Governor, 57, 206

Campbell's Highlanders. *See* 88th Regiment
Carib, Carribees, 11, 12, 21, 77, 78, 79, 81, 84, 86, 87, 88, 89, 90, 96, 175, 266
Carr, John, Private, 63, 83
Carr, Maurice, Lieutenant Colonel, 71, 96, 97
Castle William, Castle Island, 11, 52, 72, 73, 74, 75, 80, 83, 173, 174, 176
Cathcart, Charles, 8th Lord, 15
Cathcart, Charles, 9th Lord, 15, 17, 18, 46
Cathcart, Jane, 18
Cathcart, Louisa, 18
Cathcart, Margaret, 15
Cathcart, Mary (Mrs. Graham), 18, 19
Cathcart, Mary Ann, 41
Chalmers, William, Private, 171
Chislet, Stephen, Private, 171
Clinton, Henry, General, 194, 207, 211, 214, 215, 217
Cloister Camp, 29, 212
Cogliano, Frank, xi
Colden, Cadwallader, Lieutenant Governor, 36, 272
Coleman, William, Fifer, 83
Colvill, Alexander, 7th Lord of Culross, Vice Admiral, 39
Commissioners of Customs, 9, 47, 49, 51, 53, 54, 55, 56, 57, 66, 74, 96
Committee of Safety, 135, 137, 140, 141, 142, 169, 201, 278
Concord, 13, 104, 109, 111, 189
Confield, Pierce, Private, 63
Connolly, John, Lieutenant Colonel, 110
Continental Army, 67, 68, 138, 165, 195, 197, 198, 199, 205, 206, 292

Continental Congress, x, 13, 106, 125, 193, 197
Conway, Henry Seymour, Secretary of State for the Colonies, 36, 41
Cooper, David, 14th Regiment, 60, 63, 82, 83, 99, 133, 136, 140, 155, 177, 209, 210, 211
Cornwallis, Charles, General, 25, 41, 206, 214
Cornwallis, Charles, Viscount Brome, 25
Cornwallis, Edward, 41
Corrance, John, Captain, 96
Corry, Edmund Leslie, 210
Cowpens, Battle of, 214
Crocker, William, Drummer, 63, 83
Culloden, Battle of, 15, 16
Cumberland. *See* Duke of Cumberland
Curle, William, 144
Customs Commissioners. *See* Commissioners of Customs
Dalrymple, Anne, 220
Dalrymple, James, 1st Viscount Stair, 221
Dalrymple, John, 1st Earl of Stair, 41
Dalrymple, John, 5th Earl of Stair, 18
Dalrymple, John, Captain, 52, 133, 136, 140, 155, 158, 165, 167, 168, 170, 178, 180, 182, 184, 185, 208, 209, 211, 223, 230, 231
Dalrymple, John, Sir, 191, 195, 197
Dalrymple, William, Lieutenant Colonel, 12, 40, 41, 44, 54, 55, 56, 57, 58, 60, 64, 71, 73, 80, 81, 87, 88, 89, 175, 207, 217
Dalrymple-Hay, John, 212
Dana, Richard, Justice, 71
Danks, John, Private, 63

Darrah, Nicholas, Lieutenant, 88
Dartmouth, William Legg, 2nd Earl of Dartmouth, 88, 89, 90, 103, 106, 110, 112, 113, 114, 117, 118, 120, 126, 128, 130, 132, 137, 140, 143, 149, 150, 154, 156, 162, 170, 177, 182, 194, 200, 238, 239, 283
Deblois, Stephen, 66
Declaration of Independence, 198
Declaratory Act, 8, 38, 44, 112, 116, 119, 120
Dinwiddie, Robert, Lieutenant Governor, 4, 113
Dorr, Harbottle, x
Drisson, Thomas, Private, 171
Druckland, William, Private, 63, 83
Duke of Cumberland, Prince William Augustus, 15, 16
Dunmore. *See* Murray, John
Dunmore's War, 109
East India Company, 104, 221
Easterly, William, Private, 63, 83
Elliott, Joseph, Private, Corporal, 63, 83
Entwistle, Edmund, Private, 63, 83
Eppes, Francis, Lieutenant Colonel, 154, 163, 201, 202
Ethiopian Regiment, 150, 170
Fairchild, James, Private, 63, 83
Fauquier, Francis, Governor, 113, 117, 118, 119, 246, 247, 272, 274
Fellinghausen. *See* Villinghausen
Ferdinand, Prince of Brunswick-Lüneburg, 28, 29, 30, 31, 32, 33
Ferguson, Adam, Sir, 230
Findlay, Alexander, Corporal, 63
Fitzmaurice, Ulysses, Lieutenant Governor, 79
Flora, William 'Billy', 165, 241
Fontenoy, Battle of, 15
Forbes, John, Chaplin, 99, 180
Fordyce, Adam, 20, 21

Fordyce, Alexander, 15
Fordyce, Cathcart, 20, 21
Fordyce, Charles
   At Boston, 59, 60, 62, 63, 65, 66, 68, 69
   At Boston, Brigade Major, 10, 64, 65, 72, 179
   At Boston, Castle Island, 73, 83
   At Boston, mentoring Alfred Moore, 67, 68
   At Boston, Winship affair, 70, 71
   At Brucher Mühl, 32, 35, 158
   At Gosport, 134, 138, 139, 140, 141, 148, 152, 173
   At Halifax, Town Major, 9, 44, 64, 146, 179
   At Kemp's Landing, 145
   At St. Augustine, 97, 98, 100, 106
   At St. Vincent, 84
   At Virginia, 14
   Battle of Great Bridge, 158, 165, 166, 179, 180, 181, 182, 200, 226, 227, 229, 230, 233, 242
   Birth, 15
   Burial, vi, 187
   Captain, 14th Reg., v, vi, vii, viii, xii, 1, 14, 16, 41, 44, 75, 83, 155, 170, 178, 179, 180, 181, 190, 208, 210, 211, 212, 213, 215, 216, 218, 220, 221, 223, 246
   Captain, 88th Reg., 26, 30, 31, 33, 212
   Cousin of Caleb Whitefoord, 17
   Death at Great Bridge, 21, 167, 168, 174, 178, 179, 182, 183, 223, 230, 231, 234, 236, 239, 241, 247
   Death at St. Vincent, false report of, 21, 88
   Funeral, 185, 186
   Grave, 188
   In command at St. Augustine, 13, 97
   Lieutenant, 14th Reg., 26
   Links to Lord Dunmore, 47
   Links to Maxwells and Gordons, 25, 146
   Number of wounds, 223, 230, 243, 245, 246, 247
   Obituary, 184
   Relationship to 4th Earl of Loudoun, 46
   Relationship to 9th Lord Cathcart, 15, 18, 46
   Relationship to Colonel Keppel, 41
   Relationship to Earl of Dumfries, 167
   Relationship to James Dalrymple, 1st Viscount Stair, 221
   Relationship to James Lindsay, 221
   Relationship to John Dalrymple, 1st Earl of Stair, 41
   Relationship to John Dalrymple, Captain, 52, 212
   Relationship to William Dalrymple, 41, 52
   Wilkie's Independent Company of Foot, 26, 27
Fordyce, George, 20, 21
Fordyce, George, Rev., 15
Fordyce, John, xii, 7, 20, 21, 22, 24, 25, 46, 146, 147, 184, 230
Fordyce, Thomas, xi, 15, 19, 20, 21, 22, 23, 46
Franklin, Benjamin, 17
Franklin, Michael, Lieutenant Governor, 57
Fraser, Simon, Lieutenant Colonel, 28

Fraser's Highlanders. *See* 78th and 71st Regiments
Freemasons, 66
French and Indian War, 1, 2, 5, 7, 18, 36, 42, 69, 77, 123
Furlong, Jonathan, Captain and Major, 40, 65, 82, 89, 96, 97, 98, 102, 133, 134, 135, 176, 177, 208, 210
Gadsden, Christopher, 193
Gage, Thomas, General, 10, 13, 36, 44, 47, 54, 55, 56, 72, 73, 79, 80, 81, 90, 96, 102, 105, 106, 110, 111, 128, 129, 132, 133, 134, 135, 162, 208
Garlies. *See* Stewart, John
Gates' Defeat, 214
Gay, Frederick Lewis, x
Gell, John, Captain, 146, 147
Germain, George, 1st Viscount Sackville, 150, 202, 203, 204
Gifford, James, Captain, 214
Glossop, Abraham, Private, 63, 83
Goldsmith, Oliver, 16
Goodman, William, Captain, 247
Gordon, Alexander, 4th Duke of Gordon, 23, 24, 147
Gordon, George, Marquis of Huntly, 23
Gordon, George, Midshipman, 147
Gordon, Louisa, 25
Gower. *See* Levenson-Gower, Granville
Gower, Edward, Lieutenant, 82, 88, 176
Graham, Thomas, 1st Baron Lynedoch, 18
Grant, James, 95, 180
Graves, Samuel, Admiral RN, 110, 111, 129, 130, 132, 137, 163
Great Bridge, Battle of, v, vi, vii, viii, 1, 10, 14, 21, 22, 68, 98, 107, 108, 109, 111, 112, 119, 127, 139, 142, 145, 158, 162, 178, 181, 183, 185, 189, 190, 196, 198, 207, 208, 211, 212, 213, 215, 216, 220, 221, 223
Greene, Nathaniel, General, 198
Greenjud, Henry, Private, 63
Grenadier, 29, 31, 44, 62, 64, 184
Gretton or Greaten, William, Private, 63, 83
Gridley, Jeremy, 66
Grimes, Captain, 247
Guilford Court House, Battle of, 214
Gunpowder Incident, 106, 110, 113, 118, 124, 126, 197
Gwynn's Island, 198, 203
Haldimand, Frederick, Major General, 13, 95, 96, 97, 98, 100, 101, 102
Hale, Ann, 215
Hale, Sir John, General, 215
Halifax, Lord, 117, 253, 272
Hall, Charles, Surgeon, 82, 99
Hallwood, Henry, Ensign, 82, 97, 173, 176
Hamilton, Jane, 17
Harlem Heights, Battle of, 197, 199, 205
Harrison, Benjamin, Colonel, 192
Hay, Sir Thomas of Park, 211
Hayter, Thomas, Ensign, 99
Heal or Hale, Samuel, Private, Corporal, 63, 83, 170, 171
Heath, William, Captain and Major General, 68, 69
Henry, Patrick, 44, 118, 127, 141
Hesketh, Robert, Ensign, 157
Hesketh, Thomas, 157
Hessians, 29, 198, 205

Hill, Wills, Earl of Hillsborough, 10, 11, 47, 49, 53, 54, 55, 56, 57, 79, 80, 81, 89, 90, 120, 272
Holam, William, Private, 83
Holt, John, 137
Hopkins, Esek, Commodore, 193, 194
Howe, Robert, Colonel, 154, 163, 201, 213, 246
Howe, William, Colonel, 111
Howe, William, General, 129, 135, 138, 149, 151, 162, 171, 177, 190, 195, 197, 205, 207, 214
Hubbard, Thomas, v
Hudson, James, Private, 63, 83
Hulton, Ann, 66, 261, 303
Hulton, Henry, 66, 261, 303
Hunter, Katherine Leslie, 133, 147, 148
Husk, John, Colonel, 172
Huske's Regiment. *See* 23rd Regiment or Royal Welsh Fusiliers
Hutchinson, Thomas, Governor, 71, 72, 73, 106
Innes, George, 20, 23, 46
Jackson, Francis, Private, 63, 83, 170, 171
Jefferson, Thomas, 198, 199
Jefferyes, Charles, Colonel, Major General, 26, 40, 172
John Williams, John, 50, 51
Johnson, Samuel, 16
Johnston, George, Captain, 2nd Virginia, 164, 182, 185, 202, 229
Jones, John Paul, John Paul, 193
Journal of the Times, 70
Journal of The Times, 67
Kaufman, David, xi
Keith's Highlanders. *See* 87th Regiment
Kelvington, Henry, Ensign, 82

Kemp's Landing, 142, 144, 147, 162, 177, 203
Kemp's Landing, Battle of, 142, 144, 145, 150, 153, 177, 181
Kennedy, John Pendleton, 123
King George II, 15, 28, 115
King George III, 8, 12, 36, 39, 41, 78, 90, 152, 216
King James VI of Scotland, I of England and Ireland, 15
King, William, Private, 63, 83
King's Own Scottish Borderers Museum, ii, xii
Kip's Bay, 215
Kips Bay, 205
Lake, William, Private, 63
Lane, Thomas, Private, 63
Laurie, Andrew, Lieutenant, 133, 136, 140, 177, 209, 213, 214, 217
Lecky, William, 120
Lee, Charles, General, 195
Lee, Richard Henry, 195, 245
Lee, Thomas Ludwell, 245
Legg, Ellen, 216
Leslie, Edmond, 209
Leslie, Henry, 209
Leslie, Henry, Rev., 174, 209
Leslie, James, 209
Leslie, Jane, 209
Leslie, Margaret, 209
Leslie, Peter Henry, Lieutenant, 99, 134, 136, 170, 171, 174, 175, 176, 177, 178, 209, 218, 220, 231, 233, 234, 236, 239
Leslie, Peter, Rev., 209
Leslie, Samuel, Captain, vii, 99, 111, 132, 133, 134, 135, 136, 137, 138, 139, 140, 142, 147, 149, 151, 155, 156, 165, 169, 174, 175, 176, 177, 200, 209, 210, 211, 215, 216, 226, 227, 229, 230, 233, 236, 237, 238, 239, 243

Index

Leveson-Gower, Granville, 2nd Earl Gower, 45, 115, 116, 119, 120, 121
Lewis, Andrew, Brigadier General, 203
Lexington, 104, 109, 111, 189
Liberty Affair, 55
Lightbody, Elizabeth, 66
Lindsay, Colin, 221
Lindsay, James Stair, Ensign, 133, 136, 140, 174, 177, 209, 218, 219, 220, 221
Lindsay, James, 5th Earl of Balcarres, 220
Lindsey, Samuel, Captain, 40
Lockett, John, Private, 83
Long Island, Battle of, 205, 214
Lowe, William, 45, 46
MacBean, Alexander, Captain, 216
Mackay, Alexander, Brigadier General, 55, 64, 65, 181
Mackay, George, Ensign, 88
Mackenzie, Alexander, Major, 87
Malayan Emergency, xii
Malcom, Daniel, Captain, 53
Manners, John, Marquess of Granby, 30, 31, 33
Marshall, John, Culpeper Battalion, 224
Marshall, Thomas, Major, Culpeper Battalion, 164, 224, 227, 247
Martin, Josiah, Governor, 163
Martin, Thomas, Private, 63
Mason, Caleb, 223, 246
Mason, Edmund, Captain, 40, 82, 215
Mattear, Daniel, Lieutenant, 97, 173, 176
Maxwell, Edward, Lieutenant Colonel, 94, 95

Maxwell, James, Captain, 145, 146, 147
Maxwell, Jane, Duchess of Gordon, 7, 23, 24, 147
Maxwell, Katherine, Mrs. John Fordyce, xii, 7, 23, 24, 46, 147
Maxwell, William, 244
McCrery, Robert, Sergeant, 63, 84
McDouall-Crichton, Patrick, 6th Earl of Dumfries, 167, 170, 178, 183, 184, 185, 230
McKnight, James, 181
McKnight, Thomas, 181
Meade, Richard Kidder, Captain, 2nd Virginia, 164, 182, 231, 232
Meldrum, Anna, 15
Melville, Robert, Governor, 78
Milliken, Jean, 172
Mills, Benjamin, Sergeant, 83, 84
Milsom, William, Private, 83
Monongahela, the, Battle of, 5
Moore, Alfred, 67
Moore, James, 67
Moore, Maurice, 67
Moore's Creek Bridge, 67
Morris, John, Fifer, 83
Morton, Joshua, Private, 63, 83
Moultrie, Eleanor, 95
Moultrie, John, Lieutenant Governor, 94, 100, 101, 102, 104
Mulcaster, Frederick, 180
Murchieson (Murchison), Magnus, Lieutenant, 296
Murray, Alexander, Captain, 40, 213
Murray, Augusta, 207
Murray, Catherine, 114
Murray, Charles, 1st Earl of Dunmore, 109
Murray, David, 2nd Earl of Mansfield, 18

Murray, John, 1st Marquis of Atholl, 114
Murray, John, 2nd Earl of Dunmore, 47, 108, 109
Murray, John, 4th Duke of Atholl, 18
Murray, John, 4th Earl of Dunmore, v, 6, 14, 44, 47, 68, 73, 74, 75, 76, 105, 106, 107, 109, 110, 112, 113, 114, 115, 116, 117, 119, 120, 121, 123, 124, 125, 126, 127, 128, 129, 130, 131, 132, 133, 135, 137, 138, 139, 141, 142, 144, 145, 147, 149, 150, 151, 152, 154, 155, 157, 158, 160, 161, 162, 164, 169, 170, 177, 181, 182, 186, 189, 190, 191, 192, 193, 194, 195, 196, 197, 198, 199, 200, 201, 202, 203, 205, 206, 207, 210, 211, 213, 215, 217, 218, 220, 221, 224, 227, 230, 231, 235, 236, 237, 238, 239, 240, 242, 244, 245, 246, 283
Murray, Robert, 109
Murray, Thomas, 109
Murray, William, 3rd Earl of Dunmore, 109
Murray-Keith, Robert, Lieutenant Colonel, 28, 29
Napier, William, Lieutenant, 82, 99, 134, 138, 140, 170, 171, 172, 173, 174, 178, 209, 221, 231, 233, 234, 239
Napier, William, Lieutenant Colonel, 40, 172
Narin, William, Captain, 214
Navigation Act, 103
New Providence, 13, 92, 96, 97, 98, 103, 132, 133, 134, 139, 173, 175, 176, 194, 267, 285, 286, 290
North American Station, 9, 42, 110
O'Hara, Brabazon, Captain, 82, 85, 86, 88, 174, 175

Ogle, Charles, Ensign, 133, 136, 140, 177, 209, 218, 219, 220
Otis, James, 50
Otley, Mary Trant, 215
Owen, Jane (Mrs. James Boyes), 219
Parker, Peter, Admiral RN, 191
Parry, Edward, Private, 63, 83
Paxton, Charles, 51
Pendleton, Edmund, 153, 154, 226, 227
Perkins, James, Private, 63, 83
Petty, William, 2nd Earl of Shelburne, 51, 57, 78
Phillips, John, Captain, 73
Phillips, John, Sergeant, 63, 83
Pitcairn, John, Major, 111
Pitt, William (the Elder), 1st Earl of Chatham, 69
Plan of Rotation, 9, 12, 39
Pomeroy, John, Colonel, 55, 64, 67
Pratt, Charles, Lord Camden, 8
Prince of Wales's Own (West Yorkshire Regiment), iv
Purvis, John, Private, 63, 83
Quartering Act, 52, 121
Queen's Own Loyal Virginia Regiment, 150, 203
Randall, Joseph, 22
Randolph, Lorraine, xiii
Randolph, Peyton, 118, 119
Randolph, Rex, xiii
Redfern, Thomas, Private, 63, 83, 145
Redmans, Reddy, Private, 63, 83
Reeder, George, Private, 171
Restraining Act, 121
Revenue Act, 9, 44, 47, 48, 50, 53, 75, 96
Revere, Paul, 59
Reynolds, Edward, Private, 63
Reynolds, Joshua, 17, 108

Index

Ricketts, Benjamin, Private, 63, 83
Riley, John, Private, 63, 70, 83
Roberts, John, Adjutant, 98
Romans, Bernard, Captain, 96
Ross, Alexander, Lieutenant, 63, 70, 82, 83, 99, 180
Rowe, John, 50, 65, 68, 69
Rowland
    John Hamilton, Rev., 186, 187
    Thomas B., 186
Royal Welsh Fusiliers, 172, 209
Ruffin, Major, 247
Russell, John, 4th Duke of Bedford, 45, 46, 115, 119, 121
Scott, Charles, Liuetenant Colonel, 153, 164, 227
Scott, Sibbald, 62
Scott, Walter, 16
Scrimshire, Thomas, Ensign, 98
Seven Years War, 2, 4, 7, 11, 12, 28, 32, 34, 35, 36, 44, 76, 90, 212
Shedden, Robert, 279
Shelburne. *See* Petty, William
Shirley, Thomas, Governor, 96
Shirtmen, 138, 224, 227
Simpson, George, Private, 63, 83
Smelt, Cornelius, Lieutenant, 82, 136, 140, 213, 214
Smelt, William, 214
Smith, John, Private, 63
Smith, Thomas, Private, 63, 83
Sons of Liberty, 11, 50, 103
Southern Campaign, 110, 130, 159, 191, 192, 195, 199, 207, 214, 269
Spotswood, Alexander, Major, 2nd Virginia, 178, 183, 228, 241
Squire, Matthew, Captain RN, 111, 129, 137, 149, 151, 155, 166, 182, 234
Stainville, Jacques Philippe de Choiseul, General, 31

Stamp Act, 7, 8, 9, 11, 36, 38, 39, 41, 45, 48, 50, 73, 113, 114, 116, 117, 121, 272, 273, 305
Stanley, Amelia Anne Sophia, 114
Stanton, John, Captain, 82, 180, 208, 210
Stephen, Adam, General, 198
Stevenson, Jonathan, Private, 63, 83
Stewart
    Alexander, 16
    Bill, xii
    Charlotte, 46, 115
    John, 7th Earl of Galloway, 115
    Susanna, 115, 116, 119
    William, 185
Stokes, John, Private, 63, 83, 170, 171
Stokes, William, Private, 63, 83, 170, 171
Stone, William, Captain, 192, 195
Stork, William, 90, 91
Swindon, James, Private, 63
Tayler, William, Private, 83
Taylor, William, Corporal, 63
Tea Act, 13, 103
Templeman, Samuel, 247
Thornley, Thomas, Private, 63
Throop, Thomas, Private, 63, 83
Tilley, George, Private, 171
Tonyn, Patrick, Governor, 95
Townshend Acts, 9, 13, 48, 49, 75, 103
Townshend, Charles, Chancellor of the Exchequer, 9, 48
Townshend, John, Private, 83
Trapaud, Cyrus, General, 86
Travis, Edward, Lieutenant, 233, 242
Trevelyan, George, 8, 69, 120, 262, 269
Turnbull, Andrew, 92

Unwin, William, Private, 63, 83, 170, 171
Urquhart, James, Captain, 82, 99, 138, 139, 145, 152, 153, 158, 208
Villinghausen, 29, 35, 212
Villis, Edward, Private, 171
Virginia Convention, 125, 127, 135, 152, 153, 155, 163, 164, 170, 171, 178, 181, 188, 200
Virginia Convention, 2nd, 136
Virginia Resolves, 116, 123, 272
von Clausewitz, Carl, 4
Wallace, Hill (St. John), Lieutenant, 82, 99, 138, 139, 140, 153, 204, 209, 215
Walpole, Horace, 16
Walsh, Ralph, Lieutenant Colonel, 88
War of the Austrian Succession, 3
Washington, George, General, 4, 6, 157, 195, 197, 198, 199, 205
Watkinson, Robert, Private, 63, 83
Wedderburn, David, Captain, 26, 27, 40
Weir, John, Surgeon's Mate, 82, 133, 136, 140
Wells, William, 52
West, Thomas, Private, 63, 83
Whipple, Abraham, Captain, 192
White Plains, Battle of, 205
White, William, 246
Whitefoord, Adam, 1st Baronet of Blairquhan, 15
Whitefoord, Allan, 20, 21, 23
Whitefoord, Caleb, 16, 17
Whitefoord, Charles, Colonel, 16
Whitefoord, Elizabeth, 15, 16
Whitefoord, John, 2nd Baronet of Blairquhan, 16
Whitefoord, John, 3rd Baronet of Blairquhan, 16, 230
Whitfield, Herbert, Captain, 34
Wilhelmsthal, 31, 32, 35, 212
Wilkie, Francis, Lieutenant, 82
Wilkie, Patrick, Captain, 26, 27, 40
Wilkie's Independent Company of Foot, 26, 27, 40
Williamson, Peter, xii
Wilson, Thomas, Private, 63, 83
Windsor, Samuel, Private, 171
Winship, Jonathan, 70
Woodford, William Colonel, v, vi, 1, 141, 142, 144, 150, 152, 153, 154, 155, 156, 157, 158, 162, 163, 164, 165, 166, 170, 171, 174, 178, 181, 183, 185, 188, 200, 201, 203, 223, 224, 225, 226, 227, 228, 229, 230, 231, 232, 235, 236, 240, 241, 242, 243, 245, 247
Woods, Robert, Private, 63
Woolhouse, John, Private, 63
Wools, Elizabeth, 217
Wools, Thomas Appleford, 217
Wools, Thomas Appleford, Ensign, 99, 134, 136, 140, 177, 209, 216
Wreyton, Henry, Private, 63, 83
Wright, James, Governor, 13
Wyatt, Peter, Private, 170, 171
York Army Museum, iv, xii
Yorkshire Regiment, iv
Yorktown, 129, 130, 132, 206, 214, 275
Young, William, 79

Printed in Great Britain
by Amazon